intelligence

*genetic and
environmental influences*

intelligence

*genetic and
environmental influences*

edited by ROBERT CANCRO, M.D.

Professor, Department of Psychiatry
University of Connecticut School of Medicine

GRUNE & STRATTON   *New York and London*

GRUNE & STRATTON, INC.
757 Third Avenue
New York, New York 10017

Library of Congress Catalog Card Number 79-153576
International Standard Book Number 0-8089-0689-5
Printed in the United States of America (PC-B)

To Bobby and Carol

contributors

Sidney W. Bijou, Ph.D., Professor, Department of Psychology,
University of Illinois, Champaign, Illinois.

Robert Cancro, M.D., Professor, Department of Psychiatry,
University of Connecticut School of Medicine, Hartford, Connecticut.

Raymond B. Cattell, Ph.D., Professor, Department of Psychology,
University of Illinois, Champaign, Illinois.

Bruce K. Eckland, Ph.D., Associate Professor, Department of Sociology,
The University of North Carolina, Chapel Hill, North Carolina.

Benson E. Ginsburg, Ph.D., Professor and Head, Department of Biobehavioral
Sciences, University of Connecticut, Storrs, Connecticut.

Edmund W. Gordon, Ed.D., Chairman and Professor, Guidance Department,
Teachers College, Columbia University, New York, New York.

Patricia M. Greenfield, Ph.D., Research Fellow in Psychology, Center for Cognitive
Studies, Harvard University, Cambridge, Massachusetts.

Jerry Hirsch, Ph.D., Professor, Departments of Psychology and Zoology, University of Illinois, Champaign, Illinois.

Lloyd G. Humphreys, Ph.D., Professor, Department of Psychology, University of Illinois, Champaign, Illinois.

J. McV. Hunt, Ph.D., Professor, Department of Psychology, University of Illinois, Champaign, Illinois.

Arthur R. Jensen, Ph.D., Professor, Department of Psychology, University of California, Berkeley, California.

Girvin E. Kirk, Ph.D., Research Assistant Professor, Department of Educational Psychology, University of Illinois, Champaign, Illinois.

William S. Laughlin, Ph.D., Professor, Department of Biobehavioral Sciences, University of Connecticut, Storrs, Connecticut.

Ching Chun Li, Ph.D., Professor and Head, Department of Biostatistics, Graduate School of Public Health, University of Pittsburgh, Pittsburgh, Pennsylvania.

Philip R. Merrifield, Ph.D., Acting Head, Division of Behavioral Sciences, New York University School of Education, New York, New York.

Steven G. Vandenberg, Ph.D., Professor, Department of Psychology, University of Colorado, Boulder, Colorado.

David Wechsler, Ph.D., 145 E. 92nd St., New York, New York.

preface

"If a man does not keep pace with his companions, perhaps it is because he hears a different drummer. Let him step to the music which he hears, however measured or far away."

Thoreau

This book is the product of a conference on intelligence held at the University of Illinois. Ordinarily, the Preface is an appropriate place to thank the contributors for modifying their papers so as to make them suitable for publication and to acknowledge those conference participants who, for various reasons, were unable to include their manuscripts in the volume. This will be done but it would be less than candid not to say a few words about the climate in which the conference took place. Apprehension, fear, and threats were omnipresent. There was a bomb threat, not to mention a variety of threats of major disruption. It is a testimony to the courage and integrity of the vast majority of students at the University of Illinois, the members of the planning committee, and the administration that the conference was held successfully and peacefully.

This book is not a political document and should not be used as such. It is doubtful that the cause of knowledge, which is the cause of humanity, has ever been forwarded by the process of politicalization. Certain common misunderstandings became apparent during the conference and the papers attempt to resolve and clarify some of these issues. In the minds of many non-specialists, intelligence is an entity which is static or constant over time. It is almost conceived of as a dichotomous variable like pregnancy, either you are or you are not.

The papers in the first section of this volume address themselves to the different definitions of intelligence and to the variety of ways of operationalizing these concepts. Obviously, the operational definitions vary according to the values of a culture at a given time. The second section of the book discusses genetic contributions to intelligence both at an individual and population level. The final section discusses environmental contributions. Clearly, this separation is an artificial one since genetic factors operate only in an environmental context and the environment can only operate on the genotypes that are present. Yet, it seemed a division which would be pedagogically helpful and it has, therefore, been made.

I should like to acknowledge financial support for the conference from the Department of Psychology, the George A. Miller Lecture Committee, and the College of Education, all of the University of Illinois. In addition, Eli Lilly & Company gave a grant-in-aid. There were so many people who helped to make the conference and the resulting volume possible that they cannot be individually acknowledged. Yet it would be remiss to omit the efforts of Mrs. Edna Glass and Mrs. Hazel Bruce. Many of the more onerous editorial chores were kindly undertaken by my wife, Gloria, whose effort is gratefully acknowledged. Much of that which is editorially sound in this book is because of her yeoman efforts. Carl Bereiter, John R. Horn, O. Hobart Mowrer, and Morton Weir made valuable contributions to the conference but were unable to submit manuscripts for the volume.

Robert Cancro, M.D.

Hartford, Connecticut
June, 1971

contents

xii   Contents

II   genetic contributions

III   environmental contributions

part I   **theory
and measurement**

chapter 1

the structure of intelligence
in relation to the
nature-nurture controversy

RAYMOND B. CATTELL

The scientific and ethical setting of the problem

Investigation of racial differences in intelligence requires clarity on three matters: (1) the meaning of intelligence and its measurement, (2) the definition of a race, and (3) the values that should enter into social use of the results. The topic of this chapter is the first. However, the writer wishes to prevent misunderstandings of his conclusions in relation to the second and third realms; therefore, a brief statement concerning these is vital to this introduction.

A race is a people representing a gene pool that differs in a statistically significant way from that of another race. The significance, like any statistical significance, has to do with differences of means relative to the spread (sigma) in each. However, since such differences concern a whole *pattern* of elements, rather than any single dimension, the basic aim of separation and definition systematically by *actual characteristics* (rather than "ethnically" by history) requires application of the principles developed for objective numerical statistical separation of biological species and breeds (Cattell, Coulter, & Tsujioka, 1966; Sokal & Sneath, 1964). These principles have been successfully embodied and applied in the Taxonome computer program (Cattell & Coulter, 1966), to animal breeds (Cattell, Bolz, & Korth, 1971), a substantial separation of breeds of dogs being obtained on behavioral measures alone. Most of the well-known studies of human races (Coon, 1962; Darlington, 1969; Haddon, 1934; Harrison, 1961; Mourant, 1954) have, for lack of these recent aids, assisted their separation by taking account additionally of historical knowledge of migrations and inbreedings, for the branching of a parent race into distinct races has typically been accompanied by special environmental selection, or selection plus hybridization, followed by relative cultural isolation and inbreeding.

Questions of difference of intelligence arise not only among animal species and in humans among naturally segregating races, as above, but also among artificially or conceptually cutoff sections of a people, e.g., social-status categories, urban and rural areas, and so on. Here statistically significant differences may arise in intelligence even though the sections are arbitrary and do not represent truly discrete *species types*. Inasmuch as two people may differ in innate aspects of intelligence, and a race or social group is only a collection of such people, it is theoretically possible for a statistically significant difference of the average innate intelligence level to arise between any one group of people and another. However, the natures of the groups and the causes of the difference make this difference of varying practical importance, requiring special investigation in each case.

Although misunderstandings of both intelligence and race in their technical meaning have contributed to the unfortunate quality of much recent popular discussion (including the moblike attacks on Arthur R. Jensen), by far the ugliest aspect of this and other debates has sprung from the third source of misapprehension—that concerning the values that we need to bring to bear on the facts presented by science. Common assumptions from some backgrounds have been (1) that the recognition of racial differences implies hostility in the people who recognize them and (2) that, at the very least, it carries assertions of superiority and inferiority.

The first is a gratuitous assumption in which the accuser projectively exposes his own meanness of spirit. Racial differences can be as interesting as individual differences. There is no good reason to deny them in the supposed interest of human amity or cooperation. Good will can and always has been more important than differences. What is fundamentally more important is that these experimental divergences of race are necessary to the adventure of human evolution as clarified in the Beyondist philosophy (Cattell, 1971b). The second assumption by various races of their inferiority, it is true, has frequently been asserted, but any thoughtful and biologically educated person realizes at once the scientific risk—and indeed the meaninglessness—involved in asserting that a higher degree of trait X is a superiority. The story of evolution is replete with instances in which what might confidently have been admired at a given epoch, e.g., the sheer size of the great dinosaurs, turned out to be an inferiority by the final verdict of relative survival in the path of evolution.

Among the races of men, some may have a sharper hearing, others greater stature, or a better ability to memorize rhythm, or a more volatile temperament, or a better capacity to score on intelligence tests. But who knows how to balance an "excellence" in one trait against an excellence in another? In many cases we have no idea, even in *single* qualities, in which *direction* "superiority" lies, e.g., excitability of temperament, stature. Even in regard to such qualities as higher intelligence, need for little sleep, and so on, obviously advantageous in modern life, our evaluation is still in the last resort guesswork. Our *tastes* may be quite definite, but our scientific *knowledge* is not yet capable of yielding a reliable judgment on what the human being of the future will be like.

To admit that we do not *know* what traits are superior—in the sense of being the traits of the future—does not, however, contradict the fact that there *are* certain traits the higher endowment in which belongs to the future and others that should recede. The reconciliation of that fact with the fact of our own ignorance creates an emotional and philosophical problem that the present writer has attempted to solve elsewhere in his book *Beyondism: The morality of science* (1971b). What is certain is that in the interest of evolution, if races did not exist, we, as applied social scientists, should have to invent them. Indeed, racial differentiation and the creation of new types is going on as actively today as ever. "Racist" is justifiably a term of opprobrium because it points to a misguided person who takes it as a fact that his own race is superior to all others. But an even worse error is to assume that races need not exist and that innate differences between them *do not* exist. The person who dogmatically asserts that significant racial *differences* in the inherited bases of behavior cannot, do not, and should not exist deserves the still more opprobrious term of an *ignoracist*. Racists and ignoracists are equally anathema to the scientist and to the man of good will and faith in evolution.

The irrefutable record of the rocks shows that countless very diverse races have existed and have gone their way to oblivion, and if we accept cranial capacity as evidence of intelligence, they have differed substantially in intelligence. The ignoracist in academic dress has convinced himself from the beginning that differences in intelligence *cannot* exist. Sensitive investigation of the subtle and fascinating technical issues involved can hardly proceed in this atmosphere. The ignoracist's predilections make it impossible for him to accept the scheme of life in which variation, selection, and evolution are the master plan, just as the racist finds it impossible to believe that other races are probably in countless ways "superior" to his own. In this immorality of personal narcism, which is common to both the racist and the ignoracist, the ignoracist nevertheless proudly airs his moral indignation at the racist. He does so without perceiving the greater immorality—or, at the very least, the scientific dishonesty—of the ignoracist. It is necessary in the present circumstances to take time to point out that both of these intrusive, emotionalized extremes of prejudice must be excluded from the calm of the laboratory if we are to make any progress toward the intricate solutions and complex conceptual statements by which one can alone expect to approach the truth.

The problem of discussion in two languages

Having thus, we hope, followed Samuel Johnson's injunction to "clear one's mind of cant" with explicit recognition that differences in intelligence *may* exist between racial groups and that some fraction of that difference *may* prove to be innate, let us examine the basis on which the question, "Do they *actually* differ?" can be brought to an unprejudiced decision. The evidence has two parts: (1) *data* on whether the groups differ in intelligence measures; and (2) *analysis* on how much of the difference is innate. This chapter is largely concerned with the former, though it will finish with some asides on the latter.

With the jealous concern of a young would-be science to establish itself, psychology—at least among its spearhead group of researchers—has striven mightily in the last fifty years to clear up the subject of ability structure in man and lower animals. Nevertheless, the degree of success that the present writer, for one, would claim to be won, is still subject to question and still more, to misunderstanding. When Voltaire skeptically commented: "*Quand celui a qui l'on parle ne comprend pas, et celui qui parle ne se comprend pas, c'est de la metaphysique,*" he might well have been talking of the present plight of psychology rather than of metaphysics. That plight, as it affects us here, stems from the comparatively recent outgrowth of the quantitative and mathematical study of personality and ability beyond the general verbal foundation that the man in the street shares with William James or Freud. An engineer, a physicist, or a chemist realizes that he has to master basic mathematics before his bridge will stand or his rocket circle the earth. However, the man in the street and the psychology student who avoids the mathematical and experimental disciplines, because they can introspect, claim a knowledge of what goes on in the human mind.

The emergence of a quantitative, experimental, and mathematical psychology has been made concrete in the last decade by the formation of splinter groups from the American Psychological Association (APA) such as the Psychonomic Society and the Society for Multivariate Experimental Psychology. But the general public (and it is the public educated, if at all, in the Jamesian-Freudian verbal approach to psychology that is trying to discuss the present question in journalistic circles) is prepared, mainly, to handle ideas and problems only at a verbal level. For example, because there is one word "intelligence," the assumption is unconsciously—and, as it happens, erroneously—made that there is one power and that we are all talking about the same "thing." The danger of the prepsychometric morass into which discussants are likely to flounder en masse must be stressed (Bacon stressed this pitfall of words nearly four centuries ago, but still not strongly enough, apparently). Otherwise few will be willing to attempt the more arduous disciplined mathematical inquiry necessary so that some precise conclusions can be reached. In regard to the question of intelligence and race, or even of intelligence and heredity, we have now achieved a spirit (admirable when contrasted with the closed mind) of free speech and free inquiry. Even so, one would like to see the argument move on from the excitement of "Let us all stand up and debate" to the more intriguing phase of "Let us all sit down and calculate." Apart from the fact that the latter gets us much further, the computer has a calming effect on emotionality that rhetoric usually intentionally lacks.

The experimental and psychometric development of the concept of intelligence

Our purpose is to look critically at intelligence measurement; thus, let us first recognize that individual-difference measurement generally in psychology has largely passed from the construction of a priori scales, by "clinical" or "philosophical and semantic" intention, into a new phase of *structured measurement*. By correlation and factor-analytic methods one first seeks to *locate* the unitary trait structures and their interactions and use these *source traits* as the target for the construction of batteries and scales.

Actually, intelligence was the first structure to be so handled. In 1904 Spearman developed factor analysis (independently of some related developments in pure mathematics) as an answer to the perplexity and subjectivity prevalent for a generation among psychologists who were testing intelligence but were unequipped with the new methods. (These perplexities, one may add, have persisted to the present day in the reactions of many who resist the inevitable extension of the multivariate analytical experimental methods to personality and motivation.)

Spearman's theory of a unitary intelligence factor *g* in the cognitive problem-solving area is well known to every student, as also is the somewhat more complex development by Thurstone. In the latter, a dozen primary abilities (found as primary factors) themselves factor to the *same* Spearman general factor *g* but at the *second* order. Primary-ability and general intelligence tests have shown scientifically more gratifying consistencies of findings than earlier tests, for test construction can now validate itself against these uniquely determined target concepts.

However, science is continually modifying its concepts, and advances in the flexibility and penetrative capacity of factor analysis as a method (partly due to its exercise in the more complex field of personality) have more recently forced a modification in the Spearman-Thurstone model of a set of primaries and a single broad secondary *g*. The new development was first expressed at the APA Annual Meeting in 1940, when two papers were given, one by the present writer (published in 1941) on factor-analytic evidence and one by Hebb (published in 1942) on neurological evidence. The two viewpoints were later combined into the concept of *two* kinds of general intelligence. The reader who wishes to follow the development of the concept of fluid and crystallized general intelligences in depth and with detailed supporting evidence may do so in the present writer's *Abilities: Their structure, growth, and action* (1971a). In this brief chapter only the highlights of the nature, origins, and relations of these two new concepts can be given.

Briefly, if one factor analyzes (with the obliqueness necessary for full simple structure), say, fifty different variables representing fairly diverse aspects of cognitive performance, he is likely to get—as Thurstone (1938), Adkins (1952), French (1951), Horn (1965), and many others have shown— some fifteen to twenty primary abilities, such as numerical, verbal, spatial, mechanical, perceptual closure, etc. When these again are factored, not one "general" ability, but *two or three or more* are actually found—though in Thurstone's day psychometrists were content to stop at one. Although these are "general" factors affecting virtually all cognitive performance, they are very different in respect to the area in which they place their main loading influence. For example, there is a general cognitive speed factor, loading speeded measures but not complexity, and a general fluency or retrieval factor having to do with access to the bank of memory. But the two big factors that concern us most here have a twinlike quality and clearly have equal claim to some such title as intelligence, for both are concerned with those processes of abstract thinking, adaptability in problem solving, and capacity to acquire new capacity (rapid learning) that have always possessed a semantic right to the word intelligence.

Since exact description is the first necessary step to explanation, let us look in Table 1 at the precise nature of the loading pattern upon primaries of these two g factors. Now, especially through the fine analyses by Horn, we have parallel studies at different age levels, and it is becoming clearly evident that the duality persists developmentally throughout an individual's entire school life and his adult range.

Characteristically, that which shall henceforth be designated g_c, the *crystallized*-intelligence factor, loads the well-known primary abilities, such as verbal, numerical, spatial, and mechanical aptitudes and others. The second general factor, g_f, *fluid* ability, also loads these primaries to some degree; but, as Horn, Nesselroade, and others have shown, it loads most highly of all the relatively culture-free performances in abstraction and relation eduction, which shall be illustrated in test form in more detail later.

If you ask in surprise why this duality was not found sooner, the perhaps redundant reply is offered that all new things are found later rather than sooner. But, more specific reasons can be cited for the delay in the recognition

Table 1. Comparison of loading patterns of fluid (g_f) and crystallized (g_c) Intelligence factors on various performances in good experiments

	g_f	g_c
5–6-year-olds (114) (Cattell, 1967a)		
Culture Fair (Fluidity Markers)	.58	−.11
Reasoning	.10	.72
Verbal	−.17	.74
Numerical	.43	.49
Personality 2	.04	−.05
Personality 3	.07	−.08
Personality C	−.07	−.09
Personality H	.15	.17
Personality Q_2	.01	.02
9–12-year-olds (306) (Cattell, 1967b)		
Culture Fair (All)	.78	.09
Reasoning*	.30	.40
Verbal	.22	.63
Numerical	.47	.35
Spatial	.73	.03
Exvia	.01	.29
Anxiety	.05	.00
Pathemia	.04	.04
Neuroticism	−.09	.06
13–14-year-olds (277) (Cattell, 1963)		
Culture Fair (Classification)	.63	−.02
Reasoning	.08	.50
Verbal	.15	.46
Numerical	.05	.59
Spatial	.32	.14
Personality F	−.05	.09
Personality C	.21	−.07
Personality H	.21	−.04
Personality Q_2	−.06	.05
Personality Q_3	.05	−.02
Adults (477) (Horn, 1965)		
Culture Fair (All)	.48	−.08
Reasoning	.26	.30
Verbal	.08	.69
Numerical	.20	.29
Spatial	.04	−.04
Mechanical Knowledge	−.15	.48
Speed of Perceptual Closure	.18	−.05
Ideational Fluency	−.03	.25
Inductive Reasoning	.55	.12
Personality, U.I. 16	−.04	.18
Personality, U.I. 19	.05	.07
Personality, U.I. 21	−.03	−.08
Personality, U.I. 36	.01	.43
Personality Anxiety, U.I. 24	−.05	−.26

Note: The variables have, for ease of comparison, been arranged in the same order, not in g_f and g_c blocks.

*In this case since reasoning was not a separate primary, an estimate (rounded) was made from tests known to load it.

of the duality: (1) technical advances in multiple-factor analysis, notably regarding communalities and the number of factors to extract, had to be awaited; (2) the present definition of higher-order factors in abilities could not proceed until much more was known about the neighboring personality factor domain; and (3) a strategy of putting in background data for the pattern (technically, *hyperplane stuff*) had to be learned before the experiment could be successfully done.

A moment must be taken to expand on the last issue because its importance in the strategy has evidently not yet been widely understood. It makes simple sense to some investigators to seek primary abilities by factoring a batch of cognitive-ability variables only. At the first order, i.e., when looking for *primaries*, this limitation produces no serious source of distortion. However, if a second-order factoring should produce a broad factor common to all primaries, then there is no means of rotating it to a unique position, for it has nothing outside itself to act as hyperplane. Consequently, *whatever* general factor is found, it turns out to be as unstable and dependent on choice of primaries as is any principal axis. Indeed, the chief reason why the existence of more than one second-order factor has been so long overlooked is that the *background* material against which the distinct *patterns* could be visible—that is, the diverse extradimensionality of hyperplane stuff—was not added. (As in many fields, for that matter, we then fail to understand something because we know only the thing but nothing about its relation to what stands *outside* it.) Good experimental strategy requires that markers for at least half a dozen known different dimensions of personality will still be *available at the second order* to permit rotation of the two or more factors that may be expected to extend themselves across *all*, or most, ability primaries. Figure 1 shows more concretely what this means, and, incidentally, it brings out the significant positive correlation that typically obtains between g_c and g_f. This correlation, of about 0.5, is an important fact for checking some later theories.

Although the main discussion turns on the meaning of the duality presented by these intelligence factors, perspective requires that we glance briefly at their setting in the broader domain of what I have designated the *triadic theory of ability structure* (1971a). The triadic theory recognizes three classes of structures. First, there are primary abilities that functionally belong to a class which may be called *agencies* because they are the means of expression of general abilities or generate "tools" within particular domains. Second, the theory recognizes a class of neurologically organized powers local to sensory and motor cortical areas, for example, the factors found for visualization, motor dexterity, and, presumably, auditory analysis, kinesthetic sensitivity, and others. Third, there are *general capacities* running throughout cognitive performances. Thus far only two of the latter have been set out clearly in Table 1, namely, g_c and g_f, but the work of Horn, particularly, indicates an equally broad generalized cognitive speed factor, g_s, a generalized fluency or retrieval efficiency factor,

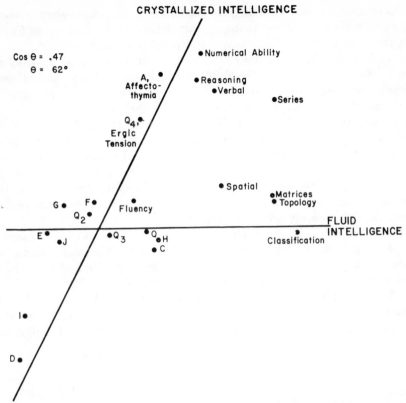

Figure 1. Plot of g_f and g_c intelligence factors showing simple structure and correlation of abilities. Capital letters refer to primary personality factors. (From Horn & Cattell, 1967.)

g_r, and some other general parameters of all cognitive action, briefly mentioned above.

Higher-order factorizations, i.e., factorings of primary-ability correlations, carried out with due attention to the technical requirements just mentioned are, in fact, now typically yielding as many as five or six of these general cognitive factors. But only two of them have the character of determining those complex judgment, abstraction, and relation eduction proficiencies to which the term intelligence has commonly been applied since the time of Herbert Spencer and Francis Galton. It is on these two that the discussion will concentrate henceforth.

The properties of the fluid- and crystallized-intelligence capacities

Once the fluid- and crystallized-ability patterns have been behaviorally (factor analytically) demonstrated as separate unitary influences, many other characteristics accrue around them, as can be shown thereafter by experimental designs simpler than factor analyses. Among the characteristics that further confirm their distinctive natures and independent qualities are:

1. The two ability patterns have different neurological associations, which has been pointed out by Hebb (1942), Lansdell (1968), and others—namely, that brain injury at *any* cortical locality produces impairment in fluid general intelligence, roughly proportional to the size of the injury, whereas crystallized ability has its various expressions more localized so that verbal aphasia, for example, can result from a Broca area injury without significant impairment of other localized habit skills, e.g., the spatial or numerical abilities.

2. A striking difference in the standard deviation of the IQ exists, such that the value calculated on fluid-ability mental ages is about 50 percent larger than that for crystallized intelligence.

3. An equally striking difference in the life curve plots is shown in Figure 2.

4. In general, the tests exclusively loaded on the fluid-ability factor are more readily applicable cross-culturally, while the crystallized-ability subtests obviously are not. They are deeply culturally embedded.

5. The indications are—in these cases needing a wider check—that the nature-nurture variance ratio has a noticeably higher value for g_f than for g_c.

Since statement 5 is a central issue in the present volume, I shall return

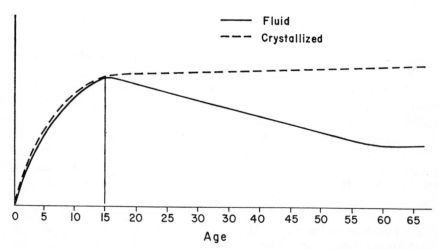

Figure 2. Growth curves of fluid (—) and crystallized (−−) general intelligence factors. The work of Schaie & Strather and that of Wackwitz suggest that if persons born in the same year are taken as subjects, both curves after 15 are raised relative to the above.

shortly to develop it. The reader has probably already recognized that one implication of Spearman's *g* being considered a component of what later turned out to be g_f and g_c is that most traditional intelligence tests are, in fact, measuring varying and usually unknown *mixtures* of the two intelligences. Consequently, we are saddled with disputes about the exact magnitude of the inheritance of intelligence which are as unreal as those formerly arising, for instance, over the atomic weight of helium before it was realized that two or more different isotopes were involved in any ordinary specimen.

Before we consider the specific genetic and other issues on intelligence under examination in this volume, it is desirable to round out the general theoretical picture regarding the total cognitive structure which seems best to fit the above wide range of areas of evidence and the hypothetico-deductive checking possible among them. We shall begin with the definition of fluid intelligence. It is *a capacity for insight into complex relations*, accounting for that part of the test variance which seems *independent of the sensory or cultural area in which the tests are expressed*. The theory is that this capacity for relation eduction is neurologically determined and a function of the size and functionality of the *general association mass*—i.e., the areas not devoted to specific sensory, motor, vegetative, and emotional control functions (Cattell, 1971a). However, to assert that it is neurologically determined is not the same as saying it is wholly *genetically* determined. Also, it should be noted that although fluid intelligence determines the capacity to perceive complex relations in *any* area of behavior, as already pointed out, the construction of a good fluid-intelligence test involves finding areas of behavior, e.g., spatial resolution, in which all persons are likely to be *overlearned* in knowing the fundaments themselves and in which all thus start from the same basis before the relational complexity is built up.

The other general capacities—we have spoken notably of speed and fluency —are, of course, independent in their levels in a given individual of fluid intelligence. They decide respectively the speed of most cognitive performances, especially the simpler forms, e.g., cancellation of letters test and the fluency with which the individual can retrieve ideas. For example, one might have the analogy 4:3 as square is to ————. A good fluid intelligence might get the idea triangle but not be as readily able to find the word quickly.

We would not expect the crystallized-intelligence factor to be so inde-pendent of other capacities as is the fluid factor because of its mode of origin. By the *investment theory*, which has been developed to fit the above facts, the more culturally Protean general crystallized-ability factor arises as the result of the investment of fluid intelligence, over the years, in whatever higher-level cultural skills the individual is exposed to. One can see that such capacities as fluency might also contribute to the success in general *acquisition* of skills and that in consequence some positive correlation might exist between g_c and these other capacities. Actually, in the principal hypothesized case (the investment of fluid in crystallized) the hypothesis of a causal connection is supported by repeated findings of a correlation of about $+0.5$ between g_c and g_f persisting across all age levels experimented upon.

The problems that have always faced the psychologist regarding the origin of the crystallized general-ability factor are those involved in accounting for its appearing as an independent *factor* (source trait) rather than as a mere *correlation cluster* (surface trait) and for the generality of its loading, i.e., for the evenness of loading across so many higher-level skills in a given culture. The investment of a unitary fluid intelligence in all learning of complex judgmental skills would account for *some* of the latter, but that generality would be undone if the learning experiences were all very different for different people. The fact that most successful traditional, crystallized-intelligence tests have been couched in verbal, numerical, and kindred skills gives us the clue that the second contributor to the commonness or generality of a general factor is the standardness of content in the school curriculum. The fact that all children are exposed to the same pattern of higher "intellectual" skills, but to varying lengths of time and with varying interest in school work, explains the origin of the common variance which puzzled us above.

That this development appears as a third factor, rather than as a cluster of variables created by common loading on two factors—g_f and intensity of school curriculum experience—involves more technical arguments. A new factor means not only that we have been given a *statistical* verdict that a new dimension is needed, but also the graphical appearance of a new *hyperplane*, indicating that some causal action is associated with the newly appearing cluster of variables. The implication of these revelations (important for the theory of g_c) is that crystallized intelligence once formed takes on a "life of its own." In other words, it begins, presumably by transfer of training effects, itself to influence new domains of growth of skill. Since this property is that assigned in the triadic theory of abilities (Cattell, 1971a) to *agencies*, i.e., to skills which begin as means to ends and then develop a (factorial) unity of their own, we are conceptually required in the end to switch from writing crystallized intelligence as g_c (expressing its reflection of g_f) to writing it as a_g (which more correctly expresses its nature as the most general of all agencies—a).

The total picture of developmental relations embraced in the investment theory of the development of crystallized general intelligence is most easily set out diagrammatically, as in Figure 3. Here the strata essentially represent factor *orders*, as empirically found in factor analysis, though connections are added of a causal nature, their existence being derived from wider evidence than experiment only by factor analysis.

After this developmental period the crystallized judgmental skills remain (as a persistent general factor determining performance) offering as a general factor the necessary target for validating construction of the traditional intelligence test. However, the increasing dissatisfaction of psychologists with the traditional intelligence test when used in middle adult years points up

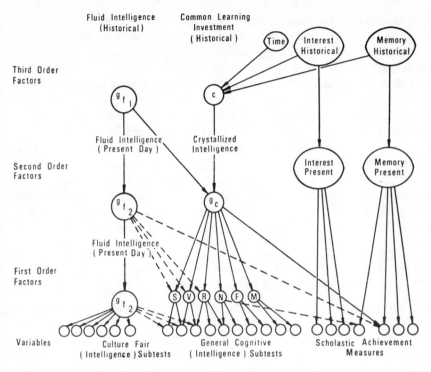

All arrows indicate direction of influence, literally loadings. Continuous arrows show major loadings.

Figure 3. The causal relations hypothesized between fluid- and crystallized-ability factors.

that this general factor is at its best at the end of the schooling period; it ceases to have such good predictive generality as men become engineers, farmers, businessmen, and so on, investing their skills in many different areas.

Many other questions will occur to the reader that the present researcher has attempted to handle more systematically elsewhere (1971a). For example, how is the line to be drawn between *total* cultural acquisition (which Humphreys seems satisfied to call intelligence but which most of us call cultural know-how) and that part originating with g_f action only, and not including acquisitions from rote memory which appear in crystallized-intelligence tests? It is a historical fact that for reasons of cultural life our schools have, from at least medieval times, concerned themselves relatively strongly with the teaching of abstract and symbolic skills. Thus, the overlap of the general "fluid" factor, g_f, and the area of the curriculum pattern is substantial; on the contrary, those fragments of the curriculum (multiplication tables, spelling) that are sheer rote learning lack this common variance with g_f and thus do not enter the new a_g (g_c) factor pattern.

In summary, the a_g pattern requires that its common variance be produced, first, by the common requirement in these intellectual skills of g_f and, second, by the fact of unequal school experience and interest across a uniform set of "intellectual" performances. The latter inequality produces a *common* advance or retardation in all of the skills, i.e., a general factor is induced by their being the common core of the teaching curricula of schools. Any individual gets either a smaller or greater dose of learning simultaneously in all of these intellectual skills. Both sources—g_f and the general, common curriculum—are needed to give substantial unitary character to the a_g factor. Consequently, it is not surprising that when the second ingredient is absent—as in the correlations found in a group of children from different subcultures or those found when using traditional tests with middle-aged adults from very different occupations—the power of a_g as a general factor (and, therefore, its practical utility as a measure of intelligence, i.e., a predictor) begins to decline.

Fluid intelligence as a first basis for culture-reduced intelligence tests

Those who wish to pursue further the specific evidence for the relations, in various circumstances, of g_f to school performance in itself must be referred to *The prediction of achievement and creativity* (Cattell & Butcher, 1968), for in the remaining space discussion has to be extended in other directions—particularly, in the direction of social and genetic inquiry and discussion of the interpretation of the results of culture fair intelligence tests. It is vital to do so in order to avert some misunderstandings that might arise in the use of these concepts in their main applications to the present debate. The first bone of contention concerns the sheer practicability of developing *culture fair* or, at least, "culture-reduced" tests of intelligence. Such measures would have great social and educational value in making individual and group comparisons of intelligence, i.e., of learning potential, possible despite the compared individuals or groups differing in major ways in their culture or subculture. The claim that the IPAT Culture Fair tests (Cattell & Cattell, 1949; Horn & Cattell, 1971) or Raven's matrices (1947) have produced a relatively culture fair test has been quite curtly dismissed by some writers acting as psychological authorities to the press. They have assured readers, who would rather like the whole question of real group differences to be forgotten, that such things simply cannot be constructed. Their reaction is on a par with those newspaper editorials in 1903 which assured their readers that the Wright brothers' plane could never be anything but a toy. The fact is that in actual tryouts, the culture fair test has met most of the requirements that could be demanded of such an instrument—namely, that it be capable not only of giving *equal* scores in people of remotely different cultures, but also of yielding *unequal* scores in people of the same culture, and that it satisfy the validity requirement of high loading on the fluid general-intelligence factor. The last is important, for there has been a tendency in this area, as with performance tests (see Cattell, Feingold, & Sarason, 1941) or the Davis-Eells (Eells, Davis, Havighurst, Herrick, & Cronbach, 1951) tests, to be satisfied with the criterion that a test does not show any difference of mean between cultures. This misses the positive requirement of *concept validity*, by demonstration against the appropriate factor, while setting up a merely negative criterion which may be wrong. In the case of a culture fair test the criterion employed for validation can be only the general cognitive-ability factor in the form of g_f. Obviously, no simple comparisons of intelligence could be made of the scores on the two different g_c factors, each from a different culture. Actually, *all three* of the above criteria have been shown to be met by the IPAT Culture Fair scales as given to subjects in several different cultures, e.g., in the United States, Germany, Japan, France, and China, and by control experiments showing that other types of tests do *not* meet these requirements (Cattell, Feingold, & Sarason, 1941).

Virtual freedom from cultural influence can be shown to obtain for these tests, but what is the *principle* by which the cultural content has been successfully reduced or virtually eliminated in subtest construction? A priori there are two theoretically acceptable ways of getting rid of test variance due to culture: (1) to couch the relation eduction processes in fundaments, i.e., perceived elements, that are *equally strange* to members of the cultures to be compared; and (2) to couch them in fundaments that are so overlearned and *equally familiar* that there is no variance left among the groups in regard to their perception. The approach that Line, Raven, and the present author independently started in the early nineteen-thirties recognized the first as a doubtful approach and worked on the latter. A rather special initial approach (Cattell, 1940) was to set up relation eduction problems among parts of the human body, among celestial objects—sun, moon, stars—earth, water, etc., judging these common things to be universally recognizable. However, a more complete escape from cultural associations soon suggested itself in perceptual tests of the kind shown in Figure 4, and they proved more satisfactory.

The pursuit of measurement devices that will prove minimally affected by culture has had the useful by-product of sharpening the theoretical conception of intelligence. Applied to Chinese high school boys the same, identical IPAT Culture Fair test has about the same correlation (0.3 to 0.4) with success in the Chinese language among Chinese as it does with success in English when applied to American high school boys. The language content is totally different and the structure appreciably different, but apparently the complexity of relations to be perceived is roughly the same in both.

From this and other experiments one is forced to a definition of intelligence as *the capacity to perceive relationships (regardless of content)*. Effective *comparative* measures of intelligence can be made, however, only if the content is overlearned by, i.e., fully familiar to, *both* groups and *all* individuals, and if the

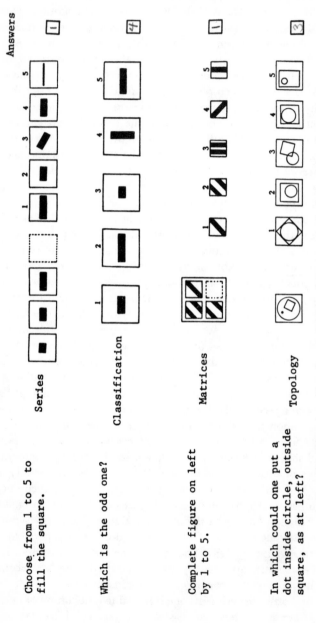

Figure 4. Examples of four forms of culture fair, perceptual relation-educative subtests of proven validity for fluid intelligence. (Excerpts from Culture-Fair Intelligence Scales 1, 2, and 3, by permission of The Institute for Personality and Ability Testing, Champaign, Illinois.)

degree of complexity of the relationships is in a range in which individuals in those groups are working fairly near the limits of their powers of insight. As far as the latter is concerned, practical difficulties have not arisen in attempting to design out of the culture fair type of fundaments items of the required level of intellectual complexity to load the general factor well. Moreover, the verdict of the factor structure is that we are still not encountering any specificity, such as a purely spatial ability (though *some* subtests share moderate spatial loadings too). Indeed, tests of this perceptual kind typically have the highest loading on the fluid general-intelligence factor. However, one does find some high-loaded subtests for g_f in *cultural* material, even in verbal analogies, *if the words involved in the complex relations are themselves very simple and well known.* Also, the tests of short-distance memory span, which Jensen and Horn have used and which appear in the Furneaux letter series as used by Horn, appear to be of high validity on g_f.

It has just been stated that a culture fair intelligence test, by definition, has to satisfy two conditions: that it be a valid intelligence test and that the performances in it are not significantly affected by culture. The first, it has been pointed out, is evaluated by determining the test's saturation with the general factor (g_f) and by its power to predict various life criteria. There is no question that the culture fair type of test meets the primary validity requirements about as well as does any good traditional intelligence test. The concept of *indirect* validity (Cattell & Warburton, 1967) is valuable here. It states that the test and the criterion (in addition to any direct correlation validity between them) yield evidence on validity through the *comparison* of the series of correlations which *each* has with a *representative set* of diverse concrete criteria. For validity (indirect) to be high, the *correlation of these two series of correlations* must be high.

Use of the IPAT Culture Fair tests (the subtests being classification, analogies, series, and topology) in France, Germany, Italy, Mexico, India, the Congo, Japan, and China has shown (1) good indirect validity, in that the correlations of the test with language success, etc., in each culture approximates that of intelligence tests peculiar to the culture, and (2) that the group means and sigmas in most of these are almost indistinguishable. Taking a remote pair of cultures—the United States midwestern high school and the Chinese-speaking and -writing high school of Taiwan—we find absolutely no evidence of any significant difference of mean or sigma between them. Evidence of the first issue is given by the work of McArthur and Elley (1963), Rodd (1958), and Weiss (1968) and is shown in Tables 2 and 3. Evidence on the second comes from several sources (see Krug's excellent summary, 1967) but especially from the Rodd studies (1958). Excerpts from the Taiwanese and Hong Kong Chinese results mentioned above are shown in Table 4.

One must distinguish, of course, between *culture fairness*, on the one hand, which means that the same test will yield no significant differences among

Table 2. Conceptual (construct) validities and concrete criterion relations of culture fair and traditional intelligence tests

    a. Construct validity against the general factors, g_f and a_g

(i) Culture fair (IPAT scale 3: Adult)

	Factor Loading on g_f
American sample (200 undergraduates)	
Form A	.84
Form B	.83
Full Test (A+B)	.96
German sample (100 business school students)	
Form A	.86
Form B	.91
Full Test (A+B)	.97

Source: Data from R. Weiss, 1968.

Validities of eight culture fair subtests ($2\frac{1}{2}$ to 3 min. each) on g_b

	Series	Class	Matr.	Topol.
A	58	56	67	51
B	70	53	63	56

Source: Data from R. Weiss, 1968.

(ii) More traditional test (WAIS)

Subtest	Factor loading on a_g
Information	83
Comprehension	72
Arithmetic	71
Digit span	62
Vocabulary	83
Digit symbol	65
P. Completion	75
Block design	70
P. Arrangement	70
O. Assembly	64

Percentage of variance due to g factor, 52.3 percent
Source: Data from J. Cohen, 1957.

Table 2.—continued

(iii) Loadings of culture fair and traditional with a single general factor
(McArthur and Elley's method)

Test	Presumed* g_f	Presumed crystallized or eductive factor
IPAT Culture Fair (Scale 2A)	.75	
Raven's Progressive Matrices	.71	
Lorge-Thorndike Fig. Class.	.58	
Lorge-Thorndike No. Series	.55	
Lorge-Thorndike Fig. Anal.	.74	
Holz-Crowder Fig. Ch.	.50	
Holz-Crowder Series	.46	.21
Holz-Crowder Spatial	.40	
Occupational Status Parent	.25	
Home Index	.25	.21
Reading Vocabulary	.34	.74
Reading Comprehension	.50	.62
Arithmetic Reasoning	.46	.34
Arithmetic Fundaments	.45	.44
Language	.42	.59
Spelling	.20	.62
Laycock Intelligence	.68	.51
Calif. Test Ment. Matur. Spatial	.61	
Calif. Test Ment. Matur. Logical	.66	
Calif. Test Ment. Matur. Number	.64	.20
Calif. Test Ment. Matur. Verbal	.46	.66

b. **Correlations of different intelligence tests with achievement and social status**

Test	g Loading	Social status	Achievement tests
IPAT Culture Fair	.79	.24	.35
Raven's Matrices	.78	.23	.41
Lorge-Thorndike Fig. Class.	.58	.15	.31
Lorge-Thorndike No. Series	.55	.19	.41
Lorge-Thorndike Fig. Anal.	.74	.26	.39
Lorge-Thorndike Total	.75	.27	.47
Holz-Crowder Series	.46	.31	.49
Holz-Crowder Fig. Ch.	.52	.22	.39
Calif. Test Ment. Matur. Nonlang.	.62	.18	.38
Calif. Test Ment. Matur. Lang.	.58	.41	.66
Calif. Test Ment. Matur. Total	—	.38	.65
Laycock Intelligence	.68	.35	.64

*McArthur & Elley conclude: (1) culture-reduced tests sample the general intellectual ability factor as well as or better than conventional tests; (2) most culture-reduced tests show negligible loadings on verbal and numerical factors; (3) culture-reduced tests show significantly less relationship with socioeconomic status than do conventional tests; (4) a conventional verbal test (Cal. Test Ment. Matur.) showed significant increase in relationship with socioeconomic status over four years, whereas the culture-reduced test showed no change.

21

Table 3. Degree of measurement of intelligence, school achievement, and social status by types of intelligence tests (N = 271, 12- & 13-year-olds)

	Validity, against general factor g	Correlation with school marks	Correlation with standard achievement tests	Correlation with social status
IPAT Culture Fair Intel. g	.79	.34	.35	.24
Calif. Test Ment. Mat.	.58	.66	.65	.38
Lorge-Thorndike Intel. g	.52	.43	.35	.27

Source: From McArthur & Elley, 1963.

Table 4. Magnitude of differences associated with cultural differences

Scale 2

Study 1

	Mainland Chinese ($N = 525$)		Taiwanese ($N = 765$)		American* ($N = 1100$†)	
	Mean	Std. Dev.	Mean	Std. Dev.	Mean	Std. Dev.
Culture Fair A	22.88	4.47	21.99	4.50	24.00	4.50
Culture Fair B	27.33	4.53	26.95	4.47	27.00	4.50

Mean age 213 months (17 years, 9 months), Rodd

Study 2

	Chinese ($N = 1007$)		American ($N = 1007$)	
	Mean	Std. Dev.	Mean	Std. Dev.
Culture Fair A	24.04	5.70	23.50	6.66
Culture Fair B	28.28	5.14	25.50	6.82

10-year-old, fourth grade, Godman

*The American results on 17-year-olds are given approximately (with a possible correction) because the test used by Dr. Rodd was printed with two items differing from those of the Culture Fair Scale 2 as now standardized on the American population. Those on 10-year-olds are precise.

†This is the 14 and over group. The total age range standardization is 4,328 boys and girls.

Note: The gain due to *test sophistication*, i.e., that between A and B, is about the same for Chinese and American in *Study 1*, though conceivably the larger size for the former (about 4½ instead of 3) is due to the initial experience of tests being less.

cultures, and insusceptibility to *test sophistication* effects, on the other. On any test, whether of g_f or g_c, subjects show improvement of performance with repetition, i.e., through test sophistication. This appears, for example, in the United States and Chinese results when comparing the scores of the first and second administration of the equivalent tests. Sophistication is nothing more than "getting used to the game." Studies show that because of this factor researchers should ideally readminister the equivalent forms of a test four or five times before considering results comparable across groups divergent in their previous test experience.

The evaluation that some culture fair tests have come far toward essential goals does not conclude that there is not still room for improvements in such tests. Several studies (e.g., Horn and Anderson) show various new possibilities. For example, it seems desirable that the fundaments should not only be nonverbal and nonpictorial, but that they should not even possess names. Work in Germany has revealed that if subjects are taught names for the shapes, they may do better than if the shapes are nameless. It is also possible that even with the culture fair material there may be cultural differences in natural tempo of working and in gain from level of motivation. There are, however, ways of separately measuring and allowing for motivation, as shown by Butcher and the present writer in *The prediction of achievement and creativity* (1968); indeed, a whole technology of separation of motivation, ability, and personality effects in any given performance is in the making. In short, when the unbelieving anthropologist contends that there is no such thing as a culture fair measure of intelligence, or a culture fair test of basic metabolism, or any other human endowment, he is only making an equivalent to the obvious remark that there is no such thing as a glass of "pure water." The real question regarding the water is, Does our drinking supply depart sufficiently from 100 percent H_2O to matter more than trivially, and can a chemist using tap water in experiments allow accurately for the impurities known to be in it?

Fluid and crystallized intelligence in relation to the nature-nurture question

The developments considered in the previous pages, beginning with the factor analysis of ability and learning performances, leading to the concepts of fluid and crystallized intelligence in the nineteen-forties, and culminating in the investment theory of their relationship and the general triadic theory of ability structure (in the 1960s, see summary in Cattell, 1971a), have proceeded with the usual debates but, on the whole, with acceptance.

Only as the storm has blown up over genetic and racial aspects of intelligence, and only as the implications of culture fair tests for giving much less ambiguous results in this area have been perceived, has a hostility developed in some sociological circles to the whole theory of intelligence as set forth here.

The conceptions of intelligence as used by the sociologist, or by the environmentalist in psychology, have always been vague and verbal. There seems to be an unmistakable trend in the literature of these professionals to keep it vague. In some cases (see the writers examined in Glass's, "Educational Piltdown Man," 1968) one cannot be sure whether this stems from ignorance or is a resolute stand. In a scholarly work such as that done by Hunt (1961) it comes out explicitly as an argument that the writer can see no basis or need for the concept of an innate difference in learning potential among different human beings. Hunt's view is, of course, as old as Watson (and perhaps Locke). There has been a revival of it in the nineteen-sixties particularly in connection with the Head Start program where there has been an attempt to get along without the idea of intelligence altogether.

The difficulties that psychologists have had in their complex subject in developing unassailable concepts *anywhere* has often resulted in a retreat from abstraction and general laws to a safe (but dreary) particularism. In the retreat of pure environmentalism from the scientific field it is now adopting a scorched-earth policy of obscurantism or even downright conceptual nihilism. A sad instance of a masquerade of scientific caution occurred in the Society for the Psychological Study of Social Issues', (SPSSI, 1969) manifesto in response to Jensen's paper which asserts: "A more accurate understanding of the contribution of hereditary to intelligence will be possible only when social conditions for all races are equal and when this situation has existed for several generations." In brief, the question can be answered only when impossible conditions are met, wherein the answer would be so obvious that methods of scientific analysis and experimental ingenuity would be superfluous. One is reminded of those critics of Copernicus who pointed out that the question of whether the earth or the sun is the center of the solar system would be answerable only when human beings could be transported to make observations from both vantage points! "Scientific caution" is sometimes the last refuge of an intellectual nihilist. In any case, it is no compliment to psychology to state, as the SPSSI manifesto does, that this science has no methods or techniques potent enough to conclude more than that the man in the street can do without them.

Let no one confuse the above conceptual and methodological arguments for the practicability of valid cross-cultural measures of the fluid general-intelligence factor with any uncritical assumption that fluid intelligence is itself wholly innate. Furthermore, for an exact comparison of group means even with fluid-intelligence, culture fair measures, some special technical attention must be given to appropriate weighting of subtests.[1] The final question

---

[1] Two conceptually and technically different bases have been proposed for comparing the mean scores of two groups on a common factor. The use of a *transcultural* pattern (Cattell, 1957) is the first. Here the two groups are among many whose mean scores on n variables have been correlated and factored to k factors. Here there is no question that the weights on the

of how innate g_f and g_c may or may not be is one the answering of which has come to depend—in recent years—on quite complex statistical methods. The main answer has to be in some kind of ratio of the variance contributed respectively by hereditary causes of intelligence variation and environmental causes of intelligence variance in our population. A ratio of this kind—briefly called a nature-nurture ratio—is admittedly not the answer that we eventually want. We would like a statement about the number of genes operative, their Mendelian character, and the different interactions that they have with the environment at various stages of maturation. But that is out of our reach at present. The nature-nurture ratio, duly determined for different ages and cultures, is the first and necessary stepping stone to such knowledge. With the polygenic inheritance of the population and a substantial environmental influence producing a continuum rather than discrete phenotypes, the appropriate initial attack is by variance ratios.

In this area we undoubtedly need more systematic and large sample investigation than we now have, as well as an advance from the twin method of determining heritability to the more comprehensive *multiple-abstract variance analysis* (MAVA) method. Thus far the twin method has been the mainstay of human behavior genetics research, but, as pointed out elsewhere (Cattell, 1953b, 1966; Cattell & Nesselroade, 1971), it is obsolete except as a preliminary "reconnaissance" method. It is obsolete in the sense that it does not give us socially and biologically valuable information on parameters that the newer MAVA method can provide. Notably it gives only the within family hereditary and environment ratios, omitting the *between family* hereditary and environmental components, as well as the *correlations* between hereditary and environmental effects. In this connection one must point out that what Hirsch's chapter (see Chapter 8) treats as a new and desirable piece of information—that concerning interaction of hereditary and environment in relation to the life period at which interaction occurs, as in imprinting—is supplied by MAVA. This information, now available through the use of MAVA, has not received much discussion by experimental human behavior geneticists because formerly no one had any more idea of how to isolate it methodologically than apparently Hirsch does. There is no simple road for directly apprehending the characteristic maturational-interactional life course of a genetic endowment. It can be traced—in various means and standard deviations of the environment

variables are "fair" because they *are* common across all cultures. However, it can be objected that it factors only intergroup not intragroup covariance. The second group is the so-called isopodic (and equipotent) methods (Cattell, 1969, 1970), which accept different weights for each of the two groups, but make them equivalent in factor score outcome. There is little doubt that general intelligence may take different weights in different groups, some being more verbally, others more spatially gifted, and so on (see Jensen, 1968). The definition of intelligence by the two bases above implies a concept which takes the common core of these manifestations, and thus deals with a concept that is demonstrably identical for the two groups.

—only by using the more complex, interactive form of the MAVA model (Cattell, 1953; Jinks & Fulker, 1953) and by obtaining samples of the various heredity-environment family constellations at different ages and different cultural conditions, which makes the whole research an expensive and arduous undertaking. (See methods in Cattell & Nesselroade, in preparation.)

However, the MAVA method presents a comparatively straightforward way of determining the nature-nurture ratio for a given culture and race and for a sample of a given age. And the *comparison* of these ratios and correlations for strategically chosen groups, is, as indicated, the basis for inferences about ages of imprinting and many other interactional concepts. Although the only existing use of the full MAVA method with culture fair tests is inadequate as to sample (500 pairs of subjects in various constellations; Cattell, Stice, & Kristy, 1957), the indications are clearly that the hereditary determination is higher (roughly 85 percent hereditary to 15 percent environmental influence) than the values, ranging in typical studies from 60 percent to 80 percent, found with *traditional* intelligence tests. (However, Cyril Burt's technically superb analysis [1967] of crystallized intelligence does approach the same value; though the greater environmental uniformity of the London child and the efficiency of the London school system might have something to do with the reduction of environmental influence which he found.)

Since many enthusiasts for the power of environment have shown a one-track-mind habit of equating environment with education, it should be pointed out that the environmental variance in fluid ability could be substantially due to prenatal, natal, and postnatal brain injury[2] and that no effect of *education* per se on fluid intelligence has yet been demonstrated. Parenthetically, it is consistent with the above conclusions regarding fluid and crystallized intelligence that striking differences are found between the change of mean population level over a generation obtained by traditional and by culture fair tests. The present writer, using the identical culture fair test tested on two occasions the entire population of 10-year-old children of a large English city (Leicester, 250,000 population). The second test was administered more than a decade after the first. The results showed no significant change of intelligence between the generations (Cattell, 1949). Tuddenham (1948), on the other hand, and Finch (1946), who used traditional tests, found substantial upward movement in a period where there was undoubtedly much improvement in schools. (This fits Figure 1, where the second factor, school curriculum learning intensity, at the higher order would contribute more, though g_f would have stood still.)[3] The inferences from this remarkable difference of studies with

---

[2]These include nutrition or drug damage in the mother during gestation, childhood fevers (measles is a culprit), anesthetic accidents, arteriosclerosis, and even simple blows on the head (as in the jousting field accident which at least one history research specialist has associated with the sudden decline in the intelligence of Henry VIII's policies after his fortieth year).

[3]Incidentally, Godfrey Thomson's Scottish council retest (1961) in northern Britain could

culture fair and traditional intelligence tests (each on very adequate samples) seem for some reason to have escaped discussants in this field.

First, from the practical standpoint in testing the inference would be that g_c but not g_f, measures shift their meaning and *standardization values* with cultural changes across time as well as place and that both historical time and sociocultural place should be embraced in our investigations of environmental effects. The theoretical expectation would be that, except where major migration or birth rate effects intrude, the intelligence of a population by g_f measures will remain constant over periods of appreciable cultural change.[4] Since it has taken some millions of years for the slow uphill trend in cranial capacity from Australopithecus through Neanderthal and Cro-Magnon man to the average racial mixtures in our modern world, an apparent constancy over so short a period as two or three hundred years would, within the limits of our instruments, surely be expected. And if, by g_f measures, regional population differences in level are established, these population differences also would be expected to persist, no matter in what direction the breezes of cultural fashion happen to blow the curriculum or the butterfly of socially preferred g_c expression.

In any case, when we talk about the environmental effects on intelligence, be it crystallized (a_g) or fluid (g_f), the statistical fact must be kept in mind that whatever the experiment yields as the *percentage* of environmental variance, it still has to be divided between *behavioral* influences (e.g., school, home, and social culture) and *physiological* influences. The same is true of any shift in the *mean*. If there had been a shift in the mean of g_f as well as a_g over the generation studied in Leicester, we might begin to ask, for example, whether better delivery methods at birth might be reducing head injuries and so on.

With the striking increase in the decade of the 1960s in the subject of behavioral genetics and with such methodological improvements as in the MAVA method, we may confidently look forward to greater precision and breadth of knowledge concerning hereditary and environmental influences on intelligence. However, the argument of this chapter has been that the narrowing of these margins of error, which now give such scope for emotionality of comment, requires not only attention to nature-nurture methodology, but, far more importantly, attention to the structure of abilities and the developments regarding fluid and crystallized intelligence.

Indeed, the arguments of this chapter may bring embarrassed and embarrassing stares from both the prosecuting and defending attorneys in the case. Both those favoring hereditary emphases and those enthusiastically claiming

---

be considered consistent with my own, for his test, like Burt's, was closer to a g_f test. I suspect that the British school system did not have scope for so fundamental an improvement as did the American in the same period.

[4] I have preserved the actual culture fair test with which I cross-sectioned the city of Leicester in 1936 and 1949 in the hope that some enterprising young psychologist will check another generation's effect on the same city.

so much for environment are in fact being told that they have worked up their briefs for the wrong character. This is not a pleasant thing to have to say, but it does explain some of the extreme discrepancies in the conclusions about that character. The only rational action at this point is to dissolve the court, cut short the heat of debate, and ask the participants to address themselves to, say, a decade of assiduous gathering of data under new concepts and radically improved methods.

References

Adkins, D. C., & Lyerly, S. B. *Factor analysis of reasoning tests.* Chapel Hill: University of North Carolina Press, 1952.

Burt, C. Intelligence and achievement. *Mensa Register,* December 1967, 1–2.

Butcher, J. *Human intelligence: Its nature and assessment.* London: Methuen, 1968.

Cattell, R. B. A culture free intelligence test. I. *Journal of Educational Psychology,* 1940, *31,* 161–179.

——. Some theoretical issues in adult intelligence testing. *Psychological Bulletin,* 1941, *38,* 592.

——. The dimensions of culture patterns by factorization of national characters. *Journal of Abnormal and Social Psychology,* 1949, *44,* 443–469.

——. A quantitative analysis of the changes in the culture pattern of Great Britain 1837–1937, by P-technique. *Acta Psychologica,* 1953, *9,* 99–121. (a)

——. Research designs in psychological genetics with special reference to the multiple variance analysis method. *American Journal of Human Genetics,* 1953, *5,* 76–93. (b)

——. *Personality and motivation: Structure and measurement.* New York: Harcourt Brace Jovanovich, 1957.

——. Theory of fluid and crystallized intelligence: A critical experiment. *Journal of Educational Psychology,* 1963, *54,* 1–22.

——. (Ed.) *Handbook of multivariate experimental psychology.* Chicago: Rand McNally, 1966.

——. The theory of fluid and crystallized general intelligence checked at the 5–6-year-old level. *British Journal of Educational Psychology,* 1967, *37,* 209–224. (a)

——. La theorie de l'intelligence fluide et cristallisee sa relation avec les tests —culture fair—et sa verification chez les enfants de 9 a 12 ans. *Revue de Psychologie Appliquee,* 1967, *17,* 135–154. (b)

——. Comparing factor trait and state scores across ages and cultures. *Journal of Gerontology,* 1969, *24,* 348–360.

——. The isopodic and equipotent principles for comparing factor scores across different populations. *British Journal of Mathematical and Statistical Psychology,* 1970, *23,* 23–41.

——. *Abilities: Their structure, growth, and action.* Boston: Houghton Mifflin, 1971. (a)

——. *Beyondism: The morality of science.* New York: Pergamon, 1971. (b)

————, Bolz, C., & Korth, B. The segregation of types of behavior in breeds of dogs, demonstrated by the taxonome program. *Journal of Behavioral Genetics*, in press.

————, & Butcher, H. J. *The prediction of achievement and creativity*. Indianapolis: Bobbs-Merrill, 1968.

————, & Cattell, A. K. The IPAT Culture Fair Intelligence Scales 1, 2, and 3. Champaign, Ill.: The Institute for Personality and Ability Testing, 1949.

————, & Coulter, M. A. Principles of behavioral taxonomy and the mathematical basis of the taxonome computer program. *British Journal of Mathematical and Statistical Psychology*, 1966, *19*, 237–269.

————, ————, & Tsujioka, B. The taxonometric recognition of types and functional emergents. In R. B. Cattell (Ed.), *Handbook of multivariate experimental psychology*. Chicago: Rand McNally, 1966.

————, Feingold, S., & Sarason, S. A culture-free intelligence test: II. Evaluation of cultural influence on test performance. *Journal of Educational Psychology*, 1941, *32*, 81–100.

————, & Nesselroade, J. *The methodology of human behavior genetics*. In preparation.

————, Stice, G. F., & Kristy, N. F. A first approximation to nature-nurture ratios for eleven primary personality factors in objective tests. *Journal of Abnormal and Social Psychology*, 1957, *54*, 143–159.

————, & Warburton, F. W. *Objective personality and motivation tests: A theoretical introduction and practical compendium*. Urbana: University of Illinois Press, 1967.

Cohen, J. The factorial structure of the WAIS between early childhood and old age. *Journal of Consulting Psychology*, 1957, *21*, 283–290.

Coon, C. S. *The origin of races*. New York: Knopf, 1962.

Darlington, D. C. *The evolution of man and society*. New York: Simon and Schuster, 1969.

Eells, K., Davis, A., Havighurst, R. J., Herrick, R., & Cronbach, L. J. *Intelligence and cultural differences*. Chicago: University of Chicago Press, 1951.

Finch, F. H. Enrollment increases and changes in the mental level of the high school population. *Applied Psychology Monographs*, 1946, *10*, 1–75.

French, J. W. *The description of aptitude and achievement tests in terms of rotated factors*. Chicago: University of Chicago Press, 1951.

Glass, J. Educational Piltdown man. *Phi Delta Kappan*, 1968, *50*, 148–151.

Haddon, A. C. *History of Anthropology*. London: Watts, 1934.

Harrison, G. A. *Genetic variations in human populations*. New York: Pergamon, 1961.

Hebb, D. O. The effects of early and late brain injury upon test scores and the nature of normal adult intelligence. *Proceedings of the American Philosophical Society*, 1942, *89*, 275–292.

Horn, J. L. Fluid and crystallized intelligence: A factor analytic study of the structure among primary mental abilities. Unpublished doctoral dissertation, University of Illinois, 1965.

————. Organization of abilities and the development of intelligence. *Psychological Review*, 1968, *75*, 242–259.

————, & Cattell, R. B. Refinement and test of the theory of fluid and crystallized intelligence. *Journal of Educational Psychology*, 1966, *57*, 253–270.

————, & ————. Extended forms of the IPAT Culture Fair Intelligence Tests. Champaign, Ill.: The Institute for Personality and Ability Testing, 1971.

Hunt, J. McV. *Intelligence and experience*. New York: Ronald, 1961.

Jensen, A. R. Social class, race, and genetics: Implications for education. *American Educational Research Journal*, 1968, *5*, 1–42.

Jinks, J. L., & Fulker, D. W. Comparison of the biometrical, genetical, MAVA, and classical approaches to the analysis of human behavior. *Psychological Bulletin*, 1970, *73*, 311–349.

Kidd, A. H. The culture fair aspects of Cattell's test of *g*: Culture fair. *American Psychologist*, 1961, *7*, 374.

Krug, S. Psychometric properties of the culture fair intelligence scales: Reliability and validity. Information Bulletin No. 14. Champaign, Ill.: Institute for Personality and Ability Testing, 1967.

Lansdell, H. Evidence for a symmetrical hemispheric contribution to an intellectual function. *Proceedings of the 76th Annual Convention of the American Psychological Association*, 1968, *3*, 337–338.

McArthur, R. T., & Elley, W. B. The reduction of socio-economic bias in intelligence testing. *British Journal of Educational Psychology*, 1963, *33*, 107–119.

Mourant, A. E. *The distribution of the human blood groups*. Oxford: Blackwell, 1954.

Raven, J. C. *Progressive matrices*. London: Lewis, 1947.

Rodd, W. G. A cross-cultural study of Taiwan's schools. Unpublished doctoral dissertation, Western Reserve University, 1958.

Scottish Council for Research in Education. *Gaelic-speaking children in Highland school*. London: University of London Press, 1961.

Society for the Psychological Study of Social Issues. Psychologists comment on current IQ controversy: Heredity versus environment. *News Release*, May 2, 1969.

Sokal, R. R., & Sneath, P. H. *Principles of numerical taxonomy*. San Francisco: Freeman, 1964.

Spearman, C. "General intelligence," objectively determined and measured. *American Journal of Psychology*, 1904, *15*, 201–293.

Thomson, G. *The Northumberland intelligence tests*. London: Harrap, 1935.

Thurstone, L. L. *Primary mental abilities*. Chicago: University of Chicago Press, 1938.

Tuddenham, R. D. Soldier intelligence in World Wars I and II. *American Psychologist*, 1948, *3*, 54–56.

Vernon, P. E. *Intelligence and cultural environment*. London: Methuen, 1969.

Weiss, R. Die Brauchbarkeit des culture free intelligence tests Skala 3. (CFT 3) bei Begabungspsychologischen Untersuchungen. Unpublished doctoral dissertation, University of Würzburg, 1968.

Wrightstone, J. W. A study of the Raven Progressive Matrices and the IPAT Culture-Fair Intelligence Test with 8th grade pupils. Research Report No. 17. New York: New York City Board of Education, Bureau of Educational Research; June 1958.

chapter 2

theory of intelligence

LLOYD G. HUMPHREYS

It is necessary, as a first step, to formulate a definition of intelligence. The usual criterion for a definition is, of course, that the term in question in conjunction with other terms in the theory lead to testable hypotheses. The definition must lead to scientifically useful consequences. On occasion it is also reasonable to employ a secondary criterion. Since intelligence tests are in common use and since these tests have become firmly entrenched in this society, the definition of intelligence should be tied directly to available measuring devices. This second criterion is compatible with a philosophy of science that does not dictate an operational definition for every concept in the theory, but it is more convenient to have operational definitions for certain terms in the theory than for others.

Definition of intelligence

Intelligence is defined as the entire repertoire of acquired skills, knowledge, learning sets, and generalization tendencies considered intellectual in nature that are available at any one period of time. An intelligence test contains items that sample the totality of such acquisitions. Intelligence so defined is not an entity such as Spearman's "mental energy." Instead the definition suggests the Thomson "multiple-bonds" approach. Nevertheless, for the sake of convenience, intelligence will be discussed as if it were a unitary disposition to solve intellectual problems.

There is one important difference from Thomson's multiple-bonds approach, at least as the Thomson theory has at times been interpreted, that should be clarified. It is not essential that the person whose intelligence is measured has acquired a specific response to each stimulus or set of stimuli presented. Learning sets and generalization tendencies were introduced in the definition to preclude critical interpretations of this type.

The definition of intelligence here proposed would be circular as a function of the use of "intellectual" if it were not for the fact that there is a consensus among psychologists as to the kinds of behaviors that are labeled intellectual. Thus, the Stanford-Binet and the Wechsler tests can be considered examples of this consensus and define the consensus. It is also true that a present consensus does not rigidly define intellectual for all time to come. One should expect change to occur. This change will come slowly, however, because the process of changing the definition of a test in terms of the items composing it is a slow one. As the empirical basis for change, primary reliance must be placed on functional relationships involving the total score on the test.

Contrast with older operationalism

The definition presently set forth differs from the statement that intelligence is what intelligence tests measure. When the intercorrelations of several different intelligence tests do not closely approximate unity after correction for attenuation, the strict operationalist is left with as many different definitions of intelligence as there are tests. From the present point of view, however, one would not expect different tests to be perfectly correlated since each samples a domain that is fairly heterogeneous with a limited number of items. Parallel forms of the same test should be more highly correlated than different intelligence tests, for in the former there is no item sampling error and there is near identity of parallel items.

A problem arises in trying to set a desired height of intercorrelations of tests sampling from the same domain. There is no easy answer. Since a great deal depends on the number of items in each test and the degree of homogeneity of the domain, an a priori approach is not possible. A combination of a rational analysis of the content of the tests in question plus a distribution of the intercorrelations of the proposed tests provides a partial answer. Tests of satisfactory reliability but whose correlations with other intelligence tests are not a part of the main distribution of such correlations can be considered inadequate representatives of the domain. By this criterion a typical culture fair test of intelligence is not an acceptable measure of intelligence at this point in time.

A second difference between the two approaches to definition is that the present one fits into a larger context. Knowledge of learning and of the constitutional bases for learning become important. As a result the definition proposed leads to testable hypotheses concerning intelligence.

A third difference between the present definition and the older, more superficial operationalism is that a distinction is made between the repertoire of responses, which is intelligence as here defined, and the eliciting of those responses on the test. A person whose repertoire of responses is for some reason not available at the time the test is administered can still be intelligent. This distinction is often phrased in the psychological literature as that between learning and performance, but the emphasis here is between acquired knowledge and skill, on the one hand, and performance on the other.

Discrepancies between intelligence and performance on an intelligence test can conceivably arise in a very large number of ways. The test constructor and the test administrator try to minimize the discrepancies by writing reliable, unambiguous items, by standardizing the conditions of test administration, and by specifying the populations of persons and the set of situations for which the test is appropriate. How successful such efforts are is an empirical matter and cannot be evaluated in the armchair. A useful generalization from a great deal of such research is that intellectual performance is relatively robust. It is not affected substantially by many of the a priori possibilities. This finding should not, however, be taken as an excuse for careless or unsophisticated use of intelligence tests.

Biological substrate

Since most theorists have defined intelligence as a capacity, generally fixed by inheritance, it is necessary to specify the reasons why this seems undesirable. It should be clearly understood at the outset that the present writer does not exclude the possibility, or rather probability, that constitutional differences among men affect the ease with which intellectual dispositions are acquired. He prefers the term biological substrate for intelligence to cover these differences while intelligence is reserved for the acquired disposition.

Biological differences can arise from many causes. In addition to genetically determined differences, biological differences can be acquired prenatally, perinatally, and postnatally. Furthermore, the genetically determined differences are far from unitary. Instead the genes are responsible for a huge complex of anatomical and biochemical factors. It is extremely doubtful that physiological psychologists are going to find a single key to the differential facility that the human possesses in the acquisition of intellectual dispositions. Bio-

logical substrate and genetic substrate, respectively, for intellectual performances are more appropriate terms than a word that suggests an entity.

From the point of view of the user of an intelligence test the most important
reason for not defining intelligence in terms of a genetic substrate is that a given
person's standing with respect to genetic factors cannot be inferred from a test
score. The test measures acquired behavior. Independent assessment of the
genetically determined biological base is presently possible for only a tiny
portion of the human population, e.g., phenylketonuria. Some few of the
acquired organic differences can be independently assessed, e.g., certain of the
birth "injuries." Experimental control is lacking in studies of human genetics
so that it is even impossible to draw conclusions about the relative contribution
to the variance of genetic factors in an analysis of variance design.

The construct of a genetic substrate for intelligence is required more by
general biological knowledge and belief in biological continuity from lower
animals to man than by good information concerning human genetics. Family
relationship and other experimentally uncontrolled studies of human genetics
are suggestive but not convincing. It is difficult to believe, however, that the
controlled breeding studies of behavioral traits in lower animals could not be
duplicated with the human if controls were possible. More basic to this line of
reasoning is the inference that any interspecies difference will also show intra-
species differences. There are clear-cut differences between man and other
primates in the genetic substrate for intelligence. It is reasonable to assume that
individual men will also differ in their genetic substrate for use of symbols,
abstract reasoning, problem solving, and so forth.

While a biological substrate for intelligence is made necessary by biological knowledge, the construct cannot at the present time enter into testable
hypotheses in any except the most general fashion. Any given organism may
have an innate capacity for the development of its intelligence, but the limits
of this are very nebulous indeed. This capacity, furthermore, is not necessarily
fixed at a given level throughout the life span. There may be genetically determined differences in the rate of maturation and of decline of the biological
substrate that will influence individual differences in intelligence. It is safe to
conclude that no amount of training will transform a chimpanzee into a human
being intellectually, or a Mongoloid into a genius, but present data do not
allow much more specific inferences than these.

Psychosocial substrate

For basically the same reason that a test user cannot draw inferences concerning
genetic causes from a test score, he cannot draw inferences concerning environmental causes from a test score. Each human being is biologically unique. Two
different biological organisms developing in seemingly identical environments
will acquire different intellectual repertoires. Identical biological organisms

developing in different environments will also acquire different intellectual repertoires. It is also true that similar repertoires can result from different mixes of heredity and environment. Therefore, it is useful to define a concept parallel to the biological substrate—namely, the psychosocial substrate. The psychosocial substrate for intelligence is just as important as the biological substrate and is almost equally difficult to assess independently. Furthermore, the two are by no means orthogonal. Probable genetic differences among social classes, for example, accompany psychosocial differences.

It was stated earlier with respect to the biological substrate that only the most general sorts of inferences could be drawn legitimately. The same is true concerning the psychosocial substrate. If a man were raised in isolation, his intelligence would be very low. Quasi-experimental approaches to this condition are furnished by canal-boat and gypsy children (Anastasi, 1958). It is also probable that one could increase the quality of the psychosocial substrate with respect to developing intelligence and obtain an increase in intellectual level, but relatively little is known experimentally about this matter. Again, a quasi-experimental approach to this problem is furnished by the comparison of intelligence of World War I and World War II draftees (Tuddenham, 1948) and of the World War II and 1963 norms of the Air Force Classification tests (Tupes & Shaycoft, 1964). The results are quite dramatic. Between the two World Wars, the increase amounted to approximately one standard deviation of the World War I distribution while subsequent to World War II the increase appears to be about one-half of a standard deviation.

In summary, response acquisition requires both a biological (including genetic) substrate and a psychosocial substrate which interact throughout the life span. Responses are acquired, and lost, during development, maturity, and decay. The test user cannot draw specific inferences from a subject's test score about either of the two substrates.

Types of behavioral repertoires

A distinction is drawn traditionally between intelligence and achievement tests. A naïve statement of the difference is that the intelligence test measures capacity to learn and the achievement test measures what has been learned. But items in all psychological and educational tests measure acquired behavior. The measures of even the simplest sensory and motor functions require a background of learning in order for the examinee to understand the directions and to provide answers.

A statement that recognizes the incongruity of a behavioral measure as a measure of capacity is that intelligence tests contain items that all examinees have had an equal opportunity to learn. This statement can be dismissed as false on its face. The psychosocial substrate is simply not equal for all. Opportunity depends on the characteristics of father and mother, siblings, other relatives, friends, the neighborhood, the schools, and other environment. There is no merit in maintaining a fiction. There is also no merit in belaboring this fiction as an argument against the use of tests.

Intelligence is here defined as the totality of responses available to the organism at any one period of time for the solution of intellectual problems. Intellectual is defined by a consensus among psychologists. The intelligence test samples the responses in the subject's repertoire at the time of testing. Thus, under this definition, there are no differences in kind between intelligence and achievement or between aptitude and achievement. Instead, there are three dimensions appropriate to the description of tests and the repertoires they sample (Humphreys, 1962). There are quantitative differences among different types of tests on these dimensions.

The most important of these dimensions is breadth. An intelligence test is much broader in coverage than individual achievement tests. Concurrent correlations between intelligence and achievement in a specific subject matter are quite high, but far from perfect. When a number of achievement tests in different subject matters are administered, thus achieving greater breadth on the achievement side, the total score obtained from the test battery is very highly correlated with measured intelligence. As a matter of fact, this correlation is about as high as the intercorrelations among recognized tests of intelligence.

A second dimension of difference is the extent to which a test is defined by a specific educational program. The achievement test is tied to a particular academic curriculum; the intelligence test samples both learning in school and out of school. An achievement test must be revised when the course of study changes; an intelligence test is more independent of what is being taught in a particular school at a particular period of time. The psychosocial substrate for the achievement test is more narrowly defined.

A third dimension of difference is the recency of the learning sampled. The achievement test measures recent learning primarily while the intelligence test samples older learning. Thus, eighth-grade arithmetic is a part of the "aptitude" section of the College Board tests and high school algebra is tapped by the "aptitude" section of the Graduate Record Examination, but similar questions administered in the eighth or ninth grade would be achievement items.

The use of aptitude requires additional clarification. The term is used commonly for one of the components of general intelligence as well as for an ability not considered a component of intelligence. The former is the sense of its use by the College Board and the Graduate Record Examination. Aptitude is also used at times in a very general sense to include both intelligence and nonintellectual abilities. No matter how used, however, there is no problem in fitting aptitude into the present analysis of differences among test items and the behavioral repertoires that they sample. When used narrowly, aptitude and intelligence tests differ on the first dimension but not on the second and third. Both aptitude and achievement tests would be classified as narrow, but an aptitude test, in contrast to an achievement test, assesses older learning that is not restricted to the classroom.

The dimensional analysis is useful in indicating why there is confusion concerning the proper category in which to place certain tests. Just because differences among test items are quantitative and not qualitative, it is possible for one man's intelligence test to be another man's achievement test. Thus, Jensen (1968) categorizes the National Merit Scholarship Examination as an intelligence test, but precisely the same items are used in the Iowa Tests of Educational Development for assessing achievement. Frequently, the distinction between achievement and intelligence (or aptitude) tests is stated in terms of the purpose for which the test is used (Wesman, 1968). Purpose is independent of type of item. A test used for the prediction of future performance is called an aptitude test while the same test used to evaluate learning is called an achievement test. Consequently, there is no conflict between the present definition of intelligence and the types of items used in measuring achievement and aptitude.

Contributions of learning to theory

Several, different well-established principles of learning contribute to the theory of intelligence being developed. The most useful ones are very broad and also independent of the nuances of various learning theories. They might be said to be within the public domain of accepted psychological knowledge.

One of the most important principles of learning for the development of intelligence is the presence of an intellectual psychosocial substrate. No one can learn to use abstract words who has had no contact with language. In the school the parallel principle is that of curriculum. A student who has had no exposure to mathematics will not acquire mathematical knowledge and skills. Note, furthermore, that it is *exposure*, not adequacy of exposure, that is the issue. In experimental attacks on type of exposure, type makes little contribution to variance. There are many cases also in which the exposure was highly idiosyncratic, e.g., Abraham Lincoln studying by fire light.

There must be motivation or incentive to learn. Motivation may be positive or negative, intrinsic or extrinsic, but it must be present in some form. This statement of principle is intended to avoid an issue important in the psychology of learning. While reinforcement for some theorists is an essential part of the mechanism of learning, for others reinforcement is necessary for performance but not for learning per se. Nevertheless, all theorists acknowledge the importance of motivation for increased effectiveness of performance. Latent or incidental learning may exist, but it is very inefficient, and motivation is required for performance.

Since we accept the fact that children differ in the type and degree of motivation for intellectual learning at a given moment in time, what is the source for these differences? Again, biological and psychosocial substrates are present for motivation as well as for intelligence. In this case the psychosocial substrate includes both the reinforcement history and current situational factors. In the absence of the ability to manipulate the genetic substrate one who is interested in changing the course of future learning must control the type of exposure and reinforce the behavior desired.

Forgetting is very slow for well-learned or overlearned behavior. With occasional rehearsal of learned behavior, practically no forgetting occurs. This means with respect to the development of intelligence that the intellectual repertoire continues to grow as long as the subject remains in an intellectual environment. The environment need not be an academic environment since an educated man cast away on an uninhabited island with a set of encyclopedias could still remain in an intellectual environment. There will be so little loss, in comparison with gain, for students during the school years that loss can be disregarded. For purposes of assessing the gain a total score uncorrected for differences in chronological age must be used; i.e., mental age units are adequate, but intelligence quotient units are not. With respect to the latter, a person who does not show as much growth as his fellows will show a loss in IQ.

Transfer of training takes place typically within a domain that the man on the street would consider quite narrow. In general, measured transfer is less than nonpsychologists assume will be the case. For the development of intelligence this means that a great many relatively specific learnings have to take place. Primates can develop learning sets, but Harlow's monkeys learn relatively narrow sets (Harlow, 1949), e.g., the odd stimulus among a set of three. It takes each monkey a relatively large number of trials to acquire each such set. While the human brings to the learning situation a different and more efficient constitutional substrate for the acquisition of learning sets, or concepts, than does the monkey, it is still necessary for the human to acquire a very large number of these within the intellectual domain. (The number of these in the human is indicated roughly by the size of his comprehensive vocabulary.) While man does not have to acquire separately and individually each specific response that psychologists would label intellectual, even the number of learning sets or generalization tendencies is very large so that a great deal of time is required for the learning.

Transfer is not only fairly narrow, but it can also be both positive and negative. Proactive inhibition is just as important as proactive facilitation. Or, to revert to terms that are more common in the literature of individual differences, a person can as readily acquire a disability as an ability. Certain disabilities are quite stable and quite resistant to change. Thus, every person acquires to a greater or less degree a disability to speak a foreign language without accent. Few adults are able to overcome this disability. There are a very large number of items in the intellectual repertoire, and each has both positive and negative effects on future response acquisition.

Contribution of biology to theory

Only the most general principles will be described in this section. Unfortunately, the number of principles and their specificity in this area are not as directly pertinent to the development of intelligence as are the principles of learning. This arises because of the difficulties attendant upon doing controlled experimental work on the functioning of the human central nervous system and upon human genetics.

The companion biological principle to the first learning principle is that the subject must have a minimally adequate biological substrate. Persons showing the lowest levels of intelligence typically have biologically inadequate organisms. Children with phenylketonuria, Mongolism, cretinism, and so forth will not be able to acquire intellectual behavior at a normal rate. Their capacity to learn is not well defined, and can be drastically underestimated, but their capacity is, nonetheless, limited by their biological limitations.

The important distinction between phenotype and genotype is meaningless unless there is independent assessment of the genotype. A diagnosis of genetically determined feeble-mindedness from a test score is not possible. The combination of psychosocial and biological substrates leading to performance at the moron level may differ widely from one person to another who test at that level. It is useful at this point to repeat the injunction presented earlier: namely, it is impossible to draw causal implications concerning any substrate from the test score alone.

Each human being is biologically unique as a function of the number of chromosomes and number of genes in the genetic substrate and the large number of biological effects of events in the prenatal, perinatal, and postnatal environments. It is not even necessary to exclude monozygotic twins in making this statement, although the uniqueness of genotypes must be discarded for such twins. In spite of the uniqueness of genotypes, it is also true that there is a clustering of sorts among genotypes. This arises from the partial segregation of gene pools in subpopulations of the human species.

The biological substrate for intelligence includes a very large number of specific anatomical structures, physiological functions, and biochemical agents. It is highly probable that there are genetically determined individual differences in each of these and that these individual differences are for the most part independent of each other. The characteristics of all synapses in a given organism probably cannot be determined from those of a particular synapse, or the characteristics of one ganglion in a given organism are not those of all ganglia. A multitude of environmental effects on the biological organism that start at the moment of conception and extend throughout the life span are also possible.

Developmental principles

At least two important principles for a theory of intelligence cannot be clearly distinguished as either learning principles or biological principles. Both maturation and learning are presumably involved.

A person's present behavioral repertoire is an imperfect predictor of a future repertoire. This principle has been well documented by Fleishman and associates for motor learning (1954, 1955, 1960). Early trials are not correlated nearly as highly with later trials as adjacent trials are to each other. For the intellectual repertoire the principle has been substantiated by Anderson (1940) and Roff (1941). These investigators found that gains in mental age from year to year were independent of the base mental age at the start of the year.

Ample a priori rationale exists for this principle. There is a great deal of seeming randomness in anyone's environment that will affect the psychosocial substrate, and even at times the biological substrate, for intelligence. The school a child attends, the particular teacher to whom a child happens to be assigned, the particular peer group he happens to become intimate with, the characteristics of his parents and siblings, accidents producing nervous system injuries, illnesses leaving neural defects, all of these impinge on the developing organism and interact with his current status. Such influences (e.g., characteristics of parents and sibs) are only partially correlated at best with the characteristics of the child. Consequently, motivation to learn fluctuates somewhat unpredictably and exposure to various kinds of learning is somewhat unpredictable. Both lead to unpredictability of future learning and thus to an uncertain future repertoire.

Biological development also does not proceed at the same rate for all structures nor for all individuals. Those who arrive at sexual maturity early tend to be taller than their age mates at that time, but they achieve shorter adult height. There is a possible genetic basis for differential growth rates that would account for reduced correlations between present status and future development. Thus, unevenness in biological development as at least a partial cause of the findings of Anderson and Roff cannot be ruled out. There is a seeming randomness in both the biological and psychosocial substrates that leads to imperfect predictions of future status.

Desirable human characteristics tend to be positively correlated with each other. This principle is particularly evident in unselected samples from the entire population. For example, in an American or western European population the correlation between height and intelligence is approximately .25. There is evidence (Husen, 1959) that this relationship is not genetically determined but that it may be determined prenatally. Another example is the positive correlation of the ability to make simple perceptual discriminations with general verbal knowledge. Some of these positive correlations may be determined genetically, some by the psychosocial environment, and some by biological "accidents." Whatever the explanation may be, however, the principle is important for a theory of intelligence.

Summary

This chapter introduced a behavioral definition of intelligence that goes beyond the simple statement that intelligence is what intelligence tests measure. The behavioral repertoire that is called intelligence and that is sampled under controlled conditions by intelligence tests develops out of biological, including genetic, and psychosocial substrates. Without independent assessment of these substrates it is not possible to make inferences about them from a test score.

From the definition presented it follows that there are no qualitative differences among intelligence, aptitude, and achievement, but there are quantitative differences along three separate dimensions. These are the breadth of the repertoire, its age, and its tie or lack thereof to a specific educational experience. From these defined properties of the concept of intelligence and from some very general principles of learning, genetics, and development testable hypotheses can be derived.

References

Anastasi, A. *Differential psychology*. (3rd ed.) New York: Macmillan, 1958.

Anderson, J. E. The prediction of terminal intelligence from infant and preschool tests. In G. M. Whipple (Ed.), *Intelligence: Its nature and nurture*, Part 1. The 39th Yearbook of the National Society for the Study of Education, Bloomington, Ill., 1940.

Fleishman, E. A., & Fruchter, B. Factor structure and predictability of successive stages of learning Morse Code. *Journal of Applied Psychology*, 1960, *44*, 97–101.

————, & Hempel, W. E., Jr. Changes in factor structure of a complex psychomotor test as a function of practice. *Psychometrika*, 1954, *19*, 239–252.

————, ————. The relation between abilities and improvement with practice in a visual discrimination reaction task. *Journal of Experimental Psychology*, 1955, *49*, 301–312.

Harlow, H. F. The formation of learning sets. *Psychological Review*, 1949, *56*, 51–65.

Humphreys, L. G. The nature and organization of human abilities. In M. Katz (Ed.), *The 19th Yearbook of the National Council on Measurement in Education*. Ames, Iowa, 1962.

Husen, T. *Psychological twin research*. Stockholm: Almquist and Wiksell, 1959.

Jensen, A. R. Patterns of mental ability and socio-economic status. *Proceedings of the National Academy of Sciences*, 1968, *60*, 1330–1337.

Roff, M. A statistical study of the development of intelligence test performance. *Journal of Psychology*, 1941, *11*, 371–386.

Tuddenham, R. D. Soldier intelligence in World Wars I and II. *American Psychologist*, 1948, *3*, 54–56.

Tupes, E., & Shaycoft, M. Normative distributions of AQE aptitude indexes for high school age boys. *Technical Documentary Report* PRL-TDR-64-17. Lackland Air Force Base, Texas, 1964.

Wesman, A. G. Intelligent testing. *American Psychologist*, 1968, *23*, 267–274.

chapter 3

using measured intelligence
intelligently

PHILIP R. MERRIFIELD

Here [in Urbana, Illinois], not far from where Lincoln debated Douglas, we face once again a crisis on the issue of controlling our expansion, not westward as a nation this time, but inward as individuals. My suggestion of an expansion inward should not lead you to think that I have renounced the rewards of sensible experience. My major concerns are the mental activities involved in experience and those activities themselves as objects of thought.

We live in paradox. Our greatest rewards come mostly for excellence in total acts, complete well-rounded wholes of behavior. Yet those who strive to emulate those performances are in jeopardy that their efforts will be considered conformist, even stereotyped, and mimetic. Fixation on the old, or the current, breeds rigidity and inability to produce novel adaptive responses to developing contingencies. Projected into the domain of intelligence, this point of view implies, to the degree that socially valued behaviors are complex factorially, that single measures of such totalities are likely to lead to unwarranted establishment of past and current modes as criteria. Surely, the least that is happening is a lag, perhaps even as long as a generation, between reality as perceived by examinees and the criteria imbedded in popular aptitude and achievement tests of limited dimensionality.

Our established selection procedures for better jobs (or any job at all), for tertiary education (and for some, even secondary), and for acceptance in a social class (even in America) require rather elaborate combinations of intellectual prowess, demonstrated achievement, and social insight. Unfortunately, these goals, like a blossom on a slender stem, are most frequently approachable along a long, constrained path on which the successful all started quite early in their lives. There are few alternative pathways to these goals.

Similarly, our more personal goals for self-concept, feelings of worthiness, or satisfying leisure-time activities have become ossified. The proliferation of recreational materials and specialists suggests the inability of many individuals even to be aware of "their own thing," let alone do it.

Our schools seem oriented to training children in established skills for specific activities and membership in groups of participants; essentially, this orientation is toward the past or, at best, the present as the latest day of the past. Might it be possible to emphasize a child's awareness of his intellectual assets and train him in their utilization for his goals as an individual? My answer, perhaps more in faith than in confidence, is "Yes!"

Informing the individual

Most educators prescribe systems by which the child as input is somehow processed into the citizen as output. "To take his place in society" is probably the most frequent curriculum objective, pervasive through all content areas. The determinism lurking in that statement and the aid and comfort that we measurement specialists have given in the operationalization of "place in society" have generated a system of school testing (egalitarian as its proponents may have intended) that functions much more to inform the gatekeepers of our society about elements of the set of school outputs than it informs the individual of his own capability. He is left to infer from the decisions of the gatekeepers what his worth may be; they seldom explain, and he has not been trained to interpret their behavior in any but the most obvious ways. Is it so surprising that a man rejected for gaps of which he is not clearly aware (and has not been helped to reduce) should seek an explanation in his more obvious attributes, e.g., class or race?

In a direct way, in my opinion, much of the well-intentioned de-emphasis on intellectual abilities, presenting their development as somehow less important than striving against the bondage of societal barriers, has been a disservice to those most in need of realistic self-knowledge.

Achievement

Traditional measurement of achievement leads to differentiation of examinees in terms of demonstrated performance. The techniques of measurement are efficient in providing information to gatekeepers, who themselves have a critical role in maintaining the structure and fabric of our technological society. One might even rationalize the heavy dependence on such assessments in language, so that those less verbal are virtually certain to fail, as reflecting the utility of sophisticated verbal behavior in our society.

Yet there are many jobs for which the effective level of language behavior seems substantially lower than the level set as a selection rule. Language behavior is relatively easy to measure reliably; perhaps we have used a high cutoff in language to assure a minimum level of those other skills, capitalizing on their correlation with language. Although these skills may seem difficult and less convenient to measure directly, we should turn our talents to the task of assessing component abilities directly and establishing their validity for various complex and rewarding activities.

The reliance on differentiation in a single dimension, e.g., verbal behavior, tends to perpetuate differences arising from social and educational inequities. The role of home and community in facilitating the development of language in young children is clearly evident. We have not been outstandingly successful, as educators, in devising programs to facilitate rapidly the language development of children from "disadvantaged" homes; we have been efficient, however, in arranging for their continuing lesser level of performance, not only in language but in other skills as well.

The primary function of assessing the individual's working knowledge of content area is to inform him of his status relative to societal criteria, e.g., job selection, college admission. Those who support a no-assessment policy, even on allegedly therapeutic grounds, deprive the learner of information he requires to develop his potential toward his own goals. In the words of another context, his existential confrontation is with himself. The therapeutic objective is that such a confrontation be productive, and not intropunitive. Withholding information replaces awareness with ambiguity and is unlikely to contribute to a solution of the problem arising from the gap between current and expected performance.

Ability

Homogeneous grouping—tracking—has great promise as a preliminary to intensive remediation or acceleration; but, in the absence of well-structured programs consistent with those goals, grouping is a disaster for the child and a disgrace to the system. Even those approaches tending to increase the child's self-esteem by concentrating on, and seeming to value, what he already has experienced do not help him prepare to cope outside his neighborhood, and thus they restrict his freedom.

Homogeneous grouping, in effect, is a compromise in the interests of individualized instruction. What now is needed is the allocation of sufficient resources truly to individualize instruction, not just with regard to one or two dimensions, but multidimensionally, for a much wider array of intellectual behaviors than have generally been considered. Differentiation should not be unidimensional—except where clearly predictive of differences in specific performance. Rather, the emphasis should be on adequacy of a variety of skills and a working knowledge in a variety of content fields.

Multiple aptitude tests are widely used in industry, and less so in tertiary education. The highly specified structure-of-intellect model (Guilford, 1967) is becoming increasingly known; my own research interests focus on establishing validities for those factors, especially in children in their preschool and elementary school years. Evidence increases that differential abilities can be assessed reliably in young children; some abilities are effective predictors of school learning, even after the influence of reading comprehension is discounted.

A major issue, of course, is how different abilities come to be measurable at, for example, age 6. Two alternatives, both perhaps extreme, are what I shall call the trunk-and-branch model and the blades-of-grass model. The former has a longer history, but the latter may have a longer past. Beginning with Galton's investigations of filial regression, a unitary notion of intelligence grew rapidly in popularity and much evidence was advanced for it by Spearman and Burt. It was further extended into the American educational milieu by Terman and McNemar. The branching from this trunk is probably best represented by Vernon's (1950) description, in which the main fork is into verbal:educational abilities and spatial:mechanical abilities, with some further branching suggested. The fluid vs. crystallized conceptualization of Cattell (1965) seems more an attempt to describe different developmental phases of what may be essentially a unitary attribute. It is interesting to contemplate the possibility that each factor in Guilford's model has a fluid and a crystallized phase. Such a conjecture is not inconsistent with their distinction:[1] fluid intelligence is freer, not culturally meaningful, manifested in large part by performance in spatial content; crystallized intelligence is manifested by acculturated performance, as in reading or arithmetic problems, or achievement in history. Hierarchical models, in general, are also examples of this trunk-and-branch scheme.

In contrast, though not necessarily in opposition, the insights of Thurstone led to the idea that each of a set of factors could be considered equally valid, regardless of its psychological domain. The work of many during World War II led to the extensive work of Guilford and his associates in developing tests of the factors hypothesized from the structure-of-intellect model. Most of the early research was carried out using male military officer candidates as examinees; more recently, the usual examinee pool has been high school students, more from suburban than from inner-city areas. As noted earlier,

---

[1]The examples here scant the theory, which is much more extensive than space permits me to show.

some work has been published on factors in younger children (Ball, 1970; Sitkei & Meyers, 1969). This direction of research seems extremely promising, especially if validation for school-related academic and life-adjustment criteria can be arranged.

Intelligent introspection

For some years investigators have noted discrepancies between measured intelligence and measured achievement. Usually these discrepancies have been discussed with reference to the criterion, as overachievement and under-achievement. Inferences have been made about the performers, called over- or underachievers, and many attributes have been adduced as putative corre-lates of this condition. Most often, some quality of motivation, or drive, or need has been advanced to explain the anomaly. Regrettably, there is no operationalized construct about which we can make a conclusion other than noting that trying harder seems to help—but not always.

A possibility that seems reasonable, but has not been systematically explored, is that another kind of intelligence is involved—an intelligence that partakes of introspection and self-awareness. It is related to goal-oriented behavior and mobilization.

Introspection as a mental phenomenon ranges in recorded literature from Plato to Polonius to Portnoy. As a psychological method, it found favor with early empiricists and, I suspect, is still used occasionally by modern theorists. However, it is clear that overt manifestations of introspection, other than verbal reports by self-disciplined observers, are rare. Self-awareness is usually con-sidered in the affective domain, but in that context it is sought as a prologue to joy and/or peace. Were the dimensions of one's own intellectual capacities the objects of such intense analysis as are one's sensitivities in our current drive for confirmation of our existence, what awesome intellectual actualizations might come into being!

Goal-oriented behavior, in humans outside of conditioning rigs, is usually interpreted as problem solving, with the expectation that some kind of strategy or cognitive style underlies their behavior. Studies of problem solving have not been very successful in defining strategic thinking as a unitary factor, and most definitions of cognitive style are somewhat less than psychometrically precise. This situation reflects more the difficulty of the problem, e.g., defining problem solving as a construct, than it does the energy or acumen of those pursuing a solution. Still, the task of specifying precisely how the problem solver perceives that he has a problem remains.

Mobilization of physiological and sensory resources in the face of threat is commonly observed in animals and men. There is evidence that under favor-able conditions certain portions of the brain can take over activities previously carried out by a portion no longer functional. But very little has been reported about the mind as manager, except, of course, for the general feedback models arising from cybernetics; most studies showing feedback as effective in behavior have been restricted, for good experimental reasons, to relatively simple learning tasks over a fairly short time interval. Problem solving, on the level that interests educators, involves the assimilation of complex schemes and their consistent application over the long term.

How does the problem solver decide which of his intellectual resources to mobilize? In reacting to stress, we seem to have a built-in template, but not obviously so for dealing with problems in calmer situations. Thus, when confronting a problem, the problem solver, first, should profit from awareness of his specific abilities as well as of the requirements of the problem. Second, he should be able to build a system of his own abilities that would most effectively process his perceptions and produce a solution. Previous research, even that dealing with part-whole learning, has not addressed this issue from a truly individual point of view. Typically, components are learned to some criterion, and then the examinees are tested on a complex task, with the expectancy that all will use the combination of components that seems optimal to the experimenter.

In contrast, the individual's processing of information in problem-solving situations may be described as follows: To the degree that examinees have different abilities, they should be expected to mobilize different systems of those abilities to respond to problems that seem identical to the observer.

The ability to construct a system of one's own abilities may be defined as follows: To the degree that examinees are equally aware of their specific abilities, differences in performance remaining after differences in specific abilities are discounted are attributed to a new set of factors in the structure-of-intellect model, of which NPS-convergent productive thinking about personal systems is a leading example.

Some justification is required for assigning this new ability to a yet unopened wing in the structure-of-intellect edifice. First, the idea of a fifth content area was advanced by the writer during early discussions[2] of the domain of social intelligence, now referred to in the model as Behavioral and parallel to the earlier three—Semantic, Symbolic, and Figural. If information about the behavior of others was to be susceptible to mentation in the structure-of-intellect mode, so should be information about one's own behavior. The pursuit of other objectives was more feasible at the time, so no further definition was attempted. Subsequently the development of tests for a number of abilities in the Behavioral content area has been successful. The term Personal is the name proposed for the content area of information about one's own behavior. It is likely that abilities other than NPS will be involved; convergent productive

[2]University of Southern California, Aptitudes Research Project. Guilford was Project Director; the writer was Assistant Director.

thinking as an operation and systems as a product seem appropriate as a beginning.

Some may feel that such an overarching, managerial function should be represented by a second-order factor in a hierarchical scheme. I think not, for second-order factors derive from what first-order factors have in common, not from an influence operating on them. The statistical model for the mobilization function is more like the generation of a canonical vector, or a multiple-regression equation, than it is like a principal component. The two possibilities should be considered alternative hypotheses until sufficient data can be collected to support a confident choice between them. Designs for such studies are in preparation.

Conclusion

We return at last to our initial problem—using measures of intelligence to improve the child's performance. While emphasis on differentiation of children from each other may not be helpful, withholding information regarding differences between an individual's status and his aspiration is a definite disservice to him. The utility of information about one's level of knowledge of content was discussed.

Argument was advanced for information leading to increased awareness of one's own abilities. Speculation relating to their mobilization into systems for problem solving led to a discussion of a new content area in the structure-of-intellect model—Personal, defined as information about one's own behavior. A specific factor, NPS-convergent productive thinking about one's own systems, was considered central to the mobilization function.

Should children profit from knowledge of their own abilities and training in their mobilization, then more individualized development, based on an extended information base, may serve to ameliorate the inequities arising from some applications of measurement technology. We may come to use more measures, of more kinds of intelligence, more intelligently.

References

Ball, R. S. *The relation of certain known environment factors to the thinking abilities of three-year-old children.* U.S. Office of Education, Project 8-1-100, Final Report. Washington, D.C.: USOE, 1970.

Cattell, R. B. *The scientific analysis of personality.* Baltimore: Penguin, 1965.

Guilford, J. P. *The nature of human intelligence.* New York: McGraw-Hill, 1967.

Sitkei, E. F., & Meyers, C. E. Comparative structure of intellect in middle- and lower-class four-year-olds of two ethnic groups. *Developmental Psychology*, 1969, *1*, 592–604.

Vernon, P. E. *The structure of human abilities.* New York: Wiley, 1950.

chapter 4

intelligence: definition, theory, and the IQ.

DAVID WECHSLER

As you read the contributions which preceded mine, you may have been impressed by the diversity of the approaches to the topic and the differences in the points of view stressed. For a subject as broad and embracing as intelligence, this was perhaps inevitable. But if the topics treated in this volume are to be profitably studied, one must assume that underneath these and other differences there is a residuum of meaning to the term intelligence, acceptable to all who use it.

This does not mean that we must agree to any particular definition of intelligence nor, for that matter, abandon any preferred ones. But we must feel that, details disregarded, we are at heart talking about the same thing. It is possible to make this assumption because intelligence is not a unique entity, but a composite of traits and abilities recognizable by the goals and ends it serves rather than the character of the elements which enter into it.

The fact that intelligence has been and can be defined in many ways need not overwhelm us nor impel us to the view, sometimes advanced, that the term is best abandoned because "nobody really knows what intelligence is." Actually, we know much more about intelligence than about practically any other subject in psychology. Few topics have been as avidly researched and discussed, and at all levels of sophistication. It is a subject about which virtually everyone can speak on the basis of personal experience. I venture that nearly every person has had occasion to call somebody, justifiably or not, bright or stupid. As a matter of fact, recognizing and identifying degrees of brightness and stupidity is what intelligence testing is all about.

Of course, the last observation is an oversimplified statement. There are problems in and aspects to intelligence which perforce have to be specially considered and about which there exist and will continue to exist differences of opinion. But in discussing these one must be careful not to mistake the forest for the trees.

When one examines in depth the various definitions of intelligence, one soon discovers that they differ not so much by what they include as by what they omit. Thus, some emphasize primarily the ability to reason or to think abstractly; others, the ability to learn or to profit from experience; still others, the capacity to adapt; and, in recent years, increasing numbers, the ability to solve problems. None of these approaches can be categorized as incorrect, nor, when sufficiently elaborated, as failing to embrace basic mental operations. Taken individually, the definitions offered are restricted and incomplete because they concern themselves with only a modest range of traits and abilities that necessarily constitute the broad spectrum of intelligent behavior. Intelligent behavior, to be sure, may call upon abstract reasoning, the ability to learn, or to adapt, or to solve problems. It may manifest itself in any or all of these ways —though not necessarily at one time—and in many other ways as well. It is also dependent, to varying degrees, upon a variety of determinents which are more of the nature of connative or personality traits rather than of cognitive abilities. These connative and personality vectors are relatively independent of intellectual ability, and for this reason were originally designated by this writer, and since widely referred to, as the *nonintellective factors* of intelligence. They include such ingredients as drive, persistence, motivation, and goal awareness. Their impact on intelligence is attested to not only by direct observation, but also by statistical and factorial analytic studies.

Less often recognized than nonintellective factors of the sort just mentioned is another group which relates to the individual's capacity to perceive and respond to moral, aesthetic, and social values. These factors involve not so much knowledge and skills as the capacity to assess excellence and worthwhileness of human aims. They are manifested by such characterological traits as steadfastness to principles, respect for truth, concern with questions of right and wrong, and sensitivity to beauty in its varied manifestations. These are traits not everywhere or always esteemed, but, nevertheless, as in the case of honesty, they have been shown to correlate significantly with the more obvious and objective measures of intelligence.

General intelligence is thus a many faceted construct. It is not, as sometimes supposed, synonymous with intellectual ability; it involves much more. But if general intelligence cannot be equated with intellectual ability, neither can it be said to be independent of it. For an individual to deal effectively with certain situations may require more of one kind of ability than another. Consequently, some psychologists have found it useful to classify intelligence according to what they judge to be the major ability or abilities called for. This has suggested the view that there are in fact different kinds or types of intelligence. Cattel in Chapter 1 made a distinction between fluid and crystallized intelligence. Operationally, this distinction seems to differentiate between native and acquired intellectual capacity. More related to the type of situation than to the kind of operation involved is Thorndike's oft-cited classification of intelligence into abstract, social, and practical intelligence. Abstract intelligence, according to Thorndike, involves mostly the ability to deal with and use symbols; social intelligence, the facility to deal with people; and practical intelligence, the ability to manipulate objects. Each of these distinctions, and certain others that have been put forward, can be usefully applied.

I personally prefer to look upon general intelligence as a global capacity that manifests itself in different ways, depending upon the challenge presented and the assets which the individual possesses to meet it. But the question of a global versus special kinds of intelligence turns out to be primarily a theoretical one. In practice, i.e., when it comes to devising instruments or tests for appraising intelligence, it generally plays a minor role. Notwithstanding their theoretical views, authors of intelligence scales tend to make use of the same sort of tasks and items. Procedures may vary, but the tests themselves do not differ very much. The reason is that basically there are really not very many different ways of appraising intelligence. One is limited by the kind of reasonable tasks that can be set and the suitable questions that can be asked.

To act intelligently one must be able to perceive accurately, to recognize and recall what has been perceived, to think logically, to plan, and so on. These are not only important in and of themselves as descriptions of how the mind works, but, in addition, as manifestations of mental operations which lend themselves to objective evaluation and measurement. That is why they have been and continue to be used in tests of intelligence. When so employed, the measures involved call for such tasks as defining words, solving arithmetical problems, detecting likenesses and differences, putting blocks together, recalling words or numbers, and so on. But the abilities called for to perform these tasks do not, per se, constitute intelligence or even represent the only ways in which it may express itself. They are used and can serve as tests of intelligence because they have been shown to correlate with otherwise widely accepted criteria of intelligent behavior.

One may question whether the tests that have come to be employed are the sole or even the best ways of appraising intelligence. One will further want to know under what conditions the tests are given, the representativeness of the populations on which they are standardized, the suitability of the tests for subjects to whom they are now administered, and so forth. These questions have been asked and discussed ever since intelligence tests began to be used (more than sixty years ago). Contributors to this volume will no doubt pursue them again, particularly as they may relate to their specific topics and personal points of view. That is all to the good and fair game as a start. Hopefully, the greater parts of their discussions will not, as has so often been the case, be devoted to redundant criticisms and belabored reevaluations of the tests of intelligence in general. The validity and value of intelligence tests cannot be judged primarily by what they may or may not contribute to the nature-nurture controversy, any more than the answer to the problem of the relative importance of heredity and environment depends solely on the reported findings of intelligence tests. The role and implications of tests of intelligence are at once much broader and less crucial. It is important to distinguish between what tests are intended for and how they may be used. To do so one must know clearly what intelligence tests consist of and how they are put together.

There is nothing mysterious about tests of intelligence. Tests so designated consist ultimately of a series of questions or tasks which a subject is required to answer or perform. Depending upon the difficulty of the items used, the accuracy and speed with which they are completed, and the frequency with which they are passed, numerical values are assigned to the responses; these, in turn, are summed to give a total score. Scores so obtained are then used as a basis for defining different levels of intelligence.

The tasks or questions used in intelligence tests are, in the first instance, measures of selected skills and knowledge, like the ability to solve arithmetical problems or the size of one's vocabulary. But they differ from measures of achievement or special aptitude in that they are intended not so much to measure a particular skill or fund of information, as the degree to which successful performance on these tasks correlate with variously esteemed and otherwise desirable capacities commonly accepted as indicators of intelligence. If the tests correlate to a significant degree with any, and preferably several, of these criteria, and in addition satisfy certain other criteria, they are considered as having established themselves as valid measures of intelligence. Some of these conditions are that the tests consistently measure and reliably predict what they claim to, that the subjects employed in the standardization of the tests be representative of the population from which they were selected, and that the questions or tasks are not, for one or another reason, "unfair" to particular individuals or groups to whom they are likely to be administered.

Intelligence tests have been charged with failing in one or another, and even all, of these areas. Attacks have been both general and specific; often they have been based on political as well as scientific grounds. Particularly vehement have been the onslaughts against that widely publicized, denounced, and misunderstood feature of intelligence tests, the IQ or intelligence quotient. I believe that the opposition to the IQ is largely due to the misunderstanding of what an IQ really is and what it is intended to define.

An IQ is a numerical ratio, derived from a comparison of the score that an individual makes on a given test of intelligence with the average score which subjects of his own age have attained on the same or a similar test. In practice, this ratio is expressed in a percent notation in which the decimal point, for convenience, is left out. There are several ways in which an IQ can be computed. Sometimes the original scores are first translated into months and years and expressed as mental ages; at other times, more directly derived. However calculated, the result is an index of relative brightness. It is a measure not of absolute but only of *relative* ability. It purports to tell you how bright or dull an individual is compared to persons of his own age; or if a comparison is made between two groups, how the brightness of the average individual in the first group compares with the average individual of the same age in the second group.

All comparisons, of course, are odious, and comparing people's intelligence with one another, particularly so. Too much is at stake. Calling a child retarded or an adult mentally defective is much more serious than calling him delinquent or questioning his paternity. Education, a job, in certain situations one's legal rights may be at stake. One must obviously be careful as to how one interprets as well as how one arrives at an IQ. It is not, however, an inherent fault of the IQ that incompetent or mischievous people misuse it. Nor does the observation that educationally, economically, and otherwise deprived subjects generally score lower on IQ tests invalidate the IQ as an index. Of course, the factors that affect the IQ are important, but it is the social conditions that produce the factors and not the tests that are the culprits. No one, for example, would suggest the elimination of tests for tuberculosis in the public schools because it was found that children from deprived areas showed up more often with positive signs than children from "good" neighborhoods. Similarly, if the IQ test scores of children coming from deprived and depressed areas are significantly lower than those of children from better neighborhoods, the reason can no more be ascribed to the inadequacy of the IQ test than the greater incidence of tuberculosis to the possible limitations of the tuberculin test. The cause is elsewhere, and the remedy not in denigrating or banishing the IQ but in attacking and removing the social causes that impair it.

An equally important stricture on the IQ has to do with the trustworthiness of the measure itself—namely, its overall reliability. This is a legitimate concern. One needs to know not only by how much an IQ may diverge from its hypothetically true value, but for how long a time it may be expected to remain approximately the same. What are the changes that may be expected over time, to what extent, and in what direction? There is a vast amount of data and literature on this subject, although not all in agreement. It is too extensive for me to review here even briefly. But taken as a whole, the findings show that for most individuals an IQ once adequately obtained, does not change markedly. The average test-retest change amounts to some 5 points, or approximately one-third of a standard deviation. This is surprisingly small when compared with commonly accepted levels of variation in physical indices, like an individual's basal metabolism or electroencephalogram. Larger discrepancies than 5-point differences in IQ do occur, but with diminishing frequency the greater the difference. Thus, an IQ difference of 10 points on retest may be expected once in five times, a difference of 20 points approximately once in sixteen. These findings attest to the need of appraising each case individually and of avoiding definitive classification on the basis of a single examination. When a subject's IQ appears inconsistent with his past history, an obvious step is to retest him or reexamine him with other instruments. A large discrepancy is always suspect and should be explored. But one does not throw out the baby with the bath water. The IQ, whatever its defects, is still one of the most useful measures of intelligence available to us.

part II   **genetic contributions**

genetic contributions to
individual differences in intelligence:
an introduction

ROBERT CANCRO

As the reader of this volume has already seen in Part I, there is substantial disagreement among experts as to the definition of intelligence and appropriate methods of measuring it. Clearly, intelligence will be defined differently in different cultures according to the values of that particular culture. It is not a unitary trait, nor is it as highly visible as eye color. Intelligence is a construct, and the presence of an underlying reality is inferred by the observer. This in no way eradicates the actual and real effect of genes on individual differences in that trait. The only way we can deny a significant genetic contribution to intelligence is by denying the very existence of the trait itself. However politically palatable this pseudoposition may be, it is not scientifically tenable. If we define intelligence as a complex trait which is measured, to some practical degree, by IQ tests, we can avoid much of the fruitless debating that has so obscured this subject.

Much of the rancor produced by discussions on the genetic contribution to intelligence is a consequence of a basic but common biological confusion. This confusion derives from the traditional organic-nonorganic duality. If we wanted to paraphrase the title of a popular movie of the late 1930s, this chapter could have been called "Descartes Rides Again." Even highly educated people see genes and the environment as separate and independent sources of variance. They believe that if the determination of a characteristic is not genetic, it must be environmental, and vice versa. As Dobzhansky has emphasized, and as is developed in this section of the book, both the genetic and environmental contributions are equally important because they are both indispensable. The gene can only express itself in an environment, and an environment can only evoke the genotype that is present. In this sense it may be very misleading to speak of one or the other as more important, even in theoretical terms. This statement should not be misunderstood to mean that we cannot look at a population at a given moment in time and say that the variation in the trait measured is determined more by the genes or the environment. It does mean, however, that we must generalize very carefully from such a finding. With a different population or a radically different environment the results might be totally different. Perhaps the clearest way of presenting the value and the limitation of this approach is by recognizing that a heritability measure is only useful as long as the environment is relatively constant.

A difficult problem, which is more than semantic, is that the term environment is used to include everything from the concentration of electrolytes in contact with the genome to the sociocultural milieu in which an infant develops. The term environment simultaneously covers a range of variables from disciplines as diverse as biochemistry and cultural anthropology. This leads to much confusion since constructs from very different universes are mixed as if they were interchangeable. While there is considerable evidence that rearing patterns interact with the genotype, there must be physiologic pathways through which that interaction can occur. Some clear and legitimate examples include patterns of infant handling and sensory stimulation. There is a profound need for more research to demonstrate both the interaction of more subtle psychological factors with the genotype and the pathways through which it takes place.

One can speculate that as the environment—broadly defined—is made more constant for all, the variation between individuals will be increasingly a function of their genotypes. In this sense a perfectly "equal" environment might be the least democratic condition of all. A distinction that may be helpful can be drawn between the equivalence of the actual versus the evocativeness of the environment. The identical environment may not be equally evocative for two different people. Equal opportunity for these two individuals would *not* be accomplished through exposure to the identical environment but rather through exposure to equally evocative environments. Implicit in this approach is the desire, conscious or otherwise, to homogenize the population and erase individual differences. The expressed goal of many workers is to equalize performance. An alternative is to diversify the range of skills that is valued and rewarded by society, but this approach is usually disregarded. There is a danger that education will attempt to shape men to meet the demands of society rather than try to modify society to meet the range of individual human differences.

While we speak of maximizing each individual's potential, operationally this often means minimizing his individual difference from that neo-Platonic ideal—the "modal" man. This general point will be developed further in a later section of this chapter, albeit in a different context.

We should also consider the popular lay misconception that genes determine the trait in an inevitable manner; e.g., if you have a certain genetic make-up, you will have brown eyes. While this is true in practical terms, it is because the range of environments to which the particular genotype will be exposed is very narrow. In other words, the environment with which the genotype will interact is so probable that the phenotype can be predicted from an earlier knowledge of the genotype with great accuracy. Obviously, the same seed grown under very different conditions of temperature, barometric pressure, or sunlight would develop quite differently. The variation in environmental circumstances must be great enough to have an effect. Most genotypes can withstand some variation in the environment without being affected. The important considerations are the degree of environmental fluctuation and the developmental stage at which the exposure to the altered conditions occurs. The product of the interaction of the genotype with the *most probable environment* is highly predictable. As the probability of exposure to a particular environment decreases, there is a concomitant increase in the probability of an alteration in the final phenotype when exposure to that unlikely environment occurs. It is only through carefully controlled research that these outcomes can be predicted and environments selected so as to influence the phenotype. The relative degrees of knowledge between biochemical and "social" genetics are such that manipulation of the genotype may be both more feasible and imminent. The possibility raises profound moral and ethical questions which go beyond the scope of this chapter but which must be recognized and discussed by the people at all levels.

There are also population genetic considerations that should be included in studying intelligence. The expression "like produces like" is an over-simplification, but offspring are more likely to be similar rather than dissimilar to their parents on any genetically loaded trait. For this reason it is biologically sound as well as empirically true to say that the best predictor of an unborn child's IQ is the IQ of its biological parents independent of who rears the child.

All of the contributors to Part II of the volume subscribe to a polygenic theory of intelligence. There is no single gene for the measure called IQ, let alone for the broader construct of intelligence. Yet, that does not mean that the frequency of particular genes in a given population pool may not be directly related to the performance of that population on tests of intelligence. Even a primitive knowledge of genetics leads one to expect real differences in gene distributions between population pools on any given trait that is genetically loaded. Races are, by definition, gene pools that differ from each other in a statistically significant way. Therefore, we should expect significant racial differences on a variety of traits. This does not mean that the groups are innately different in the sense of immutability nor that one is superior in an absolute sense. It does mean that at a given time on a given trait there are differences between the gene pools that contribute to the phenotypic expression of that trait. Different groups, be they races or nationalities, have undergone different selection pressures of a variety of types. For example, the selection pressures in the arctic region were very different from those in the temperate or tropical zones. Cultural factors also play a role in population selection. If particular gene pools have been selectively bred for certain culturally valued traits, it comes as no surprise that these traits are more heavily represented in the population that has selectively bred for them. This very population, however, given a different selection pressure for an appropriate length of time, will become a radically different gene pool. It is in this sense that most geneticists believe that all human gene pools are potentially equal.

One tragic error that frequently intrudes in the mind of man is the confusion of difference with relative inferiority. As indicated earlier in this chapter, man has a long history of treating individual differences as undesirable and of attempting to eradicate them. This characteristic continues to make itself manifest. Superiority can only be defined (and arbitrarily at that) in an operational context. Even more important is the geneticist's realization that diversity between gene pools is biologically useful and, therefore, to be encouraged. Even if a particular group differs at a certain time from the other groups in its average level of performance on a particular trait measure, it does not mean that any given individual performance can be predicted. Nor does it mean that the group cannot achieve equal performance on that trait measure should it be willing to sacrifice the potential benefits of its genetic differences.

An example of difference in IQ test performance between two groups may help to illuminate some of the values and limitations of this measure in predicting the actual performance of these groups in real life. Italians and Jews, as groups, respectively score significantly below and above the mean on IQ tests. Does this result mean that Jews are smarter than Italians? Or is this the wrong question to ask of the data? The result certainly does mean that Jews, as a group, perform better on IQ tests and will, as a group, do better at those tasks that correlate highly with IQ. As would be expected, a study of the roster of scientists—particularly physicists—who have received the Nobel Prize reveals a disproportionately high representation by Jews. The excellence of Jews on tests of abstraction, and thereby in mathematics and those sciences closely related to it, cannot be explained adequately in cultural terms alone. Nor should we be surprised to find the values of a culture are determined, at least in part, by the historical strengths of that particular people. There have been relatively few great Italian mathematicians and physicists, as would be predicted from the group performance on IQ tests. However, it would be false to say that Italians represent an inferior gene pool for intelligence, particularly since their contributions to Western culture are second to no group. The population of that small peninsula has not only made unique contributions to culture in the past but continues to do so to this very day. In a variety of fields, including painting, sculpture, writing, music, architecture, and design, the Italian influence has been strongly present. These are all intellectual activities and are the product of intelligence, but they are not so highly correlated with IQ tests. The lessons to be drawn from this example are clear. IQ test performance is not the alpha and the omega of intelligence, but it can be valuable when properly used. When used improperly, we must blame the man and not the measure. The inferences that can be drawn from differences in group performance are real but limited. The need to reward a greater variety of talents is quite pressing in a technologically advanced society where the tendency is to selectively reward the individual who is outstanding in his ability to abstract. Obviously, the argument leads to social and political issues which are outside of the scope of this chapter.

There are enormously important ethical and social implications to our present-day understanding of the role of genetics in the determination of human behavior. The most powerful emotional argument against any form of genetic intervention is that man must not meddle in this delicate system. Yet, the medical advances of the last generation, e.g., antibiotics, plus the social legislation that has been passed has resulted in a radical alteration of the gene pool. Many individuals who are presently alive and actively contributing offspring to the gene pool would have been dead prior to the remarkable developments of twentieth-century medicine and/or the more liberal social legislation. We must recognize that we are in fact influencing the gene pool in very real ways. For example, keeping schizophrenics out of the hospital and encouraging them to socialize and "lead normal lives" is producing an increased number of offspring and thereby increasing the incidence of schizophrenia in the future generations. Once we recognize that we are in fact meddling with the system, we are compelled to examine in a critical manner the ways and results of our interventions. Any thoughtful consideration of these issues leads one to recognize the enormous importance of rational and humane genetic counseling for the future of our species.

In conclusion, we must avoid the Scylla of making all groups the same —be it through genetic and/or environmental manipulation—on any given trait while ignoring the human and social cost. If we believe in the value of group differences, we will not try to remove them. We must also avoid the equally dangerous Charybdis of self-righteous neglect of genetic counseling. This recognition of man's responsibility to plan and shape his destiny does not alter the fact that equality of opportunity is not negotiable, nor is a decent standard of living for all. America is too strong economically to tolerate the present extent and level of poverty. Morality alone dictates the implementation of certain social changes. These changes must be brought about because it is the morally correct thing to do, independent of their impact on IQ test performance The existence of genetic contributions to individual and group differences in IQ do not justify discrimination in any form. There are measurable differences in the mean IQ of white groups from different national backgrounds. These groups represent slightly different population pools—both genetically and environmentally. Given the identical environment, the groups may still show different relative strengths. This is the diversity that has been needed for evolution to progress, and we have no reason to believe that conditions have changed to the point where this diversity is no longer essential.

We must also identify and reward talents that are not uncovered by IQ tests but which can be of equally great value to our society. In a technologically advanced society, such as ours, it is primarily the individuals with IQs over 115 who are highly rewarded. In the white population this group is less than 17 percent of the total. When 83 percent of the white population is "disadvantaged" vis-à-vis the prestigious positions in society, the exact percentage for blacks or Orientals becomes of questionable value. There are those who believe that the abilities measured on IQ tests represent the pinnacle of human evolution. It logically follows from their view that man as a species should try to maximize this variable. Others feel that the evolution of man is far too complex and on too broad a front to permit any single trait measure to be anything more than misleading. It is hoped that the chapters that follow will assist the reader in reaching his own conclusions.

chapter 6

social class structure and
the genetic basis of intelligence

BRUCE K. ECKLAND

The present chapter deals with a proposition which some of us take for granted, to which some would take strong exception, and perhaps to which most of us just have not given much thought. The proposition is that in meritocratic societies the average difference in measured intelligence of children from different social classes has partly a hereditary basis. In other words, talent (genotypically) is not distributed randomly in each new generation across the entire class structure but tends to be disproportionately concentrated at the middle and upper levels. Middle-class children, *on the average*, tend to be innately brighter than lower-class children.

Before examining the proposition and its implications, let me make at least two concessions to those who are inclined to challenge these statements or would prefer to ignore them: (1) intelligence is not fixed at birth or at conception, since many different factors, often in combination, contribute to its development; and (2) owing to imperfect assortative mating for intelligence and sociocultural differentials, many lower-class children are much brighter than some middle-class children. Perhaps too much has been made of the point that genes do not fix the development of polygenic traits like intelligence. Many different kinds of environmental factors are involved. Nevertheless, genes are discrete entities, which in combination determine the limits of the range within which their phenotype will be expressed. The idea of an unlimited range of individual intelligence modified only by environmental factors just does not fit with reality.

Because both nature and nurture are involved and because they are never perfectly correlated, there is a considerable amount of overlap in any group distribution of intelligence. No one class has a monopoly on all the "good" genes and another on all the "bad" genes. Both low to moderate assortative mating for intelligence and mild to severe environmental deprivation guarantee a relatively substantial pool of very bright children from lower-class backgrounds. But, as we shall argue later, the amount of overlap between classes tends to diminish as assortative mating and equality of opportunity both increase.

The deprivation model

In the standard deprivation model of social class and intelligence, any observed correlation between the social status of an adult population and the intelligence of its children is explained in terms of intervening environmental factors that enhance or inhibit cognitive development and performance, factors which themselves are correlated with social status.

The model is depicted in Figure 1 by a broken arrow in the path between intelligence and social status, r_{IS}, and causal arrows in the paths connecting intelligence with environment, p_{IE}, and environment with social status, p_{ES}. We also have introduced a residual factor, R_e, which symbolizes all possible determinants of the child's environment unaccounted for by parental status.

The extent to which children's intelligence is correlated with the socio-economic status of their parents, of course, depends upon time and place as well as upon the age of the children. Nevertheless, most of the correlations reported in the literature appear to fall in the region between .35 and .40 and, according to Jensen (1969), this "constitutes one of the most substantial and least disputed facts in psychology and education [p. 75]."

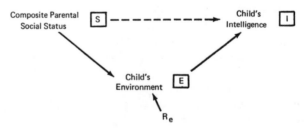

Figure 1. Standard deprivation model of social class and intelligence.

There are three basic types of environmental variables applicable to the deprivation model that may help account for these findings. One group of variables is *physical* or *biological* in nature, such as prenatal care, nutrition, and birth order. Severe prenatal stress and malnutrition both appear to impair cognitive development, and each of these conditions is found more frequently among the disadvantaged segments of the population. Birth order also may be partly responsible for the class-intelligence correlation. For whatever reasons, first-born children on the average score slightly higher on mental tests; and, owing to below average rates of fertility, there are proportionately somewhat more first-born children among higher socioeconomic groups.

A second set of correlates of social class that sometimes contribute to the variance in mental ability is *cultural*. Social classes can be viewed as "subcultures" in the sense that they confer upon their members an integrated set of norms and values which are carried down from generation to generation. The segregation, degradation, and continuity of the poor serve to insulate them from the mainstream of society. As a separate culture, the poor generally experience a relatively unique pattern of behavioral and psychological traits which may directly impair the social, emotional, and cognitive development of children raised under these conditions (Eckland & Kent, 1968).

The third general group of environmental variables that may help account for some portion of the class-intelligence correlation is *social structural*, usually defined as differential access to the institutionalized means for achieving culturally prescribed goals (Merton, 1957). Apart from the content of the subculture of poverty, deprivation frequently involves socially structured inequalities in education and other opportunities for improving a child's performance. These inequalities usually are attributed to the control one class exerts over another, i.e., the superordinate element benefits by keeping another element dependent.

Thus, numerous class-linked environmental variables have been found to contribute to individual differences in measured intelligence. Unfortunately, no serious attempt has ever been made to estimate in a direct fashion the additive effects of more than a few of these factors at one time. In what little that has been done, the effects have not been found to be strictly additive. The "independent" variables themselves are highly interrelated. But even if this were not the case, the cumulative effects of environmental variables probably would not wholly explain social class differences in intelligence since there is another set of factors which the deprivation model totally ignores.

The polygenic model

If native talent is not randomly distributed among all children at birth in the class structure, then the correlation r_{IS} cannot be entirely the result of cultural and other forms of environmental deprivation. The polygenic model in Figure 2 holds that *both* environmental and hereditarian variables are required to explain social class differences in intelligence. As long as a bona fide argument can be made that p_{SM}, p_{MP}, p_{HP}, and p_{IH} are all greater than zero, then the product of these paths constitutes a genetic loop which partly accounts for the correlation r_{IS}.

Three new variables have been introduced in Figure 2. Mid-parent's and child's *heredities* refer to the genotypes of intelligence or to that particular set of polygenes that produce quantitative variations in cognitive functioning. We have used *mid*-parent's heredity and *mid*-parent's intelligence only as a matter of simplification. Mid-parent's and child's *intelligence*, I and M, both, of course, refer to the phenotypes of intelligence or, in other words, whatever IQ tests generally measure.

We also have introduced two new residuals in the model. R_s stands for all sources of variance in the parents' composite social status unaccounted for by their intelligence. R_h stands for all sources of variance in the child's heredity unaccounted for by the mid-parent's heredity.

Let us now examine each of the main paths or links in the genetic loop. Although along the way we shall note some figures suggested by the literature, no claim will be made here regarding the true magnitude of any of the links. We need only show that a connection actually exists between each variable in the loop in order to support the model. Nevertheless, the weight of our argument obviously does depend upon their strength, and one very weak link would seriously limit our conclusions. This is because any coefficients entered in the paths are multiplicative and not additive, which also means that a small change in one of the weaker paths would contribute more to the overall effects of the genetic loop than a comparable change in one of its stronger paths.

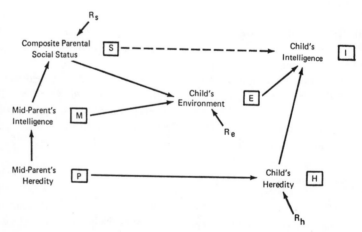

Figure 2. Simplified polygenic model of social class and intelligence.

Parental intelligence and social status

The path from parental intelligence to social status, p_{SM}, is the most critical because it is the primary link between the genetic and environmental components of the model and also because it appears to be the weakest link in the genetic loop. The zero-order correlations found in most studies range from .20 to .50, i.e., when social status is measured in terms of occupational prestige.

Although few will deny that intelligence is a bona fide cause of adult achievement, it is not entirely clear just how this operates owing to the confounding effects of education. When years of schooling are taken into account, only a small empirical relationship remains between intelligence and occupational achievement (Eckland, 1965; Bajema, 1968). This should not be interpreted, however, to mean that the relationship is spurious. Rather, it probably simply means that the educational system acts as the central mechanism in the identification of talent and the allocation of status. Success in school or college depends upon mental ability, while one's point of entry in the labor force and subsequent job promotions depend, in turn, upon prior success in school or college.

Let us inspect each of these steps, especially the first, more closely. The relationship between intelligence and educational achievement, of course, should not be surprising since IQ tests originally were designed to predict academic performance. Student performance in the classroom presumably depends, among other things, upon the kinds of mental skills which IQ tests measure. There is much evidence that they usually do (Goslin, 1963; Lavin, 1965). Yet, aside from the true validity of these tests, the association between intelligence and educational attainment is built into the educational selection process itself. That is, standardized tests of mental ability are employed as a primary basis for sorting and selecting students beginning in the primary grades and continuing on through college. In 1967 I summarized this development as follows:

(a) Virtually all schools now use standardized tests. Moreover, a large majority of the secondary schools in this country plan to expand their testing programs in the near future.

(b) Standardized tests are used to assess the potential learning ability of students, in order to provide individualized instruction, and to guide students in their decisions about school curricula, going to college, and jobs. A fairly large majority of the nation's youth actually are being placed into homogeneous classes on the basis of these tests, either by establishing completely separate programs of instruction for different students ("tracking") or by assigning students to different sections of the same course ("grouping").

(c) A majority of both students and adults believe that standardized tests measure the intelligence a person is born with; although most, at the same time, recognize that learning makes an important difference. Students and **parents** alike believe that the tests are basically accurate. While teachers essentially agree with the students and parents on these points, they also tend to believe that the tests are their best single index of a student's intellectual ability.

(d) Although public acceptance of standardized testing seems to depend largely upon the specific purposes for which the tests are used, a majority of the students believe that these tests are and should be important, especially in terms of deciding who should go to college.

This is only part of the story. For the college-going aspirants, the first two major hurdles—Educational Testing Service's Preliminary Scholastic Aptitude Test (PSAT) and National Merit Scholarship Corporation's Qualifying Test— usually come in the eleventh grade. Scores on the PSAT are not used to decide who goes to college, since that decision presumably was made some years earlier. Rather, one of the primary purposes of the test is to help decide who goes where to college by giving each student an early estimate of the probabilities of being admitted to any particular school. The National Merit examination, on the other hand, is designed to select among the uppermost two percent of the country's students those who will receive special commendation and awards. While in competition with other programs, the growth of the PSAT and National Merit programs in the past ten years has been so phenomenal that both are being administered today in roughly three-fourths of the nation's high schools.

The next major, and perhaps most important, challenge comes about a year later—the college admissions tests and, for those in accelerated programs, the Advanced Placement examinations. Whether administered nationally or locally, tests are being used today by most colleges in their admissions process or for placement. Indeed, the proportion of high-scoring students that a college can attract has become the most objective criterion available for ranking the colleges themselves. In addition, many secondary schools and colleges are participating in the Advanced Placement Program of the College Entrance Examination Board. Although presently involving fewer students and schools, its growth has closely paralleled that of the National Merit program.

As the student progresses further, the significance of educational testing does not diminish. Upon completion of most undergraduate programs, admission to nearly any reputable graduate or professional school is fast becoming dependent, in part, upon the student's sophistication on such nationally administered tests as the Graduate Record Examination, the Admission Test for Graduate Study in Business, or the Law School Admissions Test. Likewise, entry into a particular field direct from a four-year undergraduate program sometimes requires additional testing, such as the National Teachers Examination or the Foreign Service Examination. Even the Peace Corps requires the Peace Corps Entrance Tests [Eckland, 1967, pp. 185–187].

Thus, the use of IQ and closely related tests of ability can now be found at nearly every point in the educational system. In fact, as the testing movement has gained momentum, many observers are wondering if our schools place *too much* emphasis on these programs, particularly when it is recognized that culturally biased tests tend to discriminate against underprivileged groups.

Yet, notwithstanding even the restrictive legislation which has been enacted recently in some communities in order to safeguard students against the arbitrary use of tests, school and college testing programs no doubt will survive and perhaps play a still greater role in the future. I doubt that we ultimately shall decide who goes where to college or similar educational decisions by lottery, as some have suggested that we ought to do. Lotteries probably are no more "equitable" than testing programs, and they certainly are a less rational way to use human resources—although we recognize too that equal educational opportunity in its purest form might be a more compelling objective in the long run than the efficient utilization of talent.

Probably stronger than the relationship between intelligence and educational achievement is the relationship between educational and occupational achievement. (Occupational status is the most commonly used index of social status.) Commercial and industrial enterprises seem to rely very heavily upon our schools and colleges not only to train people, but also to sort out those who are less motivated and inept. Although other factors are involved too, getting to the head of the academic procession takes both persistence and "brains," and it is quite clear that graduates of the nation's best colleges and universities tend to get the most and the best job offers. Thus, just as the holder of a degree from any four-year college is almost guaranteed passage into middle-class status, graduation from a highly selective and prestigious college or university is a reasonably valid passport for entry into upper-middle-class status.

This all means that as members of the younger generation graduate from school or college, enter the labor force, and have families of their own, the relationship between intelligence and adult social status (in our model) should at least retain its present strength and quite probably become a bit stronger. The expansion of most of the school and college testing programs described earlier has been too recent to have had much effect on the vast majority of American adults. Only the most recent cohorts of students are being affected. As they move into the labor force, we should expect the path p_{SM} to increase.

The inheritance of intelligence

The next link in the genetic loop, p_{MP}, and the last link, p_{IH}, will be discussed together. In both paths we are dealing with the question, What proportion of the variance in measured intelligence is due to heredity? This proportion usually is expressed in terms of a heritability coefficient, and its magnitude will be approximately the same whether we are speaking of the child's or the parents' intelligence.

Much controversy has revolved around the concept of heritability and its measurement. But the most serious issues probably can be avoided if we remember that in the strictest sense a heritability measure is a property of a population, not of an individual or of the trait itself. Heritability simply estimates the proportion of the total phenotypic variance in a particular population at a particular point in time. We have no direct measure of heritability for individuals, per se. Moreover, a high heritability coefficient does not mean that the environment is unimportant or unnecessary for the expression of the trait. Rather, it would only mean that environmental variation does not explain very much of the *variation* in the trait that is being observed.

Heritabilities for intelligence generally fall within the range from .70 to .90, their size depending upon the population under consideration, plus the partiuclar methods, formula, and tests used.

It could be argued that the heritability of intelligence is increasing. Since the coefficient is a population statistic and always depends upon the absolute amount of variance of trait-relevant factors in the environment, any significant change in the environmental factors will change paths p_{MP} and p_{IH}. The size of these paths is inversely related to the total amount of environmental variance. This means that if either of the two direct paths from parental social status (S) and parents' intelligence (M) to the child's environment (E) declines, then, all other things being equal, we should expect an increase in the proportion of the variance in measured intelligence that can be attributed to heredity. To the extent that this nation's efforts to upgrade the environments of low SES children are successful, this should be exactly what happens. Since the genetic and environmental factors influencing intelligence presently covary in the same direction, successful efforts to decrease the excess number of children generally found in the lower region of most IQ distributions also would tend to decrease the absolute amount of variance observed and shift the population mean upward.

However, there are and would continue to be other environmental factors (in the residual, R_e) affecting cognitive development that are uncorrelated with either parental status or parental intelligence. If parents gave up altogether the care of their children to the schools or some other complex of socializing agencies, one of the major sources of environmental variation would have disappeared. On the other hand, institutionalized child rearing could conceivably create more rather than less overall diversity of trait-relevant environments, especially if highly individualized treatments of the kind being suggested by some educators were put into practice. If this were the case, heritabilities might decrease instead of increase, and the total population variance might increase instead of decrease.

There is a further complication that probably would occur. If different treatments were assigned routinely to different individuals, it is unlikely that they would be assigned randomly. The "richness" of each child's experience instead may vary directly with the unique package of genes (or potential) he brings to the situation. Just what this would do to the size and meaning of heritability has not been adequately explored.

Nevertheless, as far as our model is concerned, current heritabilities of intelligence are quite high and contribute substantially to the genetic loop.

The genetic parent-child correlation

The final link to be considered in the loop, p_{HP}, also is quite strong. And, like the other links, its size depends upon certain environmental conditions.

A child receives half of his genes from each parent. Thus, at the minimum, the genetic parent-child correlation for intelligence is .50. However, it apparently is considerably larger since this figure only applies under conditions of random mating. The additive genetic parent-child correlation for intelligence and other polygenic traits is actually .50 plus one-half the assortative mating coefficient, or, in other words, the degree to which parents on the average hold certain genes in common. The more closely the parents resemble each other, the more closely children will resemble their parents. Assortative mating also tends to increase a trait's average homozygosity and, thus, the population variance of the genes, which in the long run means reducing the trait's within-class variance while increasing its between-class variance.

Unfortunately, the size of the assortative mating coefficient for intelligence —and, consequently, the genetic parent-child correlation—is somewhat a matter of conjecture, especially for recent cohorts. One problem is that only phenotypic, not genotypic, correlations are available. Nevertheless, if the coefficient of assortative mating is as high as .60, as some authors have suggested (Jensen, 1969), then the parent-child correlation, p_{HP}, must be on the order of .80.

One possible check on the size of this path is to use some of the values that have been suggested and see if the product of the three paths, $p_{IH}p_{HP}p_{MP}$, equals the *phenotypic* parent-child correlations commonly reported in the literature. Thus, if heritability is .80 in both generations and the genetic parent-child correlation also is .80, the product of these paths is .51, which is remarkably similar to the parent-child correlation (r_{IM}) usually observed (Erlenmeyer-Kimling & Jarvik, 1963). Under conditions of random mating the expected value for this correlation would be only .32.

Due largely to educational selection and to changes in social values regarding mate selection, assortative mating for intelligence probably is increasing. Societies that value individual freedom of choice in marriage and at the same time place potential mates into relatively homogeneous social settings based on ability are likely to produce high rates of assortative mating for intelligence. Males and females of like intelligence, especially in recent generations, generally end up in similar educational niches, such as school dropouts, as college classmates, or as graduate students. These set the broad limits within which mate selection tends to occur.

Let me give one example. In 1965 a follow-up study was conducted by the National Merit Scholarship Corporation to determine the accomplishments of all female Merit Scholars who had received their awards between 1956 and 1960. These women undoubtedly were among the brightest in the nation. They were not destined to be spinsters. By 1965 the far majority had married and most of their husbands had either completed or entered graduate school (Watley, 1969). Since their husbands no doubt also are far brighter than average, their children will be well above average, and this partly will be due to the hereditary basis of intelligence.

If not already the case, education may soon become a better predictor of who mates with whom than either social class or residential propinquity. We already have argued that educational testing and similar mechanisms create relatively homogeneous pools of talent. We only need to add that our schools and colleges also function as marriage markets. I suspect that if they did not, the college-going rates for women in this country would be markedly lower than they are. But, as it is, the number of women attending college for the first time has been rising more rapidly over the past generation than the number of men attending for the first time. Yet, it is not entirely clear exactly what value a college diploma is to most women, other than attracting an eligible husband and unrestricted passage to middle-class respectability. (There are, of course, exceptions.)

Once again, assortative mating increases the genetic parent-child correlation, which, in turn, strengthens the genetic loop. Since the four paths in the loop are multiplicative, their total effect presently accounts for perhaps only a relatively small proportion of the association between parental social status and a child's intelligence—even though individually some of the paths have quite strong coefficients. Nevertheless, the polygenic model of social class and intelligence, I believe, does operate in approximately the manner described here, and the strength of the genetic loop is sufficient to warrant closer inspection. This will become increasingly true if contemporary societies continue to implement the principles of the meritocracy—a trend that, in the long run, seems inescapable.

The future of social mobility

In conclusion, I would like to consider the future of social mobility by projecting the trends outlined. Sociologists generally define social mobility as the intergenerational movement of individuals from the social class of their family of origin to the class of their family of procreation. Sometimes the individual's intelligence is considered, but only as one of several plausible mechanisms through which parental status limits or enhances the individual's future status. No genetic components of intelligence are recognized, and, like the deprivation model described earlier, the correlation between the status of father and son is usually thought to be wholly a result of social inequality. In fact, the size of the correlation sometimes is taken as a direct measure of inequality of opportunity—or the extent to which positions are socially ascribed rather than achieved in accordance with one's own effort and abilities.

However, the polygenic model of social class and intelligence suggests a quite different conclusion regarding the effects of equality of opportunity on social mobility. We already have argued that equal opportunity in the long run tends to strengthen most if not all the paths in the genetic loop between parental social status and child's intelligence. Thus, rather than leading to progressively lower correlations between father's and son's status, equal opportunity may eventually raise the correlation. Or, in other words, social mobility would not increase over time; rather, it would eventually either stabilize or decline.

In a completely open society under full equality of opportunity, a child's future position might be just as accurately predicted from the status of his biological parent as in a caste society. The basic difference between the two being that in a completely open system the casual links between generations would involve character specific or polygenic traits like intelligence, whereas in a caste system the links are consanguineous or cultural.

However, in the transition from castelike to truly open-class systems, it is not likely that a linear transformation in the rates of mobility would be observed. Initially, the correlations between father's and son's status should fall as meritocratic principles begin to operate. (This is what we still seem to be observing today.) But, at some optimal point in the not too distant future the force of the genetic loop may swing the correlations in the opposite direction.

When industrial societies emerged along with their complex division of labor, it eventually became reasonably clear that not everyone could do everything. Perhaps a noble's son could once be trusted to oversee a kingdom, but who is willing to trust the laws of primogeniture, nepotism, or even seniority in the running of today's social machinery? Thus, with the development of mass education and the demand for skilled technicians and a managerial elite, who does what now depends more upon what people are capable of doing than who their parents happen to be or other irrelevant criteria.

But what of the future? If, as suggested, the heritability of intelligence remains high while educational selection and assortative mating for intelligence increase, what then? Have we already reached the turning point, in which case we should soon expect declining rates of mobility? Or, perhaps for a variety of reasons we shall never reach this point. These are, I believe, significant questions. Unfortunately, our data are far too weak to provide even the most tentative answers.

References

Bejema, C. J. A note on the interrelations among intellectual ability, educational attainment, and occupational achievement: A follow-up study of a male Kalamazoo public school population. *Sociology of Education*, 1968, *41*, 317–319.

Eckland, B. K. Academic ability, higher education, and occupational mobility. *American Sociological Review*, 1965, *30*, 735–746.

———. Genetics and sociology: A reconsideration. *American Sociological Review*, 1967, *32*, 173–194.

———, & Kent, D. P. Socialization and social structure. In *Perspectives on human deprivation: Biological, psychological, and sociological*. Bethesda, Md.: The National Institute of Child Health and Human Development, 1968.

Erlenmeyer-Kimling, L., & Jarvik, L. F. Genetics and intelligence: A review. *Science*, 1963, *142*, 1477–1479.

Goslin, D. *The search for ability*. New York: Russell Sage Foundation, 1963.

Jensen, A. R. How much can we boost IQ and scholastic achievement? *Harvard Educational Review*, 1969, *39*, 1–123.

Lavin, D. E. *The prediction of academic performance*. New York: Russell Sage Foundation, 1965.

Merton, R. K. *Social theory and social structure*. New York: Free Press, 1957.

Watley, D. J. Career or marriage?: A longitudinal study of able young women. *National Merit Scholarship Research Reports*, 1969, *5*.

chapter 7

race and intelligence,
what do we really know?

BENSON E. GINSBURG AND
WILLIAM S. LAUGHLIN

It would seem a simple matter to collate data on ethnic origin, intelligence test scores, and economic and educational status and to do this for at least two generations on a sufficiently large sample to permit some empirical generalizations to emerge regarding the contribution of race, per se, to IQ as it is usually measured. Most of this could be handled retrospectively in a society that measures, classifies, and keeps records as devotedly as we do. In point of fact, however, it is not such a simple matter, nor is it apparent from those data that are available just what ethnicity determines in a causal sense. Some scholars have argued that the very question smacks of racism and should be taboo on those grounds alone. Others have arrived at a hands-off-the-question attitude by arguing that it invokes a hypothesis that can neither be proved nor disproved using present methods and is, therefore, not a scientific problem.

It is also possible to argue, on the other side, that many of those who would study this problem, far from being racists, are the very ones who will put in the hands of society the tools that are necessary to maximize the potential of every group and of every man and that without assaults upon hypotheses at the edge of our concepts and methods there will be no new breakthroughs. In any event, we do not have the luxury of turning our backs on this issue since it has been raised not only in this country with reference to blacks, but also elsewhere with reference to other ethnic groups. Unlike an actual fetus, an intellectual fetus cannot be aborted. It behooves us, therefore, to evaluate what evidence we have, to identify ambiguities, and to consider whether and how the question can be more profitably investigated than it has been thus far. What we need is a compass to determine where we are and a road map to instruct us on where we might go from here.

Ingle (1968) and Jensen (1969) have confronted us with data that indicate, if taken literally, that blacks in this country have a lower mean IQ than whites, even when attempts are made to equate differences in socioeconomic status and other seemingly relevant factors. Ingle has suggested that biological differences might be involved and that this possibility should be investigated. Jensen, reasoning from the high heritability of intelligence and from the knowledge that gene frequencies vary among population groups, hypothesizes that the differences in population statistics with respect to intelligence could plausibly have a genetic basis and that the history of the blacks in the United States has subjected them to a breeding structure that is behaviorally dysgenic.

Hirsch (1971) has raised some questions regarding the use and interpretation of the heritability statistic in the context of ethnic comparisons of IQ scores, and Li (1971) has analyzed the consequences of various systems of mating on the distribution of genotypes and phenotypes for a polygenic attribute, such as intelligence. In this chapter we are concerned with the relationship between genotype and phenotype under a variety of developmental circumstances in the light of our best knowledge and conceptions about these interrelations (e.g., Bloom, 1964). We are also concerned with the relationship between any existing array of phenotypes and the potential array inherent in the gene pool from which they are drawn.

Ideally, it would be instructive if we could take each subpar child, whether white or black, and reprogram his developmental history while leaving his genes intact. This would include his mother's prenatal condition—her nourishment, a uterus free of injury or disease, adequate oxygenation during delivery—as well as optimal care, emotional support, and intellectual stimulation during childhood. In many instances the child would still be mentally subnormal, though possibly happier and healthier, for the genetic potential for greater achievement simply did not exist. In other instances, however, the child might register 20 points higher in IQ under one set of circumstances as compared with another, as has been found in cases of identical twins reared apart. To say that the IQ was any more or less genetic in the two sets of circumstances would be an empty and circular play on words. To consider that the genetic potential was actualized in the second situation but not in the first is equally simpleminded and misleading. If we could take our brighter twin and reprogram him as his sib was, he should be 20 points lower. Either that or we must impute a significant proportion of the development of behavioral capacities to chance. A given genome has only those degrees of freedom that are inherent in its genes. Under controlled and specified circumstances it will develop in a particular way. Under a set of modified circumstances it will develop differently. A second genotype exposed to the same variations in conditions will have its own distinctive repertoire. Each interacting outcome is a function of the genome, as is the degree or lack of lability to changed conditions in another genotype. We refer to this phenomenon as the *genomic repertoire* of the individual. Depending on the array of genotypes comprising a population, one or another set of *phenoptions* will be presented. Given appropriate changes in environmental conditions, the phenotypic profile will also change, even if the array of genotypes remains constant.

The genotypic profile need not remain constant. In addition to changing over long periods of time due to factors of selection, mutation, migration, intermarriage, and genetic drift, it may change by recombination in a relatively short period without any concomitant change in the frequency or identity of the genes comprising the pool from which the genotypes are drawn. All that need happen is for significant portions of the population to resort to some degree of positive phenotypic assortative mating. This will produce a rapid and significant shift in the distribution of genotypes, thus leading to a change in the normative phenotypic array presented by the population. Any gene pool, if relatively large, represents a potential for producing alternative phenotypic arrays, depending on how the genes are shuffled, distributed, and recombined. Each gene pool, therefore, represents a broad series of potentials for restructuring itself within a few generations by opting, through assortative mating, for one or another system of probabilities that will determine the distribution of its genotypes as compared, for example, with the options it would have had as a result of random mating. The *phenoptions*, to which we have previously referred in the context of each individual genotype within a collective, are also a property of a gene pool which may, depending on the system of mating, result in one or another assortment of phenotypes even where environmental conditions are constant. In order to distinguish these situations, we have termed the phenoptions of an individual genotype across a spectrum of conditions that influence its potential, *geneticity*. The degrees of freedom for responding to a variable environment are inherent in the genotype. An optimally nourished Chihuahua will never reach the size of a Great Dane.

The complement to this situation is represented by the fact that a phenotype may have more than one genetic basis. From the reference point of the phenotype, these are *genoptions*, and any collection of genotypes which under a given set of developmental conditions will result in equivalent phenotypes are referred to as *isophenes* or isophenic clusters. A given genotype may, however, be *heterophenic* if it develops under different sets of conditions.

The purpose of introducing these terms is to underscore the concepts and premises that form the basis of our argument so that we shall not be mistranslated to any other set of premises that are not ours. We find it necessary to emphasize the obvious fact (see Ginsburg, 1958, p. 404) that all aspects of an organism's potential are 100 percent genetic, though not 100 percent determined, under the rubric of genomic repertoire or geneticity. Stern (1960, pp. 647 and 570–572) points out that the concept of heritability applied normatively to complex traits depending on many genes is not suitable for an individual analysis of specific genotypes, "whether the latter possess dominant, recessive, or inter-mediate alleles; whether a few or many loci; and whether two or more alleles at one locus are involved." He also calls attention to some of the limitations inherent in twin study methods where, unless we can assume that the different environments across which phenotypic comparisons are made for MZ (mono-zygotic) and DZ (dizygotic) pairs had similar effects on the expression of the different genotypes (an assumption which we find untenable in view of the data in hand), one cannot partition the variance into genetic and nongenetic categories. It would, therefore, not be justifiable to conclude on the basis of the usual statistics that X proportion of the variance of a trait in nonidentical twins is due to heredity, and $1 - X$ to environment since the value of X will vary with the genotype as well as with the range of conditions under which it develops.

Ginsburg (1966, 1968) has summarized and discussed evidence based on studies in which it has been possible to test the genomic repertoires of a number of inbred strains of mice. Each such strain was substantially isogenic so that it was possible to ascertain the potential of a given genotype across a variety of environmental circumstances. By means of ova transplant techniques, it was feasible to include prenatal genetic factors in the experimental design. A number of such strains and their equally isogenic F_1 crosses were used. The salient findings of the studies are that environmental circumstances that will alter the behavioral development of one strain will have no effect on another and the opposite effect on a third. The time during development at which an effect can be most readily induced by a given environmental circumstance is likewise a function of the strain, or genotype. Thus, it is the geneticity of the particular mouse that determines whether it will respond to an imposed environmental stress during the preweaning period by becoming more aggressive as an adult than it would have been in the absence of such stressful stimulation, or less aggressive as a result of the same stimulation. Still another genotype will remain unchanged under the same conditions. Some genotypes are most affected by stimulation during the early portion of the preweaning period, whereas others, whatever the direction and magnitude of the subsequently altered behavior, will not respond until the third week postpartum, and still others will respond maximally to cumulative experience during the entire preweaning period. A genetically mixed population would, if sampled, exhibit a central tendency, but this measure would be singularly uninformative, constituting, as it does, an amalgam of individual differences. It is just as genetically determined that the C57BL/10 male mouse is labile to a variety of environmental manipulations with respect to its aggressive behavior as that the C3H mouse is not (Ginsburg, 1967). The concept of genomic repertoire or geneticity expresses this phenomenon where the concept of heritability (which is useful in other respects) does not.

Though mutations are ultimately the source of raw materials with which selection works, there is such a profusion of genetic variability stored in species and populations that a complete cessation of new mutations would not be detectable for some time and the potential for evolutionary change would probably not be altered for thousands of generations (Crow, 1959; Dobzhansky, 1970). A major problem is the detection of cryptic or latent genetic variability: how many loci and how many alleles are there compared with those which we can detect? The fact of the matter is that we know humans are highly variable using only traits accessible to existing reagents, measurements, and observations. Using marker traits such as baldness in Europeans, the small ear of Negroes, or the shovel-shaped maxillary incisors of Mongoloids, we can see extensive variation between populations involving different tissue and organ systems and can infer that many of the genes are independent. If anything, the amount of genetic variation is probably underestimated. There is no indication that large continental populations such as Mongoloids, Negroes, and whites differ in degree of genetic variability, though they obviously differ in the frequency of genes they possess as has been especially well documented in blood-group genetics. They also differ in their phenotypic arrays.

Thus, the recombinations of existing genetic variation are clearly adequate to continue human evolution for thousands of generations. If we convert evolution into terms of years, using a generous figure of twenty-five years per generation, we may evolve for 3,000 generations, or 75,000 years (as much as the distance from Neanderthal man to modern man) without invoking new genetic materials.

We must not lose sight of a further consideration as we build our theoretical models and interpret our empirical results in the light of these models—namely, that there are multiple genetic routes to most phenotypes. Just as a particular genome has a repertoire of responses, or phenoptions, depending on its developmental circumstances but determined by the degrees of freedom inhering in its own genotype, a given phenotype contains a multiplicity of genoptions, some of which could have been otherwise expressed under a different set of circumstances, but all of which are isophenic under some circumstances (Ginsburg, 1958, 1966, 1967, 1968). A given phenotype, such as that represented by a single IQ score, would be expected to contain a multiplicity of genotypes. Nor should we assume that the normative array of genotypes which constitutes that phenotype will be the same for one population as for another. Different gene pools within the same species, in this case, our own, will differ with respect to the frequency of the genes that they contain. It must be appreciated, however, that it is not necessary for them to be equivalent genotypically in order for them to be equivalent phenotypically.

We come now to the central questions of this volume. Despite some appreciable gene flow between black and white populations in this country, the gene pools of the two populations remain distinguishable. Do differences in the means and distributions of IQ between blacks and whites, when "equated" for educational background and socioeconomic factors, reflect a corresponding difference in genetic potential, or are we dealing with a sufficiently massive deprivation experiment in the case of the black population to have distorted the phenotypic representation of its array of genomic repertoires?

Jensen (1970) cites Scarr (1970) in an evaluation of birth-weight data of twins in which the results indicate that even for birth weights over 2,500 grams the advantage in IQ lies with the larger twin. In cases of identical genotype it would mean that prenatal nutrition can program the genomic repertoire within the limits of its lability. One would expect, given a genetically diverse population of identical twin pairs, that their lability would vary as a function of genotype. An alternative interpretation of the data, which includes some instances where birth weight is positively associated with intelligence and some instances where it is not, is that each of these situations represents different geneticities and that in combining them for statistical purposes one has missed the biological point.

Population data on birth weights indicate that blacks contribute over twice the proportion of infants under 2,500 grams as whites (Meredith, 1970). If Scarr's interpretation is valid and can be generalized, this, alone, could be a significant distorting factor introducing a systematic bias in black IQ scores.

More instructive are the data of the Smilanskys as summarized by Bloom (1969). These investigators worked with the so-called European and Oriental populations in Israel. Genetic data indicate that these do, indeed, constitute distinctive gene pools (Goldschmidt, 1963). IQ and school performance separate these populations as widely as those samples of black and white populations in the United States, on the basis of which Jensen, Ingle, and others have advanced a genetic hypothesis. Compensatory education programs there, as here, have not been successful in closing the gap.

. In their attempts to find equivalent environments in which the two groups could be compared under circumstances in which ethnicity was the only significant factor in which the populations differed, the Smilanskys turned to children of Oriental and of mixed ethnicity who were born and raised on those agricultural cooperatives, or kibbutzim, in which the Europeans were the majority. Each Oriental or half-Oriental child was paired with a European child of the same age and in the same class at school for evaluation purposes. Parents were equated on the basis of educational information and of the occupational niches they occupied. Since the mothers were on the kibbutzim during their prenatal period, nutritional and prenatal care factors were comparable (cooking is communal). Children live apart from parents in nurseries, children's houses, and school, and they are attended by a specialized staff from the kibbutz. They spend some time with their parents every day. Each kibbutz is affiliated with a social or political movement, and all members, therefore, share in a prevailing ideal and set of political objectives. The Oriental and the European are, therefore, on an equal basis in the life of the settlement. Motivational factors operate equally for their children, and the relationship between education and later opportunities are comparable for both. Classroom instruction is by a project method in which various subjects may be taught together in relation to the project. Special talents and interests are fostered, although the schools themselves are noncompetitive and students help each other in their work. The 1,200 children in the study were followed into adolescence.

Under these circumstances, the Oriental children achieved and maintained a mean IQ that was the same as that of their European counterparts. They also provided as high a proportion of individuals who scored in the exceptional range on a number of separate measures as did the Europeans.

While it may be argued that self-selection for kibbutz life could introduce a bias, and that the Oriental gene pool is not the same as the Negro gene pool, the face validity of the data suggests that it is at least as plausible to argue that when most conditions of development, motivation, and education are approximately the same for the European and the Oriental gene pools, the mean differences in IQ will disappear and the proportion of individuals who score in the exceptional categories on such tests will be comparable. Further, if this obtains for the Oriental, why not also for the black?

This does not imply that the distribution of genotypes will be the same in the two groups. Neither does it denigrate the role of genetics. A comparable mean IQ level and commensurable proportions of scores over a given cutting point could represent a different array of genotypes and gene frequencies in the two populations. They are only phenotypically equivalent in a truly equivalent environment; even then, the distributions may still reveal some differences. What the kibbutz data suggest is that a polygenic adaptive trait complex can have a similar phenotypic topography under similar conditions in two genetically distinctive populations, even though the genetic underpinning for this topography may not be the same in the two cases.

It has been stated that the breeding history of the black population in the United States was and continues to be dysgenic in that it was largely random, and, when it was not, it favored brawn, not brains. To the extent that it may have been random for intelligence, the statistical consequences of the Hardy-Weinberg law would work against deterioration in that the same distributions of genotypes would be maintained indefinitely. Given the attribute of the genomic repertoire, the phenotypes might fluctuate with changes in conditions. In another paper, one of us (Ginsburg, 1970) has reasoned, as Li has argued in this volume (see Chapter 10) that if an intergrading polygenic phenotype exists, all that has to happen to keep the entire gamut of genetic repertoires intact in a population is for all of the heterozygous classes to be represented. Those at the mean of the population would be expected, as a class, to reproduce this genetic range, and to have the potential for reconstituting the phenotypic array of the entire population. When those classes on either side of the mean are also multiply heterozygous and when there is slippage between genotype and phenotype, especially in a population whose genetic potential is imperfectly nurtured and detected, there is no real evidence that it is going genetically downhill.

At the same time it must be acknowledged that if we had a society in which each genoption could achieve its optimal expression and if positive phenotypic assortative mating were to occur at the middle and upper reaches of the distribution, the phenotypic variance might well increase along with the proportion of exceptional phenotypes. The latter, if mated more generally inter se, would contribute disproportionately to their own end of the distribution. In sum, any fair-sized genetically variable population can restructure itself phenotypically in time. Seen from this point of view, the Smilansky data indicate either that the selective factors that had been operating in their populations were not all that different, or that selection for IQ in human populations is neither intense nor persistent.

Schull and Neel have developed the thesis that the outstanding "experimental" challenge in human genetics today is to understand the function and maintenance of the great number of genetic polymorphisms, and they have enumerated the principal approaches now available. Since most, if not all, of the genetic polymorphisms appear to have arisen in primitive man (if not in an earlier state of human evolution), studies on preliterate peoples with a relatively simple technology are of special relevance to the understanding of these (Neel, 1969, p. 400). Central to the study of genetic variation is the complex context of the population in which the variations occur, the breeding structure, population history, disease patterns, reproductive histories, and many more bodies of information essential to the maintenance of polymorphisms.

To the list of constraints or conditions on human evolution must be added the differences in the experiential and performance world (Laughlin, 1970).

In the urban situation where populations are sequestered in geographic sections and are further arranged in a socioeconomic hierarchy that configures mating and immigration frequencies, sampling problems are set that may vitiate the results of traditional testing for IQ or other parameters. The more successful families may abstract themselves from the groups tested by immigrating out and making themselves inaccessible. To the extent that this brain drain occurs, it introduces a systematic bias into the results.

One reason that different populations must be studied in order to understand the genetics and behavior of our species is simply that no one population system has a monopoly on variability. No single population is an adequate sample of the entire species. The total genetic repertoire of our species is deployed into many different populations which have been valuable trial runs for new combinations of genes. These populations are not incipient species but rather are part of the strategy of human evolution. Thus, the variation between races reflects the development of new combinations in which very similar phenotypic arrays rest upon genoptions that are isophenic rather than genotypically identical. The observation that no single population is an adequate sample of the entire species does not contravene our contention that any one population, if reasonably large, possesses sufficient latent genetic variability to replace any other population for whatever selective norms might be established and that, in this sense, they are equipotential.

Measures of heritability are of limited relevance to the argument regarding ethnicity and IQ owing partly to the method of partitioning effects dichotomously into hereditary and environmental components and partly to the nature of the concept itself. Three criticisms may be leveled at the use of heritability estimates in the current context (Bodmer & Cavalli-Sforza, 1970; Jensen, 1969). In brief, (1) the simple partition into two components conceals a variety of differences resident in the genetic component, and no provision is made for the diversity of interaction effects; (2) the statistic cannot be used for individual discrimination; and (3) the statistic cannot be transferred from one population to another. Stern (1960) has commented on the inadequacy of the interaction component, a factor, or factors, which we suggest is a genotypic contribution and is inherent in the genome.

Whether we set ourselves the long-range objective of the phenotypic restructuring of a population (see Ginsburg & Laughlin, 1966, 1968) or the short-term objective of extracting the maximum phenotypic potential from the array of genotypes that are with us now, our practical alternatives would be much the same. They would be to improve nutrition and prenatal care, to provide stimulation and experience to developing infants, and to maximize educational opportunities and the nurturing of individual abilities in a context where ability and achievement pay off equally for European and Oriental, black and white. The Israeli data suggest that although the total IQ distribution might not be the same from one large population group to another under such conditions, the mean differences would disappear and the proportion of high-ability individuals derived from each gene pool might be comparable. Under such circumstances, it is likely that the future would take care of itself as boy math student meets girl math student, or musician, or artist. Or, perhaps, a sufficient number will be attracted by the exotic to keep the genetic cards more randomly distributed and our phenotypic potential much as it is today. The late Herman Muller suggested that a general upgrading of the population could be achieved by the use of sperm banks—disproportionately contributed by Nobel Laureates, of course. The shadow that falls across the light from this suggestion is epitomized by the second sight of George Bernard Shaw, who, when told by dancer Isadora Duncan that they should have a child together so that "it" might inherit her incomparable body and his superb mind, reflected that "it" could turn out the other way around. Therein lies the recapitulation of the normal distribution for any intergrading phenotype.

References

Bloom, B. S. *Stability and change in human characteristics.* New York: Wiley, 1964.

———. Letter to the editor. *Harvard Educational Review,* 1969, *39,* 419–421.

Bodmer, W. F., & Cavalli-Sforza, L. L. Intelligence and race. *Scientific American,* 1970, *223,* 19–29.

Crow, J. F. Ionizing radiation and evolution. *Scientific American,* 1959, *201,* 138–160.

Dobzhansky, T. H. On natural selection in human populations. Burg Wartenstein Symposium, No. 50, Wenner-Gren Foundation for Anthropological Research, 1970.

Ginsburg, B. E. Genetics as a tool in the study of behavior. *Perspectives in Biology and Medicine,* 1958, *1,* 397–424.

———. All mice are not created equal: Recent findings on genes and behavior. *Social Service Review,* 1966, *40,* 121–134.

———. Genetic parameters in behavior research. In J. Hirsch (Ed.), *Behavior-genetic analysis.* New York: McGraw-Hill, 1967.

———. Genotypic factors in the ontogeny of behavior. *Science and Psychoanalysis,* 1968, *12,* 12–17.

———. Developmental genetics of behavioral capacities: The nature-nurture problem re-evaluated. *Merrill-Palmer Quarterly of Behavior and Development,* 1971, *17,* 59–66.

———, & Laughlin, W. S. The multiple bases of human adaptibility and achievement: A species point of view. *Eugenics Quarterly,* 1966, *13,* 240–257.

———, ———. The distribution of genetic differences in behavioral potential in the human species. In M. Mead, T. Dobzhansky, E. Tobach, & R. E. Light (Eds.), *Science and the concept of race.* New York: Columbia University Press, 1968.

Goldschmidt, E. (Ed.) *The genetics of migrant and isolate populations.* Baltimore: Williams and Wilkins, 1963.

Hirsch, J. Behavior-genetic analysis and its biosocial consequences. In R. Cancro (Ed.), *Intelligence: Genetic and environmental influences.* New York: Grune & Stratton, 1971.

Ingle, D. J. The need to investigate average biological differences among racial groups. In M. Mead, T. Dobzhansky, E. Tobach, & R. E. Light (Eds.), *Science and the concept of race.* New York: Columbia University Press, 1968.

Jensen, A. R. How much can we boost IQ and scholastic achievement? *Harvard Educational Review,* 1969, *39,* 1–123.

———. IQs of identical twins reared apart. *Behavior Genetics,* 1970, *1,* 133–148.

Laughlin, W. S. The purpose of studying eskimos and their population systems. *Arctic,* 1970, *23,* 3–13.

Li, C. C. A tale of two thermosbottles: Properties of a genetic model for human intelligence. In R. Cancro (Ed.), *Intelligence: Genetic and environmental influences.* New York: Grune & Stratton, 1971.

Meredith, H. V. Body weight at birth of viable human infants: A worldwide comparative treatise. *Human Biology,* 1970, *42,* 217–264.

Neel, J. V. Some changing constraints on the human evolutionary process. *Proceedings of the XII International Congress on Genetics,* 1969, *3,* 389–403.

Scarr, S. Effects of birth weight on later intelligence. *Social Biology,* 1970, *16,* 249–256.

Smilansky, M., & Smilansky, S. (As summarized by Bloom, 1969.)

Stern, C. *Principles of human genetics.* (2nd ed.) San Francisco: Freeman, 1960.

chapter 8

behavior-genetic analysis and its biosocial consequences[1]

JERRY HIRSCH

As a psychology student I was taught that a science was founded on the discovery of lawful relations between variables. During my student days at Berkeley the true psychological scientist was preoccupied with the major learning theories. We read, studied, and designed experiments to test the theories of Thorndike, Guthrie, Hull, and Tolman. Many of their verbally formulated laws of behavior were replaced by the mathematical models that have since come into vogue.

Afterward I learned empirically the truth of what might be the most general of all behavioral laws, the Harvard law of animal behavior: "Under the most carefully controlled experimental conditions the animals do as they damn please." Still later I discovered the low esteem in which post-World War II psychology was held by two of the best minds this century has seen. In 1947 John Dewey, eighth president of the American Psychological Association, wrote to discourage young Robert V. Daniels from studying psychology at Harvard:

[1]Reprinted with minor changes from *Seminars in Psychiatry*, 1970, 2, 89–105.

Psychology . . . is on the whole, in my opinion, the most inept and a backwards tool . . . as there is. It is much of it actually harmful because of wrong basic postulates—maybe not all stated, but actually there when one judges from what they do—the kind of problems attacked and the way they attack them [p. 570].

On the final page of the last book written before his death in 1951 Ludwig Wittgenstein, perhaps the most influential of the founders of modern philosophical analysis, observed:

The confusion and barrenness of psychology is not to be explained by calling it a "young science"; its state is not comparable with that of physics, for instance, in its beginning. (Rather with that of certain branches of mathematics. Set theory.) For in psychology there are experimental methods and *conceptual confusion*. (As in the other case conceptual confusion and methods of proof.)

The existence of the experimental method makes us think we have the means of solving the problems which trouble us; though problem and method pass one another by [1963, p. 232].

Laws of genetics

It was then while overcome by feelings of disenchantment (obviously, without laws behavior study could never be science) that I embraced genetics. There was true science! My passion became even more intense when I realized that, like thermodynamics, genetics had three laws: segregation, independent assortment, and the Hardy-Weinberg law of population equilibria. What a foundation they provided for my beloved individual differences!

Since both my teaching and research involved considerable work with *Drosophila*, I knew and would recount to my classes in somewhat elaborate detail the story of Calvin Bridge's classic experiments on sex determination as a function of a ratio between the sex chromosomes and the autosomes. As the important discoveries in human cytogenetics were made throughout the 1950s and 1960s and "abnormalities" like Klinefelter's, Turner's, and Down's syndromes and the violence-prone males with an extra Y chromosome became genetically comprehensible, I began to realize that the so-called laws of genetics were no more universal than the so-called laws of behavior. Every one of the above-mentioned clinical conditions involved, at the very least, a violation of Mendel's law of segregation. Of course, so did Bridge's experiments, but it had been too easy to rationalize them as clever laboratory tricks.

Behaviorism

Over the past two decades the case against behaviorist extremism has been spelled out in incontrovertible detail. The behaviorists committed many sins: they accepted the mind at birth as Locke's *tabula rasa*; they advocated an empty-organism psychology; they asserted the uniformity postulate of no prenatal individual differences; in short, they epitomized typological thinking. Many times we have heard quoted the famous boast by the first high priest of behaviorism, John B. Watson:

> Give me a dozen healthy infants, well-formed, and my own specified world to bring them up in, and I'll guarantee to take any one at random and train him to become any type of specialist I might select—doctor, lawyer, artist, merchant-chief and yes, even beggar-man and thief, regardless of his talents, penchants, tendencies, abilities, vocations, race of his ancestors.

However, it is only when we read the next sentence, which is rarely, if ever, quoted, that we begin to understand how so many people might have embraced something intellectually so shallow as radical behaviorism. In that all important next sentence Watson explains: "I am going beyond my facts and I admit it, but so have the advocates of the contrary and they have been doing it for many thousands of years [1959, p. 104]."

Racism

Who were the advocates of the contrary, and what had they been saying? It is difficult to establish the origins of racist thinking, but certainly one of its most influential advocates was Joseph Arthur de Gobineau, who published a four-volume *Essay on the inequality of the human races* in the mid-1850s. De Gobineau preached the superiority of the white race, and among whites it was the Aryans who carried civilization to its highest point. In fact, they were responsible for civilization wherever it appeared. Unfortunately, de Gobineau's essay proved to be the major seminal work that inspired some of the most perverse developments in the intellectual and political history of our civilization. Later in his life, de Gobineau became an intimate of the celebrated German composer, Richard Wagner. The English-born Houston Stewart Chamberlain, who emigrated to the Continent, became a devoted admirer of both de Gobineau and Wagner. In 1908, after Wagner's death, he married Wagner's daughter, Eva, settled in and supported Germany against England during World War I, becoming a naturalized German citizen in 1916.

In the summer of 1923 an admirer who had read Chamberlain's writings, Adolph Hitler, visited Wahnfried, the Wagner family home in Bayreuth where Chamberlain lived. After their meeting, Chamberlain wrote to Hitler: "My faith in the Germans had never wavered for a moment, but my hope . . . had sunk to a low ebb. At one stroke you have transformed the state of my soul! [Heiden, 1944, p. 198]" We all know the sequel to that unfortunate tale. I find that our modern scientific colleagues, whether they be biological or social scientists, for the most part, do not know the sad parallel that exists for the essentially political tale I have so far recounted. The same theme can be traced down the main stream of biosocial science.

Today not many people know the complete title of Darwin's most famous book: *On the origin of species by means of natural selection or the preservation of favoured races in the struggle for life*. I find no evidence that Darwin had the attitudes that we now call racist. Unfortunately, many of his admirers, his contemporaries, and his successors were not as circumspect as he. In Paris in 1838 Esquirol first described a form of mental deficiency later to become well known by two inappropriate names unrelated to his work. Unhappily one of these names, through textbook adoption and clinical jargon, puts into wide circulation a term loaded with race prejudice. Somewhat later (1846, 1866) Seguin described the same condition under the name "furfuraceous cretinism" and his account has only recently been recognized as "the most ingenious description of physical characteristics. . . [Benda, 1962, p. 163]."

Unfortunately, that most promising scientific beginning was ignored. Instead a regrettable event occurred—the publication in 1866 of a paper entitled *Observations on the ethnic classification of idiots* by John Langdon Haydon Down. He suggested:

> . . . making a classification of the feeble-minded, by arranging them around various ethnic standards—in other words, framing a natural system to supplement the information to be derived by an inquiry into the history of the case.
>
> I have been able to find among the large number of idiots and imbeciles which comes under my observation, both at Earlswood and the out-patient department of the Hospital, that a considerable portion can be fairly referred to one of the great divisions of the human family other than the class from which they have sprung. Of course, there are numerous representatives of the great Caucasian family. Several well-marked examples of the Ethiopian variety have come under my notice, presenting the characteristic malar bones, the prominent eyes, the puffy lips, and retreating chin. The wooly hair has also been present, although not always black, nor has the skin acquired pigmentary deposit. They have been specimens of white negroes, although of European descent.
>
> Some arrange themselves around the Malay variety, and present in their soft, black, curly hair, their prominent upper jaws and capacious mouths, types of the family which people the South Sea Islands.
>
> Nor have there been wanting the analogues of the people who with shortened foreheads, prominent cheeks, deep-set eyes, and slightly apish nose, originally inhabited the American Continent.
>
> The great Mongolian family has numerous representatives, and it is to this division, I wish, in this paper, to call special attention. A very large number of congenital idiots are typical Mongols. So marked is this, that when placed side by side, it is difficult to believe that the specimens compared are not children of the same parents. The number of idiots who arrange themselves around the Mongolian type is so great, and they present such a close resemblance to one another in mental power, that I shall describe an idiot member of this racial division, selected from the large number that have fallen under my observation.

The hair is not black, as in the real Mongol, but of a brownish colour, straight and scanty. The face is flat and broad, and destitute of prominence. The cheeks are roundish, and extended laterally. The eyes are obliquely placed, and the internal canthi more than normally distant from one another. The palpebral fissure is very narrow. The forehead is wrinkled transversely from the constant assistance which the levatores palpebrarum derive from the occipito-frontalis muscle in the opening of the eyes. The lips are large and thick with transverse fissures. The tongue is long, thick, and is much roughened. The nose is small. The skin has a slight dirty yellowish tinge and is deficient in elasticity, giving the appearance of being too large for the body.

The boy's aspect is such that it is difficult to realize that he is the child of Europeans, but so frequently are these characters presented, that there can be no doubt that these ethnic features are the result of degeneration [as reprinted in McKusick, 1962, p. 432].

And Down means degeneration from a higher to a lower race. The foregoing represents a distasteful but excellent example of the racial hierarchy theory and its misleadingly dangerous implications. That was how the widely used terms Mongolism and Mongolian idiocy entered our "technical" vocabulary. For the next century this pattern of thought is going to persist and occupy an important place in the minds of many leading scientists.

Alleged Jewish genetic inferiority

In 1884 Francis Galton, Darwin's half cousin, founder of the eugenics movement and respected contributor to many fields of science, wrote to the distinguished Swiss botanist, Alphonse de Candolle: "It strikes me that the Jews are specialized for a parasitical existence upon other nations, and that there is need of evidence that they are capable of fulfilling the varied duties of a civilized nation by themselves [Pearson, 1924, p. 209]." Karl Pearson, Galton's disciple and biographer, echoed this opinion forty years later during his attempt to prove the undesirability of Jewish immigration into Britain: ". . . for such men as religion, social habits, or language keep as a caste apart, there should be no place. They will not be absorbed by, and at the same time strengthen the existing population; they will develop into a parasitic race. . . [Pearson & Moul, 1925, p. 125]."

Beginning in 1908 and continuing at least until 1928, Pearson collected and analyzed data in order to assess "the quality of the racial stock immigrating into Great Britain . . . [Pastore, 1949, p. 33]." He was particularly disturbed by the large numbers of East European Jews, who near the turn of the century began coming from Poland and Russia to escape the pogroms. Pearson's philosophy was quite explicitly spelled out (Pearson & Moul, 1925):

Let us admit . . . that the mind of man is for the most part a congenital product, and the factors which determine it are racial and familial; we are not dealing with a mutable characteristic capable of being moulded by the doctor, the teacher, the parent or the home environment [p. 124].

The ancestors of the men who pride themselves on being English today were all at one time immigrants; it is not for us to cast the first stone against newcomers, solely because they are newcomers. But the test for immigrants in the old days was a severe one; it was power, physical and mental, to retain their hold on the land they seized. So came Celts, Saxons, Norsemen, Danes and Normans in succession and built up the nation of which we are proud. Nor do we criticize the alien Jewish immigration simply because it is Jewish; we took the alien Jews to study, because they were the chief immigrants of that day and material was readily available [p. 127].

His observations led him to conclude: "Taken *on the average*, and regarding both sexes, this alien Jewish population is somewhat inferior physically and mentally to the native population [p. 126]."

Alleged black genetic inferiority

Quite recently there has appeared a series of papers disputing whether or not black Americans are, in fact, genetically inferior to white Americans in intellectual capacity. The claims and counterclaims have been given enormous publicity in the popular press in America. Some of those papers contain most of the fallacies that can conceivably be associated with this widely misunderstood problem.

The steps toward the intellectual cul-de-sac into which this dispute leads and the fallacious assumptions on which such "progress" is based are the following: (1) a trait called intelligence, or anything else, is defined, and a testing instrument for the measurement of trait expression is used; (2) the heritability of that trait is estimated; (3) races (populations) are compared with respect to their performance on the test of trait expression; and (4) when the races (populations) differ on the test whose heritability has now been measured, the one with the lower score is genetically inferior, Q.E.D.

The foregoing argument can be applied to any single trait or to as many traits as one might choose to consider. Therefore, analysis of this general problem does *not* depend upon the particular definition and test used for this or that trait. For my analysis I shall pretend that an acceptable test exists for some trait, be it height, weight, intelligence, or anything else. (Without an acceptable test discussion of the "trait" remains unscientific.)

Even to consider comparisons between races, the following concepts must be recognized: (1) the genome as a mosaic, (2) development as the expression of one out of many alternatives in the genotype's norm of reaction, (3) a population as a gene pool, (4) heritability is not instinct, (5) traits as distributions of scores, and (6) distributions as moments.

Since inheritance is particulate and not integral, the genome, genotype, or hereditary endowment of each individual is a unique mosaic—an assemblage of factors many of which are independent. Because of the lotterylike nature of both gamete formation and fertilization, other than monozygotes, no two individuals share the same genotypic mosaic.

Norm of reaction

The ontogeny of an individual's phenotype (observable outcome of development) has a norm, or range, of reaction not predictable in advance. In most cases the norm of reaction remains largely unknown; but the concept is, nevertheless, of fundamental importance because it saves us from being taken in by glib and misleading textbook clichés such as "heredity sets the limits but environment determines the extent of development within those limits." Even in the most favorable materials only an approximate estimate can be obtained for the norm of reaction when, as in plants and some animals, an individual genotype can be replicated many times and its development studied over a range of environmental conditions. The more varied the conditions, the more diverse might be the phenotypes developed from any one genotype. Of course, different genotypes should not be expected to have the same norm of reaction; unfortunately, psychology's attention was diverted from appreciating this basic fact of biology by a half century of misguided environmentalism. Just as we see that, except for monozygotes, no two human faces are alike, so we must expect norms of reaction to show genotypic uniqueness. That is one reason why the heroic but ill-fated attempts of experimental learning psychology to write the "laws of environmental influence" were grasping at shadows. Therefore, those limits set by heredity in the textbook cliché can never be specified. They are plastic within each individual but differ between individuals. Extreme environmentalists were wrong to hope that one law or set of laws described universal features of modifiability. Extreme hereditarians were wrong to ignore the norm of reaction.

Individuals occur in populations and then only as temporary attachments, so to speak, each to particular combinations of genes. The population, on the other hand, can endure indefinitely as a pool of genes, maybe forever recombining to generate new individuals.

Instincts, genes, and heritability

What is heritability? How is heritability estimated for intelligence or any other trait? Is heritability related to instinct? In 1872 Douglas Spalding demonstrated that the ontogeny of a bird's ability to fly is simply maturation and not the result of practice, imitation, or any demonstrable kind of learning. He confined immature birds and deprived them of the opportunity either to practice flapping their wings or to observe and imitate the flight of older birds;

in spite of this, they developed the ability to fly. For some ethologists this deprivation experiment became the paradigm for proving the innateness or instinctive nature of a behavior by demonstrating that it appears despite the absence of any opportunity for it to be learned. Remember two things about this approach: (1) the observation involves experimental manipulation of the conditions of experience during development; and (2) such observation can be made on the development of one individual. For some people the results of a deprivation experiment now constitute the operational demonstration of the existence (or nonexistence) of an instinct (in a particular species).

Are instincts heritable? That is, are they determined by genes? But what is a gene? A gene is an inference from a breeding experiment. It is recognized by the measurement of individual differences—the recognition of the segregation of distinguishable forms of the expression of some trait among the progeny of appropriate matings. For example, when an individual of blood type AA mates with one of type BB, their offspring are uniformly AB. If two of the AB offspring mate, it is found that the A and B gene forms have segregated during reproduction and recombined in their progeny to produce all combinations of A and B: AA, AB, and BB. Note that the only operation involved in such a study is *breeding* of one or more generations and then, at an appropriate time of life, observation of the separate individuals born in each generation— controlled breeding with experimental material or pedigree analysis of the appropriate families with human subjects. In principle, only one (usually brief) observation is required. Thus, we see that genetics is a science of *differences*, and the breeding experiment is its fundamental operation. The operational definition of the gene, therefore, involves observation in a breeding experiment of the segregation among several individuals of distinguishable differences in the expression of some trait from which the gene can be inferred. Genetics does not work with a single subject whose development is studied. (The foregoing, the following, and all discussions of genetic analysis presuppose sufficiently adequate control of environmental conditions so that all observed individual differences have developed under the same, homogeneous environmental conditions, conditions never achieved in any human studies.)

How does heritability enter the picture? At the present stage of knowledge, many features (traits) of animals and plants have not yet been related to genes that can be recognized individually. But the role of large numbers of genes, often called polygenes and in most organisms still indistinguishable one from the other, has been demonstrated easily (and often) by selective breeding or by appropriate comparisons between different strains of animals or plants. Selection and strain crossing have provided the basis for many advances in agriculture, and among the new generation of research workers are becoming standard tools for the experimental behaviorist. Heritability often summarizes the extent to which a particular population has responded to a regimen of being bred selectively on the basis of the expression of some trait.

Heritability values vary between zero and plus one. If the distribution of trait expression among progeny remains the same no matter how their parents might be selected, then heritability has zero value. If parental selection does make a difference, heritability exceeds zero, its exact value reflecting the parent-offspring correlation. Or more generally, as Jensen (1969) says: "The basic data from which . . . heritability coefficients are estimated are correlations among individuals of different degrees of kinship [p. 48]." Though, many of the heritabilities Jensen (1967) discusses have been obtained by comparing mono- and dizygotic twins.

A heritability estimate, however, is a far more limited piece of information than most people realize. As was so well stated by Fuller and Thompson (1960), "heritability is a property of populations and not of traits." In its strictest sense, a heritability measure provides for a given population an estimate of the proportion of the variance it shows in trait (phenotype) expression which is correlated with the segregation of the alleles of independently acting genes. There are other more broadly conceived heritability measures which estimate this correlation and also include the combined effects of genes that are independent and of genes that interact. Therefore, heritability estimates the proportion of the total phenotypic variance (individual differences) shown by a trait that can be attributed to genetic variation (narrowly or broadly interpreted) in some particular population at a single generation under one set of conditions.

The foregoing description contains three fundamentally important limitations which have rarely been accorded sufficient attention. The importance of limiting any heritability statement to a specific population is evident when we realize that a gene, which shows variation in one population because it is represented there by two or more segregating alleles, might show no variation in some other population because it is uniformly represented there by only a single allele. Remember that initially such a gene could never have been detected by genetic methods in the second population. Once it has been detected in some population carrying two or more of its segregating alleles, the information thus obtained might permit us to recognize it in populations carrying only a single allele. Note how this is related to heritability: the trait will show a greater-than-zero heritability in the segregating population but zero heritability in the nonsegregating population. This does *not* mean that the trait is determined genetically in the first population and environmentally in the second!

Up to this point the discussion has been limited to a single gene. The very same argument applies for every gene of the polygenic complexes involved in continuously varying traits like height, weight, and intelligence. Also, only *genetic* variation has been considered—the presence or absence of segregating alleles at one or more loci in different populations.

Next, let us consider the ever present environmental sources of variation.

Usually from the Mendelian point of view, except for the genes on the segregating chromosomes, everything inside the cell and outside the organism is lumped together and can be called environmental variation: cytoplasmic constituents, the maternal effects now known to be so important, the early experience effects studied in so many psychological laboratories, and so on. None of these can be considered unimportant or trivial. They are ever present. Let us now perform what physicists call a *Gedanken*, or thought, experiment. Imagine Aldous Huxley's *Brave new world* or Skinner's *Walden II* organized in such a way that every individual is exposed to precisely the same environmental conditions. In other words, consider the extreme, but *un*realistic, case of complete environmental homogeneity. Under these circumstances the heritability value would approach unity because only genetic variation would be present. Even under the most simplifying assumptions, there are over 70 trillion potential human genotypes—no two of us share the same genotype no matter how many ancestors we happen to have in common (Hirsch, 1963). Since mitosis projects our unique genotype into the nucleus, or executive, of every cell in our bodies, the individuality that is so obvious in the human faces we see around us must also characterize the unseen components. Let the same experiment be imagined for any number of environments. In each environment heritability will approximate unity, but each genotype *may* develop a different phenotype in every environment and the distribution (hierarchy) of genotypes (in terms of their phenotypes) must not be expected to remain invariant over environments.

The third limitation refers to the fact that because gene frequencies can and do change from one generation to the next, so will heritability values or the magnitude of the genetic variance.

Let us shift our focus to the entire genotype or, at least, to those of its components that might covary at least partially with the phenotypic expression of a particular trait. Early in this century Woltereck called to our attention the concept of norm of reaction: the same genotype can give rise to a wide array of phenotypes depending upon the environment in which it develops (Dunn, 1965). This is most conveniently studied in plants where genotypes are easily replicated. Later Goldschmidt (1955) was to show in *Drosophila* that, by careful selection of the environmental conditions at critical periods in development, various phenotypes ordinarily associated with specific gene mutations could be produced from genotypes that did not include the mutant form of those genes. Descriptively, Goldschmidt called these events *phenocopies*— environmentally produced imitations of gene mutants or phenotypic expressions only manifested by the "inappropriate" genotype if unusual environmental influences impinge during critical periods in development, but regularly manifested by the "appropriate" genotype under the usual environmental conditions.

In 1946 the brilliant British geneticist Haldane analyzed the interaction concept and gave quantitative meaning to the foregoing. For the simplest case but one, that of two genotypes in three environments or, for its mathematical equivalent, that of three genotypes in two environments, he showed that there are sixty possible kinds of interaction. Ten genotypes in ten environments generate 10^{144} possible kinds of interaction. In general m genotypes in n environments generate

$$\frac{(mn)!}{m!n!}$$

kinds of interaction. Since the characterization of genotype-environment interaction can only be ad hoc and the number of possible interactions is effectively unlimited, it is no wonder that the long search for general laws has been so unfruitful.

For genetically different lines of rats showing the Tryon-type "bright-dull" difference in performance on a learning task, by so simple a change in environmental conditions as replacing massed-practice trials by distributed-practice trials, McGaugh, Jennings, and Thompson (1962) found that the so-called dulls moved right up to the scoring level of the so-called brights. In a study of the open-field behavior of mice Hegmann and DeFries (1968) found that heritabilities measured repeatedly in the same individuals were unstable over two successive days. In surveying earlier work they commented: "Heritability estimates for repeated measurements of behavioral characters have been found to increase (Broadhurst & Jinks, 1961), decrease (Broadhurst & Jinks, 1966), and fluctuate randomly (Fuller & Thompson, 1960) as a function of repeated testing [p. 27]." Therefore, to the limitations on heritability due to population, situation, and breeding generation, we must now add developmental stage, or, many people might say, just plain unreliability! The brilliant Englishman Ronald Fisher (1951), whose authority Jensen cites, indicated how fully he had appreciated such limitations when he commented: "the so-called coefficient of heritability, which I regard as one of those unfortunate short-cuts which have emerged in biometry for lack of a more thorough analysis of the data [p. 271]." The plain facts are that in the study of man a heritability estimate turns out to be a piece of "knowledge" that is both deceptive and trivial.

The roots of one misuse of statistics

The other two concepts to be taken into account when racial comparisons are considered involve the representation of traits in populations by distributions of scores and the characterization of distributions by moment-derived statistics. Populations should be compared only with respect to one trait at a time, and comparisons should be made in terms of the moment statistics of their trait distributions. Therefore, for any two populations, on each trait of interest, a separate comparison should be made for every moment of their score distributions. If we consider only the first four moments, from which are derived the familiar statistics for mean, variance, skewness, and kurtosis, then there are four ways in which populations or races may differ with respect to any single trait. Since we possess 23 independently assorting pairs of chromosomes, certainly there are at least 23 uncorrelated traits with respect to which populations can be compared. Since comparisons will be made in terms of four (usually independent) statistics, there are $4 \times 23 = 92$ ways in which races can differ. Since the integrity of chromosomes is *not* preserved over the generations because they often break apart at meiosis and exchange constituent genes, there are far more than 23 independent hereditary units. If instead of 23 chromosomes we take the 100,000 genes man is now estimated to possess (McKusick, 1966) and we think in terms of their phenotypic trait correlates, then there may be as many as 400,000 comparisons to be made between any two populations or races.

A priori, at this time we know enough to expect no two populations to be the same with respect to most or all of the constituents of their gene pools. "Mutations and recombinations will occur at different places, at different times, and with differing frequencies. Furthermore, selection pressures will also vary [Hirsch, 1963, p. 1441]." So the number and kinds of differences between populations now waiting to be revealed in "the more thorough analysis" recommended by Fisher literally staggers the imagination. It does not suggest a linear hierarchy of inferior and superior races.

Why has so much stress been placed on comparing distributions only with respect to their central tendencies by testing the significance of mean differences? There is much evidence that many observations are not normally distributed and that the distributions from many populations do not share homogeneity of variance. The source of our difficulty traces back to the very inception of our statistical tradition.

There is an unbroken line of intellectual influence from Quetelet through Galton and Pearson to modern psychometrics and biometrics. Adolphe Quetelet, the nineteenth-century Belgian astronomer-statistician, introduced the concept of "the average man"; he also applied the normal distribution—so widely used in astronomy for error variation—to human data, biological and social. The great Francis Galton followed Quetelet's lead and then Karl Pearson elaborated and perfected their methods. I know of nothing that has contributed more to impose the typological way of thought on, and perpetuates it in, present-day psychology than the feedback from these methods for describing observations in terms of group averages.

There is a technique called composite photography to the perfection of which Galton contributed in an important way. Some of Galton's best work in this field was done by combining—literally averaging—the separate physiognomic features of many different Jewish individuals into his composite photograph of "the Jewish type." Pearson (1924), his disciple and biographer, wrote: "There is little doubt that Galton's Jewish type formed a landmark in composite photography . . . [p. 293]." The part played by typological thinking in the development of modern statistics and the way in which such typological thinking has been feeding back into our conceptual framework through our continued careless use of these statistics is illuminated by Galton's remarks:

> The word generic presupposes a genus, that is to say, a collection of individuals who have much in common, and among whom medium characteristics are very much more frequent than extreme ones. The same idea is sometimes expressed by the word typical, which was much used by Quetelet, who was the first to give it a rigorous interpretation, and whose idea of a type lies at the basis of his statistical views. No statistician dreams of combining objects into the same generic group that do not cluster towards a common centre; no more can we compose generic portraits out of heterogeneous elements, for if the attempt be made to do so the result is monstrous and meaningless [as quoted in Pearson, 1924, p. 295].

The basic assumption of a type, or typical individual, is clear and explicit. These men used the normal curve and permitted distributions to be represented by an average because, even though at times they knew better, far too often they tended to think of races as discrete, even homogeneous, groups and individual variation as error.

It is important to realize that these developments began before 1900, when Mendel's work was still unknown. Thus, at the inception of biosocial science there was no substantive basis for understanding individual differences. After 1900, when Mendel's work became available, its incorporation into biosocial science was bitterly opposed by the biometricians under Pearson's leadership. Galton had promulgated two "laws": his Law of Ancestral Heredity (1865) and his Law of Regression (1877). When Yule (1902) and Castle (1903) pointed out how the Law of Ancestral Heredity could be explained in Mendelian terms, Pearson (1904) stubbornly denied it. Mendel had chosen for experimental observation seven traits, each of which, in his pea-plant material, turned out to be a phenotypic correlate of a single gene with two segregating alleles. For all seven traits one allele was dominant. Unfortunately, Pearson assumed the universality of dominance and based his disdain for Mendelism on this assumption. Yule (1906) then showed that without the assumption of dominance Mendelism becomes perfectly consistent with the kind of quantitative data on the basis of which it was being rejected by Pearson. It is sad to realize that Pearson never appreciated the generality of Mendelism and seems to have gone on for the next thirty-two years without doing so.

Two fallacies in the nature-nurture controversy

We can now consider the debate about the meaning of comparisons between the "intelligence" of different human races. We are told that intelligence has a high heritability and that one race performs better than another on intelligence tests. In essence we are presented with a racial hierarchy reminiscent of that pernicious "system" which Down used when he misnamed a disease entity Mongolism.

The people who are so committed to answering the nature-nurture pseudoquestion—is heredity or environment more important in determining intelligence—make two conceptual blunders. Like Spalding's question about the instinctive nature of bird flight, which introduced the ethologist's deprivation experiment, their question about intelligence is, in fact, being asked about the development of a single individual. Unlike Spalding and the ethologists, however, they do not study development in single individuals. Usually they test groups of individuals at a single time of life. The proportions being assigned to heredity and to environment refer to the relative amounts of the variance between individuals comprising a population, not how much of whatever enters into the development of the observed expression of a trait in a particular individual has been contributed by heredity and by environment respectively. They want to know how instinctive is intelligence in the development of a certain individual, but instead they measure differences between large numbers of fully, or partially, developed individuals. If we now take into consideration the concept of norm of reaction and combine it with the facts of genotypic individuality, then there is no general statement that can be made about the assignment of fixed proportions to the contributions of heredity and environment either to the development of a single individual, because we have not even begun to assess his norm of reaction, or to the differences that might be measured among members of a population, because we have hardly begun to assess the range of environmental conditions under which its constituent members might develop!

The second mistake, an egregious error, made by the nature-nurture investigators, is related to the first one. They assume an inverse relationship between heritability magnitude and improvability by training and teaching. If heritability is high, little room is left for improvement by environmental modification. If heritability is low, much more improvement is possible. Note how this basic fallacy is incorporated directly into the title of Jensen's (1969) article *How much can we boost IQ and scholastic achievement?* That question received a straightforward but fallacious answer by Jensen in the same article: "The fact that scholastic achievement is considerably less heritable than intelligence . . . . means there is potentially much more we can do to improve school performance through environmental means than we can do to change intelligence . . . [p. 59]." Commenting on the heritability of intelligence and "the old nature-nurture controversy," one of Jensen's respondents makes the same mistake in his rebuttal: "This is an old estimate which many of us have used, but we have used it to determine what could be done with the variance left for the environment." He then goes on "to further emphasize some of the implications of environmental variance for education and child rearing [Bloom, 1969, p. 419]."

High or low heritability tells us absolutely nothing about how a given individual might have developed under conditions different from those in which he actually did develop. Heritability provides no information about norm of reaction. Since the characterization of genotype-environment interaction can only be ad hoc and the number of possible interactions is effectively unlimited, no wonder the search for general laws of behavior has been so unfruitful, and *the* heritability of intelligence or any other trait must be recognized as still another of those will-o-the-wisp general laws. And no magic words about an interaction component in a linear analysis-of-variance model will make disappear the reality of each genotype's unique norm of reaction. Such claims by Jensen or anyone else are false. Interaction is an abstraction of mathematics. Norm of reaction is a developmental reality of biology in plants, animals, and people.

In Israel the descendants of those Jews Pearson feared would contaminate Britain are manifesting some interesting properties of the norm of reaction. Children of European origin have an average IQ of 105 when they are brought up in individual homes. Those brought up in a kibbutz on the nursery rearing schedule of twenty-two hours per day for four or more years have an average IQ of 115. In contrast, the mid-Eastern Jewish children brought up in individual homes have an average IQ of only 85, Jensen's danger point. However, when brought up in a kibbutz, they also have an average IQ of 115. That is, they perform the same as the European children with whom they were matched for education, the occupational level of parents, and the кibbutz group in which they were raised (Bloom, 1969). There is no basis for expecting different overall results for any population in our species.

Some promising developments

The power of the approach that begins by thinking first in terms of the genetic system and only later in terms of the phenotype (or behavior) to be analyzed is being demonstrated by an accumulating and impressive body of evidence. The rationale of that approach derives directly from the particulate nature of the gene, the mosaic nature of the genotype, and the manner in which heredity breaks apart and gets reassembled in being passed on from one generation to the next. We now have a well-articulated picture of the way heredity is shared among biological relatives.

That madness runs in families has been known for centuries. The controversy has been over whether it was the heredity or the environment supplied by the family that was responsible for the madness. Franz Kallmann and others collected large amounts of data in the 1940s and 1950s showing that monozygotic twins were much more concordant than dizygotic twins. Since David Rosenthal of NIMH (the National Institute of Mental Health) has provided some of the best criticism of the incompleteness, and therefore inconclusiveness, of the twin-study evidence for the role of heredity in schizophrenia, Rosenthal's own findings become especially noteworthy.

He has divided foster-reared children from adoptive homes into two groups: those with a biological parent who is schizophrenic and those without a schizophrenic biological parent. It was found by Rosenthal, Wender, Kety, Schulsinger, Welmer, and Østergaard (1968), and by Heston (1966) in a completely independent but similar study, that the incidence of schizophrenia was much greater among the biological children of schizophrenics. Most significantly, the two studies show that the risk of schizophrenia in offspring is four to five times greater if a biological parent is schizophrenic. Other studies in the 1960s support the Rosenthal and the Heston findings. Both Karlsson (1966) and Wender (Rose, 1969) found a high incidence of schizophrenia in the foster-reared relatives of schizophrenics.

Thinking genetically first in terms of biological relationship has already paid off in the analytical detail revealed as well as in the mere demonstration of concordance with respect to diagnostic category. Lidz, Cornelison, Terry, and Fleck (1958) reported marked distortions in communicating among many of the nonhospitalized parents of schizophrenic hospital patients. McConaghy (1959), using an objective test of thought disorder, assessed the parents of ten schizophrenic patients and compared them to a series of control subjects. Sixty percent of the patients' parents, including at least one parent in every pair, registered test scores in the range indicative of thought disturbance. In contrast, less than 10 percent of the controls had such scores.

The major features of McConaghy's findings have since been replicated by Lidz and co-workers (1962). More recently Phillips and co-workers (1965) studied forty-eight relatives of adult schizophrenics and forty-five control subjects using a battery of tests to assess thought disorder. They found cognitive disorders to be much more frequent among the relatives of schizophrenics; seventeen of eighteen parents registered "pathological" scores even though their social behavior had never been diagnosed as pathological.

In 1962 Anastasopoulos and Photiades assessed susceptibility to LSD-induced "pathological reactions" in the relatives of schizophrenic patients. After studying twenty-one families of patients and nine members of two control families, they reported "it was almost invariable to find reactions to LSD in one of the parents, and often in one or more of the siblings and uncles and aunts, which were neither constant nor even common during the LSD-intoxication of healthy persons [p. 96]."

Analogous work has been done studying the responses of the relatives of patients with depressive disorders using antidepressant drugs like imipramine (Tofranil) or an MAO inhibitor. Relatives tend to show a response pattern similar to that of their hospitalized relations.

Some very interesting human behavior-genetic analyses were done on these affective disorders by George Winokur and his colleagues in St. Louis (Rose, 1969). (The study was continued in 1970 and 1971.) Out of 1,075 consecutive admissions to a psychiatric hospital, 426 were diagnosed as primary affective disorders. These appeared to fall into two subtypes, the first of which showed manic episodes; some first-degree relatives showed similar manifestations. The other subtype was characterized by depressive episodes and lack of concordance among close relatives. Furthermore, evidence was accumulated implicating a dominant factor or factors on the X-chromosome in the manic subtype: (1) the condition is considerably more prevalent in females than in males; and (2) the morbid risk among siblings of male probands is the same for males and females, but the morbid risk among siblings of female probands is quite different—sisters of female probands are at a 21 percent risk while their brothers are only at a 7.4 percent risk. More detailed study in several appropriately chosen family pedigrees suggests that there is a dominant gene on the short arm of the X-chromosome. The condition has so far shown linkage with color blindness and the Xg blood groups, both of which are loosely linked on the short arm of the X-chromosome.

To examine the structure of the phenotypic variation in a trait whose development is in no obvious way influenced by environment and which, though ostensibly a simple trait, has been sufficiently well-analyzed phenotypically to reveal its interesting complexity, we have chosen to study dermatoglyphics, or fingerprints, in my laboratory. For his doctoral dissertation, R. Peter Johnson in 1970 was making these observations on both parents and offspring in individual families. His preparatory survey of the previous literature revealed one study which reported data on a cross-sectional sample of 2,000 males (Waite, 1915). When Johnson scored them on all ten fingers with respect to four distinguishable pattern types, the following data revealed the interesting but sobering complexity that exists in such a "simple" trait: the same type of pattern was shown on all ten fingers by 12 percent, on nine of ten fingers by 16 percent, and on eight of ten fingers by 10 percent of the men. In addition, 5 percent of the men showed all four pattern types. This included 1 percent of the individuals who had all four pattern types on a single hand.

While probably everybody has heard that there are some unusual hospitalized males who carry two Y chromosomes, are rather tall, and are prone to commit crimes of violence, few people know that when a comparison was made between the first-order relatives of both the Y-Y chromosome males and control males hospitalized for similar reasons (but not carrying two Y chromosomes), there was a far greater incidence of a family history of crime among the controls. In this control group there were over six times as many individual first-order relatives convicted and many, many times the number of convictions.

In summary, the relationship between heredity and behavior has turned out to be one of neither isomorphism nor independence. Isomorphism might justify an approach like naïve reductionism, independence a naïve behaviorism. Neither one turns out to be adequate. I believe that in order to study behavior we must understand genetics quite thoroughly. Then, and only then, can we as psychologists forget about it intelligently.

References

Anastasopoulos, G., & Photiades, H. Effects of LSD-25 on relatives of schizophrenic patients. *Journal of Mental Science*, 1962, *108*, 95–98.

Benda, C. E. "Mongolism" or "Down's syndrome." *Lancet*, 1962, *1*, 163.

Bloom, B. S. Letter to the editor. *Harvard Educational Review*, 1969, *39*, 419–421.

Castle, W. E. The laws of heredity of Galton and Mendel, and some laws governing race improvement by selection. *Proceedings of the American Academy of Arts and Sciences*, 1903, *39*, 223–242.

De Gobineau, J. A. *Essai sur l'inégalité des races humaines*. (Rééd.) Paris: Belfond, 1967.

Dewey, J. Correspondence with Robert V. Daniels, February 15, 1947. *Journal of the History of Ideas*, 1959, *20*, 570–571.

Down, J. L. H. Observations on the ethnic classification of idiots. *London Hospital Clinical Lecture Reports, III*, 1866, 259–262. Reprinted in V. A. McKusick, Medical genetics 1961. *Journal of Chronic Diseases*, 1962, *15*, 417–572.

Dunn, L. C. *A short history of genetics*. New York: McGraw-Hill, 1965.

Fisher, R. A. Limits to intensive production in animals. *British Agricultural Bulletin*, 1951, *4*, 217–218.

Fuller, J. L., & Thompson, W. R. *Behavior genetics*, New York: Wiley, 1960.

Goldschmidt, R. B. *Theoretical genetics*. Berkeley: University of California Press, 1955.

Haldane, J. B. S. The interaction of nature and nurture. *Annals of Eugenics*, 1946, *13*, 197–205.

Hegmann, J. P., & DeFries, J. C. Open-field behavior in mice: Genetic analysis of repeated measures. *Psychonomic Science*, 1968, *13*, 27–28.

Heiden, K. *Der Führer*. (R. Manheim, Transl.) London: Houghton, 1944.

Heston, L. L. Psychiatric disorders in foster home reared children of schizophrenic mothers. *British Journal of Psychiatry*, 1966, *112*, 819–825.

Hirsch, J. Behavior genetics and individuality understood: Behaviorism's counterfactual dogma blinded the behavioral sciences to the significance of meiosis. *Science*, 1963, *142*, 1436–1442.

Jensen, A. R. Estimation of the limits of heritability of traits by comparison of monozygotic and dizygotic twins. *Proceedings of the National Academy of Sciences*, 1967, *58*, 149–156.

———. How much can be boost IQ and scholastic achievement? *Harvard Educational review*, 1969, *39*, 1–123.

Karlsson, J. L. *The biologic basis of schizophrenia.* Springfield, Ill.: Charles C Thomas, 1966.

Lidz, T., Cornelison, A., Terry, D., & Fleck, S. Intrafamilial environment of the schizophrenic patient: VI. The transmission of irrationality. *AMA Archives of Neurology and Psychiatry*, 1958, *79*, 305–316.

———, Wild, C., Schafer, S., Rosman, B., & Fleck, S. Thought disorders in the parents of schizophrenic patients: A study utilizing the object sorting test. *Journal of Psychiatric Research*, 1962, *1*, 193–200.

McConaghy, N. The use of an object sorting test in elucidating the hereditary factor in schizophrenia. *Journal of Neurology, Neurosurgery and Psychiatry*, 1959, *22*, 243–246.

McGaugh, J. L., Jennings, R. D., & Thompson, C. W. Effect of distribution of practice on the maze learning of descendants of the Tryon maze bright and maze dull strains. *Psychological Reports*, 1962, *10*, 147–150.

McKusick, V. A. *Mendelian inheritance in man: Catalogs of autosomal dominant, recessive, and X-linked phenotypes.* Baltimore: Johns Hopkins Press, 1966.

Pastore, N. *The nature-nurture controversy.* New York: King's Crown, 1949.

Pearson, K. On a generalized theory of alternative inheritance, with special reference to Mendel's laws. *Philosophical Transactions of the Royal Society of London*, 1904, A 203, 53–86.

———. *The life, letters and labours of Francis Galton, volume II: Researches of middle life.* Cambridge, Eng.: At the University Press, 1924.

———, & Moul, M. The problem of alien immigration into Great Britain, illustrated by an examination of Russian and Polish Jewish children. *Annals of Eugenics*, 1925, *1*, 5–127.

Phillips, J. E., Jacobson, N., & Turner, W. J. Conceptual thinking in schizophrenics and their relatives. *British Journal of Psychiatry*, 1965, *111*, 823–839.

Rose, R. J. Department of Psychology, University of Indiana, personal communication, 1969.

Rosenthal, D., Wender, P. H., Kety, S. S., Schulsinger, F., Welner, J., & Østergaard, L. Schizophrenics' offspring reared in adoptive homes. *Journal of Psychiatric Research*, 1968, *6*, 377–391.

Waite, H. Association of fingerprints. *Biometrika*, 1915, *10*, 421–478.

Watson, J. B. *Behaviorism.* Chicago: University of Chicago Press, 1959. (C. 1930)

Wittgenstein, L. *Philosophical investigations.* (2nd ed.) (G. E. Anscombe, Transl.) Oxford: Blackwell, 1963.

Yule, G. U. Mendel's laws and their probable relations to intra-racial heredity. *New Phytologist*, 1902, *1*, 193–207, 222–238.

———. On the theory of inheritance of quantitative compound characters on the basis of Mendel's laws—A preliminary note. *Report 3rd International Conference on Genetics*, 1906, 140–142.

chapter 9

the race × sex × ability interaction

ARTHUR R. JENSEN

The Race × Sex × Ability interaction, henceforth abbreviated as R × S × A, is a convenient way of expressing the question to which this chapter is addressed. The terminology comes from the statistical technique known as the analysis of variance. The expression R × S × A poses the question of whether ability differences between the sexes are greater in one race than in another. Or, conversely, are measurable racial differences in mental ability greater for one sex than for the other?

From the outset it should be kept in mind that the term "race" is used here in its sociological sense rather than in a strictly genetic or anthropological sense. The relevant data are based entirely on the social definition of race—that is, the racial classification, white or black, that people regard themselves as belonging to and are so regarded by others in the society. There is undoubtedly a high degree of correlation between the social definition of race and the more precise genetic definition of a race as a breeding population which differs from other populations in the frequencies of a number of genes for various physical characteristics. Furthermore, we are discussing here only data derived from North American Negroes who, although having predominantly west African ancestry, must now be viewed socially and genetically as a distinctive population. (For a good discussion of these points the reader is referred to Gottesman, 1968.)

But why should the question of $R \times S \times A$ be asked in the first place? It is not fabricated out of thin air. In fact it is suggested by a host of observations with great social, economic, and educational implications. These observations call for understanding. The problem is exceedingly complex and multifaceted, and it would be ridiculous to believe at this point that it can be fully understood without examination from many angles—historical, cultural, sociological, psychological, and biological. The present chapter attempts only to highlight certain biological and psychological aspects of the problem which have not been previously considered in discussions emphasizing only cultural factors to explain the observed phenomena.

Socioeconomic evidence of sex difference

Employment and unemployment rates, occupational status, and income, although somewhat related to ability differences *within* the sexes, cannot be regarded as indicative of ability differences *between* the sexes. The different cultural roles of men and women in any society almost completely override ability factors in determining occupational roles, employment rates, income, and the like. There is no basis for inferring sex differences in ability from such data alone. Also, in any society which does not afford equal opportunities for education and employment, statistics on occupational levels, employment rates, and income are a flimsy basis indeed for inferring racial differences in ability. The same reasoning must also, therefore, apply to the $R \times S \times A$ interaction. If there are employment differences between the sexes and these sex differences vary markedly within each racial group, the explanation could well be entirely cultural: sex roles can differ in various cultures, and society can exert different forms and degrees of discrimination between men and women according to their race. On the other hand, these cultural factors do not rule out ability differences between sexes that may vary in pattern and magnitude in different racial groups. True ability differences may be operating in addition to sex role differences. To sort out these causal factors one must look to various lines of evidence and examine them for consistency.

Employment and unemployment rates of men and women in the white and black populations are very poor indices for our purposes. These rates vary as a function of too many other variables. The figures differ, for example, according to area of the country and the location of residence—rural, urban, suburban, metropolitan, central cities, etc.—and they fluctuate from one year to another. Such variable statistics could hardly be explained solely in terms of relatively stable psychological characteristics of individuals or groups, as we presume mental abilities to be. A report published by the U.S. Department

of Commerce (1969) indicates that there have been marked shifts in the employment patterns of black men and women within the 1960 decade.

> Almost half of the white men employed in central cities worked as white-collar
> workers in 1968, but only one-fifth of the Negro men were in similar occupations.
> There has been very little change in the occupational distribution of either white
> or Negro men since 1960. In contrast, there has been a marked shift in the occupa-
> tional distribution of Negro women in cities over the 8 years. While the proportion
> of employed white women engaged in white-collar work stayed steady at about
> two-thirds, the proportion of Negro women doing similar work rose sharply from
> one-fifth in 1960 to one-third in 1968. Most of this increase took place among
> clerical and sales workers. Domestic work was much less important as a source of
> jobs for Negro women in 1968 than in 1960.

The figures in this report (p. 33) also show that among all those who were
employed in central cities in 1968, 9 percent of black males as compared with
30 percent of white males were in the highest occupational category (professional and managerial workers). The corresponding figures for females were
11 percent black vs. 20 percent white. In other words, in the more skilled occupations the differences in employment between blacks and whites are much
less for women than for men. Thus, for employment in skilled occupations
there is clearly a Sex × Race interaction.

Scaling the sex difference

A brief digression into statistical methodology at this point will facilitate
further discussions of these data. Statistics presented in terms of percentages
can be very misleading as to the true magnitudes of the differences that they
represent. Percentages, like percentile scores in psychometrics, do not represent
points on an equal interval scale. It is, therefore, relatively meaningless, and
even deceptive, to compare the percentages of men and women in different
occupations, income brackets, etc. as if the figures conform to an interval
scale. For example, that a sex difference of 10 percent males vs. 20 percent
females in some employment category in 1960 represents the same difference in
employability of men and women as a difference of 40 percent males vs. 50
percent females in 1970 is an incorrect inference. There is a 10 percent difference
between males and females in each decade, but the 10 percent difference has a
very different meaning in terms of the "employability" of males and females in
1960 and in 1970. On an interval scale the difference between 10 percent and 20
percent is much greater than the difference between 40 percent and 50 percent.
For this reason it is useful to examine sex differences not only in terms of
percentages (or other measures of rate), but to view them also as points on an
interval scale. The scale of sex differences is, of course, specific to the characteristic being examined, such as employability, income level, and so forth.

We can transform percentages to an interval scale by making the one assumption that the characteristic in question (e.g., employability) has a normal (Gaussian) distribution for men and for women. The usefulness of this assumption can only be judged by the degree of order and invariance it lends to the data. We know for sure that percentages alone cannot give an accurate impression, and normalizing them to create an interval scale makes more sense than any other transformation at this initial stage of our analysis.

The procedure is straightforward: we simply convert percentages to z scores by means of a table of the areas under the normal curve. The difference between the z scores represents the magnitude of the sex difference (on the characteristic in question) expressed in sigma (σ) or standard deviation units. As an example, we can compare 10 percent vs. 20 percent. The z score beyond which 10 percent of the area under the normal distribution lies is $+1.28\sigma$; the z score for 20 percent is $+.84\sigma$. The difference is $1.28\sigma - .84\sigma = .44\sigma$. Compare this with the difference between 40 percent and 50 percent, which, on the z scale, is $.25\sigma - .00\sigma = .25\sigma$.

We can now apply this procedure to the employability data for professional and managerial occupations, showing 9 percent black male vs. 11 percent for black females in 1968. These correspond to z scores of 1.34 and 1.23, respectively, making a mean sex difference of $.11\sigma$ in favor of females. The corresponding figures for the white population are 30 percent males vs. 20 percent females, with the z scores equal to .52 and .84, giving a mean difference of $.32\sigma$ in favor of males. Thus, the black sex difference in employability in high-level occupations is less than the white sex difference, but it is in the opposite direction. The black sex difference in 1960 in professional and managerial occupations was 6 percent males vs. 8 percent females, or a difference of $.15\sigma$ in favor of females, which is larger than the $.11\sigma$ difference in 1968.

Income

In most occupational categories black men in central cities had lower median incomes than those of white workers, but the median earnings of black women who were employed year-round equaled the earnings of white women in the same occupations (U.S. Department of Commerce, 1969). The data are shown in Table 1.

Since income within occupational categories is known to have some correlation with ability and competence on the job, the question naturally arises whether these factors play any part in the black sex difference in income, which is most pronounced in the more skilled occupations. The one occupational category that is most comparable for men and women in terms of the functions performed is the highest (professional and managerial workers); in this category black women earn 5 percent more than white women, while black men earn 35 percent less than white men. These figures are, of course, the result of

Table 1. Median earnings in 1967 of white and Negro year-round workers in central cities currently employed in selected occupation groups

	Median earnings in 1967		Negro median earnings as a percent of white	Year-round workers as a percent of all workers in group	
	White	Negro	1967	White	Negro
Male					
Professional and managerial workers	$9,542	$6,208	65	86	87
Clerical and sales workers	6,878	5,515	80	78	84
Craftsmen and foremen	7,545	5,962	79	80	76
Operatives	6,475	5,414	84	72	75
Nonfarm laborers	5,355	4,492	84	63	62
Service workers, exc. private household	5,536	4,159	75	75	69
Female					
Professional and managerial workers	$5,910	$6,209	105	69	66
Clerical and sales workers	4,312	4,425	103	68	59
Operatives	3,590	3,296	92	61	66
Private household workers	880	1,410	160	26	62
All other service workers	3,061	2,905	95	54	59

Source: Trends in Social and Economic Conditions in Metropolitan Areas. Special Studies. *Current Population Reports*. U.S. Department of Commerce. Series P–23, No. 27, February 7, 1969, p. 49.

multiple causes. Note that the actual income difference for black men and women is the same for the highest occupational category and that women actually earn less than men in the less skilled occupations. It is the black-white difference as a function of sex that is of primary interest here. The difference in the case of females at the highest occupational level may be due largely to differences in career orientation for white and black women, the higher incomes going to those who remain longer in their careers. A larger proportion of black women than of white women in skilled occupations may be the chief source of family income and therefore are more likely to remain longer in their career, thereby advancing to a higher level of earnings. The Moynihan Report stated: "In 44 percent of the Negro families studied, the wife was dominant, as against 20 percent of white wives. Whereas the majority of white families are equalitarian, the largest percentage of Negro families are dominated by the wife [Rainwater & Yancey, 1967, p. 77]." Moynihan goes on to note that "Negro males represent 1.1 percent of all male professionals, whereas Negro females represent roughly 6 percent of all female professionals. Again, in technician occupations, Negro males represent 2.1 percent of all male technicians while Negro females represent roughly 10 percent of all female technicians. It would appear, therefore, that there are proportionately four times as many Negro females in significant white collar jobs than Negro males [Rainwater & Yancey, 1967, p. 78]."

Comparison of the incomes of blacks and whites in any occupational category permits no sound inferences about ability differences since we do not know to what extent the income differences are due to discrimination or to regional differences in income that are correlated with different percentages of black and white workers in a given occupational category. It is interesting in this connection, however, that black women fare at least as well as white women. One explanation that has been put forward is that there is less prejudice and discrimination against black women than against black men, and this, combined with a sex prejudice against white women in the world of work, results in a much smaller race differential in earnings for women than for men. But data such as those in Table 1 leave much to be desired since they are too complexly determined and, therefore, permit a great variety of speculative interpretations. They can suggest questions, but they cannot test hypotheses as to causal explanations.

Educational differences

Evidence on the educational levels attained by black men and women as compared with white men and women is consistent with the occupational and income data reviewed above, but it is hardly any more interpretable as to causal factors. The Moynihan Report summarizes some of the typical findings:

> The matriarchal pattern of so many Negro families reinforces itself over the generations. This process begins with education. Although the gap appears to be closing at the moment, for a long while, Negro females were better educated than Negro males, and this remains true today for the Negro population as a whole. . . . The difference in educational attainment between nonwhite men and women in the labor force is even greater; men lag 1.1 years behind women [Rainwater & Yancey, 1967, p. 77].

The Moynihan Report gives some percentage figures for males and females that can be converted to z scores to permit comparisons on an interval scale, as described in the previous section. In 1963 among black youths between the ages of 16 and 21 who were out of school, 66.3 percent of males and 55 percent of females did not graduate from high school. The corresponding z scores for males and females are $-.42$ and $-.13$, with a difference of $.29\sigma$ in favor of females. At the college level 4.5 percent of black males completed one to three years of college as compared with 7.3 percent of females. The z score difference

Table 2. Percent of nonwhite youth enrolled in school who are one or more grades below mode for age, by sex, 1960

Age	Male	Female	Difference in σ units
7 to 9 years old	7.8	5.8	−.15
10 to 13 years old	25.0	17.1	−.28
14 and 15 years old	35.5	24.8	−.31
16 and 17 years old	39.4	27.2	−.34
18 and 19 years old	57.3	46.0	−.28

Source: 1960 Census, School Enrollment, PC (2) 5A, Table 3, p. 24.

is .25σ, in favor of females. Note that the .29σ sex difference for high school dropouts does not differ appreciably from .25σ sex difference for college attendance. Thus, sex differences measured on an interval scale lend much more consistency to the data.

Sex differences in scholastic performance show a comparable magnitude when measured on an interval scale, as shown in Table 2. The mean sex difference is .27σ in favor of females.

The disparities between black boys and girls in scholastic achievement are reflected even more strongly in selection for higher education. According to Moynihan:

> In 1960, 39 percent of all white persons 25 years of age and over who had completed 4 or more years of college were women. Fifty-three percent of the nonwhites who had attained this level were women. . . . There is much evidence that Negro females are better students than their male counterparts. Daniel Thompson of Dillard University writes: "As low as is the aspirational level among lower-class Negro girls, it is consistently higher than among boys. For example, I have examined the honor rolls in Negro high schools for about 10 years. As a rule, from 75 to 90 percent of all Negro honor students are girls." Dr. Thompson reports that 70 percent of all applications for the National Achievement Scholarship Program financed by the Ford Foundation for outstanding Negro high school graduates are girls, despite special efforts by high school principals to submit the names of boys. . . . The finalists for this new program for outstanding Negro students were recently announced. Based on inspection of the names, only about 43 percent of all the 639 finalists were males. However, in the regular National Merit Scholarship program, males received 67 percent of the 1964 scholarship awards [Rainwater & Yancey, 1967, p. 78].

Data from the National Merit Scholarship Corporation show that 62 percent of the nominees for the National Achievement Scholarship Program (for outstanding Negro high school graduates) in 1964 were girls. These figures are based on 4,288 nominees from 1,280 high schools (Roberts & Nichols, 1966). The sex ratio for scholarship winners among blacks, therefore, is opposite to that found in the white population, in which the majority of scholarship winners are males. Sex differences in college enrollments in the United States show the same thing: among whites males exceeded females by almost 2 to 1 between the years 1953 and 1962, while among blacks the reverse was true. This holds also for college graduates, although the black sex difference (in favor of females) in number of graduates is not nearly so extreme as the white sex difference (in favor of males) (Davis, 1966, pp. 383–385).

Sex × SES × Education

Is the Sex × Race difference in college attendance explainable in terms of the lower average socioeconomic status (SES) of blacks rather than in terms of factors peculiar to the black population? If the Sex × SES × Education inter-action in the white population were similar to the Sex × Race × Education interaction we noted in the previous section, it could mean that we are dealing with an SES factor that operates similarly in white and black populations but creates the appearance of a racial cultural difference because of the greatly unequal proportions of blacks and whites of lower SES. The data from Project TALENT throw some light on this question (Flanagan & Cooley, 1966, p. 96). Tables 3 and 4 show the probabilities of white males and females entering college as a function of the SES of their parents and of their ability level as measured by tests of scholastic aptitude. These tables reveal that at every level of ability and at every level of SES females have a lower probability of entering college than males. Also, at the lower SES levels there is a slightly lower probability of a female's going to college as compared with a male of

Table 3. Probability of a male entering college (N = 17,738; grade-11 males)

Ability quarter	Socioeconomic quarter				
	Low 1	2	3	High 4	Mean
Low 1	.06	.12	.13	.26	.14
2	.13	.15	.29	.36	.23
3	.25	.34	.45	.65	.42
High 4	.48	.70	.73	.87	.70
Mean	.22	.33	.40	.54	.37

Source: From Flanagan & Cooley, 1966, p. 96.

Table 4. Probability of a female entering college (*N* = 20,368; grade-11 females)

Ability quarter	Socioeconomic quarter				
	Low 1	2	3	High 4	Mean
Low 1	.07	.07	.05	.20	.10
2	.08	.09	.20	.33	.18
3	.18	.23	.36	.55	.33
High 4	.34	.67	.67	.82	.63
Mean	.17	.26	.32	.48	.31

Source: From Flanagan & Cooley, 1966, p. 96.

comparable ability. So the sex difference for whites is still the opposite of that for blacks, even when we take account of SES.

An analysis of variance of the data in Tables 3 and 4 shows that ability is more than three times as important as SES in determining probability of entry for both males and females and that the interaction of SES and ability is a more important source of variance for females than for males. The percentage of variance in probability of college attendance as a function of ability and SES and their interaction, as derived from Tables 3 and 4, is shown for males and females in Table 5.

The sex differences in data such as these, of course, do not necessarily reflect ability differences, but neither can ability factors be ruled out entirely. The question calls for investigation in its own right. In the white population, at least, the difference in educational level attained by men and women is much greater than any evidence we have concerning sex differences in ability.

Table 5. Percentage of variance in probability of college attendance attributable to ability, socioeconomic status (SES), and their interaction for white males and females

Source of variance	Percentage of variance	
	Males	Females
Ability	76.1	71.4
SES	21.0	21.8
Ability × SES	2.9	6.8
Total	100.0	100.0

Source: Based on Project TALENT data (Flanagan & Cooley, 1966).

Cultural values and social customs regarding sex roles can obviously override and mask ability factors as they are manifested in educational and occupational attainments. Therefore, sex differences in abilities and in achievement in situations where there is equality of opportunity must be studied directly.

Sex differences relevant to abilities

Physical health

From the moment of birth, or even before, girls are healthier than boys. There is hardly any type of physical or emotional disorder that does not show a higher incidence for boys than for girls. There is a greater incidence among males for many childhood illnesses. In Scotland it has been established, for example, that pneumonia is 35 percent more frequent in boys than in girls under 5 years of age, and eight times as many boys die from this disease (Stott, 1966, p. 138). Stott reports that nearly twice as many boys as girls suffered serious nonepidemic illnesses in their first three years. He also notes that in severely culturally deprived (or culturally disintegrated in Stott's terminology) families, there are 22.6 percent more girls than boys. Comparing this figure with control groups and the sex ratio at birth, Stott concludes: "This would mean an excess childhood loss of approximately 29 percent for the boys." In summary, Stott states: "Virtually all nonlethal congenital malformations are more frequent among boys. The same applies to mental deficiency, including mongolism, and educational subnormality [1966, p. 140]." Boys are generally more susceptible to all forms of physical trauma. It was found, for example, that the effects of the atomic bomb in Hiroshima and Nagasaki caused boys to suffer more than girls in growth retardation and in length of the ill effects (Bayley, 1966b, p. 105).

Learning and behavior disorders

It is a well-established fact that neurological disorders resulting from complications of pregnancy and birth are significantly more frequent for males than females. This difference is probably a major factor contributing to the consistent sex differences found in the incidence of learning and behavior disorders in children, which are three to ten times more frequent among males than females of the same age (Bentzen, 1963). For reading disorders the ratio of boys to girls is 8 to 1. For stuttering the ratio is 4 to 1; boys stutter more severely than girls; and fewer boys than girls outgrow stuttering. Bentzen (1963) summarizes the sex ratios of other behavior disorders: adjudicated delinquency, 4.5:1; predelinquency, 3.4:1; personality disorders, 2.6:1; mental disease, 2.3:1; behavior problems, 9.4:1; and school failure, 2.6:1. Bentzen adds that there are similar sex ratios in the incidence of blindness, limited vision, deafness, and hardness of hearing, as well as other types of physical handicaps. Bentzen concludes:

> In a culture such as that of the United States, however, the social system not only fails to recognize the greater vulnerability of the male organism to stress but also admits only covertly the existence of a developmental differential between the sexes. Under such circumstances, it seems reasonable to assume that the predominance of males to females in learning and behavior disorders results from the failure to make realistic provisions for the male organism's greater susceptibility to stress. It also seems reasonable to assume that, unless our educational system groups children on the basis of their instructional readiness for learning, we may unwittingly be putting boys at a grave disadvantage [Bentzen, 1963, p. 98].

Developmental differences

Bentzen asserts that "at the chronological age of six, when most youngsters begin to attend school, girls are approximately 12 months ahead of boys in developmental age; by the time they are nine years of age, this developmental difference increases to about 18 months [1963, p. 96]." Bentzen is here referring to physiological indices of growth, such as rate of bone development and the eruption of permanent teeth. There is little evidence that ability differences between the sexes are as pronounced as the physiological growth rates noted by Bentzen.

N. Bayley (1966b) has reviewed evidence showing that boys' mental development is more strongly conditioned by environmental factors than is the case for girls. Girls show a higher correlation with their parents' IQs, and "the relation of girls' scores to socioeconomic status is not only stronger but stabilizes at a younger age than in boys [Bayley, 1966b, p. 103]." That these correlations reflect genetic resemblance between parents and children is shown in the Skodak and Skeels (1949) study of adopted children; the girls showed consistently higher correlations than boys with their biological parents' IQs, although they never knew their biological parents. Bayley concludes from her own studies:

> The findings in the Berkeley study of higher parent-daughter correlations in mental abilities, contrasted with higher mother-son relationships between maternal behavior and children's mental abilities, have led to a hypothesis of a genetic sex difference in resistance to, or resilience in recovery from, environmental influences. . . . It is only the boys who show, for both maternal and child behavior, persistent correlation between early behavior and later IQ [Bayley, 1966b, p. 105].

Mental retardation

The higher incidence of mental deficiency in males has been well known for many years. Commonly reported sex ratios for mild retardation are in the range of 1.2:1 to 1.3:1 and for severe mental defect, 1.3:1 to 2:1.

Intrinsic psychological sex differences

Thus far we have mentioned what might be referred to as *extrinsic* sex differences, which are those due to culturally conditioned sex roles and to the male organism's greater vulnerability to physical and psychological stress. *Intrinsic* sex differences are those arising from basic physiological differences between males and females which have differential effects on brain functioning. While good evidence does exist for these intrinsic differences, it is not yet clear to what extent they are important sources of variance in terms of practical educational, social, and economic criteria. It is possible that intrinsic sex differences, which are detected in specially devised laboratory testing situations, are more or less completely masked by the extrinsic differences in most gross practical circumstances.

Laboratory testing has shown quite conclusively that females excel in tasks requiring alertness, rapid shifts of attention, and perceptual speed and accuracy and in simple overlearned perceptual-motor tasks; males do relatively better on more complex tasks requiring an inhibition of immediate responses to less obvious attributes. A hypothesis, based on considerable physiological evidence, has been advanced that these sex differences are due to the differential effects of the sex hormones—estrogens and androgens—on the sympathetic central nervous system, which controls the balance between adrenergic activating and cholingergic inhibitory neural processes (Broverman, Klaiber, Kobayashi, & Vogel, 1968). These intrinsic sex differences in psychological functioning appear to extend across mammalian species. Nothing is known concerning a Race × Sex interaction on these intrinsic sex differences, but it is a worthy subject for investigation.

General intelligence

The general conclusion of those who have reviewed the evidence on sex differences in intelligence tests is that in the white population sex differences in overall score are negligible, although there are consistent sex differences in particular subtests. In general, differences in favor of males have been found on tests of spatial and mechanical ability, and differences in favor of females have been found in tests of verbal or linguistic functions. One of the most thorough reviews of the research on this topic came to the following conclusion regarding sex differences in intelligence test performance:

> A survey of the results abstracted from acceptable studies has yielded largely negative conclusions. When large unselected groups are used, when age is taken

into account, when possibilities of bias in test content are allowed for, startling differences between the sexes either in average tendency or in variation fail to emerge. While such a conclusion is not new to the psychological literature, it is significant that recent carefully worked-out studies substantiate earlier opinions in this regard. It should be noted that the present conclusions are restricted to overall measurements of mental status. Similar comparisons on more specific types of performance may, and in fact do, reveal systematic differences between the sexes [Kuznets & McNemar, 1940, p. 217].

A more recent review by Miner (1957) comes to the same general conclusion, but it even casts doubt on sex differences in verbal ability as measured by a vocabulary test. In samples of 721 men and 779 women who were quite representative of the United States population, the t value for the difference between the means on the vocabulary test was only .17, which is totally nonsignificant; the standard deviations also showed no significant difference.

The majority of studies, however, have found a slightly larger variance of scores for males than for females. The largest and methodologically most adequate epidemiological survey of the incidence of mental retardation shows a marked difference in the proportions of males and females (Lemkau & Imre, 1966). At the upper extreme, Terman (1926), in screening a school population of 168,000 for children with IQs 140 and over (the top 1 percent), found a sex ratio of 1.2:1 in favor of boys. Another study, by Lewis, which selected the top 10 percent of 45,000 grade-school children on a verbal test reported a sex ratio of 1.46:1 in favor of girls (L. E. Tyler, 1965, p. 249). The Terman and Lewis results can be viewed as compatible if there is a sex difference in mean score in favor of girls and a greater variance for boys. Thus, in the region of the mean girls would excel boys, but at the extremes of the distribution there would be a greater percentage of boys.

The construction of most standard intelligence tests has explicitly tried to minimize sex differences in overall score. In the Stanford-Binet, for example, items showing large sex differences were eliminated and the remaining items with small sex differences were selected so as to balance out in the composite score. Such tests, therefore, are not suited to investigating sex differences per se. But it is still of importance if they reveal a Sex × Race interaction. Interpretations of the Sex × Race interaction would seem less difficult, however, in tests which were not devised with a view to minimizing or eliminating sex differences in the normative population.

It was once believed that girls scored higher than boys up until puberty, beyond which a reverse trend was manifested. This result has not been found in data that is free of sampling bias associated with differential dropout rates in secondary schools. For example, the Scottish National Survey, which sampled all children equally at all age levels, found no sex difference at any age in Stanford-Binet IQs.

Scholastic differences

Sex differences in scholastic performance and assessments are much more pronounced than in intelligence test results. F. T. Tyler (1960, p. 685) has listed seven conclusions in this realm that are strongly supported by much research: (1) girls get higher grades in school; (2) girls get higher scores on scholastic achievement tests, but these are not as high as their school grades; (3) the direction of sex differences varies with specific subjects with girls doing better in language and boys in arithmetic and science; (4) a larger number of girls are accelerated in grade level; (5) a smaller percentage of girls is found in special classes for the retarded; (6) more boys than girls are not promoted at the end of the first year in school; and (7) reading disabilities and speech handicaps occur more commonly among boys than among girls.

Environmental correlates of IQ

Bayley (1966b) has noted a sex difference in parent-child correlations for IQ, the girls showing a higher correlation with parental IQ. The hypothesis that the parent-child IQ correlation is higher for girls because they are more subject to environmental influences associated with parental IQ is contradicted by the study of Skodak and Skeels (1949), which showed consistently higher parent-child correlations for girls than for boys, despite the fact that the children were adopted and never knew their natural parents with whose IQs they were correlated. Of the 63 correlations between parental and child IQs reviewed by Bayley (1966b), 78 percent show a higher correlation for girls than for boys, a difference which by a chi square test is significant beyond the .001 level. Bayley also notes that "the relation of girls' scores to socio-economic status is not only stronger but stabilizes at a younger age than in boys [1966b, p. 103]." An explanation of this finding, which is most consistent with the parent-child correlations, is that there is a genetic component in SES IQ differences, and girls' IQs reflect their genotypic values more closely than is the case for boys. Bayley has found more significant environmental correlates of boys' IQs than of girls' IQs; the environmental influences reflected most strongly in boys' mental development are associated with various aspects of maternal behavior in early childhood. Bayley states:

> The findings in the Berkeley study of higher parent-daughter correlations in mental abilities, contrasted with higher mother-son relationships between maternal behavior and children's mental abilities, have led to a hypothesis of a genetic sex difference in resistance to, or resilience in recovery from, environmental influences. . . . It is only the boys who show, for both maternal and child behavior, persistent correlation between early behavior and later IQ [1966b, p. 105].

This evidence suggests that boys are more vulnerable than girls to environmental influences, both physically and psychologically. Males are apparently less well buffered against the environment.

Chromosomal basis for sex differences

The male's greater vulnerability to environmental stress, prenatally and post-natally, seems to be a general mammalian characteristic. The only attempt to explain this phenomenon in biological terms makes reference to the sex chromosomes (Stern, 1949). Females inherit two X chromosomes (XX), each of which carries a full complement of genes, while males inherit an X and a Y chromosome (XY). The Y chromosome is much smaller than the X and carries very little genetic material. For every gene locus on one X chromosome there is a corresponding locus on the other X chromosome. If the alleles (different forms of the gene) are the same at each locus, they are said to be *homozygous*; if they are different, they are *heterozygous*. If they are heterozygous and one allele is recessive, it will be "dominated" by the allele on the other X chromosome. Since mutant and abnormal genes are usually recessive, when they occur in the heterozygous state, their undesirable effects are dominated by the normal allele at the corresponding locus on the homozygous chromosome, and no genetic disadvantage results. In the case of males, however, the XY combination is said to be *hemizygous*. The Y chromosome does not have corresponding gene loci which can dominate recessive alleles on the X chromosome. This condition results in so-called sex-linked inheritance, whereby genetic defects carried on the X chromosome, such as color blindness and hemophilia, are only carried by the female and are expressed in the male. (In a small percentage of cases the female will be homozygous for the condition, receiving a recessive gene at the same locus on the X chromosome from both parents.) In short, the male's Y chromosome is unable to dominate or counteract un-favorable mutant alleles on the X chromosome. This definitely accounts for sex-linked genetic defects and may account also for many birth defects and inadequate buffering or resistance against physical trauma, infections, and the like.

Mating between persons who are genetically related increases the likeli-hood that recessive alleles will occur at the same loci in the maternal and paternal chromosomes. The effects of these recessives will not be counteracted and will be manifested in characteristics of the offspring. The closer the genetic relationship between parents, the higher is the probability of pairing recessive alleles. This applies to all 22 pairs of chromosomes called autosomes and to the sex chromosomes. (There are 23 pairs of chromosomes in all.) In the case of polygenic characters (i.e., those conditioned by the effects of many genes), the effect of the mating of genetically related parents is manifested as "in-breeding depression" in the offspring, that is, a depression or lowering of characteristics under polygenic control. Thus, physical stature, the quality of dentition, intelligence, and other polygenic characters are diminished in the offsprings of consanguinous matings. This has been amply proven in cousin matings (Schull & Neel, 1965). Their offsprings are several points lower in IQ than the offsprings of a matched control group of unrelated parents.

We should expect the effects of inbreeding depression to affect girls' IQs more than boys, since the inbreeding effect has more chromosomes to work on in girls, who possess XX. That is to say, inbreeding depression can occur in 23 out of 23 chromosome pairs in girls; therefore, they are liable to 100 percent of the inbreeding effect. Boys, on the other hand, cannot show any additional effect on the XY combination due to inbreeding; they can show it only on the 22 autosomal chromosome pairs and thus will be liable to only 22/23, or 96 percent, of the inbreeding effect. In a large study of the IQs of 2,111 children of cousin marriages in Japan girls showed significantly greater inbreeding depression for IQ than did boys. Inbreeding in this sample lowered Wechsler (WISC) IQs 6.87 percent for boys and 7.90 percent for girls as compared with control children born to unrelated parents who were matched with the cousin matings for IQ, SES, age, and other relevant variables (Schull & Neel, 1965).

Because of the male's greater vulnerability to stress—physical and emotional, prenatally, perinatally, and postnatally—we can state the following hypothesis: Any segment of the population which is subjected to greater stress than the rest of the population should show greater sex differences in favor of females, and the sex differences should increase, up to a point, in proportion to the unfavorableness of the environmental conditions.

Black and white sex differences: physical sex ratio at birth

The sex ratio at birth is defined as the number of male live births per 100 female live births. The sex ratio in all human populations is over 100 and is very close to 105–106 in European and North American Caucasian populations. It is close to 102 for Negro populations in Africa, the West Indies, and the United States. It is as high as 113 in Koreans.

If males are more vulnerable to stress and more liable to genetic defects, some of which may be lethal, it seems reasonable to argue that more males than females will be aborted at some time between conception and birth and also that this should occur to a greater degree in populations that are subject to greater prenatal hazards due to maternal nutritional deficiencies, infections, early age of primaparas, close spacing of pregnancies, poor prenatal care, and the like. It was once believed that the primary sex ratio (i.e., the ratio at the time of conception) is about 135 males per 100 females. The fact that the live-birth sex ratio is 105 to 106 was accounted for by the greater fetal mortality for males than females. This hypothesis seems consistent with such observations as the fact that in England, for example, the sex ratio for live births is 106, but

it is 110 for the stillborn (Carter, 1962, p. 47). The hypothesis that socioeconomically depressed populations have a lower sex ratio because of differential fetal mortality associated with environmental disadvantages was clearly
expressed by an early student of the problem, Amos H. Hawley: "as a rule,
the sex ratio at birth exceeds 100 and varies inversely with the frequency of
prenatal losses . . . where prenatal losses are low, as in the high level-of-living
areas of the West, the sex ratios at birth are usually around 105 to 106. On
the other hand, in low level-of-living areas where the frequencies of prenatal
losses are relatively high, sex ratios vary around 102 [quoted by Visaria, 1967,
pp. 133–135]."

This hypothesis, once generally accepted, has encountered difficulty in
recent years because it fails to accord with a number of crucial facts. In reviewing all studies of sex ratios in sixty-two territories of the world with complete
birth registrations between 1949 and 1958, Visaria (1967) has found a correlation of −.15 between the sex ratio for late fetal deaths and the sex ratio of live
births. The correlation is in the expected direction, but it is so low as to be
nonsignificant at the .05 level. This low correlation casts great doubt on an
explanation of population differences in sex ratio based on differential fetal
mortality rates due to the male's greater vulnerability to stress. Another
difficulty with the hypothesis is the fact that sex ratios appear to be relatively
independent of geography and socioeconomic conditions but closely related
to racial classification. The low sex ratio of 102 in the black population in the
United States is approximately the same in all regions of the country (and the
same as for blacks in Africa and the West Indies), and it has not shown any
systematic change between 1940 and 1967, despite great improvements in
health care, as reflected in a markedly declining rate of infant mortality in the
black population during the same period. The black sex ratio in 1940 was
101.9; in 1967 it was 102. The white sex ratio in 1940 was 106; in 1967 it was
105.6 (U.S. Department of Health, Education, and Welfare, 1969). The
fluctuations throughout this period are irregular and minute. The mean sex
ratio for whites is 105.71; for blacks it is 102.34.

The lack of change in sex ratios during the same period of great reduction
in infant mortality rates is a puzzle, as yet unresolved, but it throws into question
the explanation of sex ratios in terms of greater male vulnerability to unfavorable prenatal environmental effects. Visaria concluded from his review of the
evidence up to 1967, "on the basis of the impressive evidence from the United
States and the West Indies, one can conclude that, probably, there operates,
among the negroid populations, some genetic or racial factor, which leads to a
somewhat lower sex ratio at birth than in the usual range of 104.0–107.0
[1967, p. 139]."

Sex × Race × Infant mortality

Unlike the sex ratio at birth infant mortality rates, in whites and blacks, have shown a marked decline over the last fifty years or so, undoubtedly reflecting improvements in health and medical care of the newborn. Despite a great decrease in infant mortality for both racial groups, however, the difference in mortality rates between the groups has remained relatively constant since 1915 (Davis, 1966, p. 156). The infant mortality rate for blacks has been approximately double that for whites since 1915.

The question of major interest to the present discussion concerns the sex ratio for infant mortality. Analysis of vital statistics data for the United States between 1960 and 1966 shows a higher rate of infant mortality for males than for females but no systematic change over the years. The death rate in the first year per 1,000 live births is 24.9 boys vs. 18.8 girls for whites and 45.2 boys vs. 36.7 girls for blacks. Mean death rates per 1,000 live births in the first twenty-eight days after birth are 18.9 boys vs. 14 girls for whites, and 29 boys vs. 22.9 girls for blacks (U.S. Department of Health, Education, and Welfare, 1967).

The best method for comparing the magnitude of the sex difference across the two racial groups is to convert these rates into z scores, by the method described earlier, and compare the differences between male and female z scores. This method depends upon the assumption that viability in infancy is normally distributed and has equal variances within each racial group. Without this assumption there is no proper way of comparing the magnitude of the sex differences in mortality from one racial group to another, since their overall rates differ so markedly. Table 6 shows the 1965 infant mortality rates per 1,000 live births for various racial groups, their corresponding z scores, and the difference between z scores for males and females. (Higher z scores indicate higher viability.) The z score differences between racial groups shown in Table 6 are much larger than the year-to-year fluctuations (between 1960 and 1966) within racial groups, which were computed but are not presented here. Since the sample sizes are in the tens of thousands for each group, most of the differences observed here are statistically significant. We note in Table 6 that there are overall racial differences in infant viability and also sex differences. The sex difference when viewed in terms of z scores (i.e., $z_F - z_M$) is slightly *less* for blacks than for whites. Note also that the z sex difference is close to .10 for both blacks and whites; in other words, both racial groups show a sex difference in infant viability equivalent to about one-tenth of a standard deviation when viability is assumed to be continuously and normally distributed as are most other multidetermined biological characters. It is interesting that mortality rates are so exceptionally low in the Chinese and Japanese populations as compared with the other racial groups. The only population subgroup that has lower infant mortality rates are Jews. Even when matched with other immigrant and native-born groups on general environmental conditions, Jews show the lowest infant mortality rates of all ethnic groups (Graves, Freeman, & Thompson, 1968). Such findings raise the question of whether there are genetic as well as environmental factors involved in infant viability. Whatever

Table 6. U.S. Mortality rates (1965) per 1,000 live births and z transformations

Group	Under 1 year			Under 28 days			28 days to 11 months		
	Male	Female	M-F	Male	Female	M-F	Male	Female	M-F
All races	26.6	20.6	6.0	19.5	14.8	4.7	7.2	5.9	1.3
White	23.5	17.7	5.8	17.9	13.2	4.7	5.6	4.4	1.2
Negro	44.0	36.2	7.8	28.8	23.0	5.8	15.3	13.2	2.1
Indian	39.0	34.7	4.3	17.7	15.1	2.6	21.2	19.6	1.6
Chinese	10.5	9.3	1.2	8.0	5.7	2.3	2.4	3.6	-1.2
Japanese	12.2	8.9	3.3	8.9	7.1	1.8	3.3	1.8	1.5
Other races	21.3	18.1	3.2	16.5	14.1	2.4	4.9	4.0	0.9

z transformation of mortality rates (higher z scores indicate higher viability)

Group	Under 1 year			Under 28 days			28 days to 11 months		
	Male	Female	$z_F - z_M$	Male	Female	$z_F - z_M$	Male	Female	$z_F - z_M$
All races	1.93	2.04	.11	2.06	2.18	.12	2.45	2.52	.05
White	1.99	2.10	.11	2.10	2.22	.12	2.54	2.62	.08
Negro	1.71	1.80	.09	1.90	2.00	.10	2.16	2.22	.06
Indian	1.76	1.82	.06	2.10	2.17	.07	2.03	2.06	.03
Chinese	2.31	2.35	.04	2.41	2.53	.12	2.82	2.69	-.13
Japanese	2.25	2.37	.12	2.37	2.45	.08	2.72	2.92	.20
Other races	2.03	2.09	.06	2.13	2.20	.07	2.58	2.65	.07

Source: U.S. Department of Health, Education, & Welfare, 1967.

the cause, it is clear from Table 6 that there is a sex difference in mortality in the first year of life, favoring girls by about one-tenth of a standard deviation in white and black populations.

Birth weight, skin color, and sex differences

There is a complex of interrelated factors involving birth weight, skin color, and sex differences which is scarcely understood but should be pointed out as an area deserving much further investigation. Dreger and Miller (1968) in their comprehensive review of comparative studies of blacks and whites note that light-skinned black mothers have heavier babies than darker-skinned mothers, even when there was no relation between skin color and the length of the gestation period or parity. Naylor and Myrianthopoulos (1967) have found that black and white differences in birth weight (white neonates being heavier) cannot be explained solely in terms of socioeconomic factors but probably involve a genetic racial difference. The association between maternal skin color and child's birth weight reported by Dreger and Miller might be explained in terms of differing proportions of Caucasian genes in American Negroes (see Reed, 1969). That birth-weight differences, independently of genetic factors, are related to later mental development as assessed by IQ tests has been shown in studies of identical twins who differ in birth weight (Scarr, 1969). The heavier twin at birth generally has the advantage in later IQ. This effect in identical twins is not genetic but is entirely a result of differences in prenatal environment.

The picture is further complicated by the findings of a sex difference in skin color in various black populations (Harrison, Owen, Da Rocha, & Salzano, 1967; Mazess, 1967). Females have lighter skin as determined by spectro-photometer measures of reflectance on various parts of the body. The sex difference is not attributed to differential exposure to the sun. For unknown reasons the sex difference is considerably greater in Bahamian blacks than in United States blacks. In reviewing all the existing evidence on the relationship of skin color to intelligence in black populations, Shuey (1966) found that in twelve of eighteen comparisons, those groups of lighter skin color scored higher than the darker; and in four other studies the lighter groups scored the higher in the majority of the tests given. In only two studies was there no evidence whatever of a relationship between skin color and intelligence. The fact of a *sex* difference both in skin color and in intelligence, however, raises the question of whether any correlation between skin color and intelligence can be explained entirely in terms of racial hybridization, as Shuey is inclined to interpret the evidence, or whether there might be some more direct connection between pigmentation and mental development. There may be social concomitants of skin color which could affect intellectual development. But there could also be a somewhat more direct biological connection between pigmentation and brain processes in view of the fact that the production of melanin, which is the main substance of skin pigmentation, involves the same metabolic pathway by which the protein phenylalanine is converted to tyrosine. Tyrosine is utilized by the skin in forming melanin and is also directly involved in the brain's metabolic processes and development. The nature and meaning of the network of relationships between birth weight, skin color, sex, and IQ is not known, but the unquestionable intercorrelations among these variables should prompt further investigations in this realm.

Psychological test scores

Infant tests

The largest comparative study of perceptual-motor abilities in black and white infants from the ages of 1 to 15 months is based on 1,409 infants—680 boys, 729 girls; 55 percent white, 42 percent black (Bayley, 1965). The samples are quite representative of the black and white populations in the United States. All were given the California First Year Mental Scale developed by Bayley. The scale yields both mental (i.e., perceptual-attentional alertness) and motor scores. Bayley's data reveal no sex differences for either scale between 1 and 15 months of age in either white or black samples. Bayley concludes:

> It would appear that the behaviors which are developing during the first 15 months of life, whether they are motor skills or the early perceptual and adaptive forms of mental abilities, are for the most part unrelated to sex, race, birth order, geographical location, or parental ability. The one possible difference is in motor development in which the Negro babies tend to be more advanced than the whites during the first 12 months. Although there is considerable overlap of scores among whites and Negroes of the same age, a genetic factor may be operating. That is, Negroes may be inherently more precocious than whites in their motor coordinations [Bayley, 1965, p. 408].

No studies have found the contrary. Japanese and Chinese infants, on the other hand, are found to be less precocious motorically than Caucasian infants (Candill & Weinstein, 1968; Freedman & Freedman, 1969). Similar differences in the same direction have been found between Mayan Indian infants of southern Mexico and Caucasian newborns (Brazelton, Robey, & Collier, 1969).

Although Bayley (1965) found no sex differences in level of performance on the infant scales, she did find a striking sex difference in the pattern of intercorrelations of these scales with other variables (Bayley, 1966a). For example, boys show a negative correlation between infant motor precocity and later IQ, while girls show no correlation. Vocalization between 7 and 15 months is highly positively correlated with later IQ in girls and slightly negatively correlated in boys. A variety of maternal behaviors in the first three years are significantly correlated with later IQs in boys but not in girls. These different patterns of correlations for boys and girls indicate differences in the development and organization of their mental abilities and greater susceptibility of boys' intellectual development to environmental influences. Bayley concludes:

> These striking sex differences [in correlations] in early childhood call for a much more complete analysis and study. . . . The differences are not complete dichotomies, but they are, nevertheless, very considerable. I do not believe they can be explained entirely by cultural expectations or differential environmental experiences and pressures [Bayley, 1966a, p. 130].

As yet no study has been made of similar correlational patterns in non-Caucasian children.

Intelligence tests

One of the first applications of the Binet-Simon intelligence scale (Goddard version) to black children, in 1914, noted a sex difference (Phillips, 1914). Acceleration was defined as having a mental age one year above chronological age. Only 2 percent of black boys as compared with 12.5 percent of girls were accelerated. In z score units this is a difference of $.85\sigma$. Subsequent studies reveal a much smaller sex difference. In fact, the largest normative study of black Stanford-Binet IQs, based on 1,800 black children from first to sixth grade in five southeastern states, shows a negligible sex difference in mean IQ: 80.99 for males and 80.43 for females (Kennedy, Van De Reit, & White, 1963). The 1960 Stanford-Binet, unlike the older Goddard adaptation of the original Binet-Simon scale, was specifically devised to eliminate a sex difference in overall IQ in the white normative population. This attempt apparently generalizes to the black school population sampled in the five southeastern states by Kennedy *et al.*

Unfortunately, from the standpoint of this review, very few of the extensive studies of black intelligence have analyzed the data by sex. The studies summarized below are virtually the total information available on the Race × Sex × Ability interaction. The only studies that are strictly usable for looking at the Race × Sex interaction are those in which the same tests were administered to whites and blacks at approximately the same time under approximately the same test conditions.

Henmon-Nelson tests of mental ability. Items on general information, proverb interpretation, figure analogies, and following directions make up the Henmon-

Nelson battery, a group-administered thirty-minute test. The data of Table 7 are based on a study by Wilson (1967), who administered the Henmon-Nelson tests to large samples of pupils in the public schools of Richmond, California. Wilson's IQs were reported by family socioeconomic status and by sex. (He reports IQ means but not standard deviations.) The data are summarized in Table 7 in terms of unweighted and weighted means. The weighting factor for the separate means is the number of subjects on which they are based. The weighted means are more representative of the total population sampled in the study. It can be seen that the sex difference, in favor of females for both blacks and whites, is greater for blacks—but only slightly. The overall Race × Sex difference amounts to less than 1 IQ point for this test.

Stanford-Binet and primary mental abilities. In Table 8 the Stanford-Binet test is compared with Thurstone's Primary Mental Abilities test since both tests were administered to essentially the same black and white populations in the rural South (Baughman & Dahlstrom, 1968, pp. 41, 50). These data require no further interpretation at this point. The total score of the Primary Mental Abilities is based on a composite of five subtest scores: Verbal Meaning, Perceptual Speed, Number Facility, Spatial Relations, and Reasoning.

A word is in order about the several statistics presented in Table 8 and subsequent tables. The mean difference between whites and blacks (W-N) is expressed in z score units based on the standard deviation of the white group. Z scores are directly comparable from one test to another. The ratio of white to black (Negro) variance (W/N Variance Ratio) is given for each test to permit examination of the hypothesis that the variance of scores on mental tests is greater in the white than in the black population. The sex variance ratio (M/F) is determined within each racial group. It permits examination of the hypothesis that males are more variable than females. Sex differences (M-F) are expressed in z score units. For blacks the sex difference is expressed both in z units based on the white SD and on the black SD for the given test. The first indicates the magnitude of the black sex difference on the same scale as that of the white sex difference; the second indicates the magnitude of the sex difference relative to the spread of scores in the black group.

Lorge-Thorndike intelligence test. Both verbal and nonverbal IQs are attained from the Lorge-Thorndike, which is a group test of general intelligence. The test has a high g loading when factor analyzed with other ability tests. The results are from all the black and white children in the Berkeley elementary schools, excluding all those in special classes for the retarded and educationally handicapped. All the tests were administered by trained psychometrists whose aim was to insure uniformity of testing procedures in all classes. As can be seen in Table 9, the overall sex difference on this test is over twice as great for blacks as for whites. Even so, the average sex difference for blacks amounts to only about 0.2σ, which is equivalent to 3 IQ points.

Table 7. Henmon-Nelson IQ test

Family Status*	Grade	Number White	Number Negro	Percent males White	Percent males Negro	W-N IQ diff. Male	W-N IQ diff. Female	Sex diff. (M-F) in IQ White	Sex diff. (M-F) in IQ Negro
High 1	1	294	59	71	53	14	15	−2	−1
2		397	236	70	60	12	5	−3	−4
3		426	253	71	51	7	9	−2	0
Low 4		275	665	69	53	4	5	0	1
Weighted mean		(1,392)	(1,213)	70	54	8.32	7.18	−.18	−.28
Unweighted mean				70	54	9.25	8.50	−.25	−1.00
High 1	6	344	73	71	51	16	14	−1	−3
2		468	264	71	57	16	12	−2	−6
3		515	280	71	51	8	10	−3	−1
Low 4		320	746	69	55	6	7	−2	−1
Weighted mean		(1,647)	(1,363)	71	54	10.55	9.76	−2.10	−2.15
Unweighted mean				70	54	11.50	10.75	−2.00	−2.75
High 1	8	402	84	71	52	18	17	0	−1
2		539	306	71	57	16	12	−1	−5
3		579	327	70	52	10	13	−2	−1
Low 4		371	836	67	54	9	9	−3	−3
Weighted mean		(1,891)	(1,553)	70	54	12.44	11.68	−1.49	−2.44
Unweighted mean				70	54	13.25	12.75	−1.50	−2.00
High 1	11	191	27	70	52	8	20	−2	10
2		251	121	72	56	15	10	1	−4
3		286	112	68	50	14	9	1	−4
Low 4		159	315	68	54	12	10	1	−1
Weighted mean		(887)	(575)	70	54	12.70	11.03	.35	−1.70
Unweighted mean				70	53	12.25	12.25	.25	.25
Weighted grand mean				70	54	10.92	9.92	−1.07	−1.71
Unweighted grand mean				70	54	11.56	11.06	−.88	−1.38

*1. Professional and managerial   3. Semiskilled and skilled manual
 2. White-collar   4. Lower class

Source: Wilson, 1967.

Table 8. Stanford-Binet and primary mental abilities

	Number		Percent males		Mean W-N diff.*	W/N Variance ratio	Sex (M/F) variance Ratio		Sex difference† (M-F)		
	White	Negro	White	Negro			White	Negro	White	Negro/W	Negro/N
Stanford-Binet	464	542	49.6	49.8	.92	1.23	1.12	.97	.14	−.13	−.14
Primary mental abilities	437	642	48.5	50.2	1.21	1.01	1.23	1.15	.02	−.27	−.27
Weighted mean			49.1	50.0	1.07	1.12	1.17	1.07	.08	−.21	−.21

*$(\overline{X}_w - \overline{X}_n)/SD_w$

†The mean difference is divided by the total white SD for Negro/W and by the total Negro SD for Negro/N.

Source: Baughman & Dahlstrom, 1968, pp. 41, 50.

131

Table 9. Lorge-Thorndike IQ test—nonverbal (NV) and verbal (V)

Form	Grade	Number		Percent males		Mean W-N diff.*	W/N variance ratio	Sex (M/F) variance ratio		Sex difference† (M-F)		
		White	Negro	White	Negro			White	Negro	White	Negro/W	Negro/N
Primary battery (NV) 1	K	530	391	57.0	47.8	1.14	1.10	1.20	1.23	−.05	−.06	−.07
	1	586	402	51.2	52.5	1.35	1.03	1.06	1.39	.16	.15	.15
Primary battery (NV) 2	2	620	489	51.8	49.3	1.24	1.25	.86	1.15	−.13	−.20	−.22
	3	508	395	54.1	46.3	1.29	1.06	.99	1.15	−.13	.03	.04
	4	507	412	50.1	52.2	1.55	1.03	.96	1.38	.03	−.36	−.37
Nonverbal IQ	5	472	389	55.3	51.4	1.76	.86	1.36	1.01	−.14	−.52	−.48
	6	544	403	50.2	54.6	1.84	.88	1.70	1.29	−.19	−.18	−.16
	4	492	370	52.0	49.5	1.51	1.15	1.16	1.59	−.12	−.32	−.37
Verbal IQ	5	469	391	55.6	50.1	1.52	1.32	1.12	1.05	−.15	−.33	−.38
	6	528	359	49.2	53.8	1.88	1.21	1.32	1.45	−.09	−.12	−.13
Unweighted mean				52.6	50.8	1.51	1.09	1.17	1.27	−.08	−.19	−.20
Weighted mean				52.6	50.7	1.50	1.09	1.17	1.26	−.08	−.19	−.20

*$(\overline{X}_w - \overline{X}_n)/SD_w$
†The mean difference is divided by the total white SD for Negro/W and by the total Negro SD for Negro/N.

Figure copying test. The Gesell Institute of Child Study at Yale University developed the Figure Copying Test as a means for measuring developmental readiness for the traditional school learning tasks of the primary grades (Ilg & Ames, 1964, Ch. 8). The test consists of ten geometric forms, arranged in order of difficulty, which the child is simply asked to copy. The test involves no memory factor, since the figure to be copied is before the child at all times. The test is administered without time limit, although most children finish in between ten and fifteen minutes. It is probably best regarded as a developmental scale of mental ability. It correlates substantially with other IQ tests, but it may be regarded as considerably less culturally loaded than many standard IQ tests. It is not primarily a measure of perceptual-motor ability but of cognitive development.

Each of the ten figures is scored on a 3-point scale, from 0 to 2. A score of zero is given if the child's attempted drawing (they are asked to attempt all the figures) totally fails to resemble the model. A score of 1 is given if there is fair resemblance to the model—the figure need not be copied perfectly, but it must be clearly recognizable as the figure which the child has attempted to copy. A score of 2 is given for an attempt which duplicates the figure in all its essential characteristics, though it need not have draftsmanlike accuracy—this is an essentially adult level performance. Thus the possible range of scores is 0 to 20.

Girls do slightly better on the test than boys, and the difference is greater in the white sample. Oriental children do significantly better than white children of the same age. Black children perform about one year below white and Oriental children at the kindergarten and first grade levels, and by fourth grade are about two years below. Fourth-grade black children average about the same score on this test as second-grade white and Oriental children.

The high level of motivation on these tests is suggested by the fact that the minimum score obtained in each racial group at each grade level increases systematically with grade. This indicates that all children were making an attempt to perform in accordance with the instructions. Another indication that can be seen from the test protocols themselves is that nearly 100 percent of the children in every group at every grade level attempted to copy every figure. The attempts, even when unsuccessful, usually show considerable effort, as indicated by redrawing the figure, erasures, and drawing over the figure repeatedly in order to improve it. It is also noteworthy about this test that normal children are generally not successful in drawing figures beyond their mental age level, as indicated by tests such as the Stanford-Binet, and that special instructions and coaching on the drawing of these figures hardly improves their performance.

The results of the Race × Sex comparison on Figure Copying are shown in Table 10.

Table 10. Figure copying test

Grade	Number		Percent males		Mean W-N diff.*	W/N variance ratio	Sex (M/F) variance ratio		Sex difference† (M-F)		
	White	Negro	White	Negro			White	Negro	White	Negro/W	Negro/N
K	543	479	54.7	50.1	.90	1.34	.96	1.29	−.24	−.13	−.15
1	622	484	50.8	52.1	.91	1.07	1.13	1.09	−.20	−.03	−.03
2	610	490	51.6	49.0	.82	1.15	1.00	1.44	−.10	−.10	−.10
3	546	379	53.8	46.4	.74	1.18	.85	1.28	−.09	−.08	−.08
4	411	418	49.6	49.8	.89	1.00	.93	1.15	−.21	−.16	−.16
Unweighted mean			52.1	49.5	.85	1.15	.97	1.25	−.17	−.03	−.03
Weighted mean			52.2	49.6	.85	1.15	.98	1.25	−.17	−.10	−.10

*$(\bar{X}_w - \bar{X}_n)/SD_w$

†The mean difference is divided by the total white SD for Negro/W and by the total Negro SD for Negro/N.

Table 11. Wechsler intelligence scale for children and Raven's progressive matrices

Test	Age	Number		Percent males		Mean W-N diff.*	W/N variance ratio	Sex (M/F) variance ratio		Sex difference† (M-F)		
		White	Negro	White	Negro			White	Negro	White	Negro/W	Negro/N
WISC	5	26	26	73.1	50.0	1.57	1.03	2.12	.89	−.04	.07	.07
	6	37	26	59.4	53.8	.58	1.12	5.67	2.46	−.06	.92	.98
	7	27	24	44.4	50.0	.67	.96	2.51	.43	.05	−.01	−.01
	8	27	34	55.6	58.8	.52	2.11	1.05	.78	−.04	.11	.16
	9	24	24	50.0	50.0	.59	2.37	.72	.48	−.28	.29	.45
Unweighted mean				56.5	52.5	.79	1.52	2.41	1.01	.04	.28	.33
Weighted mean				56.7	53.0	.77	1.51	2.68	1.01	−.07	.27	.32
Progressive matrices	7	27	24	44.4	50.0	.52	.72	1.09	.93	.10	−.39	−.33
	8	27	34	55.6	58.8	.36	1.89	2.35	1.08	.40	.18	.25
	9	24	24	50.0	50.0	.20	.88	1.31	1.08	−.12	.40	.38
Unweighted mean				50.0	52.9	.36	1.16	1.58	1.03	.13	.06	.10
Weighted mean				50.0	53.6	.36	1.21	1.59	1.04	.14	.08	.12

*$(\bar{X}_w - \bar{X}_n)/SD_w$

†The mean difference is divided by the total white SD for Negro/W and by the total Negro SD for Negro/N.

Source: Semler & Iscoe, 1966.

Wechsler intelligence scale for children (WISC) and progressive matrices. Semler and Iscoe (1966) administered the Wechsler Intelligence Scale for Children (WISC) and Raven's Progressive Matrices to small groups of white and black children in Texas. The WISC is an individually administered test of general intelligence comprised of Verbal (Information, Comprehension, Digit Span, Similarities, Arithmetic, and Vocabulary) and Performance (Picture Arrangement, Picture Completion, Block Design, Object Assembly, and Digit Symbol) subtests. Raven's Progressive Matrices is a nonverbal test of reasoning; it is the purest measure of the g factor of any of the tests reported here and is rivaled only by Cattell's Culture Fair Test of g as a measure of the general factor common to all tests of complex mental abilities. The results in those tests are shown in Table 11. We note that, unlike most of the other tests, the Matrices show a sex difference in favor of boys. So does the WISC in the case of blacks. Unfortunately, because of the relatively small samples used by Semler and Iscoe, we cannot be very confident whether these are *test* differences or *sample* differences.

A much larger sample of individually administered Colored Progressive Matrices was obtained from the schools of Riverside, California.[1] These results (Table 12) also show a sex difference in favor of males, and a larger sex difference for whites than for blacks, but the difference is consistent with the general finding that, relative to females of the same race, white males do better than black males. The same comparison can be made in the Riverside data between white and Mexican-American children (Table 13). These results, too, show a male advantage. The hypothesis that the magnitude of the sex difference is related to the degree of environmental deprivation of the population group under consideration should lead to the prediction that the sex difference for the Mexican-American groups should be similar to that in the black group, since both are environmentally disadvantaged as compared with the white group. Because of the considerable variability of the sex difference among the various age groups, no strong interpretation can be made of the data in Tables 12 and 13.

Peabody picture vocabulary test (PPVT). The PPVT consists of 150 sets of four pictures each. The examiner names one of the pictures and asks the testee to point to it. The sets are graded in difficulty; the more difficult items consist of pictures and words of increasing rarity. Thus, "cup" would be an easy item and "chalice" a more difficult item. The PPVT can be regarded, therefore, as more "culturally loaded" than most other tests, especially nonverbal tests such as the Matrices. The PPVT was obtained on representative samples of

[1]I am indebted to Dr. Mabel C. Purl, Director of Research and Evaluation, Riverside Unified School District, Calif., for these data.

white, black, and Mexican-American children in the public schools of River-side, California.[2] The results are shown in Tables 14 and 15.

It is surprising that this verbal test shows a sex difference in favor of males, and the difference is quite substantial (.4σ or 6 IQ points) in the white group. One wonders if the PPVT is not only "culture-loaded" but "sex-loaded" as well, in the sense that it might contain more items familiar to masculine experiences. An item analysis of the PPVT is called for to answer this question.

Listening-attention test (LAT) and memory for numbers test (MNT). The LAT is intended as a screening test for the MNT which is administered immediately after the LAT. In the LAT the child is presented with an answer sheet containing 100 pairs of digits in sets of ten. The child listens to a tape recording which speaks one digit every two seconds. The child is required to write an X over the one digit in each pair which has been heard on the tape recorder. The purpose of the Listening-Attention Test is to determine the extent to which the child is able to pay attention to numbers spoken on a tape recorder, to keep his place in the test, and to make the appropriate responses to what he hears from moment to moment. Low scores on this test (less than 90 percent correct) indicate that the subject is not yet ready to take the Memory for Numbers Test, which immediately follows it. High scores on the LAT indicate the necessary prerequisite skills for the MNT. The LAT itself makes almost no demands on the child's memory—only on his ability for listening carefully, paying attention, and responding in accord with instructions, all prerequisites for the digit memory test that follows. The results of the LAT, based on the Berkeley school population, are shown in Table 16. Contrary to what one might expect, black boys do slightly better than girls on the test. There is virtually no sex difference in the white group. The *median* score for both black and white groups from grades two through six is 100 percent, and the lower quartile is never below 98 percent in either group at any grade! This means that nearly all subjects were sufficiently motivated and attentive to comply with the requirements of the LAT. Group differences on other tests, therefore, are not easily explained in terms of motivational and attentional factors operating in the test situation.

The Memory for Numbers Test is a measure of digit span, or, more generally, short-term memory. It is made up of three parts. Each part consists of six series of digits going from four digits in a series up to nine digits in a series. The digit series are presented on a tape recording on which the digits are spoken clearly by a male voice at the rate of precisely one digit per second. The subjects write down as many digits as they can recall at the conclusion of each series,

[2]I am indebted to Dr. Mabel C. Purl, Director of Research and Evaluation, Riverside Unified School District, Calif., for these data.

Table 12. Raven's colored progressive matrices (White vs. Negro comparisons)

Age range (in years and months)	Number		Percent males		Mean W-N diff.*	W/N variance ratio	Sex (M/F) variance ratio		Sex difference† (M-F)		
	White	Negro	White	Negro			White	Negro	White	Negro/W	Negro/N
5-5- 6-6	91	64	51.6	40.6	.72	1.49	1.98	.83	.22	.14	.17
6-7- 7-6	143	76	56.6	56.6	.77	1.17	1.38	1.25	.24	-.11	-.12
7-7- 8-6	79	66	48.1	33.3	1.33	1.05	.84	1.04	.49	.22	.25
8-7- 9-6	96	42	46.9	59.5	1.35	1.27	.71	2.24	-.03	.10	.10
9-7-10-6	83	55	53.0	52.7	1.59	1.00	.72	.90	.14	-.08	-.07
10-7-11-6	71	45	54.9	51.1	1.43	.65	1.61	1.09	.03	.93	.86
11-7-12-6	69	27	47.8	48.1	.97	.96	.65	.57	.15	-.27	-.26
Unweighted mean			51.3	48.8	1.17	1.07	1.13	1.13	.18	.13	.13
Weighted mean			51.7	48.2	1.12	1.10	1.16	1.46	.18	.11	.13

*$(\bar{X}_w - \bar{X}_n)/SD_w$

†The mean difference is divided by the total white SD for Negro/W and by the total Negro SD for Negro/N.

Table 13. Raven's colored progressive matrices (White vs. Mexican-American Comparisons)

Age range (in years and months)	Number		Percent males		Mean W-M diff.	W/M variance ratio	Sex (M/F) variance ratio		Sex difference (M-F)		
	White	Mex	White	Mex			White	Mex	White	Mex/W	Mex/M
5-5– 6-6	91	110	51.6	51.8	.48	1.03	1.98	1.63	.22	.04	.04
6-7– 7-6	143	84	56.6	48.8	.87	1.23	1.38	.52	.24	−.02	−.02
7-7– 8-6	79	91	48.1	51.6	1.31	1.28	.84	.77	.49	−.21	−.23
8-7– 9-6	96	89	46.9	43.8	1.20	1.03	.71	.93	−.03	−.04	−.04
9-7–10-6	83	83	53.0	49.4	1.30	.84	.72	1.62	.14	.47	.43
10-7–11-6	71	81	54.9	59.3	1.11	.82	1.61	.74	.03	.04	.03
11-7–12-6	69	68	47.8	60.3	.87	.96	.65	.82	.15	.13	.13
Unweighted mean			51.3	52.1	1.02	1.03	1.13	1.00	.18	.06	.05
Weighted mean			51.7	51.8	1.00	1.04	1.16	1.03	.18	.05	.04

139

Table 14. Peabody picture vocabulary test (White vs. Negro comparisons)

Age range (in years and months)	Number		Percent males		Mean W-N diff.*	W/N variance ratio	Sex (M/F) variance ratio		Sex difference† (M-F)		
	White	Negro	White	Negro			White	Negro	White	Negro/W	Negro/N
5-5- 6-6	91	64	51.6	40.6	1.37	.80	1.28	1.63	.12	−.17	−.15
6-7- 7-6	142	75	56.3	56.0	.93	1.17	1.05	1.23	.45	.43	.47
7-7- 8-6	79	66	48.1	33.3	1.56	1.13	.81	1.18	.69	.56	.59
8-7- 9-6	96	42	46.9	59.6	1.10	2.57	.86	1.99	.12	.42	.68
9-7-10-6	83	55	53.0	52.7	1.25	1.67	1.11	.64	.51	−.16	−.21
10-7-11-6	71	45	54.9	51.1	1.14	1.13	1.02	3.06	.70	.80	.84
11-7-12-6	69	27	47.8	48.1	1.58	.80	.66	2.19	.49	.20	.18
Unweighted mean			51.2	48.8	1.28	1.32	.97	1.70	.44	.30	.34
Weighted mean			51.6	48.1	1.24	1.33	.99	1.58	.42	.29	.33

*$(\bar{X}_w - \bar{X}_n)/SD_w$
†The mean difference is divided by the total white SD for Negro/W and by the total Negro SD for Negro/N.

Table 15. Peabody picture vocabulary test (White vs. Mexican-American comparisons)

Age range (in years and months)	Number		Percent males		Mean W-M diff.	W/M variance ratio	Sex (M/F) variance ratio		Sex difference (M-F)		
	White	Mex	White	Mex			White	Mex	White	Mex/W	Mex/M
5-5- 6-6	91	110	51.6	51.8	1.77	.55	1.28	1.22	.12	.17	.13
6-7- 7-6	142	84	56.3	48.8	1.76	.66	1.05	.90	.45	.02	.02
7-7- 8-6	79	91	48.1	51.6	1.92	.72	.81	.91	.69	.43	.36
8-7- 9-6	96	89	46.9	43.8	1.40	1.32	.86	.94	.12	.09	.11
9-7-10-6	83	83	53.0	49.4	1.85	1.30	1.11	.80	.51	.48	.55
10-7-11-6	71	82	54.9	59.3	1.72	1.38	1.02	1.03	.70	.17	.20
11-7-12-6	69	67	47.8	61.2	1.96	1.10	.66	.71	.49	.57	.59
Unweighted mean			51.2	52.3	1.77	1.00	.97	.93	.44	.28	.28
Weighted mean			51.6	51.8	1.76	.97	.99	.95	.42	.26	.26

Table 16. Listening-attention test

Grade	Number		Percent males		Mean W-N diff.*	W/N variance ratio	Sex (M/F) variance ratio		Sex difference† (M-F)		
	White	Negro	White	Negro			White	Negro	White	Negro/W	Negro/N
2	673	497	51.4	48.5	.53	.37	1.92	.91	−.13	.13	.06
3	519	423	53.9	47.0	.66	.12	1.19	.24	.03	.54	.19
4	504	411	50.4	51.3	.08	2.45	.75	2.74	.02	−.03	−.04
5	477	416	53.0	51.4	.11	1.03	.61	.44	.00	.16	.17
6	442	387	49.3	53.2	.08	.77	.14	.11	.06	.06	.05
Unweighted mean			51.6	50.3	.29	.95	.92	.89	−.00	.17	.08
Weighted mean			57.6	50.3	.31	.92	1.01	.89	−.01	.17	.09

*$(\overline{X}_w - \overline{X}_n)/SD_w$
†The mean difference is divided by the total white SD for Negro/W and by the total Negro SD for Negro/N.

142

Table 17. Memory for numbers test
Immediate (I), repeated (R), and delayed (D)

Test	Grade	Number White	Number Negro	Percent males White	Percent males Negro	Mean W-N diff.*	W/N variance ratio	Sex (M/F) variance ratio White	Sex (M/F) variance ratio Negro	Sex difference† (M-F) White	Sex difference† (M-F) Negro/W	Sex difference† (M-F) Negro/N
Immediate	2	604	496	52.0	48.4	.64	1.29	1.11	1.17	−.17	−.07	−.08
Repeat						.44	.91	1.07	1.14	−.24	−.28	−.27
Delay						.57	2.10	1.30	1.07	−.18	−.20	−.21
Immediate	3	519	423	53.9	47.0	.52	.97	1.03	1.11	−.09	−.07	−.07
Repeat						.53	.87	.93	1.39	−.14	−.19	−.18
Delay						.72	.94	1.07	1.14	−.11	−.05	−.05
Immediate	4	504	411	50.4	51.3	.62	1.03	1.00	1.15	−.11	−.19	−.19
Repeat						.49	.94	1.09	1.03	−.22	−.29	−.28
Delay						.67	.78	1.35	1.31	−.27	−.33	−.29
Immediate	5	477	416	53.0	51.4	.73	.79	1.25	1.00	−.14	−.14	−.12
Repeat						.67	.63	1.00	1.21	−.26	−.33	−.26
Delay						.85	.53	1.08	1.51	−.19	−.42	−.31
Immediate	6	511	388	48.9	53.4	.80	.78	1.14	.86	−.10	−.22	−.19
Repeat						.63	.65	1.30	1.03	−.13	−.18	−.15
Delay						.61	.67	.90	1.13	−.09	−.11	−.09
Unweighted mean I						.66	.97	1.11	1.06	−.12	−.14	−.13
R						.55	.80	1.08	1.16	−.20	−.25	−.23
D						.68	1.00	1.15	1.23	−.17	−.22	−.19
Total				51.6	50.3	.63	.92	1.11	1.15	−.16	−.20	−.18
Weighted mean I						.66	.99	1.10	1.06	−.12	−.13	−.13
R						.55	.81	1.08	1.16	−.20	−.26	−.23
D						.68	1.05	1.15	1.23	−.17	−.22	−.19
Total				51.6	50.2	.63	.95	1.11	1.15	−.16	−.20	−.18

*$(\overline{X}_w - \overline{X}_n)/SD_w$

†The mean difference is divided by the total white SD for Negro/W and by the total Negro SD for Negro/N.

143

which is signaled by a "bong." Each part of the test is preceded by a short practice test of three digit series in order to permit the tester to determine whether the child has understood the instructions, etc. The practice test also serves to familiarize the subject with the procedure of each of the subtests. The first subtest is labeled Immediate Recall (I). Here the subject is instructed to recall the series *immediately* after the last digit has been spoken on the tape recorder. The second subtest consists of Delayed Recall (D). Here the subject is instructed not to write his response until after ten seconds have elapsed after the last digit has been spoken. The ten-second interval is marked by audible clicks of a metronome and is terminated by the sound of a bong which signals the child to write his response. The Delayed Recall condition invariably results in some retention decrement. The third subtest is the Repeated Series test (R), in which the digit series is repeated three times prior to recall; the subject then recalls the series immediately after the last digit in the series has been presented. Again, recall is signaled by a bong. Each repetition of the series is separated by a tone with a duration of one second. The repeated series almost invariably results in greater recall than the single series presentation. This test is very culture fair for children in second grade and beyond who know their numerals and are capable of listening and paying attention, as indicated by the Listening-Attention Test. There is only about one-half to one-third as much difference between black and whites on the digit memory test as on most other ability measures, such as Lorge-Thorndike, PPVT, and Matrices. Table 17 shows the sex comparisons, based on the Berkeley school population. Girls have the advantage on this test to an approximately equal extent for the white and black groups.

Summary of cognitive ability tests. The mean statistics for the tests of cognitive abilities are summarized in Table 18.

The overall weighted mean sex difference favors females and is about twice as great for blacks as for whites. These results represent a broad sampling of tests and substantial sample sizes. However, it should be recognized that the magnitude of these Sex × Race differences is partly a function of the particular tests that have entered into this composite. Even in those few tests where the sex difference is reversed (in favor of males), however, the reversal is not as extreme in the black as in the white group, with the one exception of the Wechsler Intelligence Scale for Children (Table 11, p. 135).

Motivation: Speed and persistence test

The only motivational measure on which we have Race × Sex comparisons is a test of speed and persistence in a test-taking situation; it is called the Making Xs Test. This test gives an indication of the subject's willingness to comply with instructions in a group testing situation and to mobilize effort in following those

Table 18. Summary statistics on cognitive ability tests

Table	Number White	Number Negro	Percent males White	Percent males Negro	Mean W-N diff.*	W/N variance ratio	Sex (M/F) variance ratio White	Sex (M/F) variance ratio Negro	Sex difference† (M-F) White	Sex difference† (M-F) Negro/W	Sex difference† (M-F) Negro/N
14	631	374	51.6	48.1	1.24	1.33	.99	1.58	.42	.29	.33
12	632	375	51.7	48.2	1.12	1.10	1.16	1.46	.18	.11	.13
8	901	1,184	49.1	50.0	1.07	1.12	1.17	1.07	.08	−.21	−.21
7	5,817	4,704	70.0	54.0					−.07	−.11	
11											
WISC	141	134	56.7	53.0	.77	1.51	2.68	1.01	−.07	.27	.32
Matrices	78	82	50.0	53.6	.36	1.21	1.59	1.04	.14	.08	.12
9	5,256	4,001	52.6	50.7	1.50	1.09	1.17	1.26	−.08	−.19	−.20
10	2,732	2,250	52.2	49.6	.85	1.15	.98	1.25	−.17	−.10	−.10
17	2,615	2,134	51.6	50.2	.63	.95	1.11	1.15	−.16	−.20	−.18
Weighted mean			62.9	51.3	1.10	1.09	1.13	1.23	−.07	−.13	−.09

* $(\bar{X}_w - \bar{X}_n)/SD_w$
† The mean difference is divided by the total white SD for Negro/W and by the total Negro SD for Negro/N.

instructions for a brief period of time. The test involves no intellectual component of ability, although it may involve a motor skill component, especially in younger children. Children who have already had one year of schooling and are familiar with the use of paper and pencil should perform on this test in accord with their willingness to exert effort under instructions to do so. For children without sensorimotor handicaps, the test probably measures very little in the way of skills of mental ability beyond the first-grade level. The wide range of individual differences among children from second to sixth grade, therefore, reflects motivation and test-taking attitudes in a group situation. The test also serves partly as an index of classroom morale, and it can be entered as a moderator variable into correlational analyses with other ability and achievement tests. Children who do very poorly on this test, it can be suspected, are likely not to put out their maximum effort on ability tests given in a group situation; therefore, their scores are not likely to reflect their true level of ability.

The Making Xs Test consists of two parts. On Part I the subject is asked simply to make Xs in a series of squares for a period of ninety seconds. In this part the instructions say nothing about speed. (Since there are 150 squares provided for making Xs, the maximum score is 150.) After a two-minute rest period the child turns to page 2 of the test booklet. Here he is asked to show how much better he can perform than he did on Part I. He is urged to work as rapidly as possible. Again ninety seconds are allowed for filling the boxes with Xs. The results are shown in Table 19. (Parts I and II are labeled 1st Try and 2nd Try, and the Gain Score is the difference of the 2nd try minus the 1st try.) Girls do better on this test and the Race × Sex difference is negligible. This suggests that if the test measures test-taking effort or motivation, girls' superior performance on other tests may be attributable, at least in part, to this factor. The Making Xs Test might also measure fine motor skill and reflect a sex difference in this component.

It is noteworthy that beyond first grade black children on the average perform better than white children on this test. Group differences on this test are smaller than on any other, although there is a wide range of individual differences. This suggests that test-taking attitudes and motivation are probably not lower for black than for white children.

Scholastic achievement tests

Psychometrists administered the Stanford Achievement Tests under standardized conditions to all students in the Berkeley schools in grades four, five, and six. Table 20 shows the results for the eight areas covered by the tests. The overall picture is quite similar to that of the intelligence tests. The mean race difference and the Race × Sex difference are so much like the results of the cognitive ability tests that no additional factors need be invoked in the interpretation of the achievement scores.

Table 19. Speed and persistence test (making Xs)

Test	Grade	Number White	Number Negro	Percent males White	Percent males Negro	Mean W/N diff.*	W/N variance ratio	Sex (M/F) variance ratio White	Sex (M/F) variance ratio Negro	Sex difference† (M/F) White	Sex difference† (M/F) Negro/W	Sex difference† (M/F) Negro/N
1st Try	1	642	499	50.6	51.5	−.44	2.58	.70	1.10	−.14	.15	.18
2nd Try						.40	1.23	.83	1.07	−.24	−.08	−.09
Gain						−.02	1.09	.78	1.00	−.17	−.37	−.38
1st Try	2	610	497	52.0	47.9	−.08	.80	.93	.81	−.14	−.06	−.06
2nd Try						−.06	.77	.93	.93	−.27	−.22	−.20
Gain						.22	.85	.90	.97	−.19	−.24	−.22
1st Try	3	538	412	53.7	47.1	−.20	.91	1.07	1.26	−.26	−.19	−.18
2nd Try						−.16	.95	1.06	1.35	−.34	−.19	−.18
Gain						−.09	.75	1.08	1.00	−.08	.04	.03
1st Try	4	542	432	50.6	50.7	−.37	1.01	.86	.90	−.14	−.15	−.15
2nd Try						−.44	1.23	.97	1.32	−.19	−.16	−.18
Gain						−.06	.76	.99	.87	−.06	.01	.01
1st Try	5	498	419	55.8	50.8	.00	.84	.96	1.05	−.24	−.36	−.33
2nd Try						−.11	1.14	.93	1.12	−.27	−.41	−.44
Gain						−.20	.57	1.11	1.03	−.04	−.07	−.05
1st Try	6	548	391	49.1	52.9	.07	.72	.82	1.00	−.28	−.41	−.35
2nd Try						−.06	.78	1.05	1.13	−.31	−.40	−.35
Gain						−.24	.73	1.02	1.18	−.00	.07	.06
Unweighted Means	1st			52.0	50.2	−.14	1.14	.89	1.02	−.20	−.17	−.15
	2nd					−.31	1.02	.96	1.15	−.27	−.24	−.24
	Gain					−.21	.79	.98	1.01	−.09	−.09	−.09
	Total					−.22	.98	.94	1.06	−.19	−.17	−.16
Weighted Means	1st			51.9	50.1	−.12	1.18	.88	1.02	−.20	−.15	−.13
	2nd					−.36	1.02	.96	1.14	−.27	−.24	−.23
	Gain					−.27	.96	.97	1.00	−.09	−.11	−.11
	Total					−.25	1.05	.94	1.05	−.19	−.17	−.16

*($\bar{X}_w - \bar{X}_n$) SD_w

†The mean difference is divided by the total white SD for Negro/W and by the total Negro SD for Negro/N.

Table 20. Stanford achievement test

Test	Grade	Number White	Number Negro	Percent males White	Percent males Negro	Mean W-N diff.*	W/N variance ratio	Sex (M/F) variance ratio White	Sex (M/F) variance ratio Negro	Sex difference† (M-F) White	Sex difference† (M-F) Negro/W	Sex difference† (M-F) Negro/N
Word meaning	4	533	430	50.5	50.7	1.41	1.26	1.00	1.28	.04	−.06	−.07
	5	497	435	55.1	50.3	1.60	1.66	1.25	.81	.07	−.15	−.20
	6	558	417	50.2	54.2	1.94	.84	.92	1.30	.03	−.06	−.06
Paragraph meaning	4					1.33	2.12	.84	1.14	−.06	−.05	−.07
	5					1.44	1.91	1.25	.69	−.17	−.26	−.35
	6					1.95	.95	1.60	1.15	−.15	−.04	−.03
Spelling	4					1.05	1.22	1.05	1.04	−.22	−.27	−.30
	5					1.02	1.59	1.00	.59	−.46	−.38	−.48
	6					1.22	.83	1.38	1.16	−.39	−.41	−.38
Word study skills	4					1.45	1.13	1.20	1.26	−.22	−.16	−.17
Language	4					1.34	1.21	.90	1.30	−.26	−.33	−.36
	5					1.89	.76	1.28	.61	−.40	−.37	−.32
	6					1.77	.86	1.48	1.19	−.40	−.40	−.37
Arithmetic computation	4					1.01	2.28	.95	.93	−.11	−.08	−.13
	5					.92	2.09	1.17	.61	−.08	−.20	−.29
	6					1.19	2.15	1.15	1.23	−.27	−.15	−.22
Arithmetic concepts	4					1.49	1.63	1.09	1.08	.17	.07	.09
	5					1.30	3.24	1.29	.79	.21	.00	.00
	6					1.79	1.11	1.28	1.12	.21	.02	.02
Arithmetic applications	4					1.35	2.25	1.12	1.13	.18	.00	.00
	5					1.44	2.60	1.43	.83	.18	−.06	−.10
	6					1.82	1.72	1.19	1.03	.16	.08	.10
Unweighted mean						1.45	1.61	1.18	1.00	−.10	−.15	−.17
Weighted mean				51.8	51.7	1.44	1.60	1.17	1.01	−.09	−.15	−.17

*$(\bar{X}_w - \bar{X}_n)/SD_w$

†The mean difference is divided by the total white SD for Negro/W and by the total Negro SD for Negro/N.

148

Table 21. California achievement test ($N = 300$ at each grade level) Negro sex difference [$(M-F)/SD_N$] as a function of grade level

Measure	Grade 1	2	3	4	5	6	Mean
Percent males	53.3	53.3	48.0	50.3	45.7	50.3	50.2
Reading vocabulary	.00	−.11	−.24	−.36	−.27	−.36	−.22
Reading comprehension	.02	−.19	−.38	−.39	−.34	−.41	−.28
Reading grade	.04	−.12	−.33	−.39	−.27	−.50	−.26
Arithmetic reasoning	−.13	.04	−.33	−.25	−.20	−.48	−.22
Arithmetic fundamentals	.10	.21	.08	−.18	−.13	−.44	−.06
Arithmetic grade	−.03	.13	−.12	−.22	−.15	−.49	−.15
Mechanics of English	.12	−.19	−.30	−.33	−.33	−.62	−.27
Spelling grade	−.15	−.21	−.38	−.36	−.35	−.55	−.33
Language grade	.16	−.20	−.40	−.39	−.35	−.65	−.30
Battery grade	.00	−.09	−.31	−.34	−.30	−.57	−.27
Mean	.01	−.07	−.27	−.32	−.27	−.50	

Grand mean = −.24

Source: Kennedy, Van De Riet, & White, 1963.

149

All subject areas do not show the same results. The sex difference is reversed in favor of boys for Arithmetic Concepts and Arithmetic Applications, which are the more abstract parts of the arithmetic subtest. Girls outperform boys on Arithmetic Computation. These results are completely consistent with the intrinsic sex differences studied by Broverman *et al.* (1968) reviewed earlier in the discussion.

There is virtually no sex difference among blacks on Arithmetic Concepts and Applications, although in the white group the sexes differ by about 0.2σ. All significant differences among the eight subtests favor females in the black group.

The white vs. black differences vary significantly among the subject areas. They are smallest for Spelling and Arithmetic Computation and largest for Language and Word Meaning.

There is 60 percent greater variance in scholastic achievement among white than among black pupils, and the sex (M/F) variance ratio shows 17 percent greater variance among white males than females, but virtually no overall sex difference in variance in the black group.

Grade level and achievement. The Berkeley data in Table 20 reveal little if any consistent difference in the magnitude of sex differences across grade levels from four to six. There is, however, a consistent trend from grade four to six for an increase in the white vs. black difference; it appears on every subtest. Scholastic achievement data from black pupils in five southeastern states (Table 21) show a marked increase in the sex difference at higher grade levels (Kennedy *et al.*, 1963). The sex difference in achievement in this southern black population is more than double the sex difference found in the Berkeley black population at comparable grades in school. This probably reflects more on the education provided in the southern schools than on any other single factor, in view of the fact that in the same southern sample, Kennedy *et al.* (1963) found virtually no sex difference in Stanford-Binet IQs. Why, then is there such a large sex difference in scholastic achievement? Any answers at this point are bound to be speculative.

Scholastic achievement and socioeconomic status. The Kennedy *et al.* (1963) data also permit analysis of sex difference across socioeconomic levels, as shown in Table 22. With the exception of SES level 1, which has too few cases to be reliable, there appears to be no relationship of sex difference to SES. These data, then, appear inconsistent with the environmental deprivation hypothesis to explain the sex difference.

From Table 20 we note that males show almost 20 percent greater variance in achievement than females, and females show a higher mean level of achievement. This suggests the hypothesis that male achievement is a result of more

Table 22. California achievement test. Negro sex difference $[(M—F)/SD_N]$ as a function of socioeconomic level

| Measure | Socioeconomic level | | | | | | Unweighted mean Weighted mean |
	High 1	2	3	4	Low 5	Unknown	
Number	6	28	112	304	918	432	
Percent males	83.3	42.8	44.6	54.6	49.4	50.0	
Reading vocabulary	—.07	—.35	.00	—.33	—.31	—.20	—.21 / —.27
Reading comprehension	—.11	—.50	.10	—.33	—.28	—.19	—.22 / —.25
Reading grade	—.07	—.50	.05	—.39	—.29	—.19	—.23 / —.26
Arithmetic reasoning	.14	—.21	.14	—.25	—.28	—.19	—.11 / —.22
Arithmetic fundamentals	—.19	—.09	.10	—.13	—.15	.00	—.08 / —.09
Arithmetic grade	.00	—.14	.10	—.24	—.20	—.06	—.09 / —.15
Mechanics of English	—.13	—.47	—.15	—.35	—.22	—.25	—.26 / —.25
Spelling grade	.37	—.17	.13	—.39	—.27	—.32	—.11 / —.27
Language grade	.16	—.33	—.05	—.33	—.28	—.31	—.19 / —.28
Battery grade	.00	—.24	.00	—.33	—.22	—.20	—.16 / —.22
Mean	.01	—.30	—.33	—.31	—.25	—.19	

Unweighted Grand Mean = —.16   Weighted = —.25

Source: Kennedy, Van De Riet, & White, 1966.

factors in addition to intelligence than is female achievement, and these non-intellectual factors are positively correlated with ability, thereby creating greater variance in scholastic performance. Also, it suggests that overall more of these factors act in an unfavorable than in a favorable direction for males, resulting in lower mean achievement for boys than for girls, at least at the elementary school level. (Older age groups are practically impossible to assess in this respect due to differential dropout rates for the sexes in secondary school.) There are three lines of evidence relevant to this hypothesis. Stanley and Porter (1967) have shown higher predictive validities (for college grades) of scholastic aptitude tests for women than for men, a difference between approximately .70 for women vs. .60 for men. (This was found to be true for white women; black women did not differ significantly from black or white men in the predictive validity of their scholastic aptitude scores.) It appears to be a general finding (Seashore, 1962). It could be explained if nonintellectual personality factors were less correlated with aptitude test performance for females than for males. If personality factors have a low correlation with academic aspirations and performance, as well as with ability factors, they will not much affect the correlation between aptitude and achievement. If, on the other hand, person-ality is substantially correlated with both achievement and aptitude, the predictive power of the aptitude test alone will be attenuated, especially if the personality factors are more involved in academic performance than in test measures of ability.

There is good evidence that personality traits are involved in academic aspirations and performance (Gough, 1968). If there are higher intercorrelations between ability, personality, and achievement for males, we should expect an ability test to predict achievement better for females, although we might expect a multiple correlation based on ability *and* personality to yield a better pre-diction of achievement in males. According to this hypothesis, prediction of academic performance from aptitude scores alone is higher in females because personality factors do not override the ability factors to as great an extent as in males. There is some evidence for a higher correlation between IQ and per-sonality for boys than for girls, at least in childhood. Bayley (1968) states, "A study of the personality correlates of these intelligence scores repeatedly reveals considerable independence of the girls' intelligence from their personality variables [p. 15]." No good evidence, however, is available for sex differences in the correlations between personality factors and scholastic achievement, and the explanation of sex differences in level of achievement in terms of personality and motivational variables is almost entirely speculative. Probably because the sex differences are small and of not much practical significance, investigators have not been stimulated to investigate these complexly determined phenomena. Such subjects do not yield readily to neat scientific formulations, and when the differences are of no real consequence to anyone, the investigation and explanation of them are hardly worth the effort.

Mental retardation

One prominent social-psychological theory of the Race × Sex × Ability inter-action invokes the concept of the matriarchal structure of the black family, by which males are said to be hindered in intellectual development and scholastic motivation and achievement. This theory is emphasized in the Moynihan Report (Rainwater & Yancey, 1967, pp. 76–86). It is used to help account for the greater proportion of black women, relative to whites, at higher levels of educational and occupational selection.

But let us look at the lower end of the ability spectrum to see if the ratio of males/females in the incidence of mental retardation, defined as IQs below 70, is greater for blacks than for whites. For this examination we turn to the largest and most thorough epidemiological survey of mental retardation ever made of an American community, by Lemkau and Imre (1966). The entire adult population ($N = 7,475$) of a county in Maryland was examined; 56 percent of the population were white. Table 23 shows the percentage of black males and females with IQs below 70. The table reveals that the difference in percentages between the sexes is larger for blacks than for whites. But this is an invalid method of comparison, since the total percentage of IQs below 70 is so much larger for blacks than for whites. A ratio comparison makes more sense. The table then reveals that the overall male/female ratio is 1.68 for whites and 1.31 for Negroes. In other words, the *relative* sex difference in the incidence of retardation is less for blacks than for whites. The best way of looking at this is to convert the percentages to their corresponding z scores. Then we find a *sex* difference of $.20\sigma$ for whites and $.18\sigma$ for blacks, in favor of females for both groups. The *race* difference in z score terms is 1.33σ for males and 1.25σ for females. What all this means is that the relative difference in incidence of mental retardation, as defined by IQ below 70, is consistent with a mean sex difference in both racial groups of about $.20\sigma$ and a mean difference between the racial groups of about 1.3σ. The same facts (i.e., $.20\sigma$ for sex and 1.3σ for race) are consistent with a smaller sex ratio (M/F) for blacks, as compared with whites, at the upper end of the ability spectrum.

Statistical interpretation

The picture that emerges from all the foregoing analyses is of an overall sex difference in favor of females for both white and black groups. The sex difference for ability and achievement measures among blacks is about double that among whites. In both groups, however, the sex difference is small, amounting approximately to something between $.10\sigma$ to $.20\sigma$, which on an IQ scale (with $\sigma = 15$) is about 1 to 3 IQ points. Note, however, that when sex differences for other variables in the black group were put on a z scale, as described previously, the difference generally falls in the range from $.10\sigma$ to $.30\sigma$. This was true for the employment and income figures, for mortality

Table 23. WAIS verbal IQ. Percentages below IQ 70 by race, sex, and age

| | Age group (years) | | | | | | | | |
	20–24	25–25	30–34	35–39	40–44	45–49	50–54	56–59	Mean
White males	.75	.73	1.84	2.45	2.12	1.67	1.65	2.31	1.69
White females	.74	.84	.82	1.07	.99	.78	1.13	1.75	1.02
Negro males	8.67	14.73	27.72	18.06	30.78	23.39	20.30	29.36	21.57
Negro females	12.26	12.91	19.87	12.68	18.55	22.11	19.63	13.92	16.49
Ratio (M/F), White	1.01	.87	2.24	2.29	2.14	2.14	1.46	1.32	1.68
Negro	.71	1.14	1.40	1.42	1.66	1.06	1.03	2.11	1.31
Diff. (M-F), White	.01	−.11	1.02	1.38	1.13	.89	.52	.56	.68
Negro	−3.59	1.82	7.85	5.38	12.23	1.28	.67	5.44	3.88

Source: Lemkau & Imre, 1966.

154

rates, for the incidence of mental retardation, and for college scholarship selection. These σ differences between males and females are all in the same range as the sex differences on mental abilities and scholastic achievement. This raises the question whether the sex differences in all these spheres are simply various manifestations of the same basic phenomenon. The present data unfortunately cannot answer this question. They merely point to the fact that the socially observed sex difference among blacks in areas in which mental ability and education are assumed to play an important role are quite in line with the sex differences measured by standard tests of mental ability and scholastic achievement. The actual mean difference between the sexes is so small as hardly to be in need of elaborate sociological or psychological theories for explanation. Environmental disadvantage, prenatally and postnatally, in the black population and the male's greater vulnerability to environmental stress would seem adequate to account for the small difference. Although it cannot be ruled out by the present data, the hypothesis of a genetic race difference would seem to be an implausible and nonparsimonious explanation of the slightly greater sex difference among blacks than among whites in intellectual performance and academic achievements.

But if the sex difference is as small as, say 0.2σ in the black group, as compared with, say, 0.1σ in the white group, why should it seem so conspicuous in some situations, such as in the much larger percentage of females passing examinations leading to college scholarships, the much greater percentage of black females in classes for the gifted, in skilled occupations, and the like?

The answer seems to lie in the statistical properties of the normal curve. If the means of the ability distributions for males and females differ and the distributions are approximately normal, the greater will be the sex difference when viewed as a ratio of *number of females/number of males*, the higher we place the selection criterion on the ability scale. Because of the normal curve, higher selection cutoffs have a "magnifying" effect on the female/male ratio above the cutoff point. In most selection situations this sex ratio is "magnified" more for blacks than for whites because any given selection cutoff is further above the black general mean than above the white mean. Thus, even if the mean sex difference were the same among blacks and whites, the sex ratio above a given cutoff would be more extreme for blacks than for whites. This statistical effect is illustrated in Figure 1. It can be seen that the small male-female mean difference for blacks results in quite large differences in the proportions under the curves beyond any selection cutoff that lies above the white general mean, which for intelligence measures is at least one σ above the black general mean (Dreger & Miller, 1968; Shuey, 1966). The sex ratios for the two racial groups should be just the opposite at the lower end of the ability scale, and this is exactly what was found in comparing the groups for the incidence of mental retardation, in which the male/female ratio is 1.68

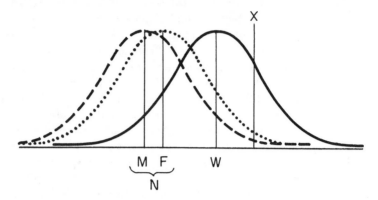

Figure 1. Normal curves for male (M) and female (F) Negroes (N) and for whites (W) (both sexes combined) to illustrate how a relatively small average sex difference can result in markedly different proportions of males and females that fall above any given selection cutoff (X).

for whites and 1.31 for blacks. Thus, seemingly opposite effects at the low and high parts of the ability spectrum are seen to be just different facets of the same basic phenomenon, which consists of a difference of about 1σ between the general racial means and a difference of about 0.1σ to 0.2σ between the sexes.

At very extreme selection cutoffs we might expect a reversal of the sex ratio, despite a mean difference in favor of females, due to the greater variance of the male population. There should be relatively more males in the extreme lower and upper tails of the distribution. The sex variance ratio (M/F) is greater for blacks on the general ability tests and greater for whites on the scholastic achievement tests. This would imply that at higher levels of academic achievement the sex ratio should increasingly favor males in the white group (because of their greater variance) but not in the black group, where females would still be increasingly favored (because of their higher mean).

Intercorrelations of statistical indexes

Intercorrelations were obtained among the following indices from Tables 8 through 23:

Race Difference	$\overline{W}\text{-}\overline{N}/SD_W$
Race Variance Ratio	$SD_W{}^2/SD_N{}^2$
White Sex Variance Ratio	$SD_M{}^2/SD_F{}^2$

Black Sex Variance Ratio	SD_M^2/SD_F^2
White Sex Difference	$\overline{M}\text{-}\overline{F}/SD_W$
Black Sex Difference	$\overline{M}\text{-}\overline{F}/SD_N$

Correlations based on eighty-one determinations of each of the above indices for different tests and samples were computed for the following pairs of variables:

$$r_{AB} = .04$$

$$r_{BD} = .09$$

$$r_{CD} = .17$$

$$r_{AF} = -.13$$

$$r_{EF} = .54, p < .01$$

$$r_{CF} = .32, p < .01$$

$$r_{DF} = .32, p < .01$$

What these correlations mean for these data is:

1. The mean race difference is unrelated to the race difference in variances ($r_{AB} = .04$, n.s.).

2. Racial differences in variance are unrelated to the sex differences in variance among blacks ($r_{BD} = .09$, n.s.).

3. The white and black sex differences in variance are not significantly correlated ($r_{CD} = .17$).

4. One of the most interesting correlations is $r_{AF} = -.13$, n.s. This means that the magnitude of the mean race difference between blacks and whites is not significantly related to the magnitude of the sex difference among blacks. If we hypothesize that the sex difference is due to greater male vulnerability to environmental stress, and that environmental disadvantages contribute to the racial difference, we should expect a correlation between black sex difference and the black-white race difference. But this is not borne out significantly by these data.

5. The sex difference in whites and blacks is significantly correlated ($r_{EF} = .54$). Those tests showing the largest sex difference among whites also show the largest sex differences among blacks.

6. The sex difference among blacks is positively correlated with greater

male/female variance ratio in whites ($r_{CF} = .32$, $p < .01$) and in blacks ($r_{DF} = .32$, $p < .01$). In other words, tests showing the greatest male variability (in whites or blacks) also show the largest sex difference in blacks.

Summary

It has been frequently noted that among blacks a greater percentage of females than males excel in school, graduate from high school, enter and succeed in college, pass high-level civil service examinations and other selection criteria, and hold their own, as compared with whites, in skilled and professional occupations. This discussion has attempted to determine on the basis of the existing evidence whether there is a larger sex difference in mental abilities and scholastic achievement in the black than in the white school-age population.

Fifteen different tests of mental ability and scholastic achievement, administered to samples totaling more than 20,000 children, were analyzed. It was found that almost all of the large female/male selection ratios for high-level scholastic achievement and occupational performance reported in the literature are consistent with a highly significant but small (about 0.2σ) average sex difference in ability and achievement. The sex difference for blacks is approximately double that for whites. But the difference shows up much more markedly for blacks, since selection cutoff criteria (for college, scholarships, civil service jobs, etc.) are further above the general mean for blacks than for whites. This results in a much higher female/male ratio in the upper tail of the distribution for blacks than in the distribution for whites. At the lower end of the ability distribution, on the other hand, whites show a higher male/female ratio among the mentally retarded (IQs under 70) than is the case in the black population.

The cause of the sex difference in abilities is not definitely known. We do know that males have a higher rate of infant mortality, are much more susceptible to contracting all communicable diseases, and are psychologically less well buffered against environmental influences, both good and bad, than are females. Boys' IQs show higher correlations with environmental factors. Since a disproportionate number of blacks as compared with whites grow up under poor conditions and are, therefore, subjected to more physical and psychological stress in the course of their early development, this could account for the slightly greater sex difference among blacks than among whites. There seems to be no need to postulate particular psychological or sociological conditions peculiar to black culture, such as the so-called matriarchal family pattern, to account for the black sex difference in IQ and scholastic achievement, which, in terms of mean difference (rather than sex ratios above a high selection cutoff), is quite small (0.1σ to 0.2σ) and at most only about 0.1σ larger than the sex difference among whites.

It is suggested that the generally lower viability of the male may be due to the fact that he has only one X chromosome, while the female has two. If recessive alleles of lower viability are carried on one X chromosome, their effects are usually overridden by dominant alleles at the same loci on the other X chromosome. But the male inherits XY instead of XX, and the Y chromosome has very few gene loci and therefore cannot counteract the undesirable recessive alleles on the X chromosome. It is probably for this reason that the incidence of various birth defects is so much greater in boys than in girls, and it definitely explains the greater incidence in males of so-called sex-linked genetic defects such as hemophilia and color blindness. Because sex differences in socioeconomically and educationally significant criteria are undoubtedly complexly determined, the present hypothesis should be considered to account for only a part of the total causation of sex differences and of the Race × Sex interaction in these realms.

References

Baugham, E. E., & Dahlstrom, W. G. *Negro and white children: A psychological study in the rural South.* New York: Academic Press, 1968.

Bayley, N. Comparisons of mental and motor test scores for ages 1–15 months by sex, birth order, race, geographical locations, and education of parents. *Child Development,* 1965, *36,* 379–411.

———. Learning in adulthood: The role of intelligence. In H. J. Klausmeier & C. W. Harris (Eds.), *Analyses of concept learning.* New York: Academic Press, 1966. (a)

———. Developmental problems of the mentally retarded child. In I. Philips (Ed.), *Prevention and treatment of mental retardation.* New York: Basic Books, 1966. (b)

———. Behavioral correlates of mental growth: Birth to thirty-six years. *American Psychologist,* 1968, *23,* 1–17.

Bentzen, F. Sex ratios in learning and behavior disorders. *American Journal of Orthopsychiatry,* 1963, *33,* 92–98.

Brazelton, T. B., Robey, J. S., & Collier, G. A. Infant development in the Zinacanteco Indians of Southern Mexico. Mimeographed paper, 1969.

Brazziel, W. F. A letter from the South. *Harvard Educational Review,* 1969, *39,* 348–356.

Broverman, D. M., Klaiber, E. L., Kobayashi, Y., & Vogel, W. Roles of activation and inhibition in sex differences in cognitive abilities. *Psychological Review,* 1968, *75,* 23–50.

Carter, C. O. *Human heredity.* Baltimore: Penguin, 1962.

Caudil, W., & Weinstein, H. Maternal care and infant behavior in Japan and America. *Psychiatry,* 1969, *32,* 12–43.

Davis, J. P. (Ed.) *The American Negro reference book.* Englewood Cliffs, N. J.: Prentice-Hall, 1966.

Dreger, R. M., & Miller, K. S. Comparative psychological studies of Negroes and whites in the United States: 1959–1965. *Psychological Bulletin Monograph Supplement,* 1968, *70,* No. 3, Part 2.

Flanagan, J. C., & Cooley, W. W. Project TALENT one-year follow-up studies. Cooperative Research Project Number 2333. School of Education, University of Pittsburgh, 1966.

Freedman, D. G., & Freedman, N. C. Behavioral differences between Chinese-American and European-American newborns. Mimeographed paper, Committee on Human Development, University of Chicago, 1969.

Gottesman, I. I. Biogenetics of race and class. In M. Deutsch, I. Katz, & A. R. Jensen (Eds.), *Social class, race, and psychological development.* New York: Holt, Rinehart & Winston, 1968.

Gough, H. G. College attendance among high-aptitude students as predicted from the California Psychological Inventory. *Journal of Counseling Psychology,* 1968, *15,* 269–278.

Graves, W. L., Freeman, M. G., & Thompson, J. D. Culturally related reproductive factors in mental retardation. Paper read at Conference on Sociocultural Aspects of Mental Retardation, Peabody College, Nashville, Tenn., June 1968.

Harrison, G. A., Owen, J. J. T., Da Rocha, F. J., & Salzano, F. M. Skin colour in Southern Brazilian populations. *Human Biology,* 1967, *39,* 21–31.

Ilg, F. L., & Ames, L. B. *School readiness: Behavior tests used at the Gesell Institute.* New York: Harper & Row, 1964.

Kennedy, W. A., Van De Riet, V., & White, J. C., Jr. A normative sample of intelligence and achievement of Negro elementary school children in the Southeastern United States. *Monographs of the Society for Research on Child Development,* 1963, *28,* No. 6.

Kuznets, G. M., & McNemar, O. Sex differences in intelligence-test scores. In G. M. Whipple (Ed.), *Intelligence: Its nature and nurture,* Part I. The 39th Yearbook of the National Society for the Study of Education, Bloomington, Ill., 1940.

Lemkau, P. V., & Imre, P. D. Epidemiology of mental retardation in a rural county: The Rose County study. Program Report, the Johns Hopkins University, Department of Mental Hygiene, July 18, 1966.

Mazess, R. B. Skin color in Bahamian Negroes. *Human Biology,* 1967, *39,* 145–154.

Miner, J. B. *Intelligence in the United States.* New York: Springer, 1957.

Naylor, A. F., & Myrianthopoulos, N. C. The relation of ethnic and selected socioeconomic factors to human birth-weight. *Annals of Human Genetics,* 1967, *31,* 71–83.

Phillips, B. A. The Binet tests applied to colored children. *Psychological Clinic,* 1914, *8,* 190–196.

Rainwater, L., & Yancey, W. L. (Eds.) *The Moynihan Report and the politics of controversy.* Cambridge: M.I.T. Press, 1967.

Reed, T. E. Caucasian genes in American Negroes. *Science,* 1969, *165,* 762–768.

Roberts, R. J., & Nichols, R. C. Participants in the National Achievement Scholarship Program for Negroes. *National Merit Scholarship Research Reports,* 1966, *2,* No. 2.

Scarr, S. Effects of birth weight on later intelligence. *Social Biology,* 1969, *16,* 249–256.

Schull, W. J., & Neel, J. V. *The effects of inbreeding on Japanese children.* New York: Harper & Row, 1965.

Seashore, H. G. Women are more predictable than men. *Journal of Counseling Psychology,* 1962, *9,* 261–270.

Semler, I. J., & Iscoe, I. Structure of intelligence in Negro and white children. *Journal of Educational Psychology,* 1966, *57,* 326–336.

Shuey, A. M. *The testing of Negro intelligence.* (2nd ed.) New York: Social Science Press, 1966.

Skodak, M., & Skeels, H. M. A final follow-up study of one hundred adopted children. *Journal of Genetic Psychology, Child Behavior, Animal Behavior, and Comparative Psychology,* 1949, *75,* 85–125.

Stanley, J. C., & Porter, A. C. Correlation of scholastic aptitude test score with college grades for Negroes versus whites. *Journal of Educational Measurement,* 1967, *4,* 199–218.

Stern, C. *Principles of human genetics.* San Francisco: Freeman, 1949.

Stott, D. H. Studies of troublesome children. London: Tavistock Publications, 1966.

Terman, L. *Genetic studies of genius.* Vol. I. *Mental and physical traits of a thousand gifted children.* Stanford, Calif.: Stanford University Press, 1926.

Tyler, F. T. Individual and sex differences. In C. W. Harris (Ed.), *Encyclopedia of educational research.* (3rd ed.) New York: Macmillan, 1960.

Tyler, L. E. *The psychology of human differences.* (3rd ed.) New York: Appleton-Century-Crofts, 1965.

U.S. Department of Commerce. Trends in social and economic conditions in metropolitan areas. *Special Studies,* Series P-23, No. 27, February 7, 1969.

U.S. Department of Health, Education, and Welfare. *Vital statistics of the United States, 1965.* Vol. II, *Mortality,* Part A. Washington, D.C.: U.S. Government Printing Office, 1967.

————. *Vital Statistics of the United States, 1967.* Vol. I, *Natality.* Washington, D.C.: U.S. Government Printing Office, 1969.

Visaria, P. M. Sex ratio at birth in territories with a relatively complete registration. *Eugenics Quarterly,* 1967, *14,* 132–142.

Wilson, A. B. Educational consequences of segregation in a California community. In *Racial isolation in the public schools,* Appendices, Vol. 2 of a report by the U.S. Commission on Civil Rights. Washington, D.C.: U.S. Government Printing Office, 1967.

a tale of two thermos bottles:
properties of a genetic model
for human intelligence

C. C. Li

Mr. Smith, a native-born American in Florida, has a thermos bottle and uses it exclusively for keeping cold drinks cold. Mr. Li, a Chinese residing in Peking, also has a thermos bottle but uses it exclusively for keeping hot water hot. In fact, the thermos bottle is known by the name "hot water bottle" in China and it has never occurred to the Chinese that it also can keep cold things cold, as he never has an occasion to use it that way.

If we have no knowledge about the transfer of heat and the principle of insulation by vacuum, it would look as if there are two different kinds of bottles with two opposite functions; hence, it requires two sets of reasons to explain the two observed phenomena. To be sure, it is not difficult at all to point out the many differences between the two bottles. We may note that they are different from the very beginning; one is made in New Jersey and one in Tientsin. Maybe the two manufacturing processes are different. Certainly the outside designs are strikingly different. I do not propose to belabor this point unduly. Suffice it to say that these differences exist and are real, but they are not the reasons why one bottle keeps cold things cold and one keeps hot things hot. It is only through physical studies that we recognize that these are not two opposite phenomena but one and the same phenomenon, to be explained by one reason, not by many different reasons. This is the nature of a scientific explanation. One basic principle explains various and sometimes apparently contradictory phenomena, thus unifying our knowledge in an orderly manner.

Early environmental influences

As to the differences among individuals and among racial groups, many authors tend to attribute them to early environmental differences for such individuals or groups. This is undoubtedly true for certain traits—but certainly not for all traits. As an example, let us consider the red-green color blindness among females and males. It has been known for many decades that there are more color-blind boys than girls. If we disregard for the moment the modern explanation for the sexual difference in color blindness, how did the "scientists" before, say, 1900 explain the phenomenon?

They did have explanations, very good ones too. Males and females have different attitudes toward color in general. When buying a new car, a young man would ask about the things under the hood; a young woman would ask, "What color is it?" In the old days (not too long ago actually) girls used to sew and embroider with colorful threads. They have early contacts with color, upon which their beauty depends so much. The boys used to ride on horses, play ball, practice fencing, or engage in some other physical activities, none of which is related to color. The difference between boys and girls in their early contacts with color and the difference in value they attach to color exists and is real. Hence, there are more boys than girls who never learned to distinguish certain colors. This explanation, based on early environmental conditions, sounds perfectly reasonable and is even appealing in many respects except one—it is untrue.

The case of color blindness brings out an extremely important general principle in scientific research; viz., the demonstration of the existence of an environmental difference does not automatically mean that it is the cause for the difference in the characteristics under study. To demonstrate that a certain factor is the cause for certain characteristics requires an independent and much more laborious research. The modern explanation for color blindness is based on a large number of detailed family pedigrees, and its predictive accuracy has been confirmed by all known families.

Two opposite phenomena

A topic that frequently arises in evening conversations among my Chinese friends is why the offspring generation of these academic Chinese (from China) are not doing as well as their fathers, or at least, do not seem to be doing as well. The performance of the offspring generation causes real anxiety for the fathers, as judged from the seriousness with which they discuss the problem. Are the

Chinese deteriorating? If so, why? Most of these Chinese are natural scientists and engineers and have considerable accomplishments in their own fields. They figured (originally) that their sons would be able to do better than themselves because of the more favorable educational and social factors for the young generation. The young do not have language difficulties and no accent, while almost all of the fathers speak English with an accent. (A few of them are hardly understandable.) Moreover, the young have better nutrition and better schooling in this country and seem to be in good health. Their fathers' early environment in China, by our present standard, would be described as nothing less than deprivation. If the young Chinese generation were doing better than their fathers, then the influence of these social factors would be accepted as reasonable explanations. But, actually, they do not seem to be doing as well. How do we account for it?

Fortunately, we shall never run out of social and environmental factors that may be invoked to explain any phenomenon. In this particular case there are presumably social factors working against the younger Chinese generation. The many reasons offered to me vary from one level to another. On the national level, one may point to the softer life in the United States. Their fathers had to struggle to survive; they had no doubt in their minds that if they did not study hard there would be absolutely no future for them. The younger generation, born and raised in this country, have taken life for granted and do not share that sense of urgency. On the individual level, one says that the fathers work too hard and do not play enough with their children, who thus do not develop well; everything about the child has been determined in the first four years of his life. Or, one may say that the fathers are so brilliant that they have completely overshadowed their children, who are thus suffering from a severe psychological handicap. And many other faults on the part of the parents, especially the father, are offered.

However, in order to show that these unfavorable factors are responsible for the comparatively inferior performance of the offspring generation, we need to show that they are stronger than the favorable factors existing at the same time. How are we to weigh them, even relatively? What complicates the matter further is that there is a group of Chinese whose offspring are doing better, much better, than their fathers. This is the group of Chinese laborers (e.g., laundry men). Many of their children are now professionals and are no longer part of Chinatown. To explain this phenomenon, one may cite again the favorable factors (English, school, health, etc.) mentioned previously and conveniently forget the unfavorable factors (soft life, etc.), apparently assuming that the laundry-men fathers play a great deal with their children. Another pseudoscientific argument is: Where can they go but up? Well, they can be unemployed and go on charity; they do not have to go up at all.

We have observed two directly opposite phenomena: (1) the children of the group of Chinese of high achievements tend to have lower achievements

than their fathers, and (2) the children of the group of Chinese of low achievements tend to have higher achievements than their fathers. To explain the two
opposing trends in terms of social factors alone, we are forced to keep in storage
a large number of social factors, including favorable and unfavorable ones of
various degrees, and pull out the right one to fit the right occasion. Then, the
explanation is necessarily a posteriori ("Monday morning quarterback"),
deficient in analytical foundation, lacking in predictive value, and not applicable
to other cases.

Need for a unified explanation

What we need is a unified explanation for the two apparently opposing trends
described in the previous section. As in the case of the two thermosbottles,
the ability to keep cold things cold and the ability to keep hot things hot are
not to be considered as two opposing abilities but one and the same phenomanon
to be explained by only one reason (insulation in this case) rather then by
various incidental reasons. Hence, we shall seek a mechanism which, if it
explains why the children of Chinese with high academic accomplishment
tend to do worse than their fathers, would also explain why the children of
Chinese with low academic accomplishment tend to do better than their fathers.
With such a mechanism these two trends will be considered as one and the
same phenomenon, to be explained by only one reason and not by many different
incidental reasons.

The usual statistical term describing the phenomena is regression. The
statistician says that the average value of a quantitative trait of the offspring
of parents of either very high or very low value tends to "regress" toward the
average value of the population as a whole. But this is merely a paraphrase
of what we have been saying all along. Regression describes the fact quantitatively
but does not explain why. Descriptive statistics seldom reveals the underlying
mechanism for a phenomenon. Even as a descriptive tool, the phrase "regression
toward the mean" is not the whole story and may easily mislead one to think
that there will be more and more individuals in the middle range and fewer
and fewer individuals in the extreme categories in subsequent generations—
which is, of course, not the case. For most quantitative traits the distribution
(its form, if not its position) is quite stable and remains very nearly the same from
generation to generation. Unless measured in an evolutionary time scale, the
difference among a few successive generations is not detectable by our usual
sample studies. For all practical purposes we may assume that the population
is in a stationary state. At this point, it should surprise nobody that the writer,
a geneticist, shall propose a genetical model to explain the two opposing trends.

Atypical pedigrees

Before outlining my population genetical model, I shall first clear up a possible misunderstanding of hereditary phenomena for which the overenthusiastic human geneticists themselves are partially responsible. The extraordinary pedigree involving Francis Galton and Charles Darwin, who were first cousins, is often cited to illustrate the heredity of mental ability in man. However, not every member of this prominent pedigree exhibits the same kind of mental ability. Moreover, the pedigree taken as a whole can also be explained by common favorable environments and chance appearance. This type of pedigree is of more historical interest than of scientific significance. To prove that a certain type of mental ability has a hereditary component involves more than producing a very rare pedigree that represents an exception rather than a rule. If the mental ability is hereditary, what should we expect to see from all pedigrees? This is a more appropriate question.

Historically, another and even more extreme pedigree is often cited to demonstrate the heredity of mental ability; it is the pedigree of the celebrated family of mathematicians—the Bernoullis. Since the idea of the heredity of

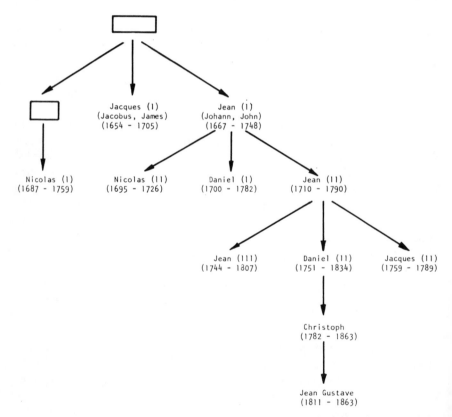

Figure 1. Simplified pedigree of the Bernoulli family. Only mathematicians are shown in the diagram.

mathematical ability, like that of musical ability, is more tolerable to the social scientists, I shall use the Bernoulli family (Figure 1) to illustrate why I object to using rare pedigrees as a proof of heredity.

The fame of the mathematical family began with Jacques Bernoulli, usually designated as Jacques (I) by historians to distinguish him from another Jacques Bernoulli (II) two generations later. We cannot mention here his many mathematical contributions, which are truly great. He was the fifth child of the family. His younger brother, Jean (I), was the tenth child of the family and thirteen years his junior; but Jean turned out to be even more prolific than Jacques. Nicolas (I), a nephew of Jacques and Jean, was also a prominent mathematician. Three of Jean's sons achieved fame in mathematics, especially Daniel. Jean (II), the youngest son of Jean (I), again had accomplished mathematician offspring. The later Bernoullis (Daniel II, Jacques II, Christoph, etc.) were also professional mathematicians but did not achieve first-class fame in history. Christoph's son, Jean Gustave, was also a mathematician.

If the pedigree of the four or five generations of mathematicians is impressive from the hereditary point of view, their family attitude is even more interesting from the environmental point of view. One would think that at least part of the mathematical tradition is due to familial environment such as the early influence of the fathers. This was not the case in the Bernoulli family. The father of the original Jacques and Jean was emphatically opposed to their study of mathematics, placing all possible obstacles in their way. After his failure to make Jacques a theologian, the father determined to make Jean a merchant and failed again. One may argue that the father, not being a mathematician, may not have influenced his sons, but his sons, being mathematicians, must have influenced the later generations. This does not seem to be true either. Jean (I), the most prolific mathematician of the Bernoulli family, had the same attitude toward mathematics as his own father, and he tried to force his own son, Daniel (I), to become a businessman. Daniel disappointed him as he had his father!

If we use the unbroken array of mathematicians over four generations in a family as a proof of heredity of mathematical ability, then what can we say about the families in which there is no such array of mathematicians? Cannot one argue that if such an array is absent, then the mathematical ability has no hereditary component? Since the great majority of families do not have such an array of mathematicians, the social scientists are perfectly entitled to be skeptical of the theory of heredity of mathematical ability. The main source of confusion is that the extraordinary pedigree outlined in Figure 1 represents a misleading rare event rather than the usual pattern that we expect of a hereditary quantitative trait. Heredity does not mean "like begets like." The relationship between parents and offspring as depicted in Figure 2 are very wrong for a human population. As will be illustrated in the next section, even if a trait is entirely determined by a few genetic factors, the variation in the

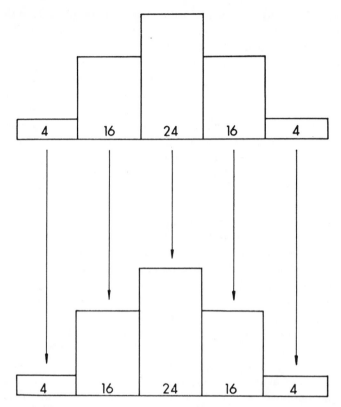

Figure 2. Wrong conception of heredity in a human population. Only very rigid social forces can make "like beget like."

offspring of any family will still be quite wide. Hence, a proper presentation of the hereditary pattern can only be achieved by the appropriate methods of population genetics.

Genetic model for quantitative traits

By way of illustration I shall outline the simplest genetic model for quantitative traits, ignoring the environmental effects for the time being. Suppose that a certain type of mental ability (e.g., intelligence, mathematics, music, etc.) is determined by two pairs of genes, (A, a) and (B, b). Although this is too simple to be realistic, it will show the general pattern of the hereditary phenomenon clearly. To further simplify our calculation, let us assume that the effects of these two pairs of genes are of the same magnitude, which we may take as unity. That is, we shall assign a value of 1 to each of the capital letters and 0 to each of the lower-case letters of each genotype. We also assume that the effects of the two pairs of genes are additive; i.e., the effect of one gene pair is to be added to that of the other. With this simple model the values of the quantitative trait for the nine genotypes are as follows:

Genotypes	aabb	Aabb aaBb	AAbb aaBB AaBb	AABb AaBB	AABB
Value	0	1	2	3	4

The point 0 in the scale above is an arbitrary origin. To reduce the arithmetic labor to almost nothing, we assume that the gene frequencies are all equal to one-half; i.e., $\text{freq}(A) = \text{freq}(a) = \frac{1}{2}$ and $\text{freq}(B) = \text{freq}(b) = \frac{1}{2}$. Then in a random-mating stationary population, such as ours, the distribution of the values of the quantitative trait is as follows:

Value	0	1	2	3	4	Total
Frequency	1	4	6	4	1	16
or	4	16	24	16	4	64

We shall use the numbers 4, 16, 24, and so on for convenience, remembering that their common denominator is 64. If this is the parental generation, what would be the offspring generation? What are the relationships between the various classes of parents and those of their offspring? It should be reiterated that the relationships between parents and offspring in a random-mating population are not like those shown in Figure 2. The correct pattern of parent-offspring relationships is shown in Figure 3.

Before we consider Figure 3 in detail, a few words about the method of constructing the diagram might be helpful. Consider the parent genotype Aabb (value 1) which produces $\frac{1}{2}$ (Ab) and $\frac{1}{2}$ (ab) gametes. In a random-mating population these gametes will unite with gametes (AB), (Ab), (aB), (ab) each with frequency $\frac{1}{4}$. Hence, the offspring of the Aabb parent will be of the following genotypes (the number below the genotype is the value of the quantitative trait of that genotype):

	(AB)	(Ab)	(aB)	(ab)
(Ab)	AABb 3	AAbb 2	AaBb 2	Aabb 1
(ab)	AaBb 2	Aabb 1	aaBb 1	aabb 0

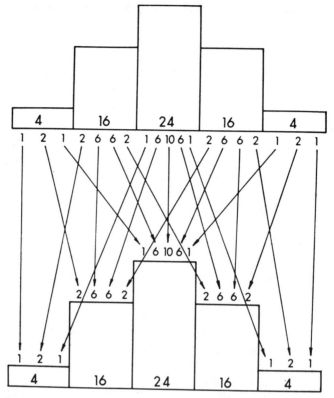

Figure 3. The connections between two random-mating generations.

Collecting the genotypes according to their quantitative values, we have the following distribution:

Value	0	1	2	3	4	Total
Frequency	1	3	3	1	0	8

A similar situation exists for the parent aaBb. Therefore, the class of parents with value 1 (Aabb and aaBb) and total frequency 16 will yield offspring of values 0, 1, 2, 3 with frequencies 2, 6, 6, 2, respectively, with an average value of 1.50. All other connecting lines in Figure 3 are calculated the same way.

A careful study of the network connecting parents and offspring is worthwhile. The diagram explains almost every question we have raised before. In particular, it shows that the children of parents of high value have a lower average value than their parents and that the children of parents of low value have a higher average value than their parents. For instance, parents of value 4 (extreme right-hand class in Figure 3) will have offspring of values, 2, 3, 4 with frequencies 1:2:1, respectively, resulting in an average value of 3. A similar situation exists for parents of value 0, whose children have an average value of 1. This diagram explains the apparently two opposite phenomena simultaneously by the same mechanism, viz., *random gene segregation and recombination*. The two seemingly opposite facts are actually the same phenomena of gene segregation, and we cannot have one without the other. The bottle that keeps cold things cold will also keep hot things hot. It is the same function. If the academic achievement is due partly to hereditary factors, then the two opposing phenomena observed in the American-Chinese population are natural events and expected to be so, as long as the social and environmental factors do not obliterate the effects of genetic factors completely. The observed phenomena show that they do not.

We may also notice the equilibrium nature derived from the connecting lines from parents to offspring in Figure 3. The resulting distribution of the quantitative trait in the offspring generation is the same as that in the parental generation, as the crisscross connecting lines balance each other, yielding a stationary state. Limiting attention to changes in one direction and ignoring

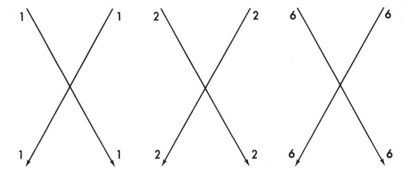

those in the other would lead to erroneous conclusions with respect to the population. The genetical model leads to the presence of the crisscross lines on account of gene segregation, while an environmental model would not only require two sets of factors working in opposite directions but also requires that they be of equal magnitude and affect equal numbers of people.

Nongeneticists may at first be amazed at the several very arbitrary assumptions involved in the genetical model. Actually, none of the assumptions are critical to the model; i.e., even if they are not exactly fulfilled the general pattern shown in Figure 3 will be modified only slightly. The assumptions are made in the interest of arithmetic simplicity, not to create an artificial network of relationships that do not exist in nature. Gene effects may not be additive, and gene frequencies are seldom equal. Matings are certainly not entirely random with respect to intelligence and education. With all these modifying factors, the essential feature of Figure 3 still remains. The most important single phenomenon of the genetic model is that for any given class of parents, their offspring will be scattered into various classes; conversely, for any given class of offspring, their parents come from various classes. Environmentalists sometimes misunderstand the implications of population genetics, thinking that heredity would imply "like class begets like class." Probably the opposite is true. Only very strong social and environmental forces can perpetuate an artificial class; heredity does not. From this point of view, social forces are more conservative than hereditary ones.

The Markov property

Of all the genetical properties that I wish to discuss with social scientists the Markov property is probably the most difficult to sell, and yet it is this property that has the most social implications. It is difficult to sell, not because it is intrinsically complicated, but because it is unbelievably simple, so simple that it contradicts the experience of social scientists, as very few, if any, social traits possess the Markov property. At the risk of oversimplification I shall present the case with the following example. Consider the heterozygote (AaBb) son from various types of families:

Father	Value		Son	Value
aabb	0	$\longrightarrow$	AaBb	2
Aabb	1	$\longrightarrow$	AaBb	2
AAbb	2	$\longrightarrow$	AaBb	2
AABb	3	$\longrightarrow$	AaBb	2
AABB	4	$\longrightarrow$	AaBb	2

The individual AaBb has a quantitative value of 2 on our scale, regardless of the type of family in which he was born. The value is determined by the genotype of the individual. The only restriction in genetics is that certain types of families cannot produce offspring of a particular genotype. Once the individual is produced, he is no different from other individuals of the same genotype from other families.

Furthermore, the future genetic behaviors of these AaBb individuals are all the same, regardless of the differences among the families from which they come. For example, in the random-mating population considered previously, the children of the AaBb individual will be in the classes 0, 1, 2, 3, 4 with relative frequencies 1, 4, 6, 4, 1, respectively, whether this AaBb individual is a product of AaBB × AABb or AABB × aabb, or any other of the many possible parental combinations. If a genotype is referred to as a "state" of an individual, we say that state 2 may be reached from several other states. The property may be summarized in more general language as follows: *The properties of an individual (or an object) depend upon the state in which he finds himself and not upon the state from which he is derived.* This is known as the Markov property (its simplest kind) in mathematics. Briefly, it says that the properties depend on where you are, not where you are from. It is essentially a property that is independent of the past. A state is a state; it has no memory. A gene is a gene; it has no memory. It is this Markov property with respect to genotypes that enables us to extend our genetic analysis and understanding of the population beyond what has been shown in Figure 3.

Consider the individuals in class 0 in Figure 3. The lines connecting the two generations show that their children will be in classes 0, 1, 2 with relative frequencies 1:2:1. We say that the transitional probabilities from state 0 to states 0, 1, 2 in the next generation are $\frac{1}{4}, \frac{1}{2}, \frac{1}{4}$, respectively. Such transitional probabilities always add up to unity, as they are the conditional probabilities for a given parental state. The transitional probabilities for all the five parental states may be arranged systematically into an array where each row gives the conditional probabilities for each given parental state:

State of Children

$$
T = \begin{array}{c} \\ \text{State of Father} \end{array}
\begin{array}{c|ccccc}
 & 0 & 1 & 2 & 3 & 4 \\\hline
0 & \frac{1}{4} & \frac{1}{2} & \frac{1}{4} & 0 & 0 \\
1 & \frac{1}{8} & \frac{3}{8} & \frac{3}{8} & \frac{1}{8} & 0 \\
2 & \frac{1}{24} & \frac{6}{24} & \frac{10}{24} & \frac{6}{24} & \frac{1}{24} \\
3 & 0 & \frac{1}{8} & \frac{3}{8} & \frac{3}{8} & \frac{1}{8} \\
4 & 0 & 0 & \frac{1}{4} & \frac{1}{2} & \frac{1}{4}
\end{array}
=
\begin{array}{ccccc}
6 & 12 & 6 & 0 & 0 \\
3 & 9 & 9 & 3 & 0 \\
1 & 6 & 10 & 6 & 1 \\
0 & 3 & 9 & 9 & 3 \\
0 & 0 & 6 & 12 & 6
\end{array}
\; \frac{1}{24}
$$

Such an arrangement of conditional probabilities is known as a stochastic matrix or a transitional matrix, designated by T. The matrix is merely an analytical way of presenting the connecting lines between two successive generations. The reason for using the transitional matrix is that the transitional probabilities for two generations, i.e., from grandparents to grandchildren, will be simply given by $T \times T = T^2$, on account of the Markov property of genotypes. Similarly, the transitional probabilities for four generations will be $T \times T \times T \times T = T^4$. The events in successive generations thus form a "Markov chain." The results of our calculations are shown in Table 1. The probabilities in each row add up to unity (except for rounding errors sometimes). It will

Table 1. Transitional probabilities from ancestor to descendant

	State of ancestor	State of descendant				
		0	1	2	3	4
T	0	.2500	.5000	.2500	0	0
	1	.1250	.3750	.3750	.1250	0
	2	.0417	.2500	.4167	.2500	.0417
	3	0	.1250	.3750	.3750	.1250
	4	0	0	.2500	.5000	.2500
T^2	0	.1354	.3750	.3542	.1250	.0104
	1	.0937	.3125	.3750	.1875	.0312
	2	.0590	.2500	.3819	.2500	.0590
	3	.0312	.1875	.3750	.3125	.0937
	4	.0104	.1250	.3542	.3750	.1354
T^4	0	.0784	.2812	.3744	.2187	.0472
	1	.0703	.2656	.3750	.2344	.0547
	2	.0624	.2500	.3752	.2500	.0624
	3	.0547	.2344	.3750	.2656	.0703
	4	.0472	.2187	.3744	.2812	.0784
T^8	0	.0635	.2520	.3750	.2480	.0615
	1	.0630	.2510	.3750	.2490	.0620
	2	.0625	.2500	.3750	.2500	.0625
	3	.0620	.2490	.3750	.2510	.0630
	4	.0615	.2480	.3750	.2520	.0635

be noticed that in the original matrix T the five rows are very different. In the matrix T^2 the five rows are still different but not to the same extent as those of T. In the matrix T^8 the five rows become almost the same. Further numerical calculations show that the five rows will indeed become identical as the number of generations (n) increases, as the theory of stochastic matrices predicts. The limiting value of T^n as n becomes large is:

$$T^n \longrightarrow \hat{T} = \begin{vmatrix} 1 & 4 & 6 & 4 & 1 \\ 1 & 4 & 6 & 4 & 1 \\ 1 & 4 & 6 & 4 & 1 \\ 1 & 4 & 6 & 4 & 1 \\ 1 & 4 & 6 & 4 & 1 \end{vmatrix} \; \frac{1}{16}$$

The rows of the T^n matrix are identical. This means that no matter what was the given initial state of the original ancestor, his distant descendants will be distributed into the various classes the same way; viz., 1:4:6:4:1, which is the equilibrium distribution of the quantitative trait in the population. Thus, the distant descendants of Jean Bernoulli are distributed into the various classes of mathematical ability exactly the same way as the distant descendants of one whose mathematical ability belongs to class 0. In practice, after only a few generations (Table 1), the transitional matrix becomes indistinguishable from its theoretical limiting value.

Figure 4 is an attempt to illustrate the biological meaning of the mathematical results. Let us first fix our attention on a particular individual, say, some one in class 3, and assume for simplicity that one father has only one son in each generation. If we follow the father-son line of descent from generation

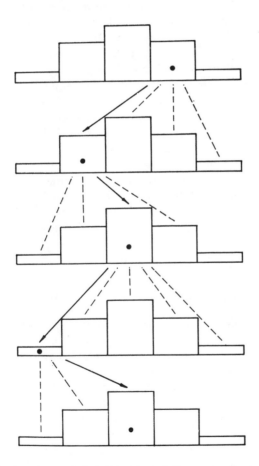

Figure 4. One possible line of descent through four generations.

to generation, we shall find the line zigzags greatly without any systematic rule. After six or eight generations, the last member of the line may end up almost anywhere along the scale 0–4. And this is true for any individual on whom we happen to fix our attention originally. In each generation the line may take one of several alternatives. The T^n matrix says that no matter which individual of which class we decided to follow, his descendants will be scattered among the classes 0–4 with eventual probabilities 1/16, 4/16, etc. These probabilities are independent of the initial position where we started the follow-up. This is one of the most important and remarkable consequences of the Markov chain events. The mathematical model fits into population genetics better than any other biological subject. In terms of genetic relationships this result means that family members six or eight generations apart are practically unrelated, even though they may retain the same family name.

For ease of understanding we have followed from father to son. Actually, the same argument applies for tracing back also. Given an individual in a class (no matter which class), if we trace his father, grandfather, etc. back to six generations, we may find his ancestor almost anywhere along the scale 0–4, with the same probabilities as indicated before.

To summarize, two individuals of the same family but several generations apart are practically uncorrelated in their genetic constitution. Given the genotype of one, we could not estimate the genotype of the other any more accurately than we can for an unrelated random individual. The hereditary forces in shaping up an individual are essentially of an immediate nature and have no long-lasting historical significance. When one tells you that his great-great-grand-uncle came to this country on the Mayflower, a historian or a social scientist may attach some meaning to that fact. A geneticist regards that as "noise," irrelevant to his own worth. It is the social forces (created by man) that tend to protect and maintain a certain class. The genetical forces (created by nature) have no such social prejudices; they obey the laws of probabilities without memory of the past.

The study of racial differences

All quantitative differences, of whatever kind, are based on measurements made under prescribed conditions, frequently under arbitrarily defined conditions. Most familiar examples are the various types of games and competitions in the sports world. Should the boxing ring be lengthened or shortened by one foot in each dimension, the outcome of the fight might be different. Similarly, if the 100-meter track is lengthened to 120 meters or shortened to 80 meters, the outcome of the competition might be quite different. Yet we define and accept the differences among the athletes under such highly artificial conditions, with full knowledge that such observed measurements and differences might be modified as soon as the rules of the game are modified.

Sports records over a long period of time show that American blacks are better runners and boxers; and this conclusion gains general acceptance without much fuss. Even the most skeptical person will readily admit that the American blacks are at least equally good in running and boxing. Nobody argues that the competition is done under artificial conditions and, therefore, not fair to the blacks or to the whites. That is the game. The running ability is defined by the rules and conditions, although nobody in the real world could or would run 100 meters straight without a turn, and certainly not between two white lines. Swimming is done under similarly artificial conditions, and American blacks are not doing so well in this sport. Purely for the sake of illustration, let us assume that the American black is superior in running and inferior in swimming. These two "tests" measure two different abilities. One's superiority as revealed by one test does not nullify his inferiority in another, or vice versa.

The discussion above by no means applies only to sports abilities. In a sense, the arbitrariness of the rules of sport is true for all types of tests for all types of abilities, including the great variety of tests for "intelligence," whatever that means. In sports one may argue (actually no one does) that the 100-meter dash does not really measure the "running ability" of an individual, as no one runs that way in natural conditions. This is purely a semantic problem. We may easily substitute some other words for running ability if that is the objection. The 100-meter dash measures the ability defined by the specified "tests" (conditions and rules of running), no matter what name we attach to that ability. And the American blacks are very high in that ability as measured by the specified tests. When we are dealing with the ability loosely known as intelligence, to be measured by certain arbitrary tests, however, we tend to lose our objectivity and standard. The ability we are measuring is defined by the tests employed, and it may be called by any name at all.

The current controversy seems to center around two questions: (1) Is intelligence (as defined by tests) determined by heredity? (2) Is there a racial difference in such a test score? Both are matters in basic science, and they must be treated and studied as such. There should be no more room for emotion than in studying the mobility of amoeba. We must face the blunt reality that for matters in basic science there is no other way to make progress except by basic research. As in all other problems in basic science, basic research may be long, slow, tedious, painstaking, expensive, and sometimes even confusing, but it is the only road to progress that we know of. Avoidance of research is certainly no road to progress.

Set it up and knock it down

In our effort to seek the true state of nature (which is unknown), we usually have one or more hypotheses (tentative assumptions) in our mind that we wish to test to determine how true or untrue are the assumptions. Suppose that the truth is T, and our initial hypothesis is H_0. In most cases the chance is remote that $H_0 = T$. The research procedure is to make our successive hypotheses $(H_1, H_2, \ldots)$ closer and closer to the truth. In order to be able to accomplish this, the research procedure must be self-policing, self-improving, or self-correcting. When the research procedure possesses these properties, we shall get closer and closer to the truth no matter where we start. That is, even if an initial H_0 is very far from the truth, we shall be able to advance in the right direction toward the truth. The ideal procedure is independent of H_0. This is somewhat analogous to the iterative methods of arriving at a mathematical solution, beginning with an initial trial value.

What is the research procedure that is self-policing and self-correcting? Briefly, it is an endless attempt to *disprove* a hypothesis. First, we set up a hypothesis so that we can initiate the research work. This should then be immediately followed by attempts to show that the hypothesis is untrue so that we may set up a new hypothesis. When the new one is disproved, we shall have a still newer one to take its place and so on. A continuous procedure of this nature will take us closer and closer to the truth even if we started out very wrong. Hence, we see, there is no good or bad hypothesis in science, but there is good or bad scientific procedure. It is the procedure, not the hypothesis, that leads us eventually to the truth. No false hypothesis can survive the self-correcting procedure very long. The continuous effort to disprove a hypothesis will help us not to go too far astray too long.

Thus, it is clear that it serves no purpose in science to set up a hypothesis that can neither be proved nor disproved. Such a hypothesis will remain still as a useless statement; it does not lead us anywhere; it adds no new knowledge; its truth or falsehood will remain unknown; it is incapable of self-improvement. An absolutely necessary feature of a hypothesis is that it is susceptible to being disproved. The scientist will then design discriminating experiments to test its degree of validity and improve the hypothesis to a hopefully truer one.

Some of us, however noble our intentions may be, are so anxious to "prove" a hypothesis that we tend to ignore the procedure of self-policing and ignore evidences unfavorable to the hypothesis. When we do so, the hypothesis ceases to be part of science and becomes ideology or dogma. In order to make progress in science we must be more interested in disproving than in proving. In my brief involvement with the social scientists concerning the hereditary and environmental components of intelligence and the possible racial differences in test scores, my review of the arguments gives me the impression that not sufficient attention has been placed on the self-correcting procedures; and some of the arguments are plainly ideological.

Discussion

After reading this chapter in Illinois a number of questions have been brought to me from various sources. A few of the most frequently raised questions are discussed below. **Q** means question and **D** means discussion.

Q1: You left me dangling as to whether the hypothesis we should disprove is that Negroes are different from Caucasians or that Negroes are the same. It might help if you would state this clearly.

D1: I shall state this clearly. It makes absolutely no difference which hypothesis you choose to attack first, as long as you adopt the self-correcting procedure. As emphasized in the text, it is the procedure (scientific method), not the hypothesis, that leads us eventually to the truth. Flip a coin or simply suit yourself. If I choose one hypothesis, that should not influence your choice at all. Personally, I should like to see various investigators, starting from many different hypotheses, eventually all reach the same conclusion. That would be a beautiful demonstration of the power of the scientific method.

Q2: You give no concrete suggestions as to how we do get around the confounding socioeconomic differences between the Negro and the Caucasian, which in my opinion continue to hinder progress in this field and will do so for the foreseeable future. Perhaps you would like to recognize in print how difficult it may be to test hypotheses in this field.

D2: I did not give concrete suggestions as to how to get around the confounding factors (not limited to socioeconomic differences) between the black and the white, as I am not writing a protocol for a research project. Obviously, there is no one single method that would overcome the effects of all confounding factors. But the situation here is no different from any other social, medical, or epidemiological study which has to face just as many confounding factors in our society. Each investigator has to make his own research design to suit the particular purpose of his project and the particular circumstances under which the project is to take place. The existence of confounding factors is certainly no excuse not to do research in this or any other field. You will encounter confounding factors in all types of research, not only in racial problems. Hypothesis testing is difficult in every field; I recognize it.

Q3: Since all tests are arbitrary devices, then should we attach any meaning to the test scores? Particularly, I mean the IQ tests.

D3: Despite the arbitrary nature of all types of tests, the results or scores do mean something. If they mean nothing else, they at least measure the scoring ability with respect to that particular test. Whether that scoring ability should play a role in society is entirely another problem. The champions in track do have better running ability than the rest of us. Whether we should make them senators or governors is a different question. A popular pitcher of the Pirates got elected to public office in the Pittsburgh area. If the IQ scores really differ between two groups (any two groups, not necessarily blacks and whites), I shall accept it as a fact without any implications. I accept a good pitcher as a good pitcher, but I do not necessarily vote for him in November, in spite of the fact that an administrator also needs a strong arm.

Q4: You are talking about science all the time. What I want to know is if you were told that the Chinese intelligence is 15 points below the whites, what would you do?

D4: Absolutely nothing! Incidentally there is no "if" about it. I have been told something like that many times since my boyhood, long before the test scores became popular. I seem to hear less and less about that as time goes by. This could be because of my age; I hear less and less about everything else too.

Summary

A systematic and unified explanation is needed for various phenomena observed in a human population or anywhere. Ad hoc explanations are a posteriori and have no predictive value. The properties of a genetical model for quantitative traits have been described and their social significance discussed. It was concluded that social factors act in a more conservative way than hereditary factors in a random-mating population. The genetic hypothesis, environmental hypothesis, or any other hypothesis on human intelligence or any other type of ability must undergo the critical self-improving research procedure. A hypothesis must be susceptible to possible disproof; otherwise it serves no purpose in science. Matters in basic science must be elucidated or resolved by basic research; no ideology can possibly help.

References

There are so many reports on the subject of environmental and hereditary components of human intelligence that a listing of a few by an author not working primarily in this field would unavoidably be very biased, if not amounting to total distortion. For this reason the author thought it is best not to list any specific technical work in an article of this nature. However, an extensive bibliography may be found in *Environment, heredity, and intelligence*. Harvard Educational Review, Cambridge, 1969. Those who are interested in the author's writings in general methodology, experimental statistics, population genetics, and its applications in human populations may consult some of the following:

Books

Li, C. C. *Population genetics*. Chicago: University of Chicago Press, 1955.

———. *Human genetics, principles and methods*. New York: McGraw-Hill, 1961.

———. *Introduction to experimental statistics*. New York: McGraw-Hill, 1964.

Articles

Glass, H. B., & Li, C. C. The dynamics of racial intermixture—an analysis based on the American Negro. *American Journal of Human Genetics*, 1953, *5*, 1–20.

Li, C. C. The correlation between parents and offspring in a random mating population. *American Journal of Human Genetics*, 1954, *6*, 383–386.

————. Some methods of studying human genetics. *Methods in Medical Research*, 1954, *6*, 1–38.

————. The concept of path coefficient and its impact on population genetics. *Biometrics*, 1956, *12*, 190–210.

————. Repeated linear regression and variance components of a population with binomial frequencies. *Biometrics*, 1957, *13*, 225–234.

————. The diminishing jaw of civilized people. *American Journal of Human Genetics*, 1961, *13*, 1–8.

————. Genetical methods for epidemiological investigations: A synthesis. *Annals of the New York Academy of Sciences*, 1961, *91*, 806–812.

————. Genetics (in Communist China). *The China Quarterly, London*, 1961, *6*, 144–152.

————. Genetic equilibrium under selection. *Biometrics*, 1967, *23*, 397–484.

————. Fisher, Wright, and path coefficients. *Biometrics*, 1968, *24*, 471–483.

————. Human genetic adaptation. In M. K. Hecht & W. C. Steere (Eds.), *Essays in evolution and genetics in honor of Theodosius Dobzhansky*. New York: Appleton-Century-Crofts, 1970.

————, & Sacks, L. The derivation of joint distribution and correlation between relatives by the use of stochastic matrices. *Biometrics*, 1954, *10*, 347–360.

chapter 11

what do we know today about the inheritance of intelligence and how do we know it?

STEVEN G. VANDENBERG

Man has probably always believed that he receives not only his existence but also his physique and part of his abilities and personality traits from his parents. Typical of such ideas is a statement by Goethe:

> *Vom Vater hab ich die Statur, des Lebens ernstes führen,*
> *Vom Mütterchen die Frohnatur und Lust zu fabulieren.*

In such ideas no distinction is made between similarity due to biological descent and similarity due to imitation. This confusion is further compounded by the fact that the words heir, hereditary, and inheritance are used in many languages for two fundamentally different processes: the legal rules governing transfer of land and movable property after the death of the owner and biological rules describing the transmission of characteristics from parents to offspring. (See the diagrams in Li's Chapter 10 for some of the consequences of these two distinct processes.)

It is no wonder that in the past the influence of social and biological factors could not be clearly separated conceptually. Most of us are at times still confused about this, especially when we talk about the relative importance

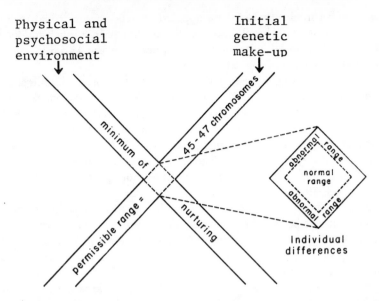

Figure 1. Individual differences in the normal range as a function of permissible variation in hereditary and environment.

of the two factors. I have in the past used Figure 1 to illustrate that in some real sense both factors are of supreme importance or, if you will, 100 percent necessary. The slightest change in the astronomically rare physical conditions on the surface of our planet Earth, or in the equally rare behavioral and social conditions that permit "babying" a newborn not only until he can toddle but actually until he can make his own "living," could wipe out the human race. Yet it is just as true that a fertilized egg with more than a few deleterious or even one lethal gene not compensated for by its partner will not grow into a viable individual but produce an early abortion or lead to a stillbirth. It is only within a very narrow range of normal conditions that the variation occurs which psychologists call individual differences. Perhaps 90 or 95 percent of the human genetic endowment (the genome) does not and cannot exhibit variation. The frequent confusion between hereditary (i.e., genetically variable) traits and instincts (i.e., innate releasing mechanisms or species-specific behaviors and structures, which are also inherited) reflects a lack of understanding of this fact. Even though the severely retarded, for example, may hardly seem human to some observers, they are vastly more similar to normal men than to any other living being.

In a volume on genetic factors in behavior Rosenthal (1968) expressed dismay that so little progress had been made in human behavior genetics since Barbara Burks' 1928 paper. I agree except that it would have been fairer if Rosenthal had added that very little work was done for the next thirty years because of an intellectual climate opposed to genetics, described in detail by Hirsch (1963, 1967). This climate paralleled, though in a much milder fashion and only in the social sciences, what happened in the U.S.S.R., though for somewhat different ideological reasons.

We can summarize research on hereditary factors in intelligence under two broad headings, which, in turn, can be further subdivided. But before we proceed, I want to make one further important introductory remark. For the purpose of this chapter only, I shall go along with the concept of a single, unitary attribute called *general* intelligence or IQ. On other occasions, I have emphasized the evidence which leads me to conclude that a model of at least four to eight major independent abilities has more pragmatic value (Vandenberg, 1968, 1970).

The two types of research that provide evidence about hereditary factors in intelligence, to be reviewed in Part I and II of this chapter, come from rather different points of view—roughly representing biometrical and Mendelian— which may be thought of as almost contrasting ones in spite of frequent demonstrations that they can be easily reconciled.

The first group includes studies of related individuals, twin studies, and adoption studies. We can call these studies of *similarity*. They are more in the psychological tradition. The second group includes studies of the effects of consanguinity, of mutant genes, and of chromosomal abnormalities. We can call these studies of gene-controlled *differences*. As is to be expected, they are usually done by geneticists and often are psychologically oversimplified.

This distinction is not identical with the familiar one between (1) the processes controlling intelligence as a continuous trait normally distributed in the population and (2) the inheritance of low IQ, which can in some respect be treated as a discontinuous or "present-absent" type of variable. Figure 2 illustrates how the distribution of intelligence in the population is thought to have two components reflecting these two separate processes. This distinction can, of course, not always be maintained as we shall see when we discuss the

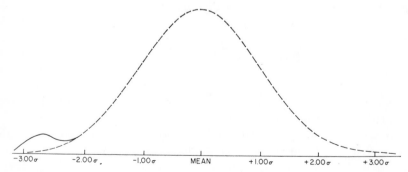

Figure 2. The actual distribution of IQs compared to a normal distribution.

effect of consanguinity which is not limited to increased production of severe retardates but also reduces the mean IQ of nonretarded offspring. For this reason and because of historical precedent, we shall distinguish instead between studies of similarity and of differences in IQ.

Part 1 : Studies of similarity in IQ

Similarity in IQ and biological relatedness

Erlenmeyer-Kimling and Jarvik (1963) published a paper that condensed in a few pages and one figure probably more information than any other publication in the history of psychology. That figure is shown here as Figure 3. Each horizontal line in the figure indicates the range of values reported for correlations between paired individuals of a given degree of biological relatedness, while the small vertical line represents the median of those values, which is the best characterization of the central tendency. From this figure a number of interesting observations can be made. The first and most important observation is that there is a near perfect correspondence between the median correlation and the degree of relatedness. In fact, the median comes close to the value to be expected from a polygenic model, i.e., a model in which a large number of genes are held to make equal cumulative contributions to intelligence. Under such a model the expected value of the correlation between relatives is equal to the percentage of genes common to the two relatives because of the same ancestor. Typical values are 0.5 for children from the same parents, 0.5 for

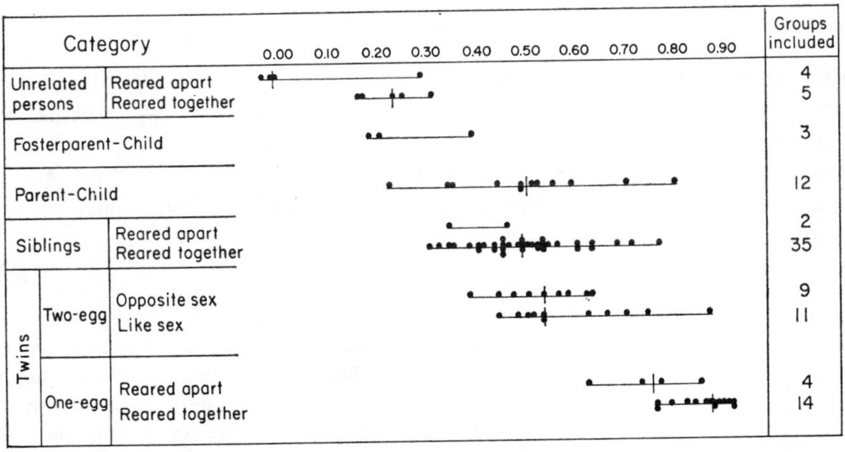

Figure 3. Correlations between IQs of paired individuals of genetic relations ranging from none to complete. (Erlenmeyer-Kimling & Jarvik, 1963.)

parent-child, 0.25 for halfsibs or grandparent-grandchild, 0.125 for first cousins, or generally $(\frac{1}{2})^n$ for relatives of the nth degree.

The values actually observed fit the model very well, but it is impossible to silence critics who may argue that similar values can be expected just as well on the basis of the degree of shared environment. The only serious difficulties for the environmental point of view are presented by the *absence* of large differences between the median values for siblings and one-egg twins reared apart versus together and the *presence* of a difference of about 0.25 between the parent-child and foster parent-child correlations.

Jensen (1969) leaned heavily on a very large study conducted over a number of years and reported in several only partially overlapping papers in which Burt obtained similar results (Burt & Howard, 1956; Burt, 1958; Conway, 1958). Formulas were developed by Burt and Howard (1956) for the expected values of correlations between relatives in which allowance was made for (1) assortative mating between the parents and (2) a small amount of dominance so that being heterozygous (having only one gene favorable for intelligence) at a given locus would confer somewhat more than half the benefit of being homozygous (having two favorable genes) at that locus. These hypothetical values were compared with the actual values obtained and provided an even closer fit. They are shown in Table 1. Burt emphasized another improvement in the fit of the data to the model, made by basing ability assessments not just on tests but also on judgments of teachers and others. While it is quite possible that such "corrected" estimates were closer to the real ability levels, a small chance for bias does creep in and the, admittedly error-prone, test scores do provide a more objective basis.

Similarity in IQ of children and foster parents and of children and biological parents

Although data about foster parent-child correlations were included in the two summaries discussed above, we shall consider these "natural experiments" in more detail. In 1928 Barbara Burks concluded from a review of data then available, plus what she learned from a large study of her own, "that about 17 percent of the variability of intelligence is due to differences in home environment [p. 223]." She further concluded:

> . . . not far from 70 percent of ordinary white school children have intelligence that deviates less than 6 IQ points up or down from what they would have if all children were raised in a standard (average) home environment; that while home environment in rare extreme cases may account for as much as 20 points of increment above the expected, or congenital, level, heredity (in conjunction with environment) may account in some instances for increments above the load of generality which are five times as large (100 points) [Burks, 1928, p. 223].

Table 1. Correlations between relatives

	Burt		Other investigators		
	Number of pairs	Corre-lation	Number of investi-gations	Median corre-lation	Theo-retical value
Direct line					
With parents (as adults)	374	.49	13	.50	.49
With parents (as children)	106	.56	—	—	.49
With grandparents	132	.33	2	.24	.31
Collaterals					
Between monozygotic twins					
Reared together	95	.92	13	.87	1.00
Reared apart	53	.87	3	.75	1.00
Between dizygotic twins					
Same sex	71	.55	8	.56	.54
Different sex	56	.52	6	.49	.50
Between siblings					
Reared together	264	.53	36	.55	.52
Reared apart	151	.44	33	.47	.52
Between uncle (or aunt) and nephew (or niece)	161	.34	—	—	.31
Between first cousins	215	.28	2	.26	.18
Between second cousins	127	.16	—	—	.14
Unrelated persons					
Foster parent and child	88	.19	3	.20	.00
Children reared together	136	.27	4	.23	.00
Children reared apart	200	− .04	2	−.01	.00

Table 2. Child's IQ correlated with environmental and hereditary factors

	Foster		Control	
Correlate	r	n	r	n
Father's mental age	.09	178	.55	100
Mother's mental age	.23	204	.57	105
Father's vocabulary	.14	181	.52	101
Mother's vocabulary	.25	202	.48	104
Whittier rating of house	.24	206	.48	104
Culture rating of house	.29	186	.49	101
Income	.26	181	.26	99
Multiple correlation	.35	164	.53	95
Multiple r corrected for attenua-tion	.42	164	.61	95

Burks reported a number of correlations between the IQ of children and various attributes of their foster parents, including IQ measured with the Stanford-Binet test, as well as similar data for a control group of parents and their own children.

Table 2 presents the most important data from that study which were included in Tables 34 and 36 in her paper. She corrected for attenuation, but because the probable errors were all close to 0.06, this may be disregarded as having only minor influence on the reported results. For the foster children the square of the multiple correlation is the portion of the variance in child IQ due to environment where the environment includes foster parents' IQs. For the control group the square of the multiple correlation is the percentage of the variance in child IQ due to the same environmental effects plus the additive genetic effects of the parents' IQ.

Next she used Sewall Wright's path analysis to obtain for the control group information about (1) the proportional contribution of total home environment to variance, (2) the unique contribution of parental intelligence to variance, (3) the estimate of total contribution of heredity to variance, and (4) the numerical estimate of the potency of home environment to raise or depress the IQ. In modern terminology (2) and (3) would be described, respectively, as the additive genetic contribution of each gene by itself and the nonadditive genetic contribution due to the particular dominance and epistatic effects of the genes for each particular child—i.e., the effect within each locus of the two alleles and the effect of the various alleles at each locus on each other. Only additive genetic effects are common to parent and offspring or to two sibs, and only they produce the correlations (only identical twins share the effects of dominance and epistasis).

Figure 4 shows the information available for calculating these values. Using the formulas of Wright (1921, 1923) Burks found that a^2, the percentage of variance associated with the direct path of influence between parental and child's IQ, was 0.3314; c^2, the contribution of the environment over and above

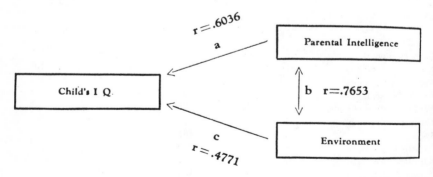

Figure 4. Correlations between child's IQ, parental intelligence, and environment.

the parental intelligence, was 0.0013; and the joint parental and environmental contribution over and above the separate contributions of each was 0.0322 for a total of 0.3649. Burks finally arrived at the following values: (1) the proportional contribution of total home environment was 0.17; (2) the unique contribution of parental intelligence was 0.33; (3) the total contribution of heredity to the variance was 0.75–0.80; and (4) an environment one standard deviation above or below the mean shifts the IQ about 6 to 9 points up or down.

The conclusions from the latter result were: (1) nearly 70 percent of school children have an actual IQ within 6 to 9 points of that represented by their innate intelligence, and (2) the maximal contribution of the *best* home environment to intelligence is about 20 IQ points. Similarly, the least culturally stimulating environment may depress the IQ by 20 points, "but situations as extreme as either of these probably occur only once or twice in a thousand times."

I have devoted so much space to Barbara Burks' study because to my knowledge it is the only one in which the genetic and the environmental contributions were assessed simultaneously, something that badly needs replication, both in the United States and elsewhere, because of the implications for social action.

The next study to be discussed is particularly impressive because the data collection was initiated with the hope of demonstrating the beneficial effects of placement in good homes on the IQ of the foster children. And, indeed, the mean IQ of the children was substantially higher than that of their biological mothers (mean IQ of 63 mothers, 85.7; of 63 children, 106). Nevertheless, it was found that the child's IQ correlated with the IQ of the biological parents but not with the IQ of the foster parents (Skodak & Skeels, 1949). In fact, when Honzik (1957) compared these results with the correlations in IQ between parents and children raised by their own parents, she obtained the results shown in Figure 5. (Parental education instead of IQ was used because some IQs were missing.)

It is clear from Figure 5 that being placed in an adoptive home does not affect the size of the child–true-parent correlation in IQ. While this provides the strongest evidence possible for hereditary factors in intelligence, no estimate can be made of the percentage of variance attributable to additive genetic factors.

Similarity in IQ of identical twins raised together and raised apart

If the environment were absolutely comparable for everyone, there would still be large differences between people because of genetic factors. Members of a set of identical twins would, however, be the same except for the lack of perfect replication of cells or uneven division of the cytoplasm in the fertilized ovum

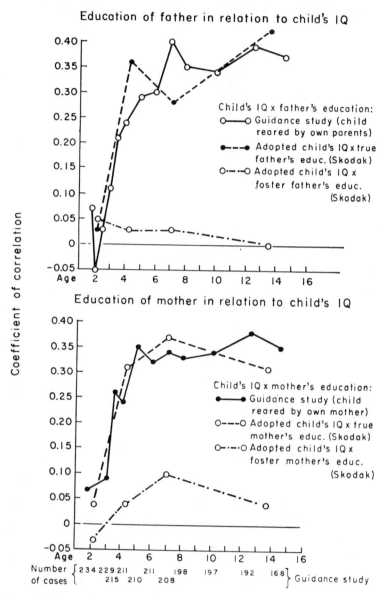

Figure 5. IQ resemblance of adopted child to foster and true parents. (After Honzik, 1957.)

from which the two or more individuals arose. For this reason the departure from perfect correlation of the IQs of identical twins provides an index of the effect of prenatal plus postnatal environmental differences with the temporal course

Table 3. Concordance in IQ of MZ twins raised apart and of MZ twins raised together

Author	MZ r	Apart n	MZ r	Together n
Newman, et al. (1937)	.77	19	.98	50
Burt (1958)	.86	53	.92	95
Shields (1962)	.77	37	.76	34
Juel-Nielsen (1965)	.62	12	not studied	
Average after z transformation	.80	121	.89	179

of such differences. This is a significant indicator of the relative weight of environmental and genetic factors. It is important to remember that between family differences are eliminated in such twin correlations. In contrast, when we compare identical twins raised apart, such differences are no longer controlled. Table 3 summarizes the results of four studies of identical twins reared apart.

It is clear from Table 3 that separation does not dramatically lower the concordance of IQ in identical twins raised apart. When we look at the actual differences between the twins that have been reported, we see why. Most differences in IQ are unimportant. Newman, Freeman, and Holzinger (1937) reported a difference of 20 points in a pair where one twin had been raised in a rural area and only went to school for four years while the other completed twelve grades in a city school. The trouble with studies of this kind is that the range of variation in the homes in which children are placed probably is not as great as in the population as a whole and that the two twins are often placed in similar homes. For these reasons we cannot place as much reliance on such studies as "hereditarians" might like to do.

The age at which twins are separated is not always a few days after birth, nor even before their first birthday. Perhaps this is not too important; at least, this is the conclusion which seems warranted from the finding of Vandenberg and Johnson (1968) that twins separated before 9 months of age were somewhat more similar in IQ than twins separated when one year of age or older. Table 4 shows their summary.

Concordance comparison of identical and fraternal twins

Francis Galton (1875) was the first to suggest that twins be studied to learn about the relative importance of nature and nurture, and this somewhat either-or formulation has colored the interpretation of twin studies ever since. Because pair differences in identical twins are due to nonhereditary factors while in

Table 4. Differences in IQ for 37 pairs of MZ twins from various studies

Age at separation	Source	IQ differences
1 day	(S & T)	4
1 day	(J–N)	6
9 days	(B)	1
½ mo.	(M)	4
3 wk.	(J–N)	1
3 wk.	(J–N)	1
1 mo.	(S)	4
1 mo.	(G & N)	3
1 mo.	(NFH)	1
1 mo.	(NFH)	6
1 mo.	(NFH)	1
6 wk.	(J–N)	11
2 mo.	(NFH)	2
3 mo.	(NFH)	15
3 mo.	(Y & B)	19
5 mo.	(NFH)	17
6 mo.	(J–N)	1
7 mo.	(J–N)	4
9 mo.	(J–N)	6
10 mo.	(J–N)	3
1 yr.	(J–N)	9
1 yr.	(J–N)	14
1 yr.	(NFH)	19
1 yr.	(NFH)	5
1 yr.	(NFH)	1
14 mo.	(NFH)	4
18 mo.	(NFH)	12
18 mo.	(NFH)	12
18 mo.	(NFH)	24
18 mo.	(NFH)	7
2 yr.	(NFH)	10
2½ yr.	(NFH)	2
3 yr.	(NFH)	8
3½ yr.	(J–N)	8
3½ yr.	(J–N)	6
5¾ yr.	(J–N)	13
6 yr.	(NFH)	9

Source key: S & T = Stephens & Thompson, 1943;
J–N = Juel-Nielsen, 1964; B = Burks, 1962;
M = Muller, 1925; S = Saudek, 1934;
G & N = Gardner & Newman, 1940;
NFH = Newman, Freeman, & Holzinger, 1937; and
Y & B = Yates & Brash, 1941.

fraternal twins they are due to nonhereditary *plus* hereditary factors, the comparison of the two sets of pair differences can indeed tell us something about the importance of hereditary factors. But this can be stated in several ways, some of which are more open to misinterpretation. One distinction is whether one wants only to test the statistical significance of the hereditary component or whether one wants to estimate the degree of hereditary determination. In the latter case statements are made about the *proportion of the variance* in the trait due to heredity; such statements are frequently mistaken to refer to the proportion of the trait due to heredity.

Lush (1945) introduced the concept of *heritability* into animal genetics. There are two definitions: one that has been called "broad," and one that has been called "narrow." The broad definition of heritability is that proportion of the total variance that is genetic, or in symbols:

$$h^2 = \frac{\sigma_g^2}{\sigma_t^2} \tag{1}$$

The narrow definition is the additive genetic component divided by the total variance or

$$h^2 = \frac{\sigma_a^2}{\sigma_t^2} \tag{2}$$

The total genetic variance consists of three components:

$$\sigma_g^2 = \sigma_a^2 + \sigma_d^2 + \sigma_e^2 \tag{3}$$

plus interaction between d and e where σ_d^2 is the variance due to dominance effects and σ_e^2 is the variance due to epistasis.

Unfortunately we know nothing about the proportional size of the effects of σ_d^2 and σ_e^2. We saw earlier that Burt and Howard (1956) assumed that genes favorable for intelligence would show a small amount of dominance. As far as I know, there are no data to support or invalidate this assumption.

To clarify what dominance refers to, let us look at Figure 6 where the amount contributed to the total IQ of three persons is depicted for various types of dominance: AA is someone who received two alleles for good intelligence at a given locus, Aa is someone who received only one "good" allele, and aa is someone who received no "good" allele at this locus. The solid line shows complete dominance: having only *one* "good" allele (Aa) results in the same contribution to IQ as having *two* "good" alleles (AA). The broken line below it shows partial dominance, which results in a value for Aa that is more than intermediate between AA and aa. The top broken line shows over-dominance, which results in a higher value for Aa than for AA. The dotted

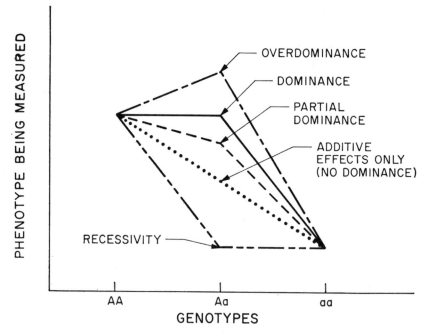

Figure 6. Relationship between phenotype and degrees of dominance.

line shows the complete absence of dominance so that additive effects only are observed, since Aa is exactly half-way between AA and aa. The very bottom line shows the exact reversal of dominance, or "recessivity."

Epistasis is the effect of alleles at one or more loci on the alleles at a given locus. A good example of epistasis in the area of behavior is formed by what has been called hygienic behavior in bees. In 1964 Rothenbuhler reported on a cross between two inbred lines, one of which had been selected for resistance to American foulbrood and the other selected for susceptibility. Bees of the resistant line remove larvae killed by foulbrood from the nest, while bees of the susceptible line do not. When the two strains were crossed, the resultant F_1 bees were found to be unhygienic, i.e., they did not remove dead larvae. When the F_1 bees were backcrossed to the original hygienic line, four types of behaviors occurred: (1) hygienic, (2) nonhygienic, (3) uncap only, and (4) remove only. Uncap means that the dead larvae were uncovered but not removed. Remove means that this line does not uncap or open up the cells with dead larvae. However, when the cells were opened by the author the remove only bees carried the dead larvae away. He concluded that there exist two loci, one with alleles U and u and the other with alleles R and r, and that the two loci together control hygienic behavior when in homozygous condition UU RR. This is illustrated in Table 5, where the results of the backcross are shown.

Table 5. Backcross between F₁ and hygienic line

	Gametes	F_1 Hygienic × nonhygienic: UuRr			
		UR	Ur	uR	ur
UURR		UURR	UURr	UuRR	UuRr
Hygienic behavior	UR	Hygienic behavior	Uncap only	Remove only	Non-hygienic

Source: Rothenbuhler, 1964.

Let us return to the two definitions of heritability. It is not known how much dominance and epistasis variance there may be in the genes controlling human intelligence. It seems intuitively correct to expect less epistasis variance the more loci there are involved. Perhaps the same is true for dominance variance. This could be estimated if data were available on identical and fraternal twins as well as on their parents. In that case one could calculate heritability from the parent-child correlations to obtain a narrow heritability as well as from the MZ-DZ concordance comparison, to obtain a broad heritability. Penrose (1969) suggested that from such data a rough estimate could be made of the number of loci involved.

Elston and Gottesman (1968) have described the first step of such an analysis involving estimation of the total variance σ^2, and the covariance of identical twins cov_{MZ}, of fraternal twins cov_{DZ}, and of nontwin sibs cov_{SS}, as well as the covariance of parent and offspring cov_{PO}. They have suggested also using data on other sibs from such families for a more complete estimation procedure. The concept of heritability was introduced for an eminently practical reason. It tells the animal or plant breeder how much room there is for improvement through selective breeding.

Holzinger (1929) attempted to find an equivalent to heritability for use in twin studies. He proposed two formulas to measure the proportion of the total variance contributed by the genetic component:

$$h^2 = \frac{\sigma_{DZ}^2 - \sigma_{MZ}^2}{\sigma_{DZ}^2} \tag{4}$$

where σ^2 is the within pair variance $1/N\,(A_i - B_i)^2$ for N pairs of twins A_i and B_i; and

$$h^2 = \frac{r_{MZ} - r_{DZ}}{1 - r_{DZ}} \tag{5}$$

where r is the intraclass correlation between the twins.

These formulas may be considered as heritability indices in the broad sense only, because no distinction is made between additive, dominance, and epistasis effects. However, both formulas are in error. In the first place they only consider the genetic variance within families. If we could be sure that the genetic component between families was equal in size to this, we could just double the value. The fact that Holzinger's h^2 frequently is greater than 0.50 demonstrates that just doubling will not do. In addition, the two formulas are not really equivalent. Clark (1956) showed that (5) is equivalent to (4) only if

$$r_{MZ} = 1 - \frac{\sigma_{MZ}^2}{V} \qquad (6)$$

and

$$r_{DZ} = 1 - \frac{\sigma_{DZ}^2}{V} \qquad (7)$$

where V is the total variance for all twins, both identical and fraternal. If

$$r_{MZ} = 1 - \frac{\sigma_{MZ}^2}{MZ} \qquad (8)$$

and

$$r_{DZ} = 1 - \frac{\sigma_{DZ}^2}{V_{DZ}} \qquad (9)$$

then formula (5) is equivalent to

$$h^2 = \frac{V_{MZ}\sigma_{DZ}^2 - V_{DZ}\sigma_{MZ}^2}{V_{MZ}\sigma_{DZ}^2} \qquad (10)$$

or, in other words, only if the total variance for the identical twins is equal to the total variance for the fraternal twins can we expect formula (5) to give the same value as formula (4). Yet it is precisely formula (5) that has generally been used in twin studies, usually without a check on the equality of the two variances.

In the same paper, Clark mentioned that while there is no significance test for Holzinger's h^2 it is a simple matter to test the statistical significance of the hereditary component by calculating

$$F = \frac{\sigma_{DZ}^2}{\sigma_{MZ}^2} \qquad (11)$$

This is the usual F-test with degrees of freedom N_{DZ} and N_{MZ}. The use of an analysis-of-variance approach was first suggested by Dahlberg (1926). It has much to recommend itself over the h^2 approach since (1) it lends itself readily to a multivariate generalization (Vandenberg, 1965); (2) it allows one to partition the variance further, for instance, between occasions if retesting is used or between several related measures; and (3) it is not readily over-interpreted (being a statistic it is more obvious that the F value refers only to the population from which one has sampled).

After this digression on heritability we are ready to return to the results of twin studies and their interpretation. Table 6 shows the results of a number of studies on heritability of IQ performed in various countries at various

Table 6. **Concordance in intelligence of MZ and DZ twins and heritabilities found in a number of twin studies**

			r_{MZ}	r_{DZ}	h^2
Germany	1930	Von Verschuer	not reported		62
U.S.A.	1932	Day	92	61	80
England	1933	Stocks & Karn	84	65	54
U.S.A.	1937	Newman, Freeman, & Holzinger[a]	90	62	74
Germany	1939	Gottschaldt[b]	not reported		82
Sweden	1952	Wictorin[a]	89	72	61
Sweden	1953	Husen	90	70	67
England	1954	Blewett	76	44	57
U.S.A.	1953	Thurstone, Thurstone, & Strandskov[c]	not reported		65
England	1958	Burt	97	55	93
France	1960	Zazzo	90	60	75
U.S.A.	1962	Vandenberg[c]	74	56	41
U.S.A.	1965	Nichols	87	63	65
England	1966	Huntley	83	66	50
Finland	1966	Partanen, Bruun, & Markkanen[d]	69	42	51
U.S.A.	1968	Schoenfeldt[e]	80	48	62

[a]Average of 2 tests.
[b]Average of 39 tests, recalculated from graph of twin differences.
[c]Average of 6 tests, recalculated from twin differences.
[d]Average of 8 tests.
[e]Data for both sexes combined.

times since 1930. Values of h^2 are reported because this is the index used in many of these studies. The values were fairly consistent across all studies, although they run from a low of 0.41 to a high of 0.93, and there seems to be no discernible correlation with geographical or chronological distribution. Table 6 demonstrates the fact that h^2 is a statistic which will vary from sample to sample and is only characteristic of a given population, not a fixed value for a given trait.

To further underline that fact, Figure 7 shows the fluctuation of h^2 over

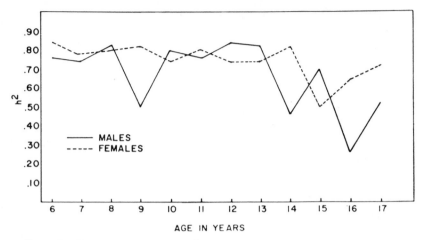

Figure 7. Changes in heritability h^2 for height at different ages for Japanese boys and girls. (After Furusho, 1968.)

time for height. It is generally known that height is largely determined by genetic factors. Environmental factors influence it very little. When children of Japanese who moved to Hawaii were compared with children of relatives who stayed at home, the Hawaiian offspring were found to be only slightly taller, even though there was no difference among their parents (Kaplan, 1954). It has also been reported that children were not permanently stunted as a result of the starvation conditions in Germany during World War II but rather that distributions for height at given ages reached their prewar shape after the conditions improved. Yet the heritability fluctuates rather dramatically. The explanation lies in part in minor differences between members of a twin pair in the exact time when growth occurs; while the final height of a pair may match exactly. they may inch ahead of one another temporarily. When all differences are small to begin with, such discrepancies in timing assume importance out of proportion to their true meaning. If such is the case for height, how much more room can there be for it in intelligence?

Part II: Studies of differences

Effects of inbreeding on intelligence

When two related individuals marry, they may have a child who receives the same gene twice from the same ancestor. The fewer steps there are between the child and the ancestor shared by his two parents, the closer the inbreeding. The coefficient of inbreeding F (Malecot, 1948) is defined as the probability that at a given locus the offspring has the identical gene twice through descent. Figure 8 shows some diagrams with the F value below them.

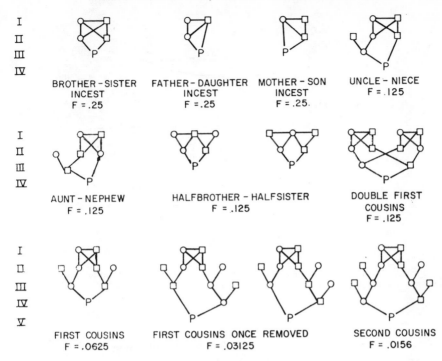

Figure 8. Coefficient of inbreeding for various types of matings.

Inbreeding generally increases the incidence of birth defects because some of the genes for which the offspring is homozygous are apt to be deleterious. For this same reason inbreeding tends to lead to lower IQs. The first report of actual data came from Böök (1957). He reported a "morbid risk" for mental retardation of 4.6 percent in cousin marriages compared with 1.3 percent for controls.

The second report consisted of a comparison of several Wechsler subtest scores of children of cousin marriages and of spouses who were not consanguineous (Cohen, Block, Flum, Kadar, & Goldschmidt, 1963). Figure 9 summarizes the findings of this report.

The largest report on inbreeding has been done by Schull and Neel (1965). In the course of their evaluating the effects of exposure to the radiation produced by the atomic explosions at Nagasaki and Hiroshima the high incidence of marriages between first and second cousins, as well as between first cousins once removed, was noted. They then decided to study the effect of inbreeding as a phenomenon in its own right. Fortunately it was possible to obtain IQ scores on a number of children. A Japanese version of the Wechsler intelligence test (WISC) was used. Results were available for 1954 Hiroshima children distributed as shown in Table 7. It was assumed that there had been

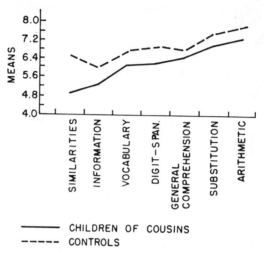

CHILDREN OF COUSINS
----- CONTROLS

Figure 9. Scores of thirty-eight children of first cousins and of forty-seven matched controls on seven subtests of the WAIS. (Cohen, *et al.*, 1963.)

Table 7. Number of children in study of effect of inbreeding on IQ

	First cousins	First cousins once removed	Second cousins	Unrelated parents
	(F = .1250)	(F = .0625)	(F = .0313)	(F = .0000)
Males	249	89	88	538
Females	237	102	100	451

no earlier consanguinity in the family (if this were the case, the F value would of course be higher).

A multivariate regression analysis was performed in which the effects of socioeconomic class and age were evaluated independent of the effect of inbreeding. (This is statistically equivalent to controlling the inbreeding for the effects of age and socioeconomic status.) Socioeconomic class was estimated by the number of tatami floor mats in the parents' houses. This number is known to the police patrol posts in each district.

Table 8 shows the changes in WISC subtest scores per month of age, per unit of socioeconomic score, and per percent inbreeding. The mean age of the children was 8 years 7 months.

Table 8. Comparison of the changes in WISC subtest scores per month of age, per unit of socioeconomic status (SES), and per percent of inbreeding (F)

WISC subtest	Age	SES	F
Information	.0418	.1230	−.0950
Comprehension	.0271	.0832	−.0742
Arithmetic	.0332	.0844	−.0602
Similarities	.0347	.1449	−.1157
Vocabulary	.0480	.1355	−.1155
Picture completion	.0138	.0817	−.0656
Picture arrangement	.0264	.0708	−.1073
Block design	.0234	.0834	−.0598
Object assembly	.0030	.0717	−.0630
Coding	.0264	.0712	−.0531
Mazes	.0080	.0260	−.0651
Verbal score	.1852	.5740	−.4418
Performance score	.0930	.3829	−.3289

Source: Schull & Neel, 1965.

Because the results shown here are a little hard to grasp, Table 9 shows the depression due to a 10 percent increase in inbreeding, expressed as a percentage of the mean score for the children of the unrelated parents ("the outbred mean"). Because the coefficient of inbreeding of children from first

Table 9. Effect of consanguinity on WISC IQ scores

	Depression as percent of outbred mean	
	Boys	Girls
Information	8.1	8.5
Comprehension	6.0	6.1
Arithmetic	5.0	5.1
Similarities	9.7	10.2
Vocabulary	11.2	11.7
Picture completion	5.6	6.2
Picture arrangement	9.3	9.5
Block design	5.3	5.4
Object assembly	5.8	6.3
Coding	4.3	4.6
Mazes	5.3	5.4
Verbal score	8.0	8.0
Performance score	5.1	5.1
Total IQ	7.0	7.1

Source: Schull & Neel, 1965.

Table 10. Expected decreases in WISC subtest scores from the outbred mean for children from incestuous marriages

Subtest	Expected decrease
Information	2.38
Comprehension	1.85
Arithmetic	1.50
Similarity	2.89
Vocabulary	2.89
Picture completion	1.64
Picture arrangement	2.65
Block design	1.49
Object assembly	1.57
Coding	1.33
Mazes	1.63
Verbal score	11.5
Performance score	8.6
Total IQ	20.1

Source: Schull & Neel, 1965.

cousin marriages is 0.125, an increase of 10 percent in F is roughly equal to being born to first cousins rather than to unrelated parents.

This analysis also allows us to predict what the results would be for higher values of F. If F were 0.25, which is the case for offspring of brother-sister or parent-child unions, the values would be as shown in Table 10.

Do we have any information about the IQ distribution of children resulting from incestuous matings? Thus far there have been only two reports. Carter (1967) reported on the offspring of six father-daughter and seven brother-sister unions when the children were 4 to 6 years of age. Three of the children had died of rare autosomal recessive diseases, one was too severely retarded to be tested, and four more were retarded (the IQs of three being 59, 65, and 76). The remaining five fell in the normal range. The second report is from the United States. Adams and Neel (1967) checked the authenticity of the reported incest by extensive blood group testing of eighteen cases. Results of IQ tests were reported by Adams, Davidson, and Cornell (1967). Each mother was carefully matched for age, race, height, intelligence, and socioeconomic background. Table 11 reports the results of the testing for the children born to the incestuous unions and the controls. If we assign an arbitrary value of 20 to the five cases which died early or are untestable, the incestuous children have a mean of 74.7 and the controls of 101.9 ($p < .01$).

It is also notable that 10 out of 18 children from incestuous unions have average IQs. In part this may be due to the fact that genetic segregation results in higher IQs for some children of lower IQ parents as illustrated in Li's

Table 11. IQs of children of incestuous and normal matings

Number	Incest	Controls
1	Died after 2 months	101
2	Died after 15 hours	100
3	Died after 6 hours	104
4	Severely retarded, seizures	107
5	Severely retarded, deaf, blind	93
6	64	100
7	64	133
8	64	109
9	85	103
10	92	81
	(68 at age 3)	
11	92	108
12	98	108
13	110	91
14	112	105
15	113	91
16	114	85
17	118	121
18	119	95

Source: Adams, Davidson, & Cornell, 1967.

diagram (see p. 170), but in part it is also due to the fact that incest is not limited to persons with low intelligence. It is not infrequent among college students or in "better" families.

Effects of single mutant genes on intelligence

We often read statements about our complete ignorance of specific genes controlling intelligence or of their number. Such pronouncements ignore the fact that we already know of a large number of genes that contribute to high intelligence, namely, the normal alleles of the various genes responsible for the many rare diseases which cause mental retardation. In 1964 Anderson listed fifty of these. There are probably very many more, some of which may be distinguished within the next few years since more and more medical centers are continually improving the techniques used in the study of retardates. In fact, Dewey, Barrai, Morton, and Mi (1965) estimated that 126 ± 88 loci were responsible for the various conditions found when the pedigrees of two large groups of retardates were analyzed by computer. Thus far no linkages have been reported between these genes, or with any blood group, or with other marker genes although there are only 23 chromosomes on which they can be located.

Of all these single gene causes of mental deficiency none is better known

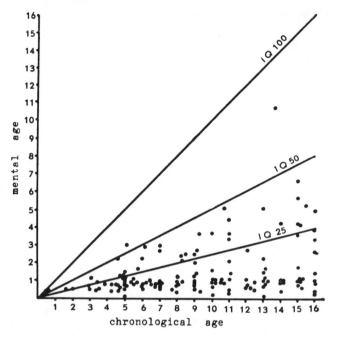

Figure 10. Distribution of IQs in PKU. (Paine, 1957.)

than phenylketonuria (PKU). PKU is an autosomal recessive condition with a frequency estimated at between 1 per 10,000 to 40,000 in most Caucasian populations. It causes severe retardation. Figure 10 shows the distribution of IQs in a study by Paine (1957). It is interesting to note that among Caucasians there is one ethnic group, the Jewish group, in which the incidence of PKU is comparatively low. Among Negro groups the incidence is also much lower, but it is found even among Orientals, at least in Japan, as Figure 11 illustrates. Because untreated patients have IQs from above 80 to less than 20, with most cases falling below 30, few PKU cases have offspring. Therefore, the frequency estimates also provide close estimates of the mutation rate (making the reasonable assumption that a Hardy-Weinberg equilibrium existed before the recently introduced treatment through diet). From the homozygous rate we can also estimate the frequency of carriers or persons who are heterozygous for PKU. Their frequency is half the square root of the rate for homozygous PKU or 1 per 50 to 100. The etiology was first described by Fölling in 1934, and the precise biochemical abnormality was specified by Udenfriend and Cooper (1952). The liver does not produce the enzyme phenylalanine hydroxylase which is needed to convert phenylalanine into tyrosine so that phenylalinine, phenylpyruvic acid, and other products are left to circulate into the

Figure 11. Japanese phenylketonuric girl aged ten years with normal Japanese girl aged eleven. (Shizume & Naruse, 1958.)

blood. While circulating in the blood, these substances apparently interfere with the normal development of the young brain, although the precise manner is not understood. It has been possible to create a condition resembling PKU in macaques so that it may be possible to study in detail the precise biochemical action in the brain.

After the enzyme deficiency was pinpointed, control of the mental retardation by a diet low in phenylalanine was introduced. It appears that conscientious observance of the diet keeps the IQ from deteriorating. After the age of six, or somewhat later, it appears that the child can be taken off the diet. Now that prevention is possible, most states have mass screening programs in which special preparations are put in the newborn infant's diaper and checked for a typical color reaction. Not all high excreters appear to suffer from PKU, however. It is also possible to detect carriers by a loading test. When an unusually high amount of phenylalanine is consumed, a carrier will start "leaking" some of it into his urine.

PKU is a classical example of an inborn error of metabolism, a term introduced by the British physician Garrod (1908) before he had any real solid basis for this brilliant guess. It is also a good example of the one gene-one enzyme concept that used to be popular when the gene was still thought of as a unitary entity. Many of the simple gene types of retardation are caused by such inborn errors of metabolism.

Thus far we have only considered genetic effects on intelligence. Most

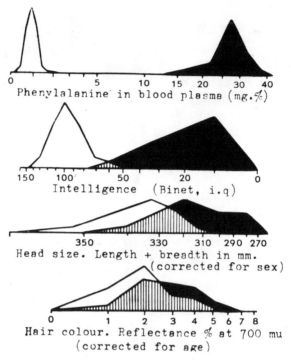

Figure 12. Distribution of phenylalanine level, IQ, head size, and hair color in PKU. (Penrose, 1951.)

likely, all genes have pleiotropic effects, i.e., they affect more than one organ or physiological function. PKU again provides a dramatic example, well illustrated by Figure 12, from a paper by Penrose (1951) which shows that PKU not only leads to lower IQ, but also to dilution of hair color, to smaller size, and, most importantly, to a new balance of metabolic processes. The new balance is not inconsistent with life though it produces a lower form of it as judged by IQ (no typical pathology has been found in the brain or any other organ). Part of the explanation of this multiple-action pattern may be found by considering the metabolic pathways involved. Blocks due to losses of four different enzymes have been found in the phenylalanine metabolism as shown in Figure 13. Two of these can be readily related to the symptoms discussed: block A produces the abnormal urinary excretion and secondarily the IQ impairment as well as a diminution of pigmentation milder but similar to the one which is produced by block D which leads to albinism. (One wonders whether it is merely an accident that these two are metabolically close or whether evolutionary selection in mammals is responsible for such a close association.) Incidentally, the diagram also shows three types of metabolic

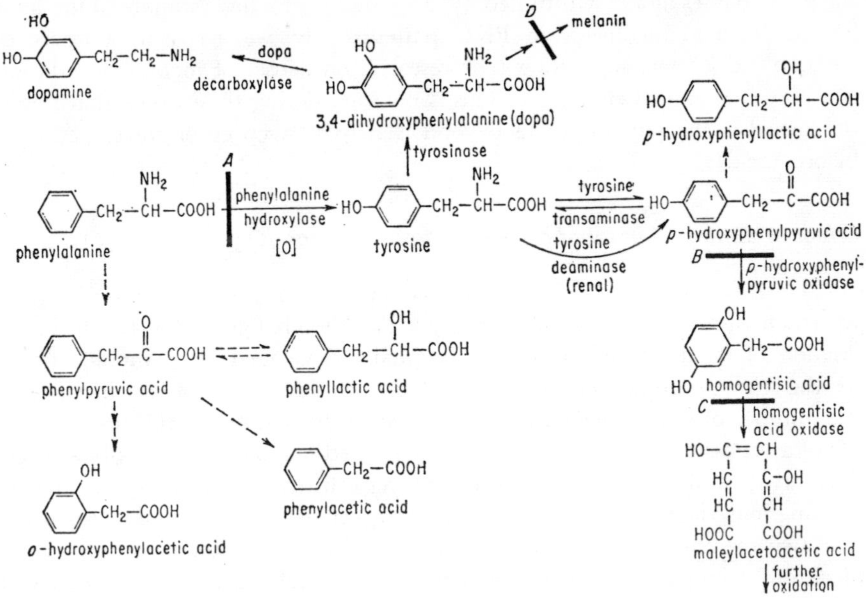

Figure 13. Metabolic pathways of phenylalanine metabolism, showing blocks in phenylketonuria (*A*), tyrosinosis (*B*), alkaptonuria (*C*), and albinism (*D*). Reactions shown by broken arrows are quantitatively unimportant in normal persons but become important in phenylketonuria. (Sutton, 1965.)

aberrations first distinguished by Haldane—an excess, an absence, or an alternate pathway, which lead to increase in another biochemical product.

Economic value of research

About 1 percent of the institutionalized retardates in the United States are PKU cases. The economic importance of the single discovery of easy treatment is clear when one calculates that the frequency mentioned leads to a minimum of 500 new PKU babies each year.

Using a conservative estimate of $10,000 a year as the cost per patient of institutional care (staff, housekeeping, food, etc.) and using a 40-year life expectancy, we arrive at $400,000 to be spent during the life of one such baby or $25,000,000 (at 1970 price levels) on the PKU babies born in any year before treatment became effective. To get the full message, we should also consider the loss of an average lifetime income of $130,000 (also at 1970 price levels) for each of these 500 babies or over $1,500,000 per year for just those 500 potential income taxpayers born each year. The potential monetary gain for the national economy to be expected from preventive measures that would turn severe retardates into taxpayers is thus close to $2,000,000 a year for the PKU babies alone. Multiplied by 20 years to get a low estimate of the total loss in personal income from PKU patients only, we arrive at a figure of $40,000,000 a year, suggesting that research on causes of mental retardation is a very economical enterprise. This is not considering the income that might be earned if the patients lived beyond a 40-year average or started earning before age 21.

Effect of abnormal number of sex chromosomes on IQ

Until recently textbooks stated that man had 2×24 chromosomes. Now we teach that the correct number is 2×23. The change is due to the introduction of an improved technique originally developed by plant geneticists for the study of human chromosomes. This technique led to a vast increase in the number of cells in which the chromosomes are visible. During most of the life of a cell, the chromosomes are tightly packed together so that only a single dark area, the nucleus, can be seen. During cell division (mitosis) this darkly staining material spreads out over most of the cell as the chromosomes separate. The two members of a pair move toward opposite sides so that the two sets of chromosomes at a given moment form two lines facing each other almost as the dancers do in a Virginia reel. That is the exact moment at which colchicine acts, preventing the next move, as if the dancers were frozen at that moment. After the colchicine is added to the cultured cell preparation, the cell division is arrested in this stage, as time goes on, in one cell after another so that when finally some of the preparation is placed on a slide, a large proportion of the cells display their chromosomes nicely spread out. Further improvements in the technique consist of tapping the cover slide gently to increase the spread by squashing the cells and by the addition of a hypotonic salt solution which swells the cells, thus making it possible to pick and choose until some really clear sets are found which are then photographed. The photographs of the individual chromosomes are then cut out and glued down in descending order of size. Such a rearranged photo is called a karyotype. Figure 14 shows a typical one, while Figure 15 shows a schematic representation of the groups that can be recognized by total size, location of the centromere relative to the arms of the chromosome, and whether or not there are satellites (small dotlike appendages). After this technique was adapted to human cell cultures, there were in rapid order a number of discoveries: (1) the correct number of chromosomes, (2) discovery of individuals with one or more extra chromosomes or one missing, (3) precise identification of groups of chromosomes, and (4) discovery of the presence or absence of part of a chromosome, the presence of excess material, and/or abnormally shaped chromosomes.

The first extra chromosome to be discovered was a number 21, an autosome (i.e., not a sex chromosome). This condition, trisomy-21, is found in patients with Down's syndrome, or Mongolism as it used to be called. Later it

Figure 14. Human chromosomes in metaphase. (Photo courtesy of Dr. Leonard Reisman.)

was found that some cases of Down's syndrome only had part of an extra chromosome attached to another chromosome. These are the so-called translocation or partial trisomics. We shall not discuss this aneuploidy (incorrect number of chromosomes) further, but rather turn to cases with an abnormal number of sex chromosomes.

In man the sex chromosomes are called X and Y (see Figure 15). A child with two Xs will become a girl, a child with one X and one Y a boy. Occasionally a child gets only one X. Such a child, designated XO, displays Turner's syndrome and, although phenotypically similar to a normal female, will be infertile, have underdeveloped breasts, and scanty pubic hair. Frequently she will have a peculiarly thick webbed neck. Her scores on the verbal parts of the Wechsler intelligence test are usually about average but on the performance parts, especially the Kohs Blocks, they tend to be low.

There are also boys who show abnormal sexual development. Some of these were found to have two Xs and a Y. This is called Klinefelter's syndrome. Such boys usually have some feminine breast development, sparse pubic hair, and less than average beard growth.

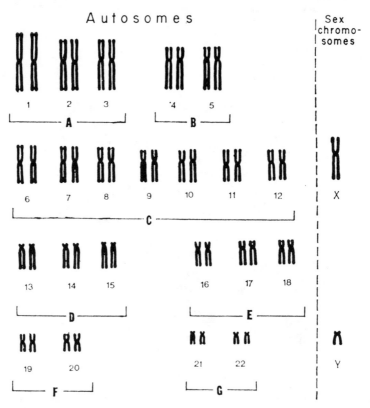

Figure 15. Schematic presentation of human chromosomes arranged in accord with the Denver convention.

The third type of abnormality shows one X and two Ys. Because it was first described by Jacobs, I shall call it Jacobs' syndrome. Such individuals are only mildly retarded, but they are reported to be unusually tall. The first reported cases came from prisons and other institutions, leading to reports of an association between XYY and uncontrolled aggression. Speculation ran rife that XYY predisposes toward crimes of violence, especially after it was found that the murderer of eight Chicago nurses in the summer of 1966 was an XYY. Since that time many XYYs have been found with normal emotional patterns. It has been suggested by Kessler and Moos (1969) that the aggressiveness may be a psychological reaction to the early arrival of adult size coupled with immaturity of sexual characteristics. There are also triple X females (XXX), sometimes mistakenly referred to as superfemales. These girls are usually infertile and somewhat retarded.

A very interesting discovery results from the fact that usually from 20 to 100 cells are karyotyped for one individual. From time to time a person has

Table 12. Average IQ for various combinations and numbers of sex chromosomes followed (in parentheses) by the number of cases

	0	Y	YY	YYY
0		unlikely to occur		
X	100 (60)	100 (∞)	76 (6)	80 (1)
XX	100 (∞)	84 (43)	58 (19)	n.r.
XXX	51 (28)	52 (12)	48 (1)	n.r.
XXXX	40 (3)	35 (22)	n.r.	n.r.
XXXXX	very low (2)	n.r.	n.r.	n.r.

n.r. = not reported
Source: Moor, 1967.

a mixture of two or even three types of cells such as XX/XO, XY/XO, XXY/XY, etc. It is important to note that XX/XY have not been reported.

A summary was reported by L. Moor (1967) of the IQ of hundreds of cases with abnormal chromosome numbers. Table 12 gives the results of her paper, rearranged somewhat, while Figure 16 presents the results in graphic form. Because of the striking similarity, Figure 17, which shows a corresponding decline in ridge counts in fingerprints with added sex chromosomes, was included here. Somewhat similar results would probably obtain for height if they were collected.

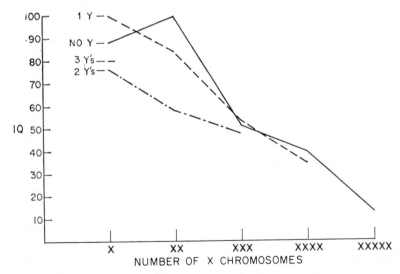

Figure 16. Mean IQ of individuals with abnormal numbers of sex chromosomes. (Moor, 1967.)

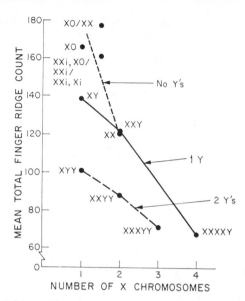

Figure 17. Total finger ridge count related to number of X and Y chromosomes. (X0/XX and XX isochromosomal constitutions are given intermediate X values.)

The similarity suggests that it would be very interesting to collect simultaneously complete information about IQ, fingerprints, and height on all persons with abnormal sex-chromosome numbers so that correlations could be obtained. It would be even more valuable to obtain similar information on parents and sibs so that estimates could be made of the departure from expected levels by comparing parent-offspring regressions of normal and affected children. In fact, it would then be possible to do a regression analysis to estimate quantitatively the depression due to each excess X or Y chromosome.

Summary and prospects for future research on the genetics of intelligence

It should be obvious from the results reported in the second part of this chapter that the emphasis in research is shifting away from exclusive reliance on biometrical studies of degree of similarity and turning to exploitation of cases selected for a common feature that will yield genetic information. That is not to say that studies of twins or of parent-offspring data will be less valuable. What it does seem to indicate is that, as usual, the most productive next step will be a thoughtful combination of the best features of both approaches: probands (persons with a genetic abnormality who come to a clinic or hospital) will have to be studied as before, but similar data will have to be collected on as many of their close relations as is possible. On the other hand, the nature of the data to be collected will have to be determined not solely on the basis of the known genetic anomaly, but also on the basis of all current behavior genetic knowledge—i.e., variables of more fundamental importance than the more or less accidentally chosen one currently used in connection with a particular anomaly must be included. It will be a frustrating experience for many clinicians because often it will not lead to immediate and medically useful results. Thus it will seem to impose an undue burden on the patient's family and on the medical staff. It may also require repeated follow-ups not entirely justified for treatment purposes. Yet such checks would permit collection of information on physical growth and changes in IQ or personality development that are urgently needed for more detailed analyses. Provision of long-term genetic counseling may provide an acceptable and worthwhile reason for such follow-ups.

Starting from the other end, the investigator of twins or of parent-offspring data should by preference include families with known genetic anomalies and not exclude them as too difficult to handle. It will be a difficult task for any single investigator and will require the cooperation of persons of rather different temperaments and of conflicting research goals and methods. Traditionally, the biometrical approach has led to clearly specified research designs and specific deadlines with relatively quick results while the clinical genetic method has to wait until enough cases have presented themselves to allow for a meaningful analysis. The somewhat unplanned nature of this kind of research has tended to lead to changes of diagnostic methods, criteria, and so on that did not permit a preordained design. This situation usually "turned off" statistically trained persons. However, the dilemma is not new. In psychiatry similar problems have existed for over fifty years. Yet it is perhaps not overly optimistic to say that during the decade of the 1960s an amalgamation has started in psychiatric research of the clinical and the statistical approaches, although there are still many places where the battle continues to rage. Surely with better training in research methods, we in behavior genetics can avoid the polarization that has hampered much research in psychiatry and not repeat this unproductive split.

Training is mentioned for a good reason. Most practitioners who have contributed to our present state of knowledge in human genetics have, with a few notable exceptions, had only one of two kinds of training—medical or genetic. Their training has been oriented either toward helping behavior or pure science. Future behavior geneticists should receive equal exposure to the techniques and philosophies of both disciplines.

Actually, genetics per se has from the beginning tried to provide such a synthesis, but today many promising students are repelled by the emphasis on fruitflies, molds, and mice. On the other hand, some of the socially oriented students badly need the discipline of the statistical concepts necessary for an understanding of genetics, as well as the tedious collection of information.

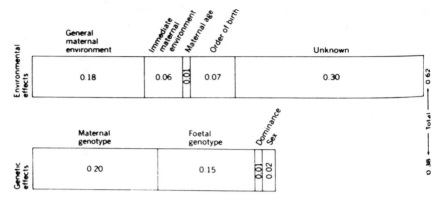

Figure 18. The human birthright. (Penrose, 1961.)

It is a hopeful sign that there are several centers where this kind of well-balanced training in human behavior genetics is provided. It is not unlikely that it will have some influence on the training of both psychologists and medical geneticists. Until the time when such separate labels and training programs will be only quaint memories of former academic divisions, we can only hope to see modest steps toward a full understanding of how genes affect behavior. Only then can a diagram be assembled of the relative proportions of types of variance that contribute, in our present society, to the distribution of IQ.

To spur our ambition and show how far we have to go, I offer as a closing display without further comment Figure 18, copied from Lerner (1968), which illustrates what Penrose (1961) was able to do for the human birthright.

References

Adams, M. S., Davidson, R. T., & Cornell, P. Adoptive risks of the children of incest —a preliminary report. *Child Welfare*, 1967, *46*, 137–142.

———, & Neel, J. V. Children of incest. *Pediatrics*, 1967, *40*, 55–62.

Anderson, V. E. Genetics in mental retardation. In H. A. Stevens & R. Heber (Eds.), *Mental retardation*. Chicago: University of Chicago Press, 1964.

Blewett, D. An experimental study of the inheritance of intelligence. *Journal of Mental Science*, 1954, *100*, 922–933.

Böök, J. A. Genetical investigation in a north Swedish population: The offspring of first-cousin marriages. *Annals of Human Genetics*, 1957, *21*, 191–221.

Burks, B. S. The relative influence of nature and nurture upon mental development; a comparative study of foster parent–foster child resemblance and true parent–true child resemblance. *The 27th Yearbook of the National Society for the Study of Education*, Bloomington, Ill., 1928.

————. A study of identical twins reared apart under differing types of family relationships. In Q. McNemar & M. A. Merrill (Eds.), *Studies in personality*. New York: McGraw-Hill, 1942.

Burt, C. The inheritance of mental ability. *The American Psychologist*, 1958, *13*, 1–15.

————, & Howard, M. The multifactorial theory of inheritance and its application to intelligence. *The British Journal of Statistical Psychology*, 1956, *9*, 95–131.

Carter, C. O. Risk to offspring of incest. *Lancet*, 1967, *1*, 436.

Clark, P. J. The heritability of certain anthropometric characters as ascertained from measurement of twins. *American Journal of Human Genetics*, 1956, *8*, 49–54.

Cohen, T., Block, N., Flum, Y., Kadar, M., & Goldschmidt, E. School attainments in an immigrant village. In E. Goldschmidt (Ed.), *The genetics of migrant and isolate populations*. Baltimore: Williams & Wilkins, 1963.

Conway, J. The inheritance of intelligence and its social implications. *British Journal of Statistical Psychology*, 1958, *11*, 171–190.

Dahlberg, G. *Twin births and twins from a hereditary point of view*. Stockholm: Tiden, 1926.

Day, E. J. The development of language in twins. II. The development of twins: Their resemblances and differences. *Child Development*, 1932, *3*, 298–316.

Dewey, W. J., Barrai, I., Morton, N. E., & Mi, M. P. Recessive genes in severe mental defect. *American Journal of Human Genetics*, 1965, *17*, 237–256.

Elston, R. C., & Gottesman, I. I. The analysis of quantitative inheritance simultaneously from twin and family data. *American Journal of Human Genetics*, 1968, *20*, 512–521.

Erlenmeyer-Kimling, L., & Jarvik, L. F. Genetics and intelligence: A review. *Science*, 1963, *142*, 1477–1479.

Fölling, A. Über Ausscheidung von Phenylbrenztraubensäure in den Harn als Stoffwechselanomalie in Verbindung mit Imbezillität. *Zeitschrift für physiologische Chemie*, 1934, *227*, 169–176.

Furusho, T. On the manifestation of genotypes responsible for stature. *Human Biology*, 1968, *40*, 437–455.

Galton, F. The history of twins as a criterion of the relative powers nature and nurture. *Fraser's Magazine*, 1875, *12*, 566–576.

Gardner, I. C., & Newman, H. H. Mental and physical traits of identical twins reared apart, case xx. *Journal of Heredity*, 1940, *31*, 119–126.

Garrod, A. E. The Croonian lectures on inborn errors of metabolism, I, II, III, IV. *Lancet*, 1908, *2*, 1–7, 73–79, 142–148, 214–220.

Gottschaldt, K. Erbpsychologie der Elementarfunktionen der Begabung. In G. Just (Ed.), *Handbuch der Erbbiologie des Menschen*. (Vol. 5) Berlin: Thieme, 1939.

Hirsch, J. Behavior genetics and individuality understood: Behaviorism's counterfactual dogma blinded the behavioral science to the significance of meiosis. *Science*, 1963, *142*, 1436–1442.

————. Behavior-genetic, or "experimental", analysis: The challenge of science versus the lure of technology. *American Psychologist*, 1967, *22*, 118–130.

Holzinger, K. J. The relative effect of nature and nurture influences on twin differences. *The Journal of Educational Psychology*, 1929, *20*, 241–248.

Honzik, M. P. Developmental studies of parent-child resemblance in intelligence. *Child Development*, 1957, *28*, 215–228.

Huntley, R. M. C. Heritability of intelligence. In J. E. Meade & A. S. Parkes (Eds.), *Genetic and environmental factors in human ability*. Edinburgh: Oliver & Boyd, 1966.

Husen, T. *Tvillingstudier*. Stockholm: Almqvist & Wiksell, 1953.

Jensen, A. R. How much can we boost IQ and scholastic achievement? *Harvard Educational Review*, 1969, *39*, 1–123.

Juel-Nielsen, N. Individual and environment. A psychiatric-psychological investigation of monozygotic twins reared apart. *Psychiatrica Scandinavica*, 1964, *40*, Suppl. *183*, 158–292.

Kaplan, B. A. Environment and human plasticity. *American Anthropologist*, 1954, *56*, 780–800.

Kessler, S., & Moos, R. H. XYY chromosomes: Premature conclusions. *Science*, 1969, *165*, 442.

Lerner, I. M. *Heredity, evolution, and society*. San Francisco: Freeman, 1968.

Lush, J. L. *Animal breeding plans*. Ames: Iowa State University Press, 1945.

Malecot, G. *Les mathématiques de l'hérédité*. Paris: Masson, 1948.

Moor, L. Niveau intellectuel et polygohosomie: confrontation du caryotype et du niveau mental de 374 malades dont le caryotype comporte un excess de chromosomes x ou y (Intellectual level and polyploidy: A comparison of karyotype and intelligence of 374 patients with an extra x or y chromosome). *Revue de Neuropsychiatrie Infantile et d'Hygiene Mentale de l'Enfance*, 1967, *15*, 325–348.

Muller, H. J. Mental traits and heredity. *Journal of Heredity*, 1925, *16*, 433–448.

Newman, H. H., Freeman, F. N., & Holzinger, K. J. *Twins: A study of heredity and environment*. Chicago: University of Chicago Press, 1937.

Nichols, R. C. The inheritance of general and specific ability. *National Merit Scholarship Research Reports*, 1965, *1*, No. 1.

Paine, R. S. The variability in manifestations of untreated patients with phenylketonuria (phenylpyruvic aciduria). *Pediatrics*, 1957, *20*, 290–301.

Partanen, J., Bruun, K., & Markkanen, T. *Inheritance of drinking behavior. A study on intelligence, personality, and use of alcohol of adult twins*. Helsinki: The Finnish Foundation for Alcohol Studies, 1966.

Penrose, L. S. Measurement of pleiotropic effects in phenylketonuria. *Annals of Eugenics*, 1951, *16*, 134–141.

———. Genetics of growth and development of the foetus. In L. S. Penrose (Ed.), *Recent advances in human genetics*. Boston: Little, Brown, 1961.

———. Effects of additive genes at many loci compared with those of a set of alleles at one locus in parent–child and sib correlations. *Annals of Human Genetics*, 1969, *33*, 15–21.

Rosenthal, D. The genetics of intelligence and personality. In D. C. Glass (Ed.), *Genetics*. New York: Rockefeller University Press and Russell Sage Foundation, 1968.

Rothenbuhler, W. C. Behavior genetics of nest cleaning in honey bees. IV. Responses of F_1 and backcross generations to disease-killed brood. *American Zoologist*, 1964, *4*, 111–123.

Saudek, R. A British pair of identical twins reared apart. *Character and Personality*, 1934, *3*, 17–39.

Schoenfeldt, L. F. Hereditary-environmental components of the project TALENT two-day test battery. In *Proceedings of the 16th International Congress of Applied Psychology*, at Amsterdam 1968. Amsterdam: Swets & Zeitlinger, 1969.

Schull, W. J., & Neel, J. V. *The effects of inbreeding on Japanese children*. New York: Harper & Row, 1965.

Shields, J. *Monozygotic twins brought up apart and brought up together*. London: Oxford University Press, 1962.

Skodak, M., & Skeels, H. M. A final follow-up study of one hundred adopted children. *The Journal of Genetic Psychology, Child Behavior, Animal Behavior, and Comparative Psychology*, 1949, *75*, 85–125.

Stephens, F. E., & Thompson, R. B. The case of Millan and George, identical twins reared apart. *Journal of Heredity*, 1943, *34*, 109–114.

Stocks, P., & Karn, M. N. A biometric investigation of twins and their brothers and sisters. *Annals of Eugenics*, 1933, *5*, 1–55.

Sutton, H. E. *An introduction to human genetics*. New York: Holt, Rinehart and Winston, 1965.

Thurstone, T. G., Thurstone, L. L., & Strandskov, H. H. *A psychological study of twins*. Chapel Hill: Psychometric Laboratory, University of North Carolina, 1953.

Udenfriend, S., & Cooper, J. R. The enzymatic conversion of phenylalanine to tyrosine. *Journal of Biological Chemistry*, 1952, *194*, 503–511.

Vandenberg, S. G. The hereditary abilities study: Hereditary components in a psychological test battery. *American Journal of Human Genetics*, 1962, *14*, 220–237.

———. Innate abilities, one or many? *Acta Geneticae Medicae et Gemellogogiae (Roma)*, 1965, *14*, 41–47.

———. The nature and nurture of intelligence. In D. C. Glass (Ed.), *Genetics*. New York: Rockefeller University Press and Russell Sage Foundation, 1968.

———. Further evidence for the pragmatic utility of several abilities rather than one unitary trait of general ability. Unpublished manuscript, University of Colorado, 1970.

———, & Johnson, R. C. Further evidence of the relation between age of separation and similarity in IQ among pairs of separated identical twins. In S. G. Vandenberg (Ed.), *Progress in human behavior genetics*. Baltimore: The Johns Hopkins Press, 1968.

Von Verschuer, O. Erbpsychologische Untersuchungen an Zwillingen. *Zeitschrift für induktive Abstammungs-und Vererbungslehre*, 1930, *54*, 280–285.

Wictorin, M. *Bidrag till Räknefärdighetens Psykologi, en Tvillingsundersökning*. Goteborg: Elanders Boktryckeri, 1952.

Wright, S. Correlation and causation. *The Journal of Agricultural Research*, 1921, *20*, 557–585.

Wright, S. The theory of path coefficients: A reply to Niles's criticism. *Genetics*, 1923, *8*, 239–255.

Yates, N., & Brash, H. An investigation of the physical and mental characteristics of a pair of like twins reared apart from infancy. *Annals of Eugenics*, 1941, *11*, 89–101.

Zazzo, R. *Les jumeaux, le couple et la personne.* (Vol. 2) Paris: Presses Universitaires de France, 1960.

part III **environmental
contributions**

chapter 12

environment and intelligence: a behavioral analysis[1]

SIDNEY W. BIJOU

In 1924 John B. Watson claimed that environmental conditions can override hereditary conditions in determining psychological behavior. Ever since then behaviorists have been classified as "environmentalists." Such a stereotype, like most, does not coincide with the facts. When Watson made this extravagant pronouncement, few behaviorally oriented psychologists subscribed to his view, and since that time many, among them Kantor (1968, 1969) and Skinner (1969) have repeatedly stressed the fallacy of Watson's contention. It is not tenable for a psychologist to take an either/or position on heredity and environment as a determinator of *any* class of psychological behavior. Heredity and environment designate sources of variables that interact with each other continuously. Dobzhansky in his book on *Heredity and the nature of man* (1964) points out, "The genotype and the environment are equally important, because they are indispensable. There is no organism without genes, and any genotype can act only in some environment [p. 63]." And with regard to the determination of

[1]This analysis was generated in large measure from the research supported by the U.S. Office of Education, Division of Research, Bureau of Education for the Handicapped, Project No. 5-0961, Grant No. OEG32-23-6002. The author wishes to thank Charles E. Ferster for reading the manuscript and offering invaluable comments on the contents.

a trait, he says, "No trait can, however, arise unless the heredity of the organism makes it possible, and no heredity operates outside of environment. Furthermore, the issue must be investigated and solved separately for each function, trait, or characteristic that comes under consideration [p. 107]."

Within this frame of reference it is reasonable and important to inquire into the relationship between changes in environmental conditions and variations in a psychological trait. The trait which will be the focus of interest here is intelligence, a concept that is very much in need of reevaluation (Liverant, 1960). Our discussion will include (1) a description of intelligence as a specifiable class of behavior, (2) an analysis of the conditions which are antecedent to intelligent behavior, (3) an analysis of the relationships between changes in environmental conditions and changes in intelligent behavior, and (4) some implications of this analysis of intelligence.

Intelligence and intelligent behavior

What is intelligence? This question, asked literally thousands of times in the psychological literature, generally produces two types of answers. One, and this has been the most frequent, is that intelligence is *something inside the individual which has mediating, causal properties*, mediating between hereditary and environmental variables, on the one hand, and extent of intelligent behavior, on the other. There are many variations on this theme. For example, intelligence is said to be (1) the capacity to perceive relationships, (2) an individual's ability to adapt to the demands of society, (3) brain or neural functioning, (4) speed of learning, (5) capacity and drive, (6) abstract thinking ability, and (7) a theoretical construct that can be changed at any time. The second kind of answer is that intelligence is a class of behavior—a behavioral trait, a behavioral characteristic, or a phenotype. Sometimes the presence or absence of this behavioral trait is based on the observer's subjective impression. A person might comment, "That was an intelligent thing for Johnny to do under the circumstances," He could have said instead, "That was the proper (sensible or moral) thing for him to do under the circumstances," and not have attributed the behavior to intelligence at all. Sometimes level of intelligence, particularly in the psychological literature, is based on performance of an individual on an intelligence test, e.g., "He has an IQ of 75."

We are not concerned here with intelligence conceived as a hypothetical mediating concept. Rather our interest is in intelligence as a class of behavior measured by performance on intelligence tests. We start by asking, What sorts of responses are required on typical intelligence tests designed for children, adolescents, and adults? The obvious answer is that the responses are primarily cognitive in nature. The term cognitive must be defined since it obviously means vastly different things to different people. (See the variety of its meaning in the volumes of the *Annual review of psychology* since 1950.) Our definition of cognitive behavior is straightforward: it means *knowing how to do things and knowing about things* (Skinner, 1968). Let us go into some detail on the nature of these categories.

Knowing how to do things refers to effective behavior, and effective behavior may conveniently be divided into abilities and skills. Abilities, for us, refer to *performances on tests or in natural situations*. We do not use the term abilities, as it is in most psychometric research, to refer to hypothetical constructs which compose an "individual's intellectual or personality structure." The term skills needs no such clarification since this concept has always referred to responses —responses associated with performances identified by their form, intensity, temporal, or durational properties.

From a behavioral point of view, abilities and skills are *operant interactional chains*. In ability chains the emphasis is on the discriminative functions of stimuli; in skill chains the focus is on the differentiated characteristics of responses. Abilities and skills may be grouped into the following categories, listed in an increasing order of complexity: (1) higher-order locomotor and manual dexterity performances, (2) self-care routines, (3) independent social behavior, (4) problem-solving (thinking and reasoning) behavior; and (5) complex verbal behavior.

Knowing about things, the second category of cognitive behavior, has been treated in a myriad of ways. In one way or another, it is generally treated as knowledge connoting something mental or intellectual. This type of conceptualization cannot be integrated in an objective analysis of behavior. One which can is: Knowledge is a description of that class of interactions which have orientational or stimulus control functions (Skinner, 1953, 1957). This class of interactions, like abilities and skills, may also be subdivided into categories and listed as follows in an increasing order of complexity: (1) distinguishing between stimulus dimensional categories (discriminative behavior) and responding to similarities within a stimulus dimension category and differences between categories (abstracting and conceptualizing behavior); (2) responding to representations of environmental stimuli (symbolizing behavior); (3) responding to complex, serially related situations in ways that will produce terminal reinforcers (describing and predicting the contingencies); and (4) responding informationally (mostly intraverbally) about past and present objects and events.

The items on even the best standardized intelligence test cannot be said to be a representative sample of the abilities, skills, and knowledge as described in the two preceding paragraphs. Anastasi's comments on the content of the intelligence tests are pertinent:

> Intelligence tests were first developed in the attempt to measure the individual's general intellectual level. It was hoped that the score on such a test would reflect a sort of over-all average of what the individual could do with different intellectual

tasks. The tasks were chosen so as to sample a wide variety of abilities. In actual practice, however, intelligence tests do not sample all abilities equally. They are overweighted with some abilities and may omit or scarcely touch upon others. Most intelligence tests measure chiefly verbal comprehension, a fact that is illustrated by the very high correlations found between total scores on intelligence tests and scores on vocabulary tests. Arithmetic reasoning and numerical computation are also frequently included [Anastasi, 1964, p. 44].

Among the factors that bias the sample of cognitive items in an intelligence test is the requirement in constructing a test that each item discriminate subjects in the reference population on the basis of age. An item finds a place in the scale if it is passed by a majority of children of that age, failed by practically all children below that age, and passed by almost all the older children. A good intelligence test, therefore, is considered one which yields progressively higher scores for children, ordered on the basis of age. Another requirement in constructing a test is that scores and school achievement have a high correlation. Hence, items which have a low correlation with school attainment tend to be replaced with others which have a high correlation with it. Consequently, many intelligence tests correlate as highly with tests of school achievement as they do with each other. A third condition mitigating against a representative sample of cognitive behaviors in intelligence tests pertains to practical considerations. For example, items that differentiate male and female responses or items that require cumbersome materials tend to be eliminated.

A score on an intelligence test has meaning only when it is compared with the performances of other children of the same age. If, for example, a 5-year-old boy were to score above the mean of the scores of his age peers, say, IQ 120, the prediction would be that his chances for doing well in school are highly favorable. Conversely, if he were to score below the mean of his age group, say, IQ 70, the prognosis for satisfactory school work would be unfavorable. The probabilities for success in school for each child are estimated on the basis of the percentage of children in the standardization group with IQ scores around 120 and around 70 who have, in the past, performed well in school. Since a child's score on an intelligence test has most meaning when it is related to probability of success in school work, or to behaviors which resemble school work, intelligence tests measure *scholastic aptitude*.

Note that the meaning of a test score is based on an *actuarial* prediction: the chances are so many in a hundred that a child with a given score will succeed in school. Since these predictions are quite accurate when based on a well-standardized test, test results provide practical information for selecting students for admission to school and for classifying them.

Another way of saying that actuarial predictions are serviceable for selecting and classifying students is to say that scores on an intelligence test tend, on the average, to be constant, i.e., those who score above the mean of their group on one test, tend to score above the mean on similar subsequent tests, and those who score below the mean tend to do the same on subsequent tests. This generalization does not exclude the possibility that some individuals may make increasingly higher scores, some increasingly lower scores, and some highly variable scores over successive administrations of a test. Sontag, Baker, and Nelson (1958) have shown that the scores of children may fluctuate as much as 25 IQ points over a period of twelve years. Constancy of IQ scores, then, means that on the average individuals tend to make scores on intelligence tests that keep them in their same relative position with respect to the others in the population from which the standardization sample was drawn. It is a concept that applies to groups of individuals.

Antecedents of intelligent behavior

Correlational analysis

We pointed out in the previous section that most psychologists claim that individual differences on intelligence tests are due to differences in mental capacity (or some similar hypothetical variable), which, in turn, is determined by heredity and environment. These relationships are shown diagramatically in Figure 1.

According to this point of view, a person's performance on an intelligence test, as shown in Figure 1 in column 3, is derived from the interactions between the test items (and setting events, e.g., instructions) and the cognitive responses (abilities, skills, and knowledge) in his repertory. Differences in scores among individuals of the same age, or differences in an individual's scores on repetitions of a test, are due to differences in mental capacity, shown in column 2. This middle term is a hypothetical construct, whether it is called a mental capacity or some kind of neural functioning, since its properties are inferred from performance on an intelligence test. Individual differences in mental capacity

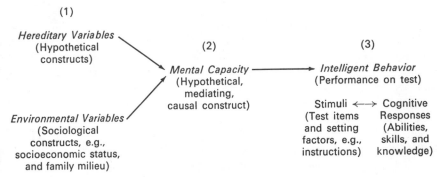

Figure 1. Correlational Analysis of Intelligence.

are attributed to everything that can influence behavior, or to hereditary and environment variables, shown in column 1. Here, hereditary variables are hypothetical constructs (like mental capacity) since they are derived from the test performances of individuals who differ in many ways but primarily in terms of their biological relatedness (e.g., identical twins). It should be noted in passing that this concept of heredity is in sharp contrast to the geneticist's concept of the term, which refers to relationships between manipulable genetic substances in plants and organisms and observable changes in their structured and physiological functioning. Finally, environmental variables in a correlational analysis of intelligence refer to sociological and epidemiological measures, e.g., the socioeconomic status of the family, educational attainment of the parents, and family milieu.

Behavioral analysis

Viewed according to a behavioral analysis, performance on an intelligence test is a function of that segment of a person's interactional history consisting of those opportunities which shape cognitive repertories. A history with a preponderance of such favorable opportunities generates large cognitive repertories; one with a dearth of situations of this order, small repertories. Before describing the kinds of conditions and processes that constitute opportunities for generating cognitive repertories, we must, for a clearer understanding, clarify the relationships between hereditary variables and biological traits, on the one hand, and between hereditary variables and psychological traits, on the other. We begin with Dobzhansky's description of a trait or phenotype:

> The phenotype is the appearance of the individual—the structure and functions of his body. The concept of the phenotype subsumes, of course, not only the external appearance, but also the physiological, normal and pathological, psychological, socio-cultural, and all other characteristics of the individual [Dobzhansky, 1964, p. 58].

Indeed, "psychological, socio-cultural, and all other characteristics of the individual" may be conceptualized as phenotypes, but since they do not evolve in the same way as do the characteristics of the structure and the functions of the body, it is imperative that we make a distinction between biological and psychological phenotypes. Biological phenotypes refer to the anatomical and physiological characteristics of the individual as a function of the continuous interaction between hereditary and environmental variables. On the other hand, psychological phenotypes refer to the behavioral characteristics of the individual, as a function of the biological phenotype interacting with the physical and social variables which make up the effective environment. In other words, the *biological phenotype contributes to the variables of which the psychological phenotype is a function and it contributes to both the response and stimulus components of a psychological reaction.*

The role that the biological phenotype plays in establishing the response component of psychological reaction is related to the fact that the kinds and range of responses an individual can make are determined by his species characteristics; but extreme variations in hereditary and environmental conditions may curtail the range and modify specific response characteristics. Nevertheless, the response possibilities of the individual constitute his "raw" reaction systems which, in the course of his psychological development, assume various topographies and come under the control of various stimulus conditions.

The individual's biological phenotype—his unique physiological functioning and anatomical makeup—provide organismic variables that interact with social and physical stimuli. For example, the absence of certain classes of stimuli from physiological processes, or their occurrence in modified forms, influences the range of responses that are possible, as in an individual's susceptibility to certain diseases, structural malformations, malfunctioning of parts and systems of his body, and cyclical deficiencies. In addition, those parts of the individual's anatomical structure and physiological functioning that are visible to him and to others provide a source of stimuli that acquire all sorts of important functions (Barker, Wright, Meyerson, & Gonick, 1953). In a given culture dark skin, almond-shaped eyes, and spasticity in limbs may be discriminative for indifference, hostility, and pity, so that persons possessing these characteristics are at a disadvantage for the development of behavior repertories—cognitive, social, and otherwise. On the other hand, facial features, body build, and speaking voice, within the norm of a social group, may be discriminative for a high frequency of approach behaviors.

To assist in the understanding and to appreciate fully the intricate and fascinating ways stimuli from the biological phenotype enter into psychological contingencies, we shall review briefly how environmental variables are typically conceptualized in psychology. Sometimes, stimuli are defined in *sociological* terms. It will be recalled that in a correlational analysis of intelligence environmental variables were defined as socioeconomic status, educational attainment, family milieu, and the like. Relationships between these measures and intelligence are usually expressed in the following form: "On the average, children from high socioeconomic families have higher intelligence test performances than children of comparable age from low socioeconomic families." Sometimes, environmental variables are defined in terms of their *physical* properties, despite the fact that it is often difficult, if not impossible, to make such measurements because of the subtleties involved in the stimulus structure as, for example, in facial expressions, or because of inaccessibility, as a pain in the stomach. In this connection it is interesting to note that Watson (1930) defined stimuli exclusively in terms of their physical properties. "So we see that the organism is constantly assailed by stimuli—which come through the eye, the ear, the nose, and the mouth—the so-called objects of our environment; at the same time, the inside of our body is likewise assailed at every moment by stimuli arising from changes in the tissue themselves [p. 12]." Sometimes environmental variables are defined in terms of their *functional* properties, i.e., the ways in which they change the behavior of an individual. According to this point of view, environmental variables may have stimulus functions (e.g., reinforcing and discriminating properties), setting factor functions (e.g., satiation and deprivation), or both.

In the analysis presented here environmental events are defined in terms of *both* their physical and functional properties. In the first set of measurement operations (actual or potential), the properties of stimuli are defined independently of the behavior of the organism studied; in the second, exclusively in relation to the behavior of the organism who is the subject for analysis. There is no stimulus without a response and there is no response without a stimulus: the stimulus-response relationship is the *basic unit* of analysis. Hence, instead of asking how much an individual is influenced by his environment, we would ask which stimuli have influenced an individual's behavior in the past and which stimuli are influencing his behavior now. Likewise, one of the classical questions in developmental psychology, "Is the individual at the mercy of his environment or is he master of it?" must be discarded because it is based on an inappropriate analogy. The environment is not something "out there" that challenges the individual to engage in an encounter, nor is the individual constituted so that he sits back and decides whether or not he wishes to accept the challenge of the environment. Instead, stimulus events that make up the individual's effective environment are constantly interacting with the response events that make up the behavioral structure of the organism. As these interactions occur, the behavior of the individual is altered, sometimes slowly, sometimes rapidly, sometimes in large units, and sometimes in small units. While this is happening, the environment is also being altered, sometimes in obvious ways and sometimes in subtle ways, sometimes immediately, and sometimes remotely. In other words, as a consequence of continuous interaction, new stimulus and response functions are acquired and old ones are eliminated or maintained. When the changes in the stimulus, response, setting events, and their contingent relationships are progressive, we refer to them as developmental (Bijou & Baer, 1961).

In Watson's zeal to eliminate everything "mental" from psychology, he overlooked the necessity for defining stimuli in terms of both their physical and functional dimensions. By viewing stimuli only in terms of their physical properties, he was left without an objective way of accounting for the influence of past interactions on current interactions. Consequently, he had no way of showing, in what he thought was an objective frame of reference, what a set of physically defined stimuli "means" to the individual. In contrast, Kantor has, since 1933, been stressing the systematic advantages of defining stimuli in terms of their functional properties.

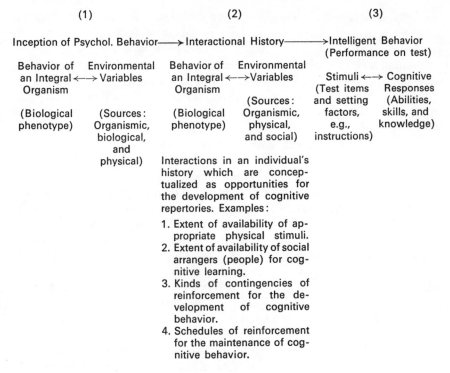

Figure 2. Behavioral Analysis of Intelligence.

A fitting summary of this discussion of the differential role of heredity in establishing biological and psychological characteristics seems to be: If we fail to distinguish between the antecedents of biological and psychological phenotypes, we are then accepting a reductionistic point of view and are in substantial agreement with Gesell that the laws of developmental psychology and of developmental embryology are one and the same (1954). Recent history has shown that Gesell's theory of human development has not been productive in advancing the field.

Let us return to a behavioral analysis of intelligence. The general formulation is outlined in Figure 2. The interactions between the test materials and the responses are represented by a test score and are a function of that segment of a person's history which consists of opportunities for the development of cognitive repertories. Such opportunities for the development of all repertories may be said to begin before birth (Bijou & Baer, 1965). In column 1 we show that the psychological responses which formed and/or came under environmental control during uterine development are a function of the interaction between the biological phenotype and environmental variables—physical, organismic, and biological (the action of surrounding substances). After birth the behavioral repertories developed are a function of the biological phenotype (at a given time) in interaction with environmental stimuli—physical, organismic, and social. Included in the biological phenotype are, of course, the potentialities for future biological growth (e.g., changes in the biological phenotype in relation to nutritional intake). Interactions after birth are shown in column 2. Also in column 2 are four examples of conditions constituting opportunities for the development of cognitive repertories. The first example listed is the extent of *appropriate physical stimuli* available for interaction. An ample supply of the physical stimuli for cognitive development would define a favorable condition; a meager supply of stimuli, a hampering situation. Degree of availability of physical stimuli does not in itself assure the development of high or low cognitive repertories. There need to be, in addition, people who manage these physical stimuli in contingent relationships. This leads to the second example, the *availability of social arrangers—people who arrange* not only the physical stimuli but all others as well. Situations enhancing the opportunities for cognitive development are those in which people, planfully or unknowingly, program contingencies to shape responses and to bring responses under stimulus control (as is necessary in teaching abstractions, conceptualizations, symbolizations, etc.). Hampering situations are those having a paucity of people who, for one reason or another (e.g., personal maladjustment, economic poverty, marital discord, etc.), do not program in ways that enhance cognitive development. The third example refers to the *kinds of reinforcers* in effect in cognitive learning situations. Favorable conditions include those in which parents and teachers mainly use positive reinforcing contingencies; unfavorable situations are those in which the adults in charge tend to use aversive, random, or neutral stimulus contingencies. A fourth and final example refers to the *schedules of reinforcement* which characterize the individual's history. Enhancing opportunities are defined by a high saturation of people who schedule contingencies of reinforcement in ways which maintain and extend the cognitive repertories acquired. In contrast, hampering opportunities refer to situations having parents, siblings, and others who, for one reason or another, provide contingencies of reinforcement on schedules which do not support the cognitive repertories acquired.

Developmental plasticity of intelligent behavior

We shall now examine the changes in intelligent behavior that may occur for an individual with a given set of biological characteristics. We may pose the question this way: What is the diversity of a *psychological phenotype*, such as intelligent behavior, for an individual with a given biological phenotype? Dobzhansky (1950) and Hirsch (1971) would cast the question in terms of norms of reaction, and Anastasi (1948) as range of response variations.

An adequate and acceptable answer to the question would take into

account findings on biologically related siblings reared in different environments (Jones, 1946). In general, there is a modest difference in the intelligence
test scores of twins reared apart, and the more divergent the environments,
the greater the difference. These data should be used cautiously in generalizing
about the range and maximum effects of environmental variables because of
the conditions under which they were gathered. Such a statement as the following is certainly unwarranted: "While environmental factors are important (as
we shall see later) in raising or lowering a child's level of intellectual performance, these studies demonstrate that they only do so within limits set by heredity
[Mussen, Conger, & Kagan, 1963, p. 52]."

One weakness of practically all such studies is that the children were not
separated until after a period of living together. The interactions shared by
both in their first phase of development could have had significant effects on
their later development. A second weakness is that the differences in the
environmental conditions were not, for the most part, extreme. The homes
were only in different areas of the same country. Finally, in all of these studies,
home environments were defined sociologically rather than functionally, e.g.,
in terms of father's occupation and educational attainment of parents rather
than in terms of observable facilitating or hampering opportunities for cognitive
development. A functionally analytic study comparing the cognitive development of twins reared apart would probably produce findings very much in
contrast to the data published to date.

A second source of data on the developmental plasticity of intelligent
behavior is the studies of intelligence test scores of young children living in
divergent socioeconomic environments. One group of studies in this category
show that children living under physical and social poverty conditions in
orphanages and in institutions for the delinquent and retarded show a gradual
decline in intelligence test performance. Another group of investigators indicate
that children living in stimulating environments tend to increase their intelligence test performance with age. Children who attend university nursery
schools (Wellman, 1945), who live in foster homes that are socioeconomically
higher than those of their natural parents (Skeels, 1965), and who attend
compensatory educational programs, all show increases in their test performances. With respect to the last group, Jensen (1969) says, "The magnitude of IQ
and scholastic achievement gains resulting from enrichment and cognitive
stimulation programs authentically range between about 5 and 20 points for
IQs, and between about one-half to two standard deviations for specific
achievement measures (reading, arithmetic, spelling, etc.) [p. 97]." Follow-up
studies show that some of the children maintained the gains made; some, part
of the gains made; and some reverted to their previous level of performance.

As with the studies of twins reared apart, the results from investigations
of the relationships between intelligence test performance and increases in
physical and social "richness" are modest. Yet one should be cautious in

drawing a conclusion, such as (Kendler, 1963), "This means simply that there seem to be definite limits beyond which no amount of stimulation or training can produce any additional improvement [p. 622]." There is no question that there are limits to the development of any class of psychological repertoires, including intelligence, but we cannot tell in advance what these limits are. To speculate that the data from current studies, the correlation between physical and cultural differences, and IQ changes represent the asymptote of development from environmental variables is to assume that the manipulations made in these studies were sufficiently extreme and highly sophisticated. In actuality, the technologies of preschool teaching, child-rearing practices, and early remediation are in their primitive states and, among other things, are still analyzed in procedural rather than functional terms. Moreover, preventative and compensatory programs for young children have just begun to be extended, as they should be, over a larger segment of the child's life (e.g., programs for mothers). In addition, they have just begun to be incorporated in schools so as to maintain the gains made (e.g., Follow-Through Program). The only reasonable conclusion that can be drawn about the results to date is that they are a function of the crude interventional programs in current use. Conclusions suggesting that we have attained the limits of change that are possible from environmental engineering can only serve to discourage investigators from further improving their experimental designs and their instructional technologies.

One final point and an important one. In discussing the relationships between changes in environmental variables and intelligence there has been a strong tendency for investigators to relate environmental manipulations to variations in test scores, mostly in the form of changes in IQs. With this kind of focus, and it is understandable because of the high interest in what lies behind measured intelligence, the question of the plasticity of behavior— the relationship between observable changes in environmental conditions and intelligent behavior—is given only cursory consideration. To avoid perpetuation of this tendency, there should be an evaluation of the effects of environmental manipulations in terms of changes in test scores *as well as* in terms of actual changes in cognitive repertoires. The second type of evaluation would become less and less formidable as interventional programs become more and more systematic and based on sound behavioral principles. Be that as it may, one would expect that when both tests and actual repertoires are assessed, the two measures would in general have a correlation (though probably not as high as the correlations between tests and school achievement) and the measures of actual behavioral gains would be higher than the test scores. The reasons behind this speculation are, first, as has been previously noted, that intelligence tests are not a representative sample of cognitive repertoires when defined as an individual's abilities, skills, and knowledge; and, second, that there is a time lag between gains in actual cognitive repertoires and increases in test scores.

This lag is because of the relationship between the amount of increase in cognitive repertories necessary to be demonstrated in an increase in test score. The plea here, then, is for assessing the effects of environmental manipulations as they relate to changes in behavioral repertories and to changes in test scores. There will be more on this topic in the next section which deals with the implications of a behavioral analysis of intelligence for individual diagnostic evaluations.

Implications of a behavioral analysis of intelligence

Theoretical

The theoretical implications of a behavioral analysis of intelligence are many. Necessarily, we must limit ourselves to a discussion of the relationship between normal and deviant development. Like all phenomena in psychology, and in the natural sciences for that matter, variations in the rates of change—retarded, normal, and accelerated—are on a continuum. The degree of retarded intelligence evolves from the diversity of restrictions on the development of cognitive repertories; in like manner, the degree of accelerated intelligence derives from the variety of specifiable favorable conditions for the development of these repertories, and the degree of normal intelligence results from conditions ranging between the two. The behavioral processes in the development of intelligence are the same; only the strengths, frequencies, and patterns of frequencies of the conditions vary. Hence, there is no need for separate theories to explain normal, retarded, and accelerated intelligence. A general theory of behavior will eventually account for development at all three rates.

A comprehensive behavioral analysis of retarded development has been presented earlier (Bijou, 1966); therefore, only a brief resume is necessary here. We have stated that the retarded child is analyzed as one who has meager repertories of cognitive behavior as a consequence of restrictions in his interactional history. Among the limiting conditions are: (1) mild to gross abnormal anatomical structure and physiological functioning; (2) inadequate programming of reinforcement and discrimination stimuli; (3) consequences of strong and frequent contingent aversive stimulation; (4) reinforcement of aversive behavior; and (5) the weakening of behavior through the loss of stimulus control, extinction, random reinforcement, time out from positive reinforcement, and the like.

On the other hand, the intellectually accelerated child is analyzed as one with a history characterized by a preponderance of conditions which foster the development of extensive repertories of cognitive behavior. Among these conditions are: (1) normal to superior anatomical structure and physiological functioning; (2) availability of stimuli for cognitive learning; and (3) high saturation of interactions with parents, teachers, and others who place a high value on cognitive achievement—(a) those who arrange contingencies for effective cognitive learning and (b) those who provide schedules of positive reinforcement which maintain the cognitive behaviors acquired. This analysis of accelerated development is supported in general by findings from many studies but particularly by the extensive longitudinal investigations by Terman and his associates on the careers of children who scored extremely high on intelligence tests (1925, 1947, 1959). The children came from all kinds of homes, but the majority were the offspring of intellectually superior parents. Below are a few of their findings:

> Nearly a third of the fathers as of 1922 were in professional occupations, and less than 7 percent in semiskilled or unskilled work. The mean amount of schooling of both fathers and mothers was approximately 12 grades, or about four grades more than the average person of their generation in the United States. A third of the fathers and 15.5 percent of the mothers had graduated from college [1959, pp. 5–6]. . . . The number of books in the parents' homes, as estimated by the field assistants, ranged from almost none to 6,000, with one home out of six having 500 or more [1959, p. 6]. . . . The results showed that the gifted children as a group exceeded the best standards at that time for American-born children in growth status as indicated by both height and weight, and that they were also above the established norms for unselected children in California [1959, p. 6]. . . . The incidence of physical defects and abnormal conditions of almost every kind was below that usually reported by school physicians in the best medical surveys of school populations in the United States [1959, pp. 7–8]. . . . Nearly half of the children learned to read before starting to school; 20 percent did so before the age of five years and 6 percent before four years [1959, p. 8]. . . . The records revealed that the average gifted child was reading about 10 books in two months by age 7, and 15 books by age 11, with little increase thereafter. Few of the control group read books below 8 years, and after 8 years the average number read in two months was less than half that of the gifted. Classification of the books read showed the gifted children reading over a considerably wider range than the control children [1959, p. 11].

Practical

The practical implications of a behavioral analysis of intelligence are most closely tied in with curriculum construction and teaching methods. The analysis of conditions producing variations in cognitive repertoires in an individual may be used as a basis for designing productive educational and training programs. Of course, one may subscribe to a behavioral analysis of intelligence but prefer to engineer an educational or training environment on the basis of cognitive theory or on an eclectic approach. It is a fair assumption, however, that educational technology would be advanced considerably if the frame of reference for the analysis of intelligence and for educational engineering were the same. The following studies exemplify practical applications of a behavioral analysis as applied to both intelligence and educational technology.

One practical implication pertains to remedial education and an example is the extended study at the Rainier School, Buckley, Washington, in which institutionalized, educable, retarded children were taught tool academic subjects (Bijou, Birnbrauer, Kidder, & Tague, 1966). The program included a contrived motivational system, programmed sequences of the beginnings of reading, writing, and arithmetic, and teaching procedures carefully designed to strengthen and maintain academic behaviors, and to weaken "problem" behaviors which interfere with academic learning. Another example is the rehabilitation work of Meyerson, Kerr, and Michael (1967). These investigators trained retarded and emotionally disturbed children in locomotion, dexterity, and self-care skills. For the most part, the steps in training were programmed on the basis of applying differential reinforcement to successive approximations to the criterion task. Still another example is the work with underprivileged preschool children by Reynolds and Risley (1968). These investigators have used behavioral principles not only to program materials and procedures for the development of preschool skills and abilities, but also to train mothers to use educational techniques that support the learning that their children have acquired in school.

A second practical implication of a behavior analysis of intelligence and instruction relates to innovations in primary education of normal children. Practically all children who are capable of going to school are capable of learning to read, write, and do arithmetic. Furthermore, there is no reason why they cannot engage in these activities with enjoyment. In other words, children who qualify for school attendance have all the biological and behavioral equipment they need to learn the tool academic subjects and to derive pleasure from learning them. There is a major prior condition: *an effective learning environment*—one which individualizes instruction so that each child, with his unique developmental history, can respond to, and can receive feedback from, each step in the learning processes. Such an environment also provides contingencies for the strengthening of prerequisite behaviors (e.g., paying attention and effective study behavior) and for the weakening of behaviors which are competitive with academic advancement (e.g., gazing out of the window, interfering with other children, etc.). Only in such an environment is it possible to institute simple record-keeping procedures which inform the teacher on an hour-by-hour and on a day-to-day basis how each child is performing. Research and demonstration projects contributing to innovation in normal, early education are concentrating on programming the beginnings of reading, writing, and arithmetic (Glaser, 1967), the development of teaching techniques (Hall, Lund, & Jackson, 1968), and procedures for efficient classroom management (Thomas, Becker, & Armstrong, 1968).

The third implication concerns educational innovations for the accelerated child. If high academic achievement and stand-out performances in the arts and sciences are indeed the consequences of interactional histories, then it is important to explore the conditions that constitute these kinds of histories and incorporate them in educational programs. Although it is at present a difficult task to design effective programs in problem-solving behavior, self-management, music composition, and the like, the strategy is, in truth, straightforward: first, specify in observable terms the terminal behavior desired; second, prepare programs that bridge the gap between a child's present and available repertories and the desired terminal behavior; and, third, utilize judiciously individually meaningful contingencies (Skinner, 1968).

The final implication of a behavior analysis of intelligence and instruction relates to educational diagnosis. Educational diagnoses based on individual tests of intelligence, such as the Stanford-Binet and the Wechsler-Bellevue, have made only an illusory contribution to remedial education (Anastasi, 1954). Individual tests of intelligence were never meant to serve as instruments for individual educational diagnosis; they were designed, as we stated earlier, to correlate high with academic achievement. The practice of presenting the teacher with a child's "mental" profile based on the variability of his test performance has not helped the teacher to help the child. To tell the teacher that Johnny has a high score in vocabulary and a low one in rote memory for numbers is of limited value because these are not subjects which typically make up her curriculum. Even if they were, the teacher would still have the task of arranging conditions so that learning in the areas of deficiency would integrate with instruction in reading, writing, and arithmetic. In other words, diagnostic procedures founded on individual intelligence tests, or on even "specialized" diagnostic tests (e.g., tests for the detection of brain damage), do not produce the kinds of information that relate meaningfully to most present-day teaching or treatment programs. These diagnostic practices are evidently based on the assumption that the teacher or clinician has at his disposal several well-developed remedial programs and that the information from the diagnostic evaluation of a child would indicate which program is most appropriate for him. This is not the case.

Obviously, some other kind of individual diagnostic procedure is needed, notably one which provides information about the *exact status* of a child's cognitive repertories. These inventories should indicate to the teacher or remedial specialist the starting points in the educational or treatment programs. If they are derived from pre- and posttests of programs in actual use, they should also point out specific areas in need of special attention. [Caldwell (1967) has devised such an inventory for preacademic education.] This new type of diagnostic test should also indicate the kinds of contingencies of reinforcement that are likely to be suitable for the child. Knowing the effective contingencies for a child would be essential particularly for the initial phase of training and also would serve as a basis for the development of reinforcers intrinsic to school achievement and associated tasks.

Perhaps we should conclude our discussion of the implications for diagnostic practices by pointing out that diagnostic tests in the form of inventories do provide information for educational planning and treatment, normal and remedial. They are most valuable when they are derived from actual instructional programs. Psychometric test results serve as a basis for placing children in academic groups and are also helpful in establishing terminal academic behaviors. For example, the target behavior for a 9-year-old boy who is referred for remedial reading might be set at the achievement expected of a child beginning in the fourth grade as determined by the intelligence and reading achievement scores of children in beginning the fourth grade in the school which the boy will attend upon completion of the remedial program.

Summary

The concept of intelligence is given an important role in contemporary psychology. One reason for its popularity is undoubtedly the fact that measurement psychologists have devised tests of intelligence that have a high correlation with school achievement. But there have been problems in integrating the concept of intelligence, which has been based primarily on correlational analyses, with the main body of knowledge in psychology founded mostly on experimental analyses. The author, rather than follow the suggestion for rapprochement suggested by Cronbach (1957), in this chapter has offered the formulation in which intelligence is analyzed in terms of an experimental analysis of behavior, an approach which is consistent with the writings of Anastasi (1948) and Humphreys (1971).

At the outset, the issue of whether heredity is more important than environment in determining an individual's level of intelligence is set aside as irrelevant in light of current knowledge of genetics and an experimental analysis of behavior. Intelligence is assumed to be a class of observable cognitive behavior— a behavioral trait, or a psychological phenotype. The antecedents of this class of behavior are formed in that segment of an individual's interactional history that sets the occasions for the development of abilities, skills, and knowledge. Organismic, social, and physical conditions participate in the development of these behaviors from the time the individual begins life as an integral biological unit. Research on the range of changes observed in cognitive repertories as a function of increases in environmental stimulation suggests that there are positive covariations of rather modest magnitudes. The question of whether the studies reported to date may be taken as estimates of maximum change must be left unanswered for the time being because the designs of most of the studies have certain deficiencies and because the so-called intervention techniques used have been primitive, at least from a technological point of view. A theoretical implication of this analysis of intelligence pertains to the ease with which it allows one to integrate, in objective terms, the concepts of retarded, accelerated, and normal development. Practical implications, provided the same analysis is applied to the educational process, include increased effectiveness in educating normal and deviant children. Some examples of practical applications are cited from the literature.

References

Anastasi, A. The nature of psychological traits. *Psychological Review*, 1948, *55*, 127–138.

———. *Psychological testing*. New York: Macmillan, 1954.

———. *Fields of applied psychology*. New York: McGraw-Hill, 1964.

Barker, R. G., Wright, B. A., Myerson, L., & Gonick, M. R. Adjustment to physical handicap and illness: A survey of the social psychology of physique and disability. *Social Science Research Council Bulletin*, 1953, No. 55 (Rev.).

Bijou, S. W. Functional analysis of retarded development. In N. Ellis (Ed.), *International review of research in mental retardation*. Vol. 1. New York: Academic Press, 1966.

———, & Baer, D. M. *Child development: A systematic and empirical theory*. Vol. 1. New York: Appleton-Century-Crofts, 1961.

———, ———. *Child development: Universal stage of infancy*. Vol. 2. New York: Appleton-Century-Crofts, 1965.

———, Birnbrauer, J. S., Kidder, J. D., & Tague, C. Programmed instruction as an approach to teaching of reading, writing, and arithmetic to retarded children. *Psychological Record*, 1966, *16*, 505–522.

Caldwell, B. *The preschool inventory*. Princeton, N.J.: Educational Testing Service, 1967.

Cronbach, L. J. The two disciplines of scientific psychology. *American Psychologist*, 1957, *12*, 671–684.

Dobzhansky, T. Heredity, environment, and evolution. *Science*, 1950, *111*, 161–166.

———. *Heredity and the nature of man*. New York: New American Library, 1964.

Gesell, A. The ontogenesis of infant behavior. In L. Carmichael (Ed.), *Manual of child psychology*. (2nd ed.) New York: Wiley, 1954.

Glaser, R. *Adapting the elementary school curriculum to individual performance*. Reprint 26, Learning R&D Center. Pittsburgh: University of Pittsburgh, 1967.

Hall, R. V., Lund, D., & Jackson, D. Effects of teacher attention on study behavior. *Journal of Applied Behavior Analysis*, 1968, *1*, 1–12.

Hirsch, J. Behavior-genetic analysis and its biosocial consequences. In R. Cancro (Ed.), *Intelligence: Genetic and environmental influences*. New York: Grune & Stratton, 1971.

Humphreys, L. G. Theory of intelligence. In R. Cancro (Ed.), *Intelligence: Genetic and environmental influences*. New York: Grune & Stratton, 1971.

Jensen, A. R. How much can we boost IQ and scholastic achievement? *Harvard Educational Review*, 1969, *39*, 1–123.

Jones, H. E. Environmental influence on mental development. In L. Carmichael (Ed.), *Manual of child psychology*. New York: Wiley, 1946.

Kantor, J. R. In defense of stimulus-response psychology. *Psychological Review*, 1933, *40*, 324–336.

———. Evolution and the science of psychology. *The Psychological Record*, 1959, *9*, 131–142.

Kendler, H. H. *Basic psychology*. New York: Appleton-Century-Crofts, 1963.

Liverant, S. Intelligence: A concept in need of re-examination. *Journal of Consulting Psychology*, 1960, *24*, 101–110.

Meyerson, L., Kerr, N., & Michael, J. L. Behavior modification in rehabilitation. In S. W. Bijou and D. M. Baer (Eds.), *Child development: Readings in experimental analysis*. New York: Appleton-Century-Crofts, 1967.

Mussen, P. E., Conger, J. J., & Kagan, J. *Child development and personality*. (2nd ed.) New York: Harper & Row, 1963.

Reynolds, N. J., & Risley, T. R. The role of social and material reinforcers in increasing talking of a disadvantaged preschool child. *Journal of Applied Behavior Analysis*, 1968, *1*, 253–262.

Skeels, H. M. Effects of adoption on children from institutions. *Children*, 1965, *12*, 33–34.

Skinner, B. F. *Science and human behavior*. New York: Macmillan, 1953.

———. *Verbal behavior*. New York: Appleton-Century-Crofts, 1957.

———. *The technology of teaching*. New York: Appleton-Century-Crofts, 1968.

———. *Contingencies of reinforcement: A theoretical analysis*. New York: Appleton-Century-Crofts, 1969.

Sontag, L. W., Baker, C. T., & Nelson, V. L. Mental growth and personality development: A longitudinal study. *Monograph of the Society for Research in Child Development*, 1958, *23*, No. 2.

Terman, L. M. *Genetic studies of genius*. Vol. I. Stanford, Calif.: Stanford University Press, 1925.

———, & Oden, M. H. *The gifted child grows up*. Vol. IV. Stanford, Calif.: Stanford University Press, 1947.

———, ———. *The gifted group at middle life*. Vol. V. Stanford, Calif.: Stanford University Press, 1959.

Thomas, D. R., Becker, W. C., & Armstrong, M. Production and elimination of disruptive classroom behavior by systematically varying teacher's behavior. *Journal of Applied Behavior Analysis*, 1968, *1*, 35–45.

Watson, J. B. *Behaviorism*. Chicago: University of Chicago Press, 1930.

Wellman, B. IQ changes of preschool and nonpreschool groups during the preschool years: A summary of the literature. *Journal of Psychology*, 1945, *20*, 347–368.

chapter 13

methodological problems and pseudoissues in the nature-nurture controversy

EDMUND W. GORDON

When I was invited to participate in the conference that resulted in this volume, I had mixed reactions. I have strong ties to the School of Education at the University of Illinois and the invitation was communicated through my friend Mort Weir, who in connection with my work with Head Start had proved very helpful to me. I could hardly say no. Yet the topic troubled me. As I indicated when invited, I have nothing new to add on the subject of hereditary and environmental contributions to intelligence, and I must add that I feel that those people who still need to hear my position repeated are probably not going to be influenced by me anyway.

I should also make it clear that I am a strongly biased witness. I am a *humanist*, I am an *educator*, and I am a *twentieth-century black man*. These characteristics make me phenotypically and genotypically different from at least most of the other conference participants. They also strongly influence the nature of my beliefs and commitments. They, added to the knowledge that I have in the field, lead me to reach certain conclusions concerning this old controversy which has been given new life by the publication of Arthur Jensen's (1969) article on compensatory education, minority group children, and the hereditary aspects of intelligence.

240

An article dealing with these issues at this time should be comprehensive and inclusive of all the evidence. There is ample reason to assert that Jensen's work is not. The political implications alone of this failure to be inclusive are frightening at this stage of our political and social development. However, the political aspects of the controversy are not my primary concern at this point. There are serious substantive problems involved in the questions that Jensen raises and the answers that he offers.

Having concluded that compensatory education and other attempts to improve the intellectual functioning of poor and minority group youngsters have been to no avail, Jensen uses this conclusion to get into a discussion of some issues with which he is preoccupied. These can be summarized in three areas: (1) determination of the relative contributions of genetic and environmental factors to the development of intellectual function, (2) possible inherent differences between racial groups in the quality and character of intellectual capacity, and (3) the possibility that these differences have important implications for the design of learning experiences and may provide a basis for explaining the failure of the schools to educate certain children.

The first of these issues, concerning the relative influences of heredity and environment on the development of intelligence, simply cannot be resolved. This, in part, accounts for the fact that it continues to be debated. The fact is that the technology of human genetic research does not permit definitive study of the genetic constitution of human organisms. We have only in 1969 isolated a single gene—and that in a bacterium. If such technology were available, our attitudes toward research utilizing human subjects would not permit it. They would at least preclude the inclusion of high-status groups in experimental, comparative studies. In addition, the economic, political, and military commitments of the society obviously do not permit the kinds of experimentation with controlled and improved environmental conditions necessary to the conduct of such studies.

Even if the question could be answered and even if it were definitively determined that a specific portion or aspect of human behavior and potential were fixed by heredity, as a humanist and as an educator, I would still have the commitment to, and the responsibility for, expanding and optimizing the influence of environmental interactions. That is what directed learning or education is all about. Educators cannot manipulate genes; we can control experience and aspects of our environments.

If and when we are able to speak intelligently about the portion of intellectual function attributable to heredity, it will only be under specific interactions or conditions. When we talk about intelligence, we are talking about phenotype, and phenotype by definition is a function of environmental interactions with genotype. It is my judgment that when and if we are able to separate genotype in human behavioral development, its function will only be determinable in relation to, or as it is expressed through, phenotype. And in that relation its function will be determinable only to the extent that the *interaction* is specified.

The rather pessimistic view of the plasticity of human potential in selected populations which is advanced by some investigators is in part a function of their limited view of the potential significance of interaction variance. As long as they view environmental interactions in "normal" or traditional terms, these investigators severely limit their perspectives and hopelessly bias their results. They seem to dismiss the possibility that interactions can be, may be, and in some instances have been made significant in specified directions. For example, Goldstein has noted that recent advances in medical science have brought under man's control several physical disorders which are clearly genetic in origin and which might, therefore, according to this limited view of the possibilities of environmental interaction, be regarded as irreversible because genetically "fixed." The discovery of insulin, the isolation of Vitamin D, and the uncovering and control of phenylketonuria, Goldstein (1969) explains:

> . . . are all those exceptional environmental changes which will make this interaction term significant. They indicate that environments everywhere are not merely supportive of hereditary potentialities, but can, at times, reverse deleterious effects. The great achievements of mankind lie in making that interaction term significant. Indeed, it could almost be a maxim for schools of education, psychology, public health, and medicine: "Make that interaction significant" [p. 20].

The nature-nurture controversy, as Birch (1968) has indicated, is a false issue perpetuated largely through ignorance of advances in scientific research, particularly regarding developmental processes. The confusion between the two concepts "genetic" and "determined" underlies much of the problem. That is, while all aspects of an organism may be thought of as 100 percent genetic, they are not 100 percent determined. Rather, phenotypic expressions are the result of a continuous biochemical and physiological interaction of the gene complex, cytoplasm, internal milieu, and external environment throughout the life of the organism.

Birch gives us more detailed information about this interaction process. Developmental influence, he notes, begins to complicate research in behavioral genetics even before birth through the influence of the maternal environment. Thus, even at birth phenotypic expressions do not correlate one to one with genotype. Another source of complication arises through differences in rates of maturation and in the patterning of maturation times among separate traits, which may lead to alterations in the patterns of phenotypic expression which do not arise from genetic differences in that trait.

In addition, Birch has noted, studies in behavioral genetics suffer equally from the fact that behavioral analysis is still at a rudimentary stage. What emerges in most research is the end product of learning a maze, the end score differences in discrimination, or mean differences between groups in intelligence test scores, and so on, and there is almost no determination of the specific characteristics of the organism that are involved in the mastery of the presented problem. The classic study by Tyron (1940) of the selective breeding of "bright" and "dull" rats illustrates the problem. Analysis of Tyron's study by subsequent investigators suggested that what the rats had been selected for was not "intelligence" but responsiveness to visual or nonvisual cues and aspects of temperament. Searle (1949), for example, showed that when visual cues were used, Tyron's "dull" rats were in some circumstances more effective learners than his "bright" strain.

As Birch points out:

> If the data of behavioral genetics permit us to draw any conclusions with respect to learning ability it is that learning ability is by no means a unitary trait, and that in different organisms different patterns of responsiveness, of motivation, of emotionality, and of antecedent history contribute substantially to determining which subgrouping will learn most effectively under conditions of different instruction and task demand. It appears, therefore, that a sober judgment would lead us to conclude that differences in learning achievements, whether measured by intelligence tests or by school achievement in human beings, represent the products of different degrees of goodness of fit between the learner, the task, and, in particular, the instructional mode. Such conclusions have positive rather than pejorative implications for a consideration of differences in learning style and achievement in human social groupings [Birch, 1968, p. 56].

Jensen's treatment of the second question that he poses for consideration —the possibility of inherent differences between racial groups in intellectual capacity—is likewise open to criticism on many grounds. According to Fried (1968), the humanistic intentions of most investigators who have studied intelligence, ability, or achievement endowment among different races do not alter the fact that their studies have invariably been based on racial constructs that are destructive and antisocial in addition to being unscientific. In almost all studies the so-called racial background of individual respondents and respondent populations has been derived in ways that show no resemblance to means used by genetic specialists. In those few cases where any information is given about criteria of assortment, one usually finds that skin color has been the sole or dominant criterion, and that as measured by the eye. In other words, the actual genetic background of the subjects is uncontrolled. The classic study by Shuey (1966) on *The testing of Negro intelligence* illustrates the racist implications of investigations conceived in this mode. In fact, there is as yet no study on a so-called racial sample that adequately links intelligence, potential ability, educability, or even achievement to a specifiable set of genetic coordinates associated with an aggregate larger than a family line or perhaps lineage.

The most useful studies linking race and certain specified socially valued traits make no pretense of dealing with biogenetic race; rather, they openly work with categories of "social race." A case in point is the massive survey by Coleman (1966), *Equality of educational opportunity*, which focused on psychological reactions of being identified and identifying oneself as a Negro in the United States. If race is to be treated as a sociocultural construct, it is important to get the individual's views on his own identification and the identification he applies to others. However, if race is to be treated as a biological construct, the lay individual's views of his own racial identity or that of anyone else are unqualified and immaterial.

These two concepts of race relate to another flaw in such research to date, most of which has given insufficient attention to the problem of control for economic condition and social-status variance, not to mention physical conditions and surroundings. Investigators conducting these studies seem to feel that they have controlled for socioeconomic variance when the two comparison groups are selected from comparable income or occupational levels. However, most students of economic and ethnic status concede that equal income for whites and blacks in the United States, or comparable occupational level, greatly camouflages differential patterns of cultural experience and social interaction. Unless one is also arguing that conditions of life have no impact on affective and cognitive development, these sources of variance cannot be ignored in equating groups.

Even when comparison groups are established on the basis of comparability of income and of life conditions within the generation being studied, the problems of intergenerational variance and its contribution to physical and behavioral development are ignored. If, for instance, one selects fifty middle-class white children in New York City and compares them with fifty middle-class black children, the likelihood is that the families of the white children will have been at the middle-class status level for a longer time. Then, when one considers the relationship between socioeconomic status and health and nutritional status, and the derivative relationship between health and nutritional status and the quality of fetal life and development, the ludicrous character of failure to control for such variation becomes obvious.

We have, then, in these efforts at studying behavioral differences in racial groups, problems that relate to the identification and specification of pure race as well as problems in control for variations in life condition. These variations so greatly confound racial effects as to make their separation impossible of solution by those who have sought to investigate the problem thus far. We might conclude that to create the social conditions necessary to make such investigation scientifically accurate and possible would be very likely to actually eliminate the problem before it could be examined!

If these questions regarding intelligence, race, and genetics are so difficult, even impossible, of solution given present scientific skill, what is the relevance of the controversy? Of course, we cannot fail to see the possible racist implications of this kind of superficially supported assertion regarding ethnic inferiority. Broader social consequences threaten if we give prevalence to those theories that posit only a limited effectiveness for environmental interaction. My argument with those who hold this more narrow view is that, despite their claim to interest in the advancement of science, few of them support the kinds and magnitude of changes in social, economic, and political conditions which could make the interaction component more significant and their own research more possible. I cannot accept this stance since it is supportive of the status quo: it means business as usual; it means limited opportunity for black and poor people. It means that we invest too little effort in trying to make the interaction significant, while the majority tries to fix the blame on the victims or on nature for differences, underdevelopment, or school failures, all of which are largely imposed on lower-status persons by man's indifference to, or abuse of, his fellow man.

It is important to acknowledge the special relevance of the investigator's theoretical stance to research carried on by specialists in the field. The manner in which investigators or practitioners approach the understanding of the organization of behavior or the modification of behavioral organization is greatly influenced by the theoretical position held with respect to the genesis of patterned behavior. Problems raised for investigation, the research design chosen, as well as the phenomena that are observed, generally reflect the theoretical bias of the investigator. The choice of goals and practices to be utilized in approaches to behavioral change are usually determined by the practitioner's view of the mechanisms underlying behavioral organization.

Theories of behavior may be divided between those which posit an essentially projective view and those which posit an essentially reflectional or interactive view of the mechanisms underlying behavioral organization. In the projective view predetermined, intrinsic patterns are thought to be released by stimulation and projected onto the environment where their specific form is facilitated or inhibited. Among persons adhering to this position, emphasis is given to hypotheses concerning the existence in the organism of intrinsic drive states which exist prior to, and independently of, life experiences and which are the basic forces in the determination of behavior. Certain behavioral patterns are seen as preformed, stored, and waiting for the proper time and condition for emergence. Capacities and traits are seen as determined by these intrinsic factors, which can only be modified somewhat by the environment. The fundamental character of patterned behavior is seen as genetically established and bound. Environmental forces are considered to influence the organization of behavior by determining (1) the directions taken by the primary energies and drives, (2) the environmental objects to which they become attached, and (3) the specific time and form in which they will emerge.

On the other hand, the interactionist or reflectionist position holds that all organized patterned behaviors are reflections of the interaction between the organism and its environment. Environmental interaction is seen as the crucial determinant and molder of patterned organismic function. Temporal and situational phenomena are not *releaser* but *causative* and *mediating* agents. Behavioral characteristics, traits, species typical behaviors—all organized patterned behavior—are seen to exist only as a result of sensory input flowing from the interaction between the organism and the environment. Behavior potentials are said to be genetically seeded in the sense that the organism includes structural responsivity which is determined by interactions between organism and environment with the nature of these interactions being critical for organized behavior.

Then, what is the relationship of this controversy to directed learning? When behavior theory is used to guide practice in directed learning, the differences in the two positions are manifested in the goals, the design, and the management of learning experiences. (Directed learning is used here as an inclusive term to cover education, counseling, and guidance.)

The dominance of the projective view in directed learning has been reflected in (1) a laissez-faire or neglectful attitude toward the training and development of intelligence; (2) a monitoring as opposed to a stimulating approach to academic and social readiness and personality development; (3) an exaggerated emphasis on the predictive value of the classification and quantification of psychological appraisal data and the neglect of qualitative appraisal data as a basis for planning, prescription, and intervention; (4) distortion of aspiration and expectation levels based upon unjustified ceilings on potentials for human development and adaptation; (5) placement of the burden of proof on the examinee rather than on the appraiser or appraisal method, on the learner rather than on the teacher or teaching method, and on the counselee rather than on the counselor or counseling method; (6) emphasis on adjustment to or acceptance of assumed realities rather than on modification of the environment and the individual's interaction with same; and (7) overemphasis on selection and placement with an underemphasis on the nurturing of interests and aptitudes and the development and training of capacities and skills.

I have tried to show some of the difficulties and dangers of a too hasty acceptance of theories and speculations that argue for the fixed nature of intelligence or behavior, or that purport to show racial differences under sloppily controlled experimental conditions. However, despite the problems of designation of subgroups, there is some research evidence and a considerable degree of logic to support the assertion that patterns of intellectual function differ within *and* across subgroups in our society, and this observation has considerable relevance for the future of compensatory programs and education in general. Although Jensen makes the mistake of regarding these differences as traits generic to, respectively, black or white subgroups, and makes little allowance for identifiable differences in patterns of function *within* the two designated ethnic groups, the work of Lesser, Fifer, and Clark (1965) supports the observation that such subgroups as urban blacks, urban Puerto Ricans, Orientals, and Caucasian (Jewish) children, separated into lower-class and middle-class groups, differentiate themselves according to predominant patterns of intellectual function identifiable in each group. When one considers the variations in life style that tend to be associated with subgroups in this society, without turning to genetic considerations it is logical to expect differential patterns of preference and style in intellectual and social functioning.

Although I consider many of Jensen's speculations ill-founded, I feel it would be unwise to dismiss the possibility that subgroups which share a number of common genetic characteristics, such as skin color or physiognomy, and also share common life experiences may have some neurologic characteristics which may be phenotypically expressed with high incidence as specific patterns of intellectual function. Thus, children in any subgroup may have certain identifiable patterns of function occurring with high frequency within that group. However, we must not forget that these studies show such patterns as emerging in statistically significant high proportion; *none* of them show specific patterns of intellectual function to be invariant within the target population. The presence of alternative patterns occurring under natural circumstances, or the possibility of such patterns occurring under contrived conditions, is consistently neglected in this research. We can say that when a specific pattern is consistently found to occur in a certain group with high frequency, it would be be unreasonable to assert that the pattern is not genetically influenced, but this possibility does *not* mean that it is genetically *fixed*.

It seems to me that this is one of the principal sources of difficulty in Jensen's position. Not only are we dealing with ethnic groups that are inadequately defined, living under conditions which have not been appropriately controlled for, but we have, in addition, the tendency of these groups to show patterns of behavior occurring in sufficiently high frequency to suggest typicality, yet reflecting considerable within-group variation. The research that Jensen has reviewed and the problems with which he is concerned are hopelessly complicated by our inability to distinguish between genetic determination and genetic influence.

Even were we able by tomorrow to attain the ability to make this distinction, in looking at what is genetically influenced one is then forced to give serious consideration to concurrent influences. Under this heading, we should have to consider environmental interactions and also subjective perceptions of self and environment. This latter influence, while initially derivative of the other two, ultimately comes to function as an independent variable. The problem with Jensen's assertions really lies in these three complex sources of influence. He has tried statistically to distill out one of them, but his statistical treatment is of questionable validity. For example, he uses twin studies to support his major claims. The test data in these studies are obviously those of individual subjects. Yet the data to which these individual scores are compared are mean scores of groups. Analyses in which individual scores and group mean scores constitute the data are not generally used to arrive at statistical conclusions. Even if his procedures were less open to question, there is still the fact that this problem does not lend itself to resolution through statistical manipulation. Such analyses can be made to support hunches, or can provide leads, but in the absence of very careful and sophisticated study of the mechanisms by which the genetic, the environmental, and the existential interact to influence behavioral outcomes, we shall continue to be limited to speculation about the issues basic to this controversy. This may, in part, account for the fact that Jensen repeatedly retreats to speculation despite his efforts at casting his arguments in the context of a research-based document.

Our failure—and possibly inability—to conduct research of this sort on problems related to the origins of behavioral adaptation and learning has contributed greatly to our failure to make greater advance in the development of scientific pedagogy. Whether we are talking about compensatory education or just good education, understanding and control of the mechanisms by which behavior develops and is changed are critically important ingredients.

The assertion that compensatory education has failed is patently inaccurate; to claim further that it has failed because its subjects are incapable of responding is particularly ludicrous when one considers that compensatory education, like ethnic integration in the schools, has never been tried. We can find several implications for *real* compensatory education in the consideration of the *true* answers to the questions that Jensen raises.

Given the fact of individual differences and the fact of subgroup differences that may influence value orientation, temperament, and style in intellectual and social function, educational programs which are not designed to complement or compensate for these in-group and between-group variations in function should hardly be expected to show positive results. In fact, some of us argue that existing patterns of academic achievement are remarkably high given the relatively low state of differentiated instructional procedures. I strongly suspect that much of what we see as standard patterns of achievement are the products of the material goodness of middle-class life conditions more than the product of the goodness of our schools or the goodness of the capacities of the youngsters attending the schools. Jensen's alleged concern with qualitative differences in intellectual function and the more serious concern with these problems reflected in Lesser's work reflect one-half of what our concern must be if we are to bring about a necessary new focus in education, the goal being the best match between these idiosyncratic learner characteristics and the essential characteristics of an effective learner environment. It is the absence of attention to this match that presents problems not only for the quality of compensatory education but also for its evaluation.

There has been a great proliferation of compensatory education programs over the past ten years. However, the major attention has been given to the expansion of these programs, with insufficient attention to their quality or the adequacy of evaluation and research. The field has been characterized by a well-intentioned but relatively low-level effort at providing for poor and minority group children many aspects of educational intervention that are thought to be effective in work with more privileged children. Emphasis is placed on guidance, remedial reading, earlier exposure to formal learning, language enrichment, and socialization efforts, and some effort has been exerted to make the learning content more relevant to the lives of the learners. All of these ideas are sensible and reasonable, but they do not represent any drastic change in pedagogy. Some of the more radical programs are beginning to give attention to individualization, contingency management, and reinforcement techniques. However, even these innovations have tended to be generically applied, without the effort to look for the right match of technique to individual learner. And, of course, the problem *is* the individual learner, a problem which must be solved before we move on to the development of group techniques. Furthermore, in order to develop techniques suitable for the characteristics of a certain group, we need first an identifiable group, not an alleged one and certainly not a conglomerate of individuals socially assigned to a specific status.

I suggest that compensatory-education evaluation data are not only discouraging because of the low quality of the programs and the wide variation in the characteristics of the target populations, but are equally complicated by wide variations in the conditions under which they are implemented. We know that teacher characteristics not only have a differential overall effect, but differential effects on individuals. We know that class composition not only influences the nature of teacher classroom behavior but influences also the nature of patterns of pupil achievement. We are beginning to appreciate the fact that there are a wide variety of instructional procedures which are equally effective depending upon the teacher who is using them and the children with whom they are used. We know that learner conditions, permanent, situational, or temporary, influence learner responsiveness. We know that organizational patterns in schools greatly influence what happens in the school.

All of these equally important variables have not been controlled for in our effort at studying compensatory education. The mistaken practice has been to ask the question "Does compensatory education make a difference?" without specifying the precise nature of the population or examining the appropriateness of the treatment actually provided to the expected and desired difference or effect and in too many instances without determining whether the designated treatment has actually been applied.

When we add to these problems and complications in the programs themselves and in the processes of evaluation the grossly inadequate monetary and human resource support that has been provided for them, our assertion that compensatory education has not been tried is more than adequately supported. Jablonsky and I (1968) estimated that it would cost $100 billion a year, or $50 billion more than what we are spending in 1970, to create an effective, quality system of education for all; Cohen's (1967) more conservative estimate of the problem was a need of an additional $10 billion annually. When we realize that the height of our investment in quality compensatory education has been $2 billion annually, the seriousness of the financial picture becomes more obvious. In addition, we can turn to an NAACP report on the way in which this $2 billion has been spent and discover that appallingly large proportions of the sum have been diverted from disadvantaged communities to serve more general purposes of school districts and in some instances even their more privileged segments.

Not only is the financial support available to the compensatory education effort totally inadequate; the human resource situation is equally discouraging. There are few educators in the country who are regarded as experts on compensatory education, and even these few are far from being able to provide complete and effective answers to the problem. In addition, those educators actually at work in the field, with the children in the schools, are kept busy with the everyday task of dealing with their own pupils and their problems. They have little chance to participate in intensive long-term training or to gain an in-depth knowledge of the problem or possible solutions. They do not even have the time to seriously study and become scholars of their own work. In the field of remedial reading, for example, many of those specializing in the area work by slowing down the teaching process in an attempt to suit the pace of the children with problems or by helping in the repetition of prescribed drills, but they know little of the principles and possibilities for individual diagnosis and prescription. While there may be as many as 50,000 people assigned to do remedial reading in this country, there are probably less than a thousand who could really qualify as experts in this specialty. We would hardly find more than one hundred who are working with disadvantaged children in compensatory education programs.

It is certainly necessary and desirable at this time that we maintain an ongoing process of questioning and evaluating the compensatory education effort. However, any effort at such analysis which does not take into account the appallingly inadequate supply of financial and human resource support cannot be regarded as a valid and accurate assessment. It is impossible to ignore the fact that we have today a social and political situation which, at best, can be accused of neglecting the problems facing the children with whom we are concerned and often can justly be accused of outright oppression and exploitation of these less privileged and less powerful segments of the population. To blame the failure of compensatory education on these children, those supposedly being served, is criminally abusive, particularly when done by those who have the intelligence to see the diseases and immorality of our society. These afflictions touch us all, but clearly they must victimize those on whom some are now attempting to place the burden of the blame for the society's failure. This attempt can at best be regarded as misguided; it is more appropriately seen as chauvinistic arrogance and blatant racism masquerading as scientific inquiry. Five years ago I predicted that our failure to take the tasks of compensatory education more seriously would open the door to this kind of antihuman and unscientific retreat. Unhappily my prediction has proved true. Let us hope that volumes like this one and the controversy which is its topic will mark the birth of a second-level concern and effort at "the improvement of education and other environments," which Bloom (1969, p. 421) has called "really the only means available to a civilized society for the improvement of the lot and fate of man."

References

Birch, H. Boldness and judgment in behavior genetics. In M. Mead, T. Dobzhansky, E. Tobach, & R. E. Light (Eds.), *Science and the concept of race.* New York: Columbia University Press, 1968.

Bloom. B. Letter to the editor. *Harvard Educational Review*, 1969, *39*, 419–421.

Cohen, D. *Policy for the public schools: Compensation or integration?* Paper presented at the National Conference on Equal Educational Opportunity in America's Cities, Washington, D.C., November 16–18, 1967.

Coleman, J. S. *Equality of educational opportunity.* Washington, D.C.: U.S. Government Printing Office, 1966.

Fried, M. H. The need to end the pseudoscientific investigation of race. In M. Mead, T. Dobzhansky, E. Tobach, & R. E. Light (Eds.), *Science and the concept of race.* New York: Columbia University Press, 1968.

Goldstein, A. C. A flaw in Jensen's use of heritability data. *Bulletin of the Information Retrieval Center on the Disadvantaged, 5* (No. 4), Fall 1969.

Gordon, E. W., & Jablonsky, A. Compensatory education in the equalization of educational opportunity, II: An organizational model for compensatory education. *The Journal of Negro Education*, 1968, *37*, 280–290.

Jensen, A. R. How much can we boost IQ and scholastic achievement? *Harvard Educational Review*, 1969, *39*, 1–123.

Lesser, G. S., Fifer, G., & Clark, D. H. Mental abilities of children from different social class and cultural groups. *Monographs of the Society for Research in Child Development*, 1965, *30*, No. 4.

Searle, L. V. The organization of hereditary maze-brightness and maze-dullness. *Genetic Psychology Monographs*, 1949, *39*, 279–325.

Shuey, A. M. *The testing of Negro intelligence.* (2nd ed.) New York: Social Science Press, 1966.

Tryon, R. C. Genetic differences in maze-learning ability in rats. In G. M. Whipple (Ed.), *Intelligence: Its nature and nurture*, Part I. The 39th Yearbook of the National Society for the Study of Education, Bloomington, Ill., 1940.

chapter 14

goal as environmental variable in the development of intelligence

PATRICIA M. GREENFIELD

I am concerned with the notion of a goal as environmental variable which makes new sense out of a lot of seemingly confusing data on cultural variation in the development of intelligence and which, at the same time, grows out of a new body of empirical data.

Teleological analysis of behavior was out during the reign of behaviorism. The reinforcer does not "cause" behavior; behavior produces the reinforcer. In this way of looking at things, means lead end, not vice versa. Research on young babies at the Center for Cognitive Studies in the 1960s has tended to show that the opposite is true; intention precedes the act, goal dictates the choice of means. A goal may, therefore, have the temporal primacy required of the stimulus in stimulus-response conceptions. Let me cite one example (Bruner, in press). Before babies have the necessary means for capturing an object manually, they reveal the oral goal of capture by vigorous mouthing movements. The reach-and-capture routine is at first indissolubly wed to the goal of bringing the object to the mouth. Only months later does reach-and-capture become an independent routine that can be run off either for itself or as a means to any number of goals. In the beginning the rule seems to be: no goal, no behavior. This very simple example may be useful for illustrating the notion of a goal as an important environmental concept. Reach-grasp-and-mouth an object may be an innate reaction pattern; nonetheless, an object is necessary to set the pattern off, to arouse the intention reflected in the baby's mouthing movements. Without appropriate objects placed in the environment an essential element of the goal is missing and the reaching skill remains untapped potential.

The reaching example illustrates a general type of relationship between inborn and environmental components of behavior, a relationship long realized by the ethologists: the most genetically specified type of behavior requires a more or less specific environmental trigger, and the trigger very often initiates a period of rapid learning (Thorpe, 1964). The importance of this learning should not be underestimated.

Another finding issuing from the same study of infant reaching, as well as from other studies carried out at the Center for Cognitive Studies, is that a given skill must be *mastered* before it can be inserted as a component in a more complex pattern of skilled behavior. Thus, the ability to deal manually with more than one object at a time depends on the perfection and modularization of the basic reach-and-grasp unit. An awkwardly carried out element evidently demands too much attention in itself and is too unpredictable to be inserted in a complex routine. In consequence, even for a highly preformed behavior like reaching, the lack of environmental opportunity and practice presumably affects future as well as present learning. Thus, the external or environmental component of an internal goal or intention can be conceived as an invitation to carry out a certain type of action—something more than opportunity, something less than compulsion.

Neurological research now supports behavioral evidence that people may be teleological machines. Pribram, Spinelli, and Kamback (1967) have found that intention—the internal counterpart of a goal—can be electrically recorded in the projection areas of the macaque monkey's brain, a phenomenon labeled feed-forward or corollary discharge, and that this mechanism facilitates the intended behavior which follows.

If a goal does have this respectable reality, how does it function in behavior? Internal goals or intentions are important in the formal organization of behavior. Means-end relationships are an important example of the hierarchical structuring that is so prevalent in human functioning. That is, responses or behavioral routines often occur in relation to higher-order goals, which in turn may be subgoals for even more remote ends. These interconnected goal structures are crucial to the temporal integration of behavior, a problem posed by psychologists as divergent as Lashley (1951) and Sartre (1956). The concept of reafference, whereby intention is compared with result and the difference between the two is used as a basis for correction, provides a mechanism by which the goal can control the form of instrumental behavior even after the behavioral sequence is initiated. This process was generalized by Miller, Galanter, and Pribram to many aspects of behavior in their book *Plans and the structure of behavior* (1960).

Goals not only hold behavior together in the formal sense; since environmental goals precede behavioral means temporally, they function as trigger and energizer as well. The psychological notion of a goal or intention is, therefore, both structural and motivational. Motivation thus becomes intrinsic to the structure of intelligent behavior, not something apart from it. Once motivation is part of the very nature of intelligent behavior, a number of social issues relating to intelligence become illuminated. Before discussing these, let me cite some experiments showing the way in which the psychological organization of behavior in terms of goals determines how much and what kind of learning takes place.

It would seem that if the concept of reafference has general applicability in learning—i.e., if even conceptual behavior is regulated by feedback from its end, then the existence of some goal is critical to learning. Furthermore, the fuller the specification of goals and subgoals, the more precise the comparison of ideal with actual and the more effective the correction procedure. My own experiments on ways to teach 2- and 3-year-olds mathematical concepts indicate that specification of the goal is indeed a critical determinant of success in instruction. Initially I used an inductive or discovery-oriented procedure to teach the quantitative concepts "fat" and "skinny." A child would be told that a raisin was under one of two cans differing in diameter. When he was being taught the concept of fat, he had to discover that the raisin was always under the fatter of the two cans. Although in this procedure the concept fat was embedded in an action sequence as a means to attaining the raisin, a negative outcome did not give much corrective information. When the child erred in this situation, all that he could learn was that the raisin was not under that can. The pedagogical problem is that the raisin is not the true goal of the task; it is actually just a way of letting the child know that he has attained the real goal of lifting the fat can. Since the environment has not specified this goal, no comparison of what happened with what was supposed to happen is possible, and corrective feedback is nil. In fact, 2- and 3-year-olds fail to learn the concept under these conditions. Even if they already know the concept, they cannot apply it in this situation. If, however, the same children are told that the "square" piece in an array of shapes will just fit into a puzzle frame placed in front of them, they will learn the concept "square" rather quickly, even if they did not know it beforehand. Here the true goal is initially represented verbally by the word square and ikonically by the square puzzle frame. An error in this situation yields much more information about the means necessary to succeed. In terms of what the child does, the square puzzle frame gives both enactive and visual feedback from the fitting process, while the adjectival position of the word square indicates that some attribute of the piece is a critical part of the goal. A series of three experiments indicated that simultaneous representation of the concept to be learned in terms of action, image, and word is ideal for teaching the meaning of a given mathematical term to 2- and 3-year-olds. A redundant specification of the goal provides a wealth of corrective information about what is wrong with the means when the goal is not realized. This redundancy appears to facilitate learning greatly at the early stages. I am not denying that extrinsic reinforcement can give yes-no information about whether a goal has been attained, but in new learning this cannot replace intrinsic feedback from the goal itself.

The difference between the nature of the object goal presented by the environment to trigger infant reaching and the complex verbal and ikonic goal used to trigger the mathematical learning tasks shows how the environmental sources of intention become more varied with age. Nonverbal demonstrations are another type of goal that are very important in certain types of learning.

Let us consider an example from the realm of perceptual learning in order to generalize the central point that what is learned is learned as a means to some end and that feedback from end to means, therefore, regulates learning. The data come from an experiment carried out in the summer of 1969 in Mexico with Carla Childs (1970). Zinacanteco Indian children were asked to reconstruct two different striped patterns using strips of wood in a frame. We found that the girls who knew how to weave the patterns did thread-by-thread representations of these patterns. This analytic type of representation is clearly requisite to the enterprise of weaving. Zinacanteco boys of the same age, by contrast, do not know how to weave, but they are concerned with the culturally defined patterns as male clothing in the case of one pattern, female clothing in the case of the other. Their representations are, typically, grossly inaccurate in terms of woven threads; they emphasize features that relate to general appearance rather than intrinsic structure. If the pattern construction task is a good index of the nature of past learning, then each group has learned what it needs to know to carry out the respective enterprises in which the patterns are embedded; perceptual learning has been regulated by feedback from the goal.

The general point is that people seem to learn what they need to know to accomplish a goal presented by the environment, that is, when the goal provides the necessary information feedback to the instrumental behavior. What is adequate feedback will vary according to age, task, and stage of learning a given activity. As experience is acquired with a particular type of enterprise, some of these complex external goal representations may become internalized and be spontaneously applied in new situations. In fact, when goals are poorly defined, the educated adult in a technical culture may even exhibit search behavior until some goal is found.

The specification of goals by the environment not only determines whether learning takes place, but also what kind of learning. When understanding a given concept is a subgoal in the service of many different ends, that concept takes a more generalized form. Thus, in the experiment on ways to teach the meaning of the term square, children who were asked to carry out three different actions with the square piece were better able to generalize their learning to new situations than were children who always carried out the same action. Indeed, Werner and Kaplan (1950) have found experimentally that younger children do not differentiate a word from its verbal context and may regard a given word as carrying the meaning of the whole or a part of the context. Variable verbal and action contexts for a given concept then provide a way of generalizing the concept by differentiating it from its context. Equally interesting, this effect of a variety of concrete goals is much larger when *no* verbal labels yet exist within the geometric domain. Thus, if the child already knows the meaning of the word "round," increasing the number of verbal and action contexts no longer is much help in establishing the meaning of the word square. The initially learned label round tends to be overgeneralized to square stimuli, and explicit correction of this overgeneralization becomes the crucial pedagogical problem. At this point in learning exposure to the contrasting labels round and square becomes more effective than using the word square as a means to carrying out a variety of activities. What this may mean educationally is that providing a wide variety of action goals is more important in the initial than in the later stages of mastering concepts in a particular domain; just as for the infant the goal was most critical to the first reaching attempts. The task or goal structure provided by the environment may play its most important role early in life and gradually decline in importance.

The general point about this study, as well as others that could be cited, is that what are learned best, that is, in the most generalized form, are those verbal concepts that function as means to many desired ends. These are concepts that have "relevance" to larger enterprises; the child thus has a "reason" (or motive) to learn about them. Surely in everyday life those concepts most important to action are the ones placed in the greatest variety of contexts and therefore learned the most thoroughly. It then follows that motivation to learn and the hierarchical structuring of a task in terms of means-end relationships are one and the same thing. The role of familiarity becomes that of providing a higher-order structure into which the unfamiliar can be fitted as a necessary component.

Generalization of this line of thought leads to the idea that the goal structure of an environment is extremely important to the development of intelligence. I should like to suggest that when the goal structure of the environment—its means-end relationships—is out of kilter, many of the intellectual phenomena labeled cultural deprivation result. This disorganization of means and ends can be of two types. The first, commonly recognized, occurs when goal attainment is constantly frustrated. In this case the natural process of mastering instrumental behavior or knowledge grinds to a halt. Failure leads to a feeling of powerlessness, to a shifting of responsibility outward, as Rotter, Seaman, and Liverant (1962) demonstrated. Decrease in a sense of self-determination, in turn, reduces means-end analysis and augments a gambling approach to problem solving. This point has been made experimentally by

Rotter and Battle (1963) who showed that people lacking a sense of self-determination failed to relate instrumental behavior to outcomes in predicting the course of future events. Instead, they treated outcomes as randomly determined. But if people generally learn the means to desired goals, then cessation of means-end analysis also means cessation of learning. Thus, a repeated negative outcome of one's projects for whatever social or personal reason would not only annihilate motivation to learn, but also annihilate the structural conditions that make learning possible.

The findings of the Coleman report (1966) on equal educational opportunity confirm this idea with respect to the learning that takes place in school. School achievement for both black and white children was found not to be a function of any objective conditions like curriculum, teacher quality, and so forth, but rather a function of whether the child felt that what he did would affect what happened to him later on—in other words, the perceived ability to determine one's own fate by the use of controllable means. The implication is that children who were continually frustrated in their attempts to achieve anything stopped treating school as a situation in which learning the material is a means to gain one's ends. Instead they started taking the passive role appropriate to a fate- or chance-controlled situation.

If a mother believes that her fate is controlled by external forces, that she does not control the means necessary to achieve her goals, what does this mean for her children? The follow-up data from the Hess group's study of the relation between maternal variables and the development of intelligence shows that the more a mother feels externally controlled when her child is 4 years old, the more likely the child is to have a low IQ and a poor academic record at age 6 or 7 (Hess, Shipman, Brophy, & Bear, 1969).

This high degree of perceived external control that exists among lower-class mothers is also one of the most difficult characteristics to modify. Such was Ira Gordon's (1969) experience from training poor black mothers to play with their babies in an educationally effective way during the first year of life; the high degree of external control felt by the mothers was not modified at all during the course of the program. This feeling of external control may thus be one of the reasons why compensatory educational changes are so difficult to effect.

Not only can people fail to realize goals, the environment can fail to provide a growth-promoting sequence of them. I suggest that the goals set for the child by his caretakers and the relation of these to the child's available means is a critical factor in determining the rate of cognitive growth in the early formative years. By goals, I mean essentially the host of possible enterprises with which a child fills up his day. The means available to him to carry out these enterprises consist of an interplay between what his mother or someone else teaches him through modeling, direct instruction, etc., and what he already knows.

Generalizing the experiment on methods of teaching the concept square, one could say that an ideal strategy for teaching the semantics of a geometric term to someone who was starting from scratch would be to set tasks where understanding the term was a means to accomplishing the enterprise. For example, a mother says to her child when he has a plate of round and square cookies in front of him, "You may eat one round cookie." Clearly, the child will learn which are the round ones. If this remains the only context, however, he will probably think that round is a name for chocolate Oreos. At some later time the mother may say to him, "Your dump truck is in the round box." The more activities in which the concept is embedded, the more generalized the definition will become.

Within this framework, let us examine some more facts about subcultural variation in cognitive development and the environments that produce these differences. Research by Bee, Van Egeren, Streissguth, Nyman, and Leckie (1969) on how mothers—lower-class and middle-class, black and white—teach their 4-year-old children to copy a house made of building blocks indicates that it is precisely the technique of setting a goal and structuring a problem to be solved that differentiates the lower- and middle-class mothers. When the mothers' verbal suggestions are classified according to three levels of specificity, it is found that middle-class mothers use the most general level significantly more than do lower-class mothers. What the middle-class mothers have in common is some mention of the model, that is, the goal. Examples are, "Look at the lady's house," and "Let's start at the front." The more specific levels of suggestion focus on the blocks, that is, they refer to the *means*, not the end. An example of the most concrete level of suggestion is "Put that one over here." The middle-class mothers certainly do not ignore the means—in fact, class differences in the rate of giving the more specific block-oriented suggestions are not statistically significant. The main difference is that middle-class mothers relate means to end, whereas lower-class mothers, on the average, deal with means alone and fail to relate it to any goal. At the same time, the middle-class mothers give their children significantly more positive and significantly less negative feedback. In view of my earlier argument about the effects of success and failure, this emphasis on positive feedback ought to augment the whole process of means-end analysis and realistic goal striving. The relatively high rate of negative feedback from the lower-class mothers, on the other hand, should be leading to feelings of failure and thence to a gambling or luck approach to the situation.

Thus, social reinforcement, as a type of extrinsic feedback vis-à-vis intellectual facts, not only can give information about success, but as a generalized pattern it will also (1) reinforce or fail to reinforce a feeling of competence and (2) select certain types of goals as being more worthwhile than others. Since the latter function is precisely that of cultural values, this view of cognitive activity in terms of a means-end relation makes values part of the very structure of intelligence, not something apart from it.

It may well be that a feeling of external control, a belief that goals cannot be attained, discourages lower-class mothers from structuring their childrens' environment in terms of problems to be solved. (Ironically, this is also a characteristic of the type of education promulgated by the so-called progressive movement. In both cases the child loses the opportunity for the rational goal striving that leads to learning. Although it may help to relax the middle-class child, it ruins the lower-class one.)

A puzzling aspect of the phenomena of cognitive development attributed to cultural deprivation is why these phenomena were not identified before the 1960s. One reason, of course, is that the level of skills demanded by our economy has risen leaving "no room at the bottom." Another reason may be the intensified pace of urbanization. A fascinating study by Graves (1969) comparing rural with urban Spanish-Americans in the Denver area and rural with urban Bagandans in Uganda seems to indicate that in poor families urbanization per se profoundly affects the pattern of enterprises to which a preschool child is exposed. In both Uganda and the United States household tasks for the preschool child are missing in the city. Furthermore, many exploratory activities of which the child is capable become too dangerous in an urban environment. Interviews with mothers revealed also that urban mothers were far less likely than rural mothers to believe that their preschool children were capable of understanding or being taught various principles or skills. The city mothers also rated their children lower in potentialities for independence, self-reliance, and ability to help within the family. When poor mothers move to the city, moreover, they have much more constant contact with small children in the context of relative isolation from adults. This situation engenders frustration and irritation, leading to an increase in the use of power-assertive techniques with children. Urban mothers also use less future-oriented teaching techniques than do their rural counterparts. Thus, it is clear that the urban environment fails to present small children from poor families with the pattern of goal-directed tasks found in a rural environment. At the same time the urban mothers stop believing in their children's efficacy. Interestingly, this belief is correlated with a lowered belief in their *own* efficacy as mothers, a lowered confidence in their own ability to produce the kind of child they desire. Thus, the absence of a sense of self-determination is present in many areas critical to giving the young child himself a sense of competence and self-determination. The lack of confidence in himself appears to be closely linked to the absence of suitable goal-oriented activities for the child to use as vehicles for learning. With more money and education mothers can both escape from the isolation of city life and use imaginative play tasks as substitutes for useful chores; but this approach demands resources unavailable to the poor, relatively uneducated urban dweller.

The findings of Zigler and Butterfield (1968) that motivational factors alone can raise the IQ scores of lower-class children 10 points on the average fits in nicely with these findings about poor urban environments. The type of motivating procedure used in this study related mainly to making sure that the child had a high degree of success before he was faced with difficult test items. A possible explanation is that a child who was prone to interpret outcomes as a matter of chance over which he had no control was made to see that he did and *does* have control in this situation. Such an attitude leads to the means-end analysis necessary for problem solving and learning; hence, the improvement in intellectual functioning manifest in the test score.

The problem of maintaining compensatory educational gains can now be seen in a new framework. Initially, it was thought that once poor children "caught up" they would respond to school like middle-class children and would continue to develop in the same way. But if it is true that people learn that which functions as a means to some end, and if it is also true that the lower-class environment fails to present such ends to its children, then it will also be true that these children will stop learning in this environment. In nursery school most learning and teaching occurs in the context of concrete tasks. In a regular school, by contrast, learning is often dissociated from any ends. In fact, ends are there; they just become more and more remote from the task at hand. In many cases, the home environment may supply the middle-class child, but not the lower-class child, with an image of the goals toward which school instruction is aimed. For example, this is often the case when it comes to learning to read; the goal is clear for the child who has been read hundreds of books by the time he reaches first grade. If specification of the goal is initially a structural as well as motivational condition for learning, the process of learning to read will be greatly impeded for the lower-class child. Where the requisite goal structure is absent, no amount of past "catching up" is going to affect the course of present and future learning.

School learning is characteristically out of the context of any concrete task. The middle-class environment provides the needed supportive goal structure through its social values and practical activities; the lower-class environment does not. In an industrial, technical society means-end chains become so long and means become so generalized in the sense of being detached from specific goals that it is easy to lose sight of an ultimate purpose. In fact, when final goals become too remote, it is easy even to stop caring what they are. This is possibly one reason why the best educated young people are complaining of lack of relevance in their intellectual training. Perhaps the way is open for educational innovations that will connect learning to the relevant goals so needed by the poor and desired by the rich.

References

Battle, E. S., & Rotter, J. B. Children's feelings of personal control as related to social class and ethnic group. *Journal of Personality*, 1963, *31*, 482–490.

Bee, H. L., Van Egeren, L. F., Streissguth, A., Nyman, B. A., & Leckie, M. S. Social class differences in maternal teaching strategies and speech patterns. *Developmental Psychology*, 1969, *1*, 726–734.

Bruner, J. S. The growth and structure of skill. In K. J. Connolly (Ed.), *The Development of Motor Behavior*. New York: Wiley, in press.

Childs, C. A developmental study of pattern representation in Zinacantan. Unpublished honors thesis, Harvard University, 1970.

Coleman, J. S. *Equality of educational opportunity*. Washington, D.C.: U.S. Government Printing Office, 1966.

Gordon, I. J. Stimulation via parent education. *Children*, 1969, *16*, 57–61.

Graves, N. B. City, country and child rearing in three cultures. Unpublished manuscript, University of Colorado, 1968.

Hess, R. D., Shipman, V. C., Brophy, J. E., & Bear, R. M. The cognitive environment of preschool children: Follow-up phase. Unpublished manuscript, University of Chicago, 1969.

Lashley, K. S. The problem of serial order in behavior. In L. A. Jeffries (Ed.), *Cerebral mechanisms in behavior: The Hixon Symposium*. New York: Wiley, 1951.

Miller, G. A., Galanter, E., & Pribram, K. H. *Plans and the structure of behavior*. New York: Holt, Rinehart and Winston, 1960.

Pribram, K. H., Spinelli, D. N., & Kamback, M. C. Electrocortical correlates of stimulus response and reinforcement. *Science*, 1967, *157*, 94–95.

Rotter, J. B., Seaman, M., & Liverant, S. Internal versus external control of reinforcement: A major variable in behavior theory. In N. F. Washburn (Ed.), *Decision, values, and groups*, Vol. 2. New York: Pergamon, 1962.

Sartre, J.-P. *Being and nothingness*. New York: Philosophical Library, 1956.

Thorpe, W. H. Some concepts of ethology. In J. Cohen (Ed.), *Readings in psychology*. London: Allen & Unwin, 1964.

Werner, H., & Kaplan, E. Development of word meaning through verbal context: An experimental study. *Journal of Psychology*, 1950, *29*, 251–257.

Zigler, E., & Butterfield, E. C. Motivational aspects of changes in IQ test performance of culturally deprived nursery school children. *Child Development*, 1968, *39*, 1–14.

chapter 15

social aspects of intelligence: evidence and issues

J. McV. HUNT AND
GIRVIN E. KIRK

The hope of improving the abilities and the lot of men through education is at least as old as Plato's *Republic.* In his dialogue on *The Laws* (Books VI and VII), moreover, Plato has the Athenian suggest that the welfare of the state depends upon parents being supervised in their begetting and rearing of children. He has the Athenian include within the domain of education both prenatal and the earliest of infantile experience. At the same time, Plato has the Athenian acknowledge that "at present there is a want of clearness in what I am saying [Book VII, 788]."

"Want of clearness" on this matter has remained throughout the ages during which the importance attributed to the effects of circumstances encountered by infants and young children on the course and rate of their development has waxed and waned and during which even the goals of education have changed. In fact, how to conceive of the obvious observables of development, anatomical and behavioral, has always been troublesome. Preformationism (see Needham, 1959) and predeterminism (see Hunt, 1961, pp. 42–49) have each known their day, and our contemporary debates appear to place us in what may well prove to be the later phases of a transition between a period of lively conflict of faith in environmentalism or empiricism with faith in hereditary predeterminism and a period of much more general under-standing of interactionism (Johannsen, 1909), of population genetics, and of the implications of plasticity in development—especially early development.

Modern faith in environmentalism probably has its historical origins in John Locke's polemic against innate principles, *An essay concerning human understanding*. Locke's concept of the infant's mind as a *tabula rasa* was expressed in Watsonian behaviorism (1914, 1924) as a concept of original nature con-sisting of an abundant repertoire of miniscule reflexes. The faith that each reflex could come to be evoked by any new stimulus, even a receptor input from an evoked reflex, paved the way for the notion of the chaining of reflexes as a basis for complex activities and thereby for the extreme environmentalism which comprised the background faith of many students of learning. The political faith of the authors of the Constitution of the United States also drew heavily upon Locke's empiricism.

Faith in hereditary predeterminism probably has its historic origins in Wolff's notion of 1759 (Needham, 1959) that a predetermined epigenesis of embryological, anatomical maturation is controlled by something like Leibniz's monads. With the nineteenth-century developments in chemistry and biology, genes became a scientific replacement for the logical construct of monads. Midway in the nineteenth century, Darwin's survival theory of evolution (1859) replaced Lamarck's view that the gains or losses due to use or disuse are transmitted from parents to offspring. Through what are probably two serious misreadings of the implications of Darwin's theory, we got what have prevailed in the twentieth century as twin faiths in traits, especially intelligence, fixed largely by heredity, and behavioral development, predetermined by heredity. These twin faiths have, in turn, given rise to widespread belief in the immutability of class differences and race differences.

Although the assumptions of fixed intelligence and predetermined develop-ment with their mistaken social implications have commonly been subsumed under the term social Darwinism, they have their origins in the thought and influence of two followers of Darwin. It was Darwin's cousin, Francis Galton (1869), who introduced the notion of genius largely fixed by heredity. It was Galton's American follower, G. Stanley Hall, who focused upon the notion that "ontogeny recapitulates phylogeny" to explain the development of behavior and thereby to assume that behavioral development is essentially predetermined.

Through their teaching of the leaders of the intelligence-testing movement and of the first outstanding investigator of child development, Galton and Hall have had a lasting influence on education and psychology. One of Galton's students was James McKeen Cattell, who brought the first mental tests to the United States. Galton also invented the statistical procedure of correlation and, through his influence upon such men as Karl Pearson, did much to shape the nature of psychological investigation in England through at least the first half of the twentieth century. Hall did much to shape the philosophy of the intelligence-testing movement in the United States through teaching its leaders (H. H. Goddard, Frederick Kuhlmann, and Lewis Terman). The implication of predeterminism in the recapitulation doctrine that he taught helped to establish the faith of American educators and psychological students of individual differences in a constant rate of development as assessed by the IQ (mental age/chronological age). Arnold Gesell, who became the leading investigator of child development in America from World War I through World War II, was another of Hall's students. Gesell's acceptance of the principle of predeterminism may be seen to underlie the normative nature of the preponderant majority of investigations of behavioral development throughout this period. This is not meant to imply that the investigative evidence had no influence on either intelligence testing or the investigations of behavioral development during this period, but this is not the place to review that evidence (Hunt, 1961, 1965, 1966, 1969b). Yet, inasmuch as thought tends strongly to control both observation and interpretive action in adults (Piaget, 1947), these ideas of fixed intelligence and predetermined development, operating as controlling faiths, have strongly influenced both the goals and methods of investigation and the interpretations of the evidence uncovered in these two domains. Moreover, these ideas have influenced greatly what has been taught in college courses of education and psychology throughout the first half of this century.

Even so, early education has been one of the prominent social innovations of the 1960s. Its prominence has been epitomized in Project Head Start, which the federal government of the United States established under the Office of Economic Opportunity and which has given many thousands of children from poor families from one summer to a year and a summer at nursery school, beginning usually at 4 years of age.

Two sets of developments following World War II appear to have combined to produce the emergence of early childhood education as a major social innovation. The first consisted of the effects of welfare policies along with the effects of technology coming to agriculture and mining. Welfare policies, established by the federal government during the depression of the 1930s and expressed in Aid to Families with Dependent Children (AFDC), tended to make the dollar value of aid in the relatively well-to-do northern cities several times that in the relatively poor regions of the southern states. When technology brought power-driven machines into agriculture and mining during and after World War II, farm laborers and miners lost their means of livelihood. Farm laborers migrated to the cities. A large share of those from the South were black. Since they were already troubled by legally sanctioned white supremacy, they tended to migrate to the cities of the North where welfare payments were larger and white supremacy had less legal sanction. Although miners were similarly affected by the introduction of power-driven machines, they were unionized, and their unions helped them obtain higher levels of welfare support. Therefore, many remained in rural poverty and dependency. Michael Harrington (1962) summarized these effects to dramatize the economic importance of competence deriving from our burgeoning technology. It was this, combined with the plight of American cities, that constituted one set of developments which brought the need for early childhood education to the fore.

The second set of developments consists of the new evidence and theorizing from various lines of investigation within the behavioral, educational, and neurophysiological sciences. These have weakened faith in fixed intelligence and predetermined development. One of the branches of investigation, stemming from the theorizing of Donald Hebb (1949), has shown that perceptual experiences during infancy affect the problem-solving ability of adult animals (see Forgays & Forgays, 1952; Forgus, 1954; Hymovitch, 1952; Thompson & Heron, 1954). Another, which comes from both the neurophysiological theorizing of Hebb and the biochemical theorizing of Hydén (1960), has shown that depriving animals of visual interaction with their circumstances by rearing them in the dark produces not only a deficiency of visual control over motor activities, but also hampers neuroanatomical maturation throughout the visual system (Brattgård, 1952; Liberman, 1962; Riesen, 1958; Valverde, 1967; Weiskrantz, 1958; Wiesel & Hubel, 1963). Conversely, enrichment of visuomotor experience produced by enlarged cages supplied with a variety of things to see and manipulate has been shown not only to improve the maze-learning ability of rats, but also to increase the thickness of their cerebral cortices and their levels of acetylcholinesterase activity (Bennett, Diamond, Krech, & Rosenzweig, 1964).

A third line of investigation consists of the assessments of apathy and retardation associated with orphanage rearing. René Spitz (1945, 1946a, 1946b) and Dennis (1960), interpreted the evidence quite differently, but, whatever the nature of their basis, they made clear that the genotype guarantees no course or rate of behavioral development. Moreover, the reports of Goldfarb (1943, 1947) strongly suggested that the effects of experience during the first three years have detectable influence on behavior at least as late as adolescence. Those investigators who have attempted to program electronic computers to solve problems (e.g., Newell, Shaw, & Simon, 1958) have concluded that the brain cannot function in the fashion of a static telephone switchboard but must include a hierarchical arrangement of active strategies for the processing of information coming in through receptor systems and collating it with that already in the memory storage. Other researchers of adult problem solving (e.g., Gagné & Paradise, 1961) consider competence in solving problems to be based upon a hierarchical organization of abilities and concepts in which those abilities and concepts high in the hierarchy depend upon the prior existence of those lower. This hierarchical view of the development of intelligence received support from Piaget's observations (1936, 1937) of the development of intelligence and the construction of reality in his own three children. Moreover, his observations strongly suggest the existence of a sequential order in the development of the hierarchical organization of abilities and concepts. Piaget's theory of encounters with circumstances producing accommodative changes in the structure of behavioral organization which are assimilated and transferred to new situations served to advance, at least to some extent, the explication of ongoing interactionism in the course of living between individuals and their circumstances.

These lines of investigation all produced evidence emphasizing the plasticity in human development. Studies indicating that the longer a young organism lives under any given kind of circumstances, the harder it is to alter the direction of its influence (see Hunt, 1969b, pp. 150–151) reenforce the conclusions of the findings discussed above. Other studies have made the evidences of plasticity, which tends to decrease with the duration of encountering a given kind of circumstances, relevant to an understanding of the difference between social classes and races in measures of intelligence. The circumstances encountered during their preschool years by children of the poor all over the world provide them with fewer opportunities to acquire the language and number skills, the motivational habits, and the standards that underlie competence (see Hunt, 1969b, pp. 202–216). This new evidence of plasticity in human development, made relevant to class and race differences and combined with the new economic importance of competence, and the urgent challenge posed by the plight of American cities produced a *Zeitgeist* that looks to early education as a promising way of raising the competence of the children of the poor to a level enabling them to succeed in school and to take their place in the mainstream of society. In this context, Project Head Start was initiated with the hope that a summer or two, or a year, of nursery schooling, beginning at age 4, would compensate the children of the poor for their previous lack of opportunities to learn and thereby enable them to succeed in regular schools. Although Project Head Start was a tremendous step in the right direction, there were those who saw the hopes for it as unrealistic because it was undertaken before an adequately effective technology of early childhood education had been developed and proven (e.g., Deutsch, 1967; Hunt, 1967).

Evaluative studies soon produced evidence confirming the unrealism of these hopes. Although many evaluative reports described immediate mean gains in IQ of from 5 to 10 points on standard tests of intelligence, the first nationwide survey, published by the U.S. Commission on Civil Rights (1967), stated that "there is little question that school programs involving expenditures for cultural enrichment, better teaching, and other needed educational services can be helpful to disadvantaged children. The fact remains, however, that none of the programs appear to have raised significantly the achievement of participating pupils, as a group, within the period evaluated by this Commission [p. 138]." More recently, the Westinghouse Learning Corporation has pubished a study (Cicarelli, 1969) designed to answer the question, "To what extent are children now in the first, second, and third grades who attended Head Start programs different in their intellectual and social development from comparable children who did not attend [p. 2]." To summarize the conclusions from the results, the report states, "The most significant conclusions reached on the basis of this study are that summer programs are ineffective and that full-year programs appear to be marginally effective [p. 245]." Elsewhere the report asserts, "In sum, Head Start children cannot be said to be appreciably different from their peers in the elementary grades who did not attend Head Start in most aspects of cognition and affective development measured in this study, with the exception of the slight but nonetheless [statistically] significant superiority of full-year Head Start children on certain measures of cognitive development [p. 8]."

What has been viewed, on the basis of such global evaluations, as the failure of Head Start and sometimes of compensatory programs of education wherever they have been initiated (see Jensen, 1969, p. 3) raises both substantive and methodological issues which call urgently for analysis.

Substantive issues

The alleged failure of Project Head Start to produce lasting improvements in the scholastic achievement of the children participating in the program prompted Jensen (1969) to write a paper for the *Harvard Educational Review* entitled "How Much Can We Boost IQ and Scholastic Achievement?" In this paper he provided an elaborate restatement of the traditional doctrine of fixed intelligence and predetermined development which raises a number of substantive issues. He defined intelligence operationally as what intelligence tests measure. Because performance on the various tests in the standard batteries shows substantial intercorrelations, he argued, as did Spearman (1904, 1923), that there must be a general factor of intelligence which "we should keep in mind . . . when we speak of intelligence [p. 10]." The IQ, he contended, has been a good measure of this general factor, and since IQs show substantial correlations with both scholastic and occupational achievement, what they measure is socially significant. Since the distribution of IQs, derived from standard test batteries, are distributed in a fashion that approximates the theoretical normal distribution, to continue Jensen's (1969) argument, and since rats can be bred selectively to show high or low error scores in maze learning and "since intelligence is basically dependent upon the structural biochemical properties of the brain, it should not be surprising that differences in intellectual capacity are partly the result of genetic factors which conform to the same principles involved in the inheritance of physical characteristics [p. 32]." Jensen argues that the educational system and the occupational hierarchy act as an intellectual "screening" process. Thus, he reasons, "If each generation is roughly sorted out by these 'screening' processes along an intelligence continuum, and, if the phenotype-genotype correlation for IQ is of the order of .80 to .90, it is almost inevitable that this sorting process will make for genotypic as well as phenotypic differences among social classes [p. 75]." In this connection Jensen asserted that in the absence of "consistent evidence for any social environmental influences short of extreme environmental isolation which have a marked systematic effect on intelligence . . . below a certain threshold of environmental adequacy, deprivation can have a marked depressing effect on intelligence. But above this threshold, environmental variations cause relatively small differences in intelligence [p. 60]." Jensen also noted that "black people, in the United States, are disproportionately represented among groups identified as culturally or educationally disadvantaged . . . they test about one standard deviation (15 points) below the average of the white population in IQ, and this finding is fairly uniform across the 81 different tests of intellectual ability used in the studies reviewed by Shuey (1966)." Such a magnitude of difference means that only "15% of the Negro population exceeds the white average [p. 81]. . . . [Though] it seems not unreasonable, in view of the fact that intelligence variation has a large genetic component [based on the existence of heritability indices of the order of .80 to .90], to hypothesize that genetic factors may play a part in this picture [p. 82]." In a nutshell, Jensen has argued that Head Start, and compensatory educational efforts in general, have failed to produce substantial effects because the indices of heritability imply that the disadvantaged children of the poor —both white and black—simply have not inherited the necessary intelligence to learn in school. Based on his own investigations, Jensen (1969) distinguished Level I, or associative learning abilities, tapped by such tests as digit memory, serial rote learning, and paired-associate learning, from Level II, conceptual learning abilities which "involve self-initiated elaboration and transformation of the stimulus input before it eventuates in an overt response [p. 111]." According to his own findings, children from parents of low socioeconomic status perform as effectively as those from parents of high socioeconomic status on Level I tasks; they show their inferiority chiefly in tasks involving Level II. From such findings he concludes that children of the poor need to be taught in a fashion different from the teaching that has been effective with children of the well-to-do.

Jensen's argument has far more than academic significance, for it received widespread attention in newspapers across the country with headlines like the following: "IQ: God-given or Man-made?" "Intelligence: Is There a Racial Difference?" "Born Dumb?" "Can Negroes Learn the Way Whites Do?" Jensen's argument has been summarized with approval several times in the *Congressional Record*, and it has become the subject of discussion of meetings of high-level policy-makers in Washington and even in corporation board rooms. This extra-academic significance of Jensen's argument lends extra importance to accurate analysis of the substantive issues raised. How much influence has the environment been found to have on IQ and academic achievement? Is it true that above some threshold environmental improvements have little effect on intelligence? Does a high heritability index for the IQ (e.g., of the order of .80 or .90) justify the hypothesis of genetic inferiority and the implication that class differences and race differences are biologically inevitable? In addition, investigators from the domain of linguistics have contended that variations in dialect may account for the scholastic failure of children of the poor, and especially of black children. Finally, among the substantive issues, are there other reasons why Head Start failed to achieve the high hopes with which it was established?

Amount of environmental influence on IQ

The most relevant evidence known to us concerning the issue of how much influence the environment can have on the IQ comes from studies by Dennis (1966) and Skeels (1966). In the study by Dennis (1966), which should be more widely known, the Goodenough Draw-a-Man Test was given to good-sized samples of typical children, 6 to 9 years of age, living in normal family environments in some fifty cultures over the world. The variations in mean Draw-a-Man IQs for these samples extended from a high of 124 to a low of 52. Mean IQs of 124 were found for suburban children in America and England, for children in a Japanese fishing village, and for Hopi Indian children. In each of these four cultures children grow up with continual contact with representative, graphic art. The low mean IQ of 52 came from a sample of children in a nomadic Bedouin tribe of Syria and the mean IQ of 53 from a nomadic tribe in the Sudan. It should be noticed in this connection that the Muslim religion prohibits contact with graphic art. Yet, even among groups of Arab Muslim children, the mean IQs for the Draw-a-Man Test ranged from 52, for the children of Syrian Bedouins who had almost no contact with graphic art, to 94, for the children of Lebanese Arabs in Beirut who have repeated contact with the graphic art of Western civilization—even that including television.

It is likely that the Draw-a-Man IQ calls for a less complex set of abilities, as these are described by factor analysis (Guilford, 1967), than does the IQ derived from either the Stanford-Binet battery or the Weschler-Bellevue battery. For American children, nevertheless, IQs from the Draw-a-Man Test correspond about as well with IQs from either of these two standard measures of intelligence as the two standards do with each other.

It should be noted that the variation of 72 points in mean Draw-a-Man IQs holds for children reared in environmental circumstances quite normal for their various cultures. Moreover, the 72 points of variation in mean IQs from such typical groups of children fall only about 18 points short of the range of individual IQs (that between 60 and 150), which includes all but a fraction of 1 percent of individuals above the pathological bulge at the low end of this distribution. Thus, variation in mean IQ associated with circumstances of rearing has a range nearly equal to that variation for individual differences in the IQ which is commonly attributed largely to genetic variation.

While Jensen (1969) acknowledged that "extreme sensory and motor restrictions in environments such as those described by Skeels and Dye (1939) and Davis (1947), in which the subjects had little sensory stimulation of any kind and little contact with adults (p. 60)" result in large deficiencies in IQ, he minimized their importance for class differences and race differences. In favor of his view that the environment has little permanent effect on the IQ, he notes that the orphanage children of Skeels and Dye gained in IQ from an average of 64 at an average age of 19 months to 96 at 6 years of age as a result of being given "social stimulation and placement in good homes at between two and three years of age (p. 60)." He notes further than when these children were followed up as adults, they were found to be average citizens in their communities, and their own children had an average IQ of 105 and were doing satisfactorily in school. They actually had a median educational attainment of twelfth grade. Four had one or more years of college work; one received a bachelor's degree and went on to graduate school.

Neglected in Jensen's (1969) report are two points of importance for interpretation. Neglected first is the fact that most of these children were well under 2 years of age when they were transferred from the orphanage to the institution for the mentally retarded. At this age the children of the poor typically average approximately 100 in DQ or IQ. It is between the age of about 18 months and the age of 5 or 6 years that the IQs of children of the poor, both black and white, drift downward (Gray & Klaus, 1970; Klaus & Gray, 1968). As long as conditions that fail to foster psychological development persist but for a short or limited time, the very plasticity of early child development permits considerable recovery when development-fostering circumstances are provided. Neglected also in Jensen's report are the results of the follow-up for the Skeels-Dye children who were left in the orphanage. When the study began, these children had a mean IQ of 87. Retested after periods varying from 20 to 43 months, all of them showed decreases that ranged from 8 to 45 points, and five of the decreases exceeded 35 points. The median of ultimate educational attainment for this contrast group proved to be less than the third grade. At the time of the follow-up, one had died in adolescence following continued residence in a state institution for the mentally retarded; five were still wards of state institutions; and all but one of the remaining six were employed in work calling for only the lowest of skills. One gleans from these studies by Skeels and Dye (1939) and Skeels (1966) that persisting environmental circumstances can make a tremendous difference. The effects of circumstances are reversible early in life; but as given circumstances endure, their effects become more and more difficult to change. This principle holds for a variety of organisms and a variety of different kinds of circumstances (see Hunt, 1969b, p. 150).

The threshold conception of environmental influence

Insofar as the genotype sets limits on both the rate and the ultimate level of intelligence to be achieved, the threshold theory of environmental influence has validity. Insofar as this threshold conception, as epitomized by "normal environmental conditions," implies that this hypothetical threshold is typically achieved in families, it is likely to be very false. Evidence from a study by Paraskevopoulos and Hunt (in press) calls this view into serious question. The investigators used versions of the ordinal scales of object construction and imitation developed by Uzgiris and Hunt (1966) with some of the landmarks marking relatively small steps in development omitted. These scales were inspired by the observations of Piaget (1936, 1937). Both object construction and imitation comprise behavioral categories that are not deliberately taught. In fact, little knowledge exists concerning the nature of the environmental encounters required for their acquisition. Although imitation can be reinforced (Miller & Dollard, 1941), it is difficult to conceive of the acquisition of object construction through the standard categories of learning. In order to test the effects of diverse circumstances on the development of object construction and imitation, Paraskevopoulos and Hunt had these scales administered to all of the children aged between 5 months and 5 years who had lived from birth in two Athenian orphanages and to a sample of home-reared children. Most of the home-reared children were obtained through day-care centers in Athens. One of the orphanages had an infant-caretaker ratio of approximately 10:1; the other, a ratio of 3:1. Inasmuch as the Uzgiris-Hunt scales are ordinal in character, passing one landmark and failing the next serves to identify a level of development that a child has achieved at the time of examination. This method permits a comparison of the ages of the children, who have developed under each set of circumstances, at each level of performance on each scale. The home-reared children achieved the various levels of object construction at somewhat younger ages than did the children at the orphanage with an infant-caretaker ratio of 3:1, but the differences were not statistically significant. Both of these groups of children, however, achieved the higher levels of object construction at much earlier ages than did the children at the orphanage with an infant-caretaker ratio of 10:1. In the case of vocal imitation home-reared children achieved the various levels of development much earlier than did the children in either orphanage. Both object construction and vocal imitation are highly important aspects of the early phases of intellectual development. The mere fact that there is a variation among the mean ages of the children living under these three rough categories of circumstances which differ for object construction and vocal imitation calls into question any simple version of the threshold concept of environmental influence.

Even more significant for the threshold concept of environmental influence are the findings of this study concerning the variances in the chronological ages of the children at various levels of development. It is hardly surprising to find these variances in age lowest for the orphanage with an infant-caretaker ratio of 3:1. Of the sets of circumstances in the two orphanages and in the homes, that set in the orphanage with the 3:1 ratio of infants to caretakers is the most constant across the children developing there. It is hardly surprising that the variances in the ages of the children at various levels at orphanage 10:1 are larger than those for the children at corresponding levels in orphanage 3:1. When a caretaker must look after ten different children, it is almost inevitable that she will develop preferences which cause her to give more attention to some of her children than to others. Such preferences become obvious to any observer of the behavior of caretakers in orphanages. These preferences constitute the most obvious explanation, albeit not a very informative one psychologically, for the fact that the standard deviations for the ages of the children in orphanage 10:1 for the upper levels of object construction are more than twice those for the ages of children in orphanage 3:1. What may be surprising is that the variances in the ages for the home-reared children at the upper levels of object construction are even larger than those for the ages of children in orphanage 10:1. For instance, in the case of that level of object construction defined by following an object hidden in a container through successive disappearances of that container in the order in which those disappearances took place without evidence of reversability, the findings are as follows: orphanage 10:1—mean = 39.4 months, SD = 7.47 months, N = 13; orphanage 3:1—mean = 27.6 months, SD = 2.59 months, N = 7; home-reared children—mean = 26.3 months, SD = 8.32 months, N = 28. The large standard deviations in the ages at which home-reared children achieve the later levels of object construction appear to indicate that variations in rearing practices within families are substantial in their effects upon this highly important intellectual achievement. Such a finding is highly dissonant with a threshold conception of environmental influence that is taken to imply that family-based rearing provides "normal environmental conditions" with little influence on psychological development.

An investigation underway at the George Peabody College for Teachers by Schoggen and Schoggen promises to be highly illuminating on this matter. The Schoggens selected three samples of eight families, one of professional people, one of the rural poor, and one of the urban poor. In each family is a 3-year-old who is the target child of the study. The method consists of having observer-recorders become so well-acquainted with each of these families that the effect of their presence on the interaction of the members of the family with the target child is unaffected. They record instances of interaction initiated by parents and the older children with the target 3-year-old and the reaction of the older members of the family to the instances of interaction initiated by the child in such functionally equivalent situations as meal time and bed time. Those interactions initiated by older members of the family they term "environmental force units." The preliminary results reported in 1968 have shown more than twice as many such units per given interval of time in the families of professional status—half black and half white (41)—as in families of either the rural poor—all white (18)—or urban poor (17)—half black and half white. Moreover, the quality of such interaction differs. According to preliminary impressions of the staff, whereas the 3-year-olds in professional families are often asked to note and compare the shape, the size, the color of objects and places, the children of the poor are called upon to do so only when they are asked to run errands, and then the request typically comes with scolding or in a vocal screech. Also, according to the impressions of the staff, children of professional families are often asked to talk of such matters in their own words, children of poverty seldom are. The reactions to the interactions initiated by the 3-year-olds also differ according to these preliminary impressions. Although restraining commands in one form or another are common in all families, they comprise a much higher proportion of the reactions in the families of the rural and urban poor. Moreover, these restraining commands come with phrases of explanation in professional families ("Shut up! Can't you see I'm on the telephone!"), but such explanations are seldom given in families of poverty. Thus, although a threshold conception of the environment may have some theoretical validity, what validity it has is quite irrelevant to the academic inadequacies of children of the poor, be they black or white.

Heritability and the concept of genetic inferiority

The idea that class differences and race differences in the IQ are biologically inevitable derives principally from the presupposition that measures of heritability are inverse indicators of educability. In general, the mean IQs of samples of children of unskilled laborers typically fall about 20 points below the mean IQs of samples of children of professional men (Anastasi, 1958, p. 517). Also, the mean IQs for samples of black children do fall about 15 points (one standard deviation) below the means for white children (Shuey, 1966). These are descriptive facts, but, as Anastasi concluded, they provide "no information regarding the causes of these observed behavioral differences [1958, p. 598]." The fact that there can be a 72-point range in mean Draw-a-Man IQs for groups of typical children from fifty cultures throughout the world not only suggests that the descriptive class differences and race differences fall far short of the possible range, but also calls into question the relevance of indices of heritability to educability. This lack of relevance can be further clarified by logical analysis.

Heritability is defined as the ratio of the hereditary or genotypic variance to the total observed variance in the trait concerned (Sinnott, Dunn, & Dobzhansky, 1958, p. 275). Thus, heritability is the correlation of the unobservable, theoretical, genotypic variance of a trait with the observed, and measured, phenotypic variance of the trait. The same genotype, however, can give rise to a wide array of phenotypes depending upon the environment in which it develops. This is the norm-of-reaction concept to which Woltereck called attention shortly after the turn of this century (see Dunn, 1965). Since the genotype is a logical construct that is not observable, estimating heritability demands that investigators find ways to estimate the genotype variance of a trait from observables. The simplest index of heritability, originally invented by Francis Galton, estimates the genotypic variability through measures of the trait in parents, based on the average measure for the two parents, and correlates these measures with measures of the trait in the offspring of these parents, based on the average measure for the children of each couple. The higher the correlation between such measures for parents and children, the greater the heritability. Because any given estimate of heritability depends completely upon the manner in which the sample was selected and the environmental circumstances operative, heritability is a property of population and not of traits, which Fuller and Thompson (1960, p. 64) have taken care to point out. Moreover, although other approaches to the estimation of genotypic variability exist, the various indices of heritability that result concern only the degree of correspondence of the rank order of the estimated variations in the genotype with the rank order of the phenotype variations of the trait. In the case of the correlation of measures of a trait in a sample of parents with measures of that trait in their children, the correlation has nothing to say about the correspondence or lack of correspondence between the average measure of that trait in the parents and the average measure of that trait in the children. One can see this more readily by noting that the rank order of one set of measures may correspond perfectly with the rank order of another set of measures even though the former set may have a mean which is either several times that of the other or but a fraction of that of the other. This is part of the analysis that has prompted behavior-geneticist Hirsch (1970) to say that "the plain facts are that in the study of man a heritability estimate turns out to be a piece of 'knowledge' that is both deceptive and trivial [p. 98]." Such indices of heritability have absolutely nothing to say about the educability of individuals, or classes, or races.

Such an argument does not make the one who makes it an environmentalist. Insofar as individual differences in genotypes set limits on an individual's potential IQ—albeit unknowable limits—the genotype must determine the amount of effect which given variations in circumstances can have. Thus, in the case of identical twin retardates, say of the type commonly called Mongoloids, the potential IQ is so limited that the cumulative effects of even the most extreme variation in circumstances could probably never produce as much as 72 points of difference between their IQs. Since a genotype with high potential does not guarantee a high IQ, the accumulative effects of life under sets of circumstances differing in the most extreme degree imaginable for pairs of identical twins would be a function of this genotypic potential.

In the light of such an analysis the polarization between faith in the importance of heredity and faith in the importance of circumstances encountered disappears. Moreover, the analysis makes clear why the predicted intellectual bankruptcy from differential fertility (Cattell, 1937) has been so regularly disconfirmed by evidences of a rising IQ. Differential fertility refers to the fact that about 60 percent of each new generation comes from the lowest third of the population in socioeconomic-educational status. From assuming such status to be a function of the heritability index and from taking into account the 20-point difference in mean IQ for the children of laborers and the children of professional people, Cattell (1937) predicted a drop of a little more than 3 points of IQ for each generation, or about one point a decade. In the paper presenting this prediction Cattell (1937) reported the distribution of IQs for the 10-year-olds living in the city of Leicester in 1936. Thirteen years later Cattell (1950a) published another study comparing the IQs of the 10-year-olds living in the city of Leicester in 1949 with those of the 10-year-olds of 1936. He used the same test and standardization for these two samples. The result was an increase of 1.28 points in mean IQ instead of the expected drop of about this same amount.

Other investigators have reported evidence showing substantially larger increases in IQ, thus invalidating Cattell's predicted drop in IQ. One study based on the children in a sample of families tested with the same test before, and then a decade after, the social changes initiated by the Tennessee Valley Authority yielded a mean increase in IQ of 10 points (Wheeler, 1942). Another study of students in a sample of Minnesota high schools tested first in the 1920s and again in the 1940s with the same test uncovered mean gains for the various high schools ranging between 10 and 15 points (Finch, 1946). Still another investigation, based on a sample of schools in Honolulu, where the children were first tested in 1924 and then again in 1938, yielded an increase in mean IQ of 20 points (Smith, 1942). Similar evidence of increases in such measures of intellectual level has come from comparing the test performances of soldiers of World War I with those of soldiers of World War II on the same military tests of intelligence (Tuddenham, 1948). Perhaps the most dramatic of such evidence comes from Puerto Rico where Albizu-Miranda (1966) has found children aged 7 and 8, who have enjoyed the advantages of the prosperity associated with the coming of industrialization, with mental ages as light as higher than those of their parents who were reared in the rural poverty characteristic of the inland portion of the island before industrialization. In this study children and parents were tested at the same time. The parents, despite their low IQs, were functioning adequately in their traditional roles.

As long as measures of heritability are regarded as indices of educability, such evidence seems incredible to those who believe in the importance of heredity. Once it becomes clear that measures of heritability of the IQ say nothing about the educability of individuals, classes, or races, this conflict of belief in the potency of hereditary influence with belief in the potency of environmental influence evaporates. Once such conflict of belief has evaporated, the observed differences between classes in mean IQ need no longer be regarded as biologically inevitable. Moreover, if one takes into account the three centuries of slavery and another century in which the predominant majority of white Americans expected very little in the way of competence of their black fellow Americans—typically permitting them only inferior opportunities for education and keeping the majority of them near or in poverty by allowing employment only in the most menial and low paying of occupations—it is really surprising to find the mean IQ of black Americans only 15 points below that of white Americans. No reason whatever exists to consider this discrepancy as biologically inevitable.

The issue of difference in dialect

Various investigators from the domain of linguistics are beginning to contend that what they term the social pathology perspective is as false as the hypothesis of genetic inferiority as an explanation for the lower average IQs and the scholastic inadequacy of black children (Baratz, 1969; Baratz & Baratz, 1970; Labov, 1969; Stewart, 1968; Wilfram, 1969). Black children, these investigators contend, have cognitive and linguistic skills which are structurally as coherent and complex as are those of children of middle-class whites. These cognitive and linguistic systems of black children they regard as defective in no way; they are merely different from those of children of middle-class whites.

Such conclusions appear to be based upon a comparison of the syntactical structures from bodies of recorded speech from children black and white. If we understand correctly the nature of this evidence, the typical urban black child is found to have a consistent linguistic system which may differ from that of a typical white child of the middle class; but the two linguistic systems are considered not to differ in complexity, and the information from either can be transmitted to the other.

Whenever the assessment of language competence is discussed, the investigators from linguistics are especially critical of the way in which educators and psychologists go about evaluating such competence in children who have learned nonstandard English. They reject the Peabody Picture Vocabulary Test because this test contains and allows only the linguistic forms of standard English. They reject findings from the Lorge-Thorndike Test for similar reasons. Thus, Stewart (1969) rejects the findings of Vera John (1963) of inferior verbal and classificatory skills in slum children and, of course, her conclusion that the acquisition of abstract and integrative language is hampered by the living conditions in the homes of poor families. His rejection is based upon the fact that the tests which she used contained only the linguistic forms of standard English.

Similarly, Shuy (1969) rejects the claims of Head Start teachers that children of the slums come to school with meager vocabularies on the ground that these teachers, who are speakers of standard English, are unaware that slum children acquire a home vocabulary which is merely different from the school vocabulary. Shuy argues that whenever investigators detect a linguistic deficiency among children of the poor, it means only that "the investigators prove to be such a cultural barrier to the interviewee that informants were too frightened and awed to talk freely, or that the investigators simply asked the wrong questions [p. 120]." In this context, Goodman (1969) has argued that "all children develop vocabulary which falls generally within the vocabulary pool of their speech community. Through repeated experience common for their culture they have begun to develop complex concepts and to express them in their mother tongue [p. 17]." According to this argument, none of the standard tests are fair to children of the poor because they have all been standardized in use of the language forms and heuristic styles of standard English. The word *fair* here refers to the presumption that such tests measure potential for learning. This, Hunt (1961) has contended, such tests cannot do. The tests can merely indicate what abilities have been achieved and made available for use (Humphreys, 1962a).

Three implications of importance for early education flow from this argument of the linguistics investigators, if it is true. First, insofar as the heard evidence of divergence in speech brings corrections and other behavioral evidences of disapproval, the child of the slums is likely to find school an unpleasant place. Second, insofar as dialects divergent from standard English and street cultures divergent from schoolroom cultures produce conflict, they are likely to interfere with the learning of children of poverty. Third, insofar as teachers get to know and to believe that test scores reflect learning ability, this knowledge is likely to destroy motivation to use ingenuity in teaching. One of the saddest teacher answers to the question "How are they doing?" is "As well as can be expected." Such a context is made to order for a self-fulfilling prophecy. Thus, Baratz and Baratz (1970) conclude that Head Start has failed because the teachers failed "to teach the mainstream language styles and usage by means of the child's already existing system [p. 42]."

But how correct is this conclusion? Is this "structurally coherent dialect" (or are these "structurally coherent dialects") of poor children an efficient device for communication? Does the dialect readily enable a child to understand and communicate prepositional relationships—the placement of objects in relation to one another, comparative lengths, comparative heights, difference in color, differences in shapes, and the placement and classification of objects and people by means of such criteria? From our observations of poor white children going to summer schools of Appalachia and of poor black children in various Head Start classes, we venture the suspicion that these dialects of poverty may be basically deficient in permitting a child to understand verbal directions concerning such matters or to communicate such matters. It is a matter for investigation; our suspicions may be wrong. Our questions cannot be answered, however, merely by examining the syntactical structure of bodies of verbal conversation. On the other hand, if our suspicion is true, it is likely to be just as characteristic of the language of white children of poverty as it is of the black children of poverty.

There is another question. If we be wrong about the limitations of these dialects to communicate prepositional relationships, comparative lengths, heights, weights, and volumes, variations in color and shape, and the placement and classification of objects in terms of such criteria, then it is important to ask if children from poverty achieve such concepts and the ability to communicate them at ages as young as do children of the middle class. Such is the nature of the information processing upon which success in school, later employability, and later participation in the mainstream of our culture depends. It does no good to complain that such concepts are culture-bound, for these are the conceptual stuff of our highly technological culture. The earlier children acquire them, the more skill they would be expected to have in utilizing them in any situation. On the other hand, on the basis of the "problem of the match" (Hunt, 1961, pp. 267–288; 1966, pp. 118–142), we would be the first to grant that one does not equalize the opportunities of children to learn merely by providing them with a given curriculum and a given mode of teaching. Whatever the basis for the differences among children, the more nearly school experiences can be individualized to take these into account, the more effective they are likely to be.

Poverty and opportunities to learn

But are the low test scores and the scholastic failure typical of children of the poor merely a matter of divergent dialects? If Goodman's contention that "the more divergence there is between the dialect of the learner and the dialect of the learning, the more will be the task of learning to read [1969, p. 14]" be true, how is it that the children of Jewish and Oriental parentage have long been observed to average as high, or possibly very slightly higher, than even white Americans in IQ and have typically managed to get along well in schools conducted in standard English? The Yiddish, Chinese, and Japanese languages differ far more from standard English than do the dialects of Appalachia or the black ghettos. Should one accept the hypothesis which puts the blame on linguistic differences despite the evidences that many children of the poor are conceived and go through the embryonic and fetal phases of their development in mothers with nutritional deficiencies and emotional stress (Cravioto, 1967; McDonald, 1966; Pasamanick, 1962), despite the fact that these children are often reared in crowded quarters where loud voices and the blare of television or radio are continuously jumbled (see Hunt, 1969b, pp. 204–205), despite the fact that their parents, by their own report, typically spend less time in verbal interaction with them than do the parents of the middle class with their children (Hess & Shipman, 1965; Keller, 1963; Milner, 1951), despite the fact that they lack a variety of opportunities in which to develop the motivational systems inherent in competence (see Hunt, 1969b, pp. 208–211), and despite the fact that, due to the troubles and work of their mothers, they depend very early upon peer groups for the acquisition of their values and standards (see Hunt, 1969b, pp. 211–214)? If the genotype guarantees neither the rate nor the course of psychological development, the ethical and political doctrine of equal opportunity applies to these children of the poor. By the mere accident of their birth, these children of the poor become deprived of such opportunities to develop those intellectual skills, motivational systems, and standards of conduct required for coping successfully in our schools, where, in turn, they acquire the skills for employability and with which to participate in the mainstream of our society.

This body of evidence, merely referred to here, is the basis for what Baratz and Baratz (1970) designate the social pathology perspective. It is true that much of this evidence of very early lack of educational opportunity in families of the poor derives chiefly from the reports of mothers. Insofar as these mothers of the poor report merely what they think the investigators expect to hear, this evidence may be suspect. Direct observations of the social and verbal interactions within families of varying educational and socioeconomic status are needed. Thus, the still quite incomplete study by Schoggen and Schoggen (1968) already referred to above, promises to be especially illuminating. Undoubtedly, middle-class families exist where the behavior of the parents more closely resembles that of parents of poverty than it resembles the behavior of professional families. Contrariwise, families with incomes well below the poverty line undoubtedly exist wherein the behavior of the parents toward their young resemble more that of professional families than it resembles the behavior typical of these parents of poverty. Yet, the evidence from direct observation in this still quite incomplete study by Schoggen and Schoggen tends to support the social pathology perspective, or the hypothesis that children accidentally born to parents of poverty commonly lack in their earliest years within the family the opportunities to acquire the cognitive, linguistic, and motivational skills more commonly provided by families of the middle class.

One basis for the "failure" of Head Start

Although Project Head Start has been a fine step in the proper direction, the evidence indicates that on the whole it has failed to achieve the unrealistically high hopes that a summer, or a year, of nursery schooling, beginning at 4 years of age, would enable children of the poor to succeed in regular schools. There were those who saw the hopes with which Head Start was initiated as unrealistic because the project was undertaken before a technology of early childhood education with proven compensatory effectiveness had been developed (e.g., Deutsch, 1967; Hunt, 1967).

Nursery schools were originally invented for the purpose of compensatory education. In the first decade of this century Maria Montessori (1909) developed a program for the culturally deprived of the San Lorenzo district of Rome which, according to the reports of those who visited, was highly successful (Hunt, 1964). It was the Roman Association of Good Building and the owners of the refurbished apartments in the San Lorenzo district who invited Montessori to apply the teaching methods that she had developed for the mentally retarded to the children of working parents (Montessori, 1909). These gentlemen were motivated in large part by the hope of keeping the unruly children occupied in a supervised atmosphere like school in order to prevent vandalism and save damage to their property. These children, aged 3 to 7 years, became avid pupils, according to the reports, and even learned the basic skills of counting, reading, and writing, often before they were 5 years old. Somewhat later, in the slums of England, Margaret McMillan (1919) established her nursery schools to give the children whom she considered to be environmentally handicapped by poverty an opportunity to learn what middle-class children learn spontaneously. According to the reports, she also achieved considerable success.

When nursery schools were brought to the United States, however, families of the poor could not pay for them, and no governmental support for them existed. In consequence, the nursery school came to be adapted for the needs of young children of the well-to-do. Two of the most prominent goals were to provide these children a part-time escape from the discipline from over-controlling mothers by giving them opportunities for exercise and learning through play. Since such children came even to nursery school with well-established linguistic number skills, special tutelage for these skills was considered quite unnecessary. Moreover, Montessori's practice of working simultaneously with children ranging in age from 3 to 6 or 7 years was dropped in most of these schools, thereby depriving younger children of a graded series of models for imitation and depriving older children of the opportunities to teach the younger ones.

In consequence of these historical developments, no ready-made practices of early childhood education existed for deployment in Project Head Start which were designed to compensate children of the poor for those missed opportunities to learn and which were designed to develop in them those skills which they often failed to acquire as a consequence of their family rearing.

Instead, that nursery schooling which was adopted for the program was largely that which had been traditional in the nursery schools for the well-to-do. Recognition of the inadequacy of such traditional nursery schooling as compensatory education has brought what might be called an explosion of innovations in curricula for young children. Reviewing the existing evaluative studies suggests that these curricula achieve little in the way of compensatory development in the children of the poor unless they focus on language and number concepts and on the motivation to extend the time interval in which these children operate psychologically (see Hunt, 1969b, Ch. 6). While these program directions are rapidly becoming more and more widely recognized, many nursery school teachers and some students of child development still disagree. Moreover, teachers with the appropriate skills for compensatory education are simply too few to permit wide-scale adoption of the curricula and methods of teaching which have appeared to be most effective.

The existing evidence indicates that compensatory education is remedial in nature even when it is given to disadvantaged children of the poor beginning at 3 or 4 years of age. Thus, Project Head Start failed to achieve the high hopes with which it was initiated because it was "too little and too late." It was too little in the sense that the nursery school techniques used were inappropriate for the compensatory function demanded. It was too late because it came after children had already had some four years of life under familial circumstances which deprived them of opportunities to learn typically prevailing in families in the middle class.

It should be noted, at least in passing, that successful compensatory programs are inevitably very expensive. They call for a very high teacher-student ratio, typically of the order of 1:5. Moreover, despite the expense of such education it appears all too often to have but a temporary effect. The fact that parents of poverty clearly love their children and are as concerned with their futures as any parents, coupled with the fact that these parents can be taught to be effective teachers of their infants and young children (Karnes, 1969; Karnes, et al., 1968; Karnes, et al., 1970; Klaus & Gray, 1968; Miller, 1968; Weikart, 1969), makes it seem highly likely that programs designed to prevent the development of incompetence in the young through education and work with the parents may prove both less expensive and more effective than programs of compensatory education (see Hunt, 1969b, Chs. 6 and 7). It may well be possible to produce a genuine program of social change in early education through the Parent and Child Centers deployed experimentally on a limited scale in 1968 (see Hunt, 1969b, 1970). Since no genotype guarantees by itself the development of competence, the ethical implications of the political doctrine of equal opportunity upon which our political system is based obligates our society to keep trying until an effective method of developing competence in the children of the poor has been created. If early experience is so important in both anatomical maturation and behavioral development as recent evidence implies, then that equality of opportunity, which our forefathers considered to be the ethical birthright of all, must somehow be extended to the early life of children of the poor.

Methodological issues

The failure of Project Head Start to achieve the compensatory educational goals with which it was initiated suggests that we need a reanalysis of what we think we know about the nature of intelligence and psychological development and of how best to test the validity of our existing beliefs. Any such reanalysis will raise basic methodological issues, but this is highly important lest we continue in a blind alley of investigative and educational effort.

The nature of traditional measurement of intelligence and cognitive development

Jensen (1969) has contended that "intelligence, like electricity, is easier to measure than to define [p. 5]." He defined intelligence operationally as what is measured by the metrical scale of intelligence devised in 1905 by Binet and Simon. He asserted, moreover, that the general factor (Spearman's g) implied by the existence of positive intercorrelations among scores for the performances on the several tests of this and other standard batteries "has stood like a rock of Gibraltar in psychometrics [1969, p. 9]." Is it wise to continue to let operations direct thought about the nature of intelligence and cognitive development? How useful has this "rock" been in guiding the education of the young? How useful also are mental age and the IQ—that ratio of mental age to chronological age which Stern (1912) proposed?

We have for the hypothetical construct that we call intelligence no such direct operations of measurement as we have for electricity. We have no such defining operations as those involved in ammeters, volt meters, and resistors with such resulting units as amperes, volts, and ohms. We have for intelligence nothing like Ohm's law, which, in branched circuits, provides for highly generalized operational control of electrical power. We have only tests which call for information and various abilities and the motivation to process information. Only very indirectly, and terribly inaccurately, do the tests indicate the effort and time required by individuals to achieve the information, the abilities, and the motives. Moreover, they cannot be accurately indicative of effort and time unless individuals have encountered essentially the same situations—which very seldom occurs.

It is customary to distinguish between tests of intelligence and tests of achievement. Humphreys (1962a), however, has demonstrated that tests of intelligence are basically similar to tests of achievement. Both kinds of tests involve performances depending upon previously acquired information, abilities, and motives. Minor differences exist. Tests of intelligence do typically call upon older learning than do tests of achievement. Tests of intelligence call upon information and skills for which learning situations can seldom be specified, while tests of achievement call upon information and abilities that have been the goals of teaching in specified curricular situations. The point is that both kinds of tests call upon the results of learning or experience.

Insofar as tests of intelligence serve to indicate the time and effort required for achieving information, abilities, and motivation, they do so through units of mental age, the IQ, and scores for general ability (Spearman's g). Have such concepts helped to identify the types of information, the learning sets which govern the structure of the abilities to process information, or the motives to process information? Have they served to show in psychological development how the structures of ability build upon one another? Have they served to tell teachers what curricular exercises to utilize with any given individual child to foster his development? An answer to such a question comes from considering what we know today that Binet and his contemporaries did not know about intellectual development, and especially what we know that they did not about intellectual development that can guide teachers in the formation of curricular circumstances to foster this development. Any candid student of the writings of Binet (see for a survey Varon, 1936) and of such other early students of intellectual development and education as Dewey (1897), Froebel (1826), and Montessori (1909) must admit that we know very little which is of use in directing education that these early investigators did not already know.

Most of that very little new information comes directly from the work of Piaget (1936, 1937, 1945, 1947) and the various studies stemming from his work (e.g., Elkind & Flavell, 1969; Fraisee & Piaget, 1969; Inhelder & Piaget, 1955; Smedslund, 1964). The evidence from these studies combines with that from other lines of investigation to suggest strongly that conceiving of intelligence as a forcelike variable is wrong. Rather, this evidence suggests that the cognitive structures that control information processing and that comprise intelligence and also the construction of concepts of reality undergo a series of epigenetic changes in which those acquired later build upon those acquired earlier. This view has become known as the hierarchical conception of intelligence.

There are several other lines of investigation that provide supportive evidence for the hierarchical conception of intelligence (see Hunt, 1961). The work on adult problem solving by such investigators as Gagné (1964a, 1964b) and Gagné and Paradise (1961) is one example. These investigators see the basis for the ability underlying adult problem solving in something akin to the learning sets described by Harlow (1949). Another source of at least indirect support is found in the work of those who have attempted to program electronic computers for problem solving (e.g., Newell, Shaw, & Simon, 1958; see Hunt, 1961, Ch. 4). The experimental studies of the effects of early perceptual experience on later ability and maze learning which were prompted by Hebb's (1949) theorizing (see Hunt, 1961, 1969b) and the various developments of the past two decades in the theory of brain function (e.g., Pribram, 1960, 1963; see Hunt, 1969a, pp. 286–288) furnish further backing for the hierarchical conception of intelligence. Thus, it is readily evident that detailed knowledge of the epigenetic changes in the structure of information processing and knowledge of reality which comprise this developmental hierarchy and of the kinds of encounters with circumstances required for their acquisition would be both highly important in understanding psychological growth and highly useful in the development of educational technology.

Despite the basic similarity of tests of intelligence to tests of achievement, traditional measurement practice has utilized only individual differences in scores, variously derived, from a battery of tests. The meaning of these scores has derived from interpersonal comparisons that give the rank of an individual among others in a sample. The fact that the scores, be they mental ages, IQs, or the raw scorings of some kind, have been numerically continuous has given the impression that what is measured is a continuous variable. It has been recognized, however, that these scores are but the indicators of an underlying reality and that these scores have limited reliability and limited validity as indicators. Most of the attempts to uncover the fundamental nature of this underlying reality have depended upon the use of correlational procedures in various forms of what has been called factor analysis. Where the tetrad difference method of treating the intercorrelations among test scores from children aged between 6 and 10 years led Spearman (1904, 1923, 1927) to his theory of a unitary general ability along with special abilities for each test, Kelley (1928) and Thurstone (1938) found the variance in the scores of college students on tests better accounted for by group factors. Thurstone (1938) proposed seven such factors, which he termed primary mental abilities. French, Ekstrom, and Price (1963) have more recently selected tests to measure twenty-four such abilities in their Kit of Reference Test for Cognitive Factors. The number of such group factors can be extended indefinitely by elaborating and fractioning tests of existing factors.

Although such group factors are separate enough to be identifiable, group factor scores are typically correlations, so that factor scores can themselves be analyzed in what has been designated second-order factoring. This fact has led to another hierarchical conception in which higher-order factors derive from the intercorrelations among lower-order factors. In this conception, something very close to Spearman's general factor emerges at the top (Burt, 1967; Humphreys, 1962b; Vernon, 1961). The hierarchical theory of factors, however, is radically different from the hypothetical hierarchy of learning sets, which presumably underlie the sequential epigenesis in the structure of information processing.

The correlational procedures of factor analysis have led also to a third way of viewing the organization of human abilities, which is exemplified in Guilford's (1956, 1967) structure-of-intellect model. Guilford's concern has been to uncover the units of intellect and to provide a system for classifying them after the fashion of Mendeleev's periodic table of elements in chemistry (see 1967, p. 47). He has not been concerned with understanding psychological development. His view has been called *facet theory*. Guilford's model is represented by a $4 \times 5 \times 6$ solid. The three dimensions represent, respectively, four kinds of *content* (figural, symbolic, semantic, and behavioral), five kinds of psychological *operations* (cognition, memory, divergent production, convergent production, and evaluation), and six kinds of *products of information* (units, classes, relations, systems, transformations, and implications). Implied is the existence of 120 unique abilities. The term facet theory derives from the use of logical dimensions, or facets, to guide the development of tests (Guttman & Schlesinger, 1965). Thus, for Guilford, the 120 unique abilities hypothesized derived from the theory rather than from exploratory factor analysis of test performances even though Guilford and his students have made such analyses in order to verify a great many of these hypothesized abilities.

The meaning of these factors of intelligence has been a matter of dispute. Some factor analysts have contended that the method uncovers genuine ability entities (Cattell, 1952; Guilford, 1940; Holzinger, 1937; Thurstone, 1935). Others have conceived of the factors only as descriptive categories (Burt, 1940; Thompson, 1939; Tryon, 1935; Varon, 1936). Some factor analysts have contended that these ability entities are essentially predetermined and fixed by heredity (Cattell, 1937, 1950b). Such a view amounts to psychological preformationism. Although Burt (1940) was unwilling to view factors as fixed causal entities of ability, nevertheless, he considered intelligence as inborn (Burt, *et al.*, 1934).

Evidence highly dissonant with the immutability of factors has come from various studies in which the factor structures of scores from given groups of tests were clearly altered by practice (Anastasi, 1936; Fleishman & Hempel, 1954; Woodrow, 1938, 1939). Moreover, a logical analysis by Ferguson (1954) results in a view diametrically opposed to that of immutability. Ferguson (1954, 1956) based his logical analysis upon a scrutiny of the terms ability and transfer. *Ability* refers, first, to measures of performance which, subject to error, locate individuals on an underlying latent variable; second, in the case of factor analysis, to the weighted additive sum of measures of performance on separate tasks which imply a latent factor variable; and third, to some attribute of the organism or person. Ferguson assumes that the various ability factors have achieved stability through overlearning and are, therefore, approaching a crude limit beyond which no systematic improvement is likely to come with further practice. *Transfer*, defined after the mathematical concept of function (Ferguson, 1956, 1959), implies that change in performance on one task is a function of change resulting from practice on another. Thus, Ferguson explains a general factor of ability and the considerable degree of positive correlation among test scores in terms of positive transfer. He also explains the group factors of ability which emerge in the performance of adults in terms of abilities which tend to facilitate rather than to inhibit one another. Humphreys (1959, 1962b) has extended this analysis by showing how experimental manipulations which have traditionally been used to study the transfer of training can account for the obtained correlations among abilities.

Despite the evidence that practice can alter the factor structures which emerge from the intercorrelations among the scores in given batteries, and despite the theory of Ferguson and Humphreys that the abilities which emerge from factor analysis represent nodes of transfer from overlearning, the results from factor analyzing the scores on tests of intelligence appear to be education-ally sterile. They provide teachers with no guidance concerning how interests and abilities build dynamically one upon another. In fact, except for some of the abilities of Guilford (1967) which derive in large part from his intuition, factored abilities lack for us intuitive reality. They are of little use in observing and understanding the behavioral development of a child. They are of little use in choosing the circumstances best calculated to foster the development of new levels of ability in children. We contend that the traditional concept of intelligence as a continuous variable measurable by mental age and the IQ and conceived as a forcelike general ability has been of highly limited use in education and in the study of the nature of psychological development. We contend that the very existence of these measurement concepts of mental age and IQ and g have stood in the way of serious consideration of the concept of intellectual development as a hierarchy of learning sets which underlie a sequential epigenesis in the structure of information processing. We contend that this traditional view of intelligence has stood in the way of investigating the behavioral landmarks in intellectual development and the kinds of encounters with circumstances upon which their development depends.

The desirability of sequentially ordinal scales

What is required is a basically new approach to the assessment of cognitive development and also motivational development. What we need are investigations which will uncover the sequential landmarks in both cognitive and motivational development and in the construction of operations which will define these behavioral landmarks and the successive structures of information processing and reality construction.

Such is the nature of the sequential, ordinal scales of psychological develop-ment in infancy devised by Uzgiris and Hunt (1966, 1968). These ordinal scales were inspired by the observations of Piaget (1936, 1937). A foreshortened version of the scale of object permanence, which gives seven of the behavioral landmarks in the acquisition of the object concept, has already been described above in connection with the study of the ages at which the various levels are achieved in children living in Athens under differing circumstances. For illustrative purposes it may be useful to give here the landmarks in the development of vocal imitation which are also being used in this same study. The first landmark consists in a positive response to vocalizations which are known to be familiar to the child. The second landmark consists in the child copying such familiar vocal models. The third landmark consists in vocal responses to an examiner's modeling of unfamiliar vocal patterns, but vocal responses which fail to resemble the model. The fourth landmark consists of progressive efforts to copy vocally an unfamiliar vocal pattern. The fifth landmark consists in copying successfully three different unfamiliar vocal patterns. Since it has been found to make little difference whether these unfamiliar vocal patterns are words of the language or nonwords, this foreshortened version of the scale uses only words. The sixth landmark consists in the child copying or repeating after the examiner such short sentences as "This is a ball." Copying such sentences puts a child beyond the sensorimotor phase of vocal imitation.

Since such landmarks are sequentially ordinal in character, success with one and failure with the next in the sequential order serves to define a child's level of acquisition for a particular line of development. It should be noted that this concept of *level* resembles in certain ways Piaget's (1947) concept of *stages,* but inasmuch as the levels defined by these scales do not correspond to the stages of Piaget, we use the term level rather than the term stage.

This capacity to define levels of development permits one to compare the ages at which children with different backgrounds of experience achieve these levels. Such information should be useful in pointing to the general nature of what kinds of experience are important for the acquisition of the successive behavioral landmarks in the line of development with which each scale is concerned. It is of significance, therefore, that the ages of the children of orphanage 3:1 in the upper levels of object construction approximate more closely the ages of home-reared children than do the children in orphanage 10:1 who are at the same upper levels of object construction. On the other hand, the ages of the children at orphanage 3:1 in the upper levels of vocal imitation resemble more closely the ages of those in orphanage 10:1 than do the ages of the home-reared children in those same upper levels of vocal imitation. Thus, it appears likely that the amount of opportunity to hear adult vocalization is more important for the development of vocal imitation than for object construction, but any such hypothesis calls for validation through careful comparisons of the frequencies of the various kinds of circumstances encountered in these two orphanages and in the homes of working-class families in Athens.

Norm-referenced tests versus criterion-referenced tests

Such methodology differs radically from the standard approach to the testing of intelligence. In their invention of "mental age" Binet and Simon (1905) utilized chronological age to obtain quantitative meaning from the performances of children. They developed this notion of mental age because there is, indeed, a rough correlation between level of achievement and chronological age and because, with appropriate circumstances, increasing levels of achievement do come with time. What is omitted in the concept of mental age, however, is any concern for how one level of achievement builds upon another. What is also omitted is any concern for the kinds of circumstances or experience required to foster new levels of achievement at each successive level of development.

Although Binet participated in the invention of the mental age, he deplored the fact that "some recent philosophers appear to have given their moral support to the deplorable verdict that the intelligence of an individual is a fixed quantity . . . we must protest and act against this brutal pessimism . . . a child's mind is like a field for which an expert farmer has devised a change in the method of cultivating, with the result that in the place of desert land, we now have a harvest [Binet, 1909, pp. 54–55]." As we have already noted, the notion of fixed intelligence was promulgated by Galton (1869) in his work on hereditary genius. It received conceptual support from the notion of predetermined development that was implicit in Hall's emphasis on the doctrine of recapitulation (see Hunt, 1961, pp. 43–49). When Stern (1912) suggested that the rate of development might be taken as a convenient measure of intelligence, he provided a handy tool of measurement (mental age/chronological age $=$ IQ) for those who came into the investigation of intelligence and into the intelligence-testing movement with the presuppositions based upon the teachings of Galton and Hall.

It should be noted, however, that neither the mental age nor the IQ carry much significance without norms to provide a basis for comparing the performance of an individual with the performances of others. The fact that the average IQ equals 100 derives directly from the fact that the mental-age value of performing a given test item successfully is based upon the fact of interpersonal comparisons wherein approximately 65 percent to 80 percent of children at a given age have been able to succeed with the item. Such considerations have prompted Glaser (1963) to refer to the standard test batteries for both intelligence and achievement as *norm-referenced*. They are norm-referenced because the scores describing performance acquire meaning from the rank given to an individual's performance in the performances of that group of individuals upon which the norms for the test are based. Glaser (1963) has drawn a contrast between these traditional norm-referenced tests and a new kind of test that he calls *criterion-referenced* tests. In this latter type of test, the meaning of any individual's performance derives from the behavioral goal of providing that individual with a given educational experience. This behavioral goal constitutes the criterion of success for the educational effort.

It should be noted that the criterion-referenced tests give new meaning to the standard concepts of reliability and validity of test scores—new meaning which is radically different from the meaning that they have had in connection with norm-referenced tests (Popham & Husek, 1969).

This distinction between norm-referenced tests and criterion-referenced tests is extremely useful. Moreover, if the effects of educational experiences are to be meaningfully assessed, the distinction is absolutely necessary. Approaching the problems of education with merely comparative measures of individual differences in intelligence or achievement has not only deprived teachers of the motivation to use their own ingenuity in teaching children who fail, but it has commonly provided the basis for that self-fulfilling prophecy, already lamented, epitomized in the judgment of teachers that their students are doing "as well as can be expected." Also, norm-based comparisons among individual children supply their teachers with no guidance about what kind of experience a given child at a given time requires to foster his progress. Great teachers appear to glean intuitively what kind of illustration or exercise will prove useful in promoting new understanding in a given student from the way that student answers his questions. Unfortunately, we know of no attempts having been made to move this art of "great" teachers toward the beginning of a science that specifies the relationships required. Probably no barrier to such effort has been greater than that deriving from what Glaser has termed norm-referenced tests.

Defining operations for sequential landmarks versus criterion-referenced tests

The approach to assessment, suggested above, via operations which will define the sequentially achieved landmarks in various lines of intellectual and motivational development resembles in certain ways the approach via criterion-referenced tests of Glaser (1963). In both cases the meaning of an individual's test performance derives from the level of achievement at which this performance places him rather than from comparison with the performances of others. On the other hand, such defining operations also differ fundamentally from criterion-referenced tests. In case of the latter the meaning of an individual's performance derives from the behavioral goal of the educational experience being provided. In the case of the ordinal scales of psychological development in infancy devised by Uzgiris and Hunt (1966) no deliberate educational effort existed to provide the criterion of meaning for an individual infant's performance. But, once the sequentially achieved landmarks have been identified, the meaning of any child's performance can derive from where that performance places him along the sequential, ordinal scale of landmarks. Inasmuch as criterion-referenced tests derive their meaning from the goals of educational experiences, they are impossible to administer before some kind of formal education begins. Moreover, insofar as the hierarchical, epigenetic conception of psychological development is true, placing an individual child on the sequentially ordinal arrangements of landmarks for a given line of psychological development should serve as a highly useful guide to readiness for given educational encounters.

Thus far, readiness has typically been conceived to be largely a function of a child's level of maturation, where maturation has been conceived to be under the control of heredity, rather than of his past experience. Time alone, however, results in neither cognitive nor motivational development. This is the lesson from Gordon's (1923) finding from the canal-boat children of England and from Dennis's (1960) finding that 84 percent of orphanage children in their fourth year still fail to walk alone. For development to be fostered, the circumstances encountered must be appropriately matched to the structure of information processing and motor abilities already achieved (Hunt, 1961, pp. 267–288; 1966). Even so, the alterations in the meaning of reliability and validity which have been described by Popham and Husek (1969) for the shift from norm-referenced tests to criterion-referenced tests probably hold also in large part for those test operations for defining the sequential landmarks in any given line of psychological development.

Operations defining sequential landmarks of development beyond infancy

Thus far, only provisional scales exist for the sequentially ordinal landmarks of some six lines of development through what Piaget has named his sensori-motor phase of psychological development. Although clinical observations strongly suggest the existence of such sequentially ordinal landmarks for that development during the preconceptual phase between the sensorimotor phase and the phase of concrete operations, almost nothing has yet been done in the way of constructing test operations to define the sequential landmarks of development in this preconceptual phase. Curricular planning for early child-hood education could profit greatly by such information. If one takes seriously Hunt's (1961, 1966) "problem of the match," teachers and parents of children in the preconceptual phase are limited to the behavioral clues of interest and surprise in their choice of circumstances for promoting the psychological development of these children. Discovering operations with which to define a series of sequentially ordinal landmarks in this preconceptual phase of develop-ment and discovering what kinds of experience are required for the acquisition of the successive behavioral landmarks must not only contribute substantially to our understanding of psychological development, but it must also be of tremendous utility in early childhood education.

During this preconceptual phase, according to Piaget's (1945) observa-tions, children acquire facility with the symbolic operations of language. They appear to achieve a coordination between two lines of development from the sensorimotor phase. One line is that of object construction wherein representational central processes, or images, give permanence to the objects encountered perceptually. The other line is that of vocal imitation, which provides the system of signs for objects and events. In the course of this coordination children become able to formulate with the symbols of language and numbers the operations that they have already achieved at the sensorimotor level.

Unfortunately, the sequential ordinality of the landmarks in this phase of development are still obscure. For this reason we have designed two batteries of test operations with which to define some of the behavior that educational experience indicates must be present or under acquisition. One is a battery of tests of information identification (Hunt & Kirk, 1970). The second is a battery of tests of information-processing abilities (Kirk & Hunt, 1970). Each battery investigates the ability of children to perceive and to act upon given kinds of information and, in turn, to communicate this information. Evidence of a child's possessing the cognitive, or information-processing, ability to perceive the model is based upon whether he can be got to imitate the examiner's actions once the cues in the product of the action have been removed. Each battery then goes on to determine whether the child can act upon the same information when it is presented to him verbally in either standard English or nonstandard English. Each goes further to determine whether the child can communicate the matters concerned to another child through either standard English or nonstandard English and then finally proceeds on through the use of reading and of writing. Thus, each of these batteries investigates the ability of children to process information in the following ten modes: (1) Perceptual Identification—Model Present; (2) Perceptual Identification—Model Removed; (3) Listening Identification—Standard English; (4) Listening Identification—Nonstandard English; (5) Speaking Identification—Standard English; (6) Speaking Identification—Nonstandard English; (7) Reading Identification—Standard English; (8) Reading Identification—Nonstandard English; (9) Writing Identification—Standard English; and (10) Writing Identification—Nonstandard English.

The Hunt-Kirk Test of Information Identification investigates the ability of children to receive, to process, and to communicate information related to such matters as (a) color, (b) positional placement, (c) number, (d) shape, (e) size, and (f) object names, each taken separately, in the various modes of perception and communication noted above.

The Kirk-Hunt Test of Information-Processing Abilities is a battery of test operations which define perceptual, conceptual, and communicational abilities to process various combinations of the kinds of information identified individually in the Hunt-Kirk Test of Information Identification. The latter battery investigates the ability of young children, and of older children and even adults, to perceive, to process, and to communicate information about perceptual patterns that vary from the very simple to the quite complex. The ability to perceive and utilize the information about the pattern to guide action involves color, shape, size, and positional placement and is based upon imitation of the manipulations of the examiner with his model present and imitation with his model removed. The ability to process such information symbolically goes also through the modes of listening to and reading directions in both standard English and in dialect, and the ability to communicate through the modes of both speaking and writing directions for others to follow. The complexity of the patterns can be extended from simply putting a single block in a single place, through putting three blocks of given colors or size into three boxes of the same colors, to such as using the next-to-the-next longest yellow stick and the next-to-the-largest flat, blue, triangular block to put the tallest of the slim, round, red blocks into the red box on the right-hand side. Both the perceptual processing of information required to imitate such complex performances and the listening to or the giving of instructions in speech or writing calls for the existence of that concrete operation which Piaget has termed *seriation*.

Such tests should be very useful in testing the hypothesis of those investigators from linguistics that the failure of the children of the poor, especially black children of the poor, occurs merely because they are required to use standard English. Comparisons of the success of the imitative performances of such children with those of children from families of the middle class coupled with comparisons of the success of their performances under directions in the dialect familiar to them with the success of their own performances under directions in standard English should tell whether their failure is merely a matter of unfamiliar language or is a matter of inability to process such information with facility. One pilot study (Kirk, 1970a) has already compared the performances on the positional identification test of a small sample of twenty children of the poor in a Head Start class with the performances of twenty privileged children in a private Montessori school. The children of each of these groups were in their fifth year. All had already had several months of preschooling. The pilot study was limited in the procedures employed to (1) perceptual identification where the child must imitate with the examiner's model of the placement of the object in view, (2) perceptual identification where the child must imitate with the placement of the object not in view, (3) listening identification where the child must follow directions given by the examiner vocally in standard English, and (4) speaking identification where the child must describe verbally where the examiner has placed the object in his own language. The test consisted in placing a single block *in, on, under,* and *in front of* one of the reference boxes and *between* the two reference boxes. Table 1 presents the results.

The children of poverty imitated these simple placements as well as did those from the private Montessori school both with the model present and with

Table 1. Performances of 20 disadvantaged children and 20 advantaged children on the test of positional identification

| | Pretest | | | Test A | | | | |
	In the ash tray	On the book	On the block	in	under	between	in-front-of	on
				Utilizing 2 reference boxes side by side				
A. Perceptual identification: imitation with the model present								
Advantaged	20	20	20	20	20	20	20	20
Disadvantaged	20	20	20	20	20	20	20	20
B. Perceptual identification: imitation with the model removed from view								
Advantaged	20	20	20	20	20	20	20	20
Disadvantaged	20	20	20	20	20	20	20	20
C. Listening identification: performance with verbal directions in standard English								
Advantaged	20	20	20	20	20	19	14	19
Disadvantaged	20	20	18	20	20	7	7	20
D. Speaking identification: reporting verbally the placement of the test object								
Advantaged	18	20	20	20	20	12	13	18
Disadvantaged	19	18	16	17	17	7	4	14

the model absent. But, despite the fact that they were over 4 years old and had experienced several months of preschooling, more than half of them failed to understand verbal directions in standard English for *in front of* and *between*. Some of the privileged children failed to follow the directions too, but substantially fewer. No directions were given in the dialect of the children, but when given a chance to say where the block had been placed by the examiner with no restraint on the matter of dialect or standard English, substantially more of the Head Start children than of the Montessori students failed. These results from such a pilot study are only illustrative of method; they are not to be taken seriously even as provisional evidence against the hypothesis posed by the investigators from the domain of linguistics.

Insofar as the matter of sequential ordinality is concerned, investigations with these batteries of tests will be exploratory. That such sequential ordinality does exist, however, is attested by observations of children utilizing the shape box of Creative Playthings. Regularly young children learn to place the round block through the round hole before they learn to place the square block through the square hole, and the latter before they learn to place the rectangular block through the rectangular hole. Regularly children show persistence in those activities for which they have newly acquired capacity. Thus, an infant of 28 months was observed to lift the lid of the shape box and pick out the round block from it eighteen consecutive times, each time thrusting the round block through the round hole. This is evidence for what Hunt (1966) calls use of motivational and emotional cues in solving the "problem of the match." Other observational evidence exists for this solution. Before children have learned to put such blocks through the properly shaped holes without trial and error, they become distressed by efforts to get them to locate on a sheet picturing nine such objects in three columns of three the same objects pictured on cards. Once children have learned to place the blocks of the shape box through properly shaped holes without trial and error, they can readily be interested in this game of finding on the sheet the objects pictured on the cards. Moreover, they play the new game for prolonged periods of time with evident pleasure (observations of Earladeen Badger, personal communication). We expect information about sequential ordinality among the information-processing abilities defined by the operations in our tests, however, to be a product of our investigations.

The diagnostic value of such tests for early childhood education should be of considerable value quite independently of the information that our investigations may yield about sequential ordinality. The abilities to receive, process, and communicate information concerning such matters as color, shape, number, and positional placement is not only typically taken for granted by 5 years of age, but they are also basic to the acquisition of later academic skills and information-processing abilities. A second pilot study (Kirk, 1970b) which has investigated the development of information on color identification with fifteen white children of poverty in attendance at a Parent and Child Center in Illinois illustrates the educational value of information from such tests. The children in this group were in the last half of their fourth year or in their fifth year. All had had several months of preschooling. The pilot study was again limited to but part of the testing procedures, namely, to (1) matching blocks by color on an imitative basis, (2) identifying the correct color on a listening basis, and (3) identifying the correct color of blocks on a speaking basis. The listening operations were in standard English, but the children were given free rein for their spoken identifications. The test included six blocks, each representing one of the following colors: *red, blue, yellow, green, purple,* and *orange*. All of the children were able to demonstrate competence in the perceptual identification of all of these colors by matching the appropriate color blocks together; yet, they demonstrated difficulty in processing word symbols for these colors in both listening and speaking communication. Over half of the children were unable to identify correctly the color name in both listening and speaking. It was interesting to note, however, that each child provided a color name (when asked, "What color is this block?") even though the color name was incorrect, thus implying that they had a crude concept of colors as a class. The teachers who had served these children for several months observed the testing. The educational value of the information was found in their surprise to see how many of these children, whom they had assumed already knew how to identify objects by color, were in fact unable to process this information on either a listening or a speaking basis. The teachers expressed a special concern for those of the children who were to enter kindergarten in the coming fall.

One of the major values to emerge from such tests will be the information of a diagnostic nature made immediately available for teachers. Thus, instead of having to translate the educationally vague information provided by a traditional test of intelligence or a norm-referenced test of achievement, such test operations will define the abilities and inform parents and teachers whether and how a child is able to process information of various kinds. The teacher provided with such information is much more readily able to decide which instructional activities should be provided for the child to match his level of development and previous experience than she would be from a mental age or an IQ. We hope that the evidence from investigation will lead also to evidence of sequential ordinality in landmarks for several lines of development in this preconceptual phase, such as Uzgiris and Hunt (1969) have already uncovered for the sensorimotor phase of psychological development.

Other methodological issues

Investigation is also urgently needed for other methodological issues. It is our hope that developing tests that provide defining operations for various abilities will yield evidence relevant to some of these issues. Several of these deserve brief consideration.

Cumulative effects of circumstances

The relation of experience to psychological development, except largely in the domains of classical and operant conditioning, which have thus far been found to have little effect on rate of development, continues to be poorly understood. The classical early studies of the effects of practice on immediate memory for digits (Gates & Taylor, 1925), stair climbing (Gesell & Thompson, 1929), and buttoning, ladder climbing, and cutting with scissors (Hilgard, 1932) found the effects of practice on these activities to be highly evanescent. Other evidence has implied that the effects of experience on intellectual development, even as measured by the IQ, is cumulative. Thus, Gordon's (1923) famous study of the English canal-boat children brought out that the IQ declines from age 4 to 6 years (mean IQ = 90) to adolescence (mean IQ = 60). In this study the correlation between IQ and age was $-.75$. Such a cumulative effect of circumstances which fail to foster intellectual development is commonly observed also in a progressive drop in the IQs for children of the poor between the ages of 15 or 18 months and 5 or 6 years (Gray & Klaus, 1970; Klaus & Gray, 1968). It is this drop which appears to be compensated in part by cognitively oriented early education and which has been prevented by teaching mothers of poverty to be better teachers of their own infants and preschool children (Karnes, *et al.*, 1968; Karnes, *et al.*, 1970; Weikart, 1969). This evidence of the cumulative effects of experience appears to be very much at variance with the evidence of the evanescence of the effects of practice.

Logical analysis of the interrelated lines of evidence can remove at least part of this dissonance. For instance, substantial variations with experience have been shown for the age at which the blink-response appears (Greenberg, Uzgiris, & Hunt, 1968) and for the age at which top-level, visually directed reaching is achieved (White & Held, 1966). As long as measurement of development is limited to the presence of such limited reactions, the ceiling of the scale is exceedingly low. The same goes for the stair climbing, buttoning, ladder climbing, and cutting with scissors used in the early studies of the effects of practice mentioned above. We would expect the effects of experience on such functions to be evanescent unless the circumstances encountered by the child were such as to enable him to use such abilities early in the process of acquiring later sequential landmarks in his psychological development. Only as the circumstances of children enable them to use each new landmark in a line of development immediately upon its acquisition to foster the development of landmarks higher in the sequence could one expect to find evidence of cumulative effects of experience. Unfortunately, this hypothesis of the cumulative process in development has not yet been investigated experimentally. It can be investigated only as sequentially ordinal landmarks for given lines of development are uncovered and only as the kind of circumstances required for the use of each landmark schema are experimentally provided as it develops so as to promote earlier achievement of the next landmark schema in the line.

Relation of cognitive structures to language

Investigators from the domain of linguistics appear to rest their various cases upon either logical analysis or evidence derived from bodies of recorded utterances by children. Chomsky (1959) made his case against Skinner's (1957) argument that verbal behavior is acquired through reinforcement, like that which has been effective in the training of animals, on the failure of this theory to account for the ability of children to produce an indefinite variety of linguistic structures that have never been previously uttered and reinforced. Chomsky's (1963) theory makes of language a system of rules rather than a system of elements, and it is typically referred to as transformational linguistics or generative grammar. The theory attempts to describe the rules of language as these rules are internalized and mastered by the child functioning as a speaker-listener. These transformational rules include (1) those syntactical, (2) those phonological, and (3) those semantic.

Unfortunately, beyond his logical analysis, Chomsky rests his theory almost entirely upon the verbal behavior that occurs after children begin to speak. As Friedlander (1970) has pointed out in an excellent paper on receptive language development, the normal baby's expressive speech is still highly primitive when "his listening admits him to a world of sophisticated language communication . . . it is almost irrelevant [therefore] to labor over the controversy of whether the child learns to speak by mimicry, by social modeling, or by creative synthesis, when any or all of these processes can only get underway in earnest a full six months to a year after the child is already an attentive listener and [receptive user of language] [p. 20]."

This influential theory of Chomsky, in its focus upon the three kinds of rules mentioned, omits consideration of the formation of central processes which represent objects, persons, places, and events and the role which sequential organizations of these representational processes play in the acquisition of both receptive language and active communication. In this connection, Sigel (1970) has reported substantial differences in the classifying behavior of children from the middle class from that of children of poverty. Children of 8 or 9 years of age from middle-class backgrounds make essentially similar classifications of concrete, tridimensional objects, of pictures of those objects, and of cards with the names of those objects. But children of poverty succeed in classifying only concrete objects in a fashion resembling the classifications of children of middle-class backgrounds. The classifications which children of the poor tend to make of the pictures of those objects and of the names of those objects differ radically from the classifications which they make of the concrete objects. According to Sigel's "distancing hypothesis," the experiences of children of poverty have failed to develop from pictures and names the full range of interconnections developed for concrete objects. In other words, Chomsky's theory fails completely to take into account both the process of forming the object concept and the process of development in vocal imitation which processes appear to be the two lines of psychological development that are coordinated in the acquisition of language.

Chomsky's theory also omits consideration of possible discrepancies between perceptual ability to process information about color, shape, size, and the placement of objects and the ability to process such information symbolically through either heard or spoken language. The tests that we have constructed should help determine if there are such discrepancies—and if they differ for children of differing background.

On a priori grounds it would appear likely that an epigenesis will appear in the relationship between central representational processes and language both with increasing age and with increasing complexity of tasks. As long as the number of items of information which must be taken into account to imitate the examiner's action is small, perceptual information processing will be adequate. As the number of items of information about color, shape, and size increases, it should become more and more difficult to imitate even with the model present, and it should be additionally difficult to imitate with the model absent without language. Moreover, once that number of items passes well beyond the span of apprehension, performance under written directions will probably surpass performance under verbal directions.

Until these additional aspects of the development of language in communication have been investigated and until the various kinds of experiences upon which their development depends have been specified, we shall have neither a fully developed conception of language development nor one that can be very useful to the technology of education.

Relation of cognitive and communicative abilities to home experience

What we think we know about the relation between cognitive and communicative abilities to what goes on in homes comes largely from the reports of mothers. An exception to this statement is the investigation already mentioned of the social and linguistic interaction of the older persons with 3-year-olds in families representing the professional class, the rural poor, and the urban poor by Schoggen and Schoggen. This investigation, which is still in progress at this writing, appears to be uncovering evidence which will be highly illuminating. Yet, if we are ever to understand the relationship of these experiences within families to the acquisition of cognitive and communicative abilities, we shall have to compare the variation in such home experiences for children who are known to be advanced and retarded in the development of cognitive and communicative abilities. Such an approach calls for a radical change in our methodology—both the methodology for assessing the development-fostering quality of the circumstances of intrafamilial social interaction and the methodology for measuring psychological development.

Conclusion

Measured by the high and wonderful hopes with which Project Head Start was initiated, the achievement of Head Start has been a severe disappointment to many. The frustration of this disappointment is motivating some to return to a belief in the genetic inferiority of both those poor and those black. Since this belief can justify holding that the principle of equal opportunity for all cannot be applied to those infants who happen to have been born to parents of poverty and of dark skins, there is also danger that this frustration may lead to apathy about the social problems of poverty and race.

On the other hand, the frustration of this disappointment can also motivate a new concern for the evidence and the issues surrounding early psychological development. In this discussion, we have attempted to focus attention on the evidence for plasticity in early psychological development with its ethical implications. We have reexamined several of the substantive issues. We have also raised several methodological issues. Most important among these are the sterility of traditional tests of intelligence and aptitude for the study of psychological development and as a guide for educators and the need of new modes of attack. Our own suggestion is outlined along with additional issues for future consideration.

Since that "want of clearness" in these matters which Plato had his Athenian acknowledge (*Laws*, Book VII, 788) persists to our day, we pray that those who are enjoying the benefits of our highly affluent culture will continue to support an extended investigation of early psychological development, that they will continue to support the development of more effective technologies of early education, and that they will ultimately support a universal deployment of those technologies that prove to be effective and viable. Only thus may we be able to reduce that inequality of preschool opportunity which figures heavily in the cycle of poverty and incompetence and which fosters what James Baldwin has called "the racial nightmare" of America.

References

Albizu-Miranda, C. The successful retardate. Mimeographed technical report. Hato Rey, Puerto Rico: Division of Education, Commonwealth of Puerto Rico, 1966.

Anastasi, A. The influence of specific experience upon mental organization. *Genetic Psychology Monographs*, 1936, *18*, 245–355.

————. *Differential psychology.* (3rd ed.) New York: Macmillan, 1958.

Baratz, J. C. Language and cognitive assessment of Negro children: Assumptions and research needs. *ASHA*, March 1969.

Baratz, S. B., & Baratz, J. C. Early childhood intervention: The social science base of institutional racism. *Harvard Educational Review*, 1970, *40*, 29–50.

Bennett, E. L., Diamond, M. C., Krech, D., & Rosenzweig, M. R. Chemical and anatomical plasticity of the brain. *Science*, 1964, *146*, 610–619.

Binet, A. *Les idées modernes sur les enfants.* Paris: Ernest Flamarion, 1909. Cited from G. D. Stoddard, The IQ: Its ups and downs. *Educational Record*, 1939, *20*, 44–57.

————, & Simon, T. Méthodes nouvelles pour le diagnostic du niveau intellectuel des anormaux. *Année Psychologique*, 1905, *11*, 191–244.

Brattgård, S. O. The importance of adequate stimulation for the chemical composition of retinal ganglion cells during early post-natal development. *Acta Radiologica*, Stockholm, 1952, Suppl. 96, 1–80.

Burt, C. L. *The factors of the mind.* London: University of London Press, 1940.

————. The structure of mind. In S. Wiseman (Ed.), *Intelligence and ability.* Baltimore: Penguin, 1967.

————, Jones, E., Miller, E., & Moodie, W. *How the mind works.* New York: Appleton-Century-Crofts, 1934.

Cattell, R. B. *The fight for our national intelligence.* London: Staples, 1937.

————. The fate of national intelligence: Test of a thirteen-year prediction. *Eugenics Review*, 1950, *42*, 136–148. (a)

————. *Personality: A systematic theoretical and factual study.* New York: McGraw-Hill, 1950. (b)

————. *Factor analysis: An introduction and manual for psychologist and social scientist.* New York: Harper & Row, 1952.

Chomsky, N. Review of B. F. Skinner *Verbal behavior. Language*, 1959, *35*, 26–58.

————. Formal properties of grammar. In R. D. Luce, R. Bush, & E. Galanter (Eds.), *Handbook of mathematical psychology.* Vol. 2. New York: Wiley, 1963.

Cicarelli, V. *The impact of Head Start: An evaluation of the effects of Head Start on children's cognitive and affective development.* Vol. 1. *Text and appendices F through J.* Athens, Ohio: Ohio University and Bladensburg, Md.: Westinghouse Learning Corporation, 1969.

Cravioto, J. Malnutrition and behavioral development in the preschool child. In N. Scrimshaw & J. E. Gordon (Eds.), *Malnutrition, learning, and behavior.* Cambridge: M.I.T. Press, 1967.

Darwin, C. *On the origin of species.* London: Murray, 1859.

Davis, K. Final note on a case of extreme isolation. *American Journal of Sociology*, 1947, *57*, 432–457.

Dennis, W. Causes of retardation among institutional children: Iran. *Journal of Genetic Psychology*, 1960, *96*, 47–59.

————. Goodenough scores, art experience, and modernization. *Journal of Social Psychology*, 1966, *68*, 211–228.

Deutsch, M. Social intervention and the malleability of the child. In M. Deutsch and associates, *The disadvantaged child*. New York: Basic Books, 1967.

Dewey, J. Pedagogic creed. *The School Journal*, 1897, *54*, 77–80.

Dunn, L. M. *Expanded manual for the Peabody Picture Vocabulary Test*. Minneapolis: American Guidance Service, 1965.

Elkind, D., & Flavell, J. H. (Eds.) *Studies in cognitive development: Essays in honor of Jean Piaget*. New York: Oxford University Press, 1969.

Ferguson, G. A. On learning and human ability. *Canadian Journal of Psychology*, 1954, *8*, 95–112.

———. On transfer and the abilities of man. *Canadian Journal of Psychology*, 1956, *10*, 121–131.

———. Learning and human ability: A theoretical approach. In P. H. DuBois, W. H. Manning, & C. J. Spies (Eds.), *Factor analysis and related techniques in the study of learning*. Technical Report No. 7, Office of Naval Research Contract No. Nonr 816 (02), 1959.

Finch, F. H. Enrollment increases and changes in the mental level of the high school population. *Applied Psychology Monographs*, 1946, *10*, 1–75.

Fleishman, E. A., & Hempel, W. E., Jr. Changes in factor structure of a complex psychomotor test as a function of practice. *Psychometrika*, 1954, *19*, 239–252.

Forgays, D. G., & Forgays, J. W. The nature of the effect of free environmental experience in the rat. *Journal of Comparative and Physiological Psychology*, 1952, *45*, 322–328.

Forgus, R. H. The effect of early perceptual learning on the behavioral organization of adult rats. *Journal of Comparative and Physiological Psychology*, 1954, *46*, 331–336.

Fraisse, P., & Piaget, J. *Experimental psychology: Its scope and method. VII: Intelligence*. (T. Surridge, Transl.) New York: Basic Books, 1969.

French, J. W., Ekstrom, R., & Price, L. A. *Manual for Kit of Reference Tests for Cognitive Factors*. Princeton, N.J.: Educational Testing Service, 1963.

Friedlander, B. Z. Receptive language development in infancy: Issues and problems. *Merrill-Palmer Quarterly of Behavior and Development*, 1970, *16*, 7–51.

Froebel, F. *The education of man*. (W. N. Hailman, Transl.) New York: Appleman, 1892. (C. 1826)

Fuller, J. L., & Thompson, W. R. *Behavior genetics*. New York: Wiley, 1960.

Gagné, R. M. Problem solving. In A. W. Melton (Ed.), *Categories of human learning*. New York: Academic Press, 1964. (a)

———. The implications of instructional objectives for learning. In C. M. Lindvall (Ed.), *Defining educational objectives*. Pittsburgh: University of Pittsburgh Press, 1964. (b)

———, & Paradise, N. E. Abilities and learning sets in knowledge acquisition. *Psychological Monographs*, 1961, *75*, No. 14 (Whole No. 518).

Galton, F. *Hereditary genius: An inquiry into its laws and consequences*. London: Macmillan, 1869.

Gates, A. I., & Taylor, G. A. An experimental study of the nature of improvement resulting from practice in a mental function. *Journal of Educational Psychology*, 1925, *16*, 583–593.

Gesell, A., & Thompson, H. Learning and growth in identical twin infants. *Genetic Psychology Monographs*, 1929, *6*, 1–124.

Glaser, R. Instructional technology and the measurement of learning outcomes: Some questions. *American Psychologist*, 1963, *18*, 519–521.

Goldfarb, W. The effects of early institutional care on adolescent personality. *Child Development*, 1943, *14*, 213–223.

———. Variations in adolescent adjustment of institutionally-reared children. *American Journal of Orthopsychiatry*, 1947, *17*, 449–457.

Goodman, K. S. Dialect barriers to reading comprehension. In J. C. Baratz & R. W. Shuy (Eds.), *Teaching black children to read*. Washington, D.C.: Center for Applied Linguistics, 1969.

Gordon, H. *Mental and scholastic tests among retarded children: An inquiry into the effects of schooling on various tests*. London: Educational Pamphlets of the Bureau of Education, No. 44, 1923.

Gray, S. W., & Klaus, R. A. *The Early Training Project: A seventh-year report*. Nashville, Tenn.: DARCEE, George Peabody College for Teachers, 1970.

Greenberg, D., Uzgiris, I. C., & Hunt, J. McV. Hastening the development of the blink-response with looking. *Journal of Genetic Psychology*, 1968, *113*, 167–176.

Guilford, J. P. Human abilities. *Psychological Review*, 1940, *47*, 367–394.

———. The structure of intellect. *Psychological Bulletin*, 1956, *53*, 267–293.

———. *The nature of human intelligence*. New York: McGraw-Hill, 1967.

Guttman, L., & Schlesinger, I. M. A faceted definition of intelligence. *Scripta Hierosolymitana: Studies in psychology*. Jerusalem: The Hebrew University, 1965.

Harlow, H. F. The formation of learning sets. *Psychological Review*, 1949, *56*, 51–65.

Harrington, M. *The other America*. New York: Macmillan, 1962.

Hebb, D. O. *The organization of behavior*. New York: Wiley, 1949.

Hess, R. D., & Shipman, V. Early experience and the socialization of cognitive modes in children. *Child Development*, 1965, *36*, 869–886.

Hilgard, J. R. Learning and maturation in preschool children. *Journal of Genetic Psychology*, 1932, *41*, 36–56.

Hirsch, J. Behavior-genetic analysis and its biosocial consequences. *Seminars in Psychiatry*, 1970, *2*, 89–105.

Holzinger, K. J. *Student manual of factor analysis*. Chicago: Department of Education, University of Chicago, 1937.

Humphreys, L. G. Discussion of Dr. Ferguson's paper. In P. H. DuBois, W. H. Manning, & C. J. Spies (Eds.), *Factor analysis and related techniques in the study of learning*. Technical Report No. 7, Office of Naval Research Contract No. Nonr 816 (02), 1959.

———. The nature and organization of human abilities. In M. Katz (Ed.), *The 19th Yearbook of the National Council on Measurement in Education*. Ames, Iowa, 1962. (a)

———. The organization of human abilities. *American Psychologist*, 1962, *17*, 475–483. (b)

Hunt, J. McV. *Intelligence and experience*. New York: Ronald, 1961.

———. Montessori revisited. Introduction to Montessori, M. *The Montessori method: Scientific pedagogy as applied to child education in "The Children's Houses," with additions and revisions*. (A. E. George, Transl.) New York: Schocken, 1964. (C. 1909)

——. Intrinsic motivation and its role in psychological development. *Nebraska Symposium on Motivation*, 1965, *13*, 189–282.

——. Toward a theory of guided learning in development. In R. H. Ojemann & K. Pritchett (Eds.), *Giving emphasis to guided learning.* Cleveland: Educational Research Council, 1966.

——. Has compensatory education failed? Has it been attempted? *Harvard Educational Review*, 1969, *39*, 278–300. (a)

——. *The challenge of incompetence and poverty: Papers on the role of early education*. Urbana: University of Illinois Press, 1969. (b) See in particular: Political and social implications of the role of experience in the development of competence. (Invited address for Psi Chi, Meeting of the Midwestern Psychological Association, Chicago, May 6, 1967.)

——. Parent and Child Centers: Their basis in the behavioral and educational sciences. Paper presented at the Meeting of the American Orthopsychiatric Association, San Francisco, March 25, 1970.

——, & Kirk, G. E. *Tests of Information Identification*. Urbana: University of Illinois, 1970.

Hydén, H. The neuron. In J. Brachet & A. E. Mirsky (Eds.), *The cell: Biochemistry, physiology, morphology*. Vol. 4. *Specialized cells*. New York: Academic Press, 1960.

Hymovitch, B. The effects of experimental variations in early experience on problem solving in the rat. *Journal of Comparative and Physiological Psychology*, 1952, *45*, 313–321.

Inhelder, B., & Piaget, J. *The growth of logical thinking from childhood to adolescence: An essay on the construction of formal operational structures*. (A. Parsons & S. Milgram, Transls.) New York: Basic Books, 1958. (C. 1955)

Jensen, A. R. How much can we boost IQ and scholastic achievement? *Harvard Educational Review*, 1969, *39*, 1–123.

Johannsen, W. *Elemente der exakten Erblichkeitslehre*. Jena: Fischer, 1909.

John, V. P. The intellectual development of slum children: Some preliminary findings. *American Journal of Orthopsychiatry*, 1963, *33*, 813–822.

Karnes, M. B. *A new role for teachers: Involving the entire family in the education of preschool disadvantaged children*. Urbana: University of Illinois, 1969.

——, Studley, W. M., Wright, W. R., & Hodgins, A. S. An approach for working with mothers of disadvantaged preschool children. *Merrill-Palmer Quarterly of Behavior and Development*, 1968, *14*, 173–184.

——, Teska, J. A., Hodgins, A. S., & Badger, E. D. Educational intervention at home by mothers of disadvantaged infants. *Child Development*, 1970, *41*, 925–935.

Keller, S. The social world of the urban slum child: Some early findings. *American Journal of Orthopsychiatry*, 1963, *33*, 823–831.

Kelley, T. L. *Crossroads in the minds of man: A study of differentiable mental abilities*. Stanford, Calif.: Stanford University Press, 1928.

Kirk, G. E. Pilot studies with the Hunt-Kirk Test of Information Identification. I. Positional identification in preschool children—Montessori and Head Start. Urbana: University of Illinois, 1970. (a)

————. Pilot studies with the Hunt-Kirk Test of Information Identification. II. Color identification and naming in disadvantaged preschool children. Urbana: University of Illinois, 1970. (b)

————, & Hunt, J. McV. *Tests of Information-Processing Abilities*. Urbana: University of Illinois, 1970.

Klaus, R. A., & Gray, S. W. The early training project for disadvantaged children: A report after five years. *Monographs of the Society for Research in Child Development*, 1968, *33*, No. 4.

Labov, W. The logic of nonstandard dialect. In J. Alatis (Ed.), *School of Languages and Linguistics Monograph Series*, 1969, *22*, 1–43.

Liberman, R. Retinal cholinesterase and glycolysis in rats raised in darkness. *Science*, 1962, *135*, 372–373.

McDonald, D. Our invisible poor. In L. A. Ferman, J. L. Kornbluh, & A. Haber (Eds.), *Poverty in America*. Ann Arbor: University of Michigan Press, 1966.

McMillan, M. *The nursery school*. (Rev. ed.) London: J. M. Dent, 1930. (C. 1919)

Miller, J. O. *Diffusion of intervention effects in disadvantaged families*. Occasional paper. Urbana: University of Illinois, Coordination Center, National Laboratory of Early Childhood Education, 1968.

Miller, N. E., & Dollard, J. *Social learning and imitation*. New Haven: Yale University Press, 1941.

Milner, E. A study of the relationship between reading readiness in grade one school children and patterns of parent-child interactions. *Child Development*, 1951, *22*, 95–122.

Montessori, M. *The Montessori Method: Scientific pedagogy as applied to child education in "The Children's Houses," with additions and revisions*. (A. E. George, Transl.) New York: Schocken, 1964. (C. 1909)

Needham, J. *A history of embryology*. New York: Abelard-Schuman, 1959.

Newell, A., Shaw, J. C., & Simon, H. A. Elements of a theory of human problem solving. *Psychological Review*, 1958, *65*, 151–166.

Paraskevopoulos, J., & Hunt, J. McV. Object construction and imitation under differing conditions of rearing: 1. Athens. *Journal of Genetic Psychology*, in press.

Pasamanick, B. Determinants of intelligence. Paper presented at Symposium on Man and Civilization: Control of the Mind—II. University of California San Francisco Medical Center, January 27, 1962.

Piaget, J. *The origins of intelligence in children*. (M. Cook, Transl.) New York: International Universities, 1952. (C. 1936)

————. *The construction of reality in the child*. (M. Cook, Transl.) New York: Basic Books, 1954. (C. 1937)

————. *Play, dreams, and imitation in childhood*. (C. Gattegno & F. M. Hodgson, Transls.) New York: Norton, 1951. (C. 1945)

————. *The psychology of intelligence*. (M. Piercy & D. E. Berlyne, Transls.) Paterson, N. J.: Littlefield, Adams, 1960. (C. 1947)

Popham, W. J., & Husek, T. R. Implications of criterion-referenced measurement. *Journal of Educational Measurement*, 1969, *6*, 1–9.

Pribram, K. H. A review of theory in physiological psychology. *Annual Review of Psychology*, 1960, *11*, 1–40.

———. Reinforcement revisited: A structural view. *Nebraska Symposium on Motivation*, 1963, *11*, 113–159.

Riesen, A. H. Plasticity of behavior: Psychological aspects. In H. F. Harlow & C. N. Woolsey (Eds.), *Biological and biochemical bases of behavior*. Madison: University of Wisconsin Press, 1958.

Schoggen, P. H., & Schoggen, M. F. Behavior units in observational research. Paper presented at Symposium on Methodological Issues in Observational Research, American Psychological Association, San Francisco, September 1968.

Shuey, A. M. *The testing of Negro intelligence*. (2nd ed.) New York: Social Science Press, 1966.

Shuy, R. W. A linguistic background for developing reading materials for black children. In J. C. Baratz & R. W. Shuy (Eds.), *Teaching black children to read*. Washington, D.C.: Center for Applied Linguistics, 1969.

Sigel, I. Language of the disadvantaged: The distancing hypothesis. In G. B. Lavatelli (Ed.), *Promising practices in language development*. Urbana: University of Illinois Press, 1970.

Sinnott, E. W., Dunn, L. C., & Dobzhansky, T. *Principles of genetics*. New York: McGraw-Hill, 1958.

Skeels, H. M. Adult status of children with contrasting early life experiences. *Monographs of the Society for Research in Child Development*, 1966, *31*, No. 3.

———, & Dye, H. B. A study of the effects of differential stimulation of mentally retarded children. *Proceedings of the American Association on Mental Deficiency*, 1939, *44*, 114–136.

Skinner, B. F. *Verbal behavior*. New York: Appleton-Century-Crofts, 1957.

Smedslund, J. Concrete reasoning: A study of intellectual development. *Monographs of the Society for Research in Child Development*, 1964, *29*, No. 2.

Smith, S. Language and non-verbal test performance of racial groups in Honolulu before and after a fourteen year interval. *Journal of Genetic Psychology*, 1942, *26*, 51–93.

Spearman, C. "General intelligence," objectively determined and measured. *American Journal of Psychology*, 1904, *15*, 201–293.

———. *The nature of intelligence and the principles of cognition*. London: Macmillan, 1923.

———. *The abilities of man*. New York: Macmillan, 1927.

Spitz, R. A. Hospitalism: An inquiry into the genesis of psychiatric conditions in early childhood. *The Psychoanalytic Study of the Child*, 1945, *1*, 53–74.

———. Hospitalism: A follow-up report. *The Psychoanalytic Study of the Child*, 1946, *2*, 113–117. (a)

———. Anaclitic depression. *The Psychoanalytic Study of the Child*, 1946, *2*, 313–342. (b)

Stern, W. *The psychological methods of testing intelligence*. (G. H. Whipple, Transl.) Baltimore: Warwick & York, 1914. (C. 1912)

Stewart, W. A. Continuity and change in American Negro dialects. *The Florida FL Reporter*, 1968, *6* (No. 1), 3–4, 14–16, 18.

———. On the use of Negro dialect in the teaching of reading. In J. C. Baratz & R. W. Shuy (Eds.), *Teaching black children to read*. Washington, D.C.: Center for Applied Linguistics, 1969.

Thompson, G. H. *The factorial analysis of human ability.* Boston: Houghton Mifflin, 1939.

Thompson, W. R., & Heron, W. The effects of restricting early experience on the problem-solving capacity of dogs. *Canadian Journal of Psychology,* 1954, *8,* 17–31.

Thurstone, L. L. *The vectors of the mind.* Chicago: University of Chicago Press, 1935.

———. *Primary mental abilities.* Chicago: University of Chicago Press, 1938.

Tryon, R. C. A theory of psychological components—an alternative to "mathematical factors." *Psychological Review,* 1935, *42,* 425–454.

Tuddenham, R. D. Soldier intelligence in World Wars I and II. *American Psychologist,* 1948, *3,* 54–56.

U.S. Commission on Civil Rights. *Racial isolation in the public schools,* Vol. 1. Washington, D.C.: U.S. Government Printing Office, 1967.

Uzgiris, I. C., & Hunt, J. McV. An instrument for assessing infant psychological development. Mimeographed paper. Urbana: University of Illinois, Psychological Development Laboratory, 1966.

———, ———. Ordinal scales of infant psychological development: Information concerning six demonstration films. Mimeographed paper. Urbana: University of Illinois, Psychological Development Laboratory, 1968.

———, ———. Toward ordinal scales of psychological development in infancy. Unpublished monograph, 1969.

Valverde, F. Apical dendritic spines of the visual cortex and light deprivation in the mouse. *Experimental Brain Research,* 1967, *3,* 337–352.

Varon, E. J. Alfred Binet's concept of intelligence. *Psychological Review,* 1936, *43,* 32–49.

Vernon, P. E. *The measurement of abilities.* New York: Philosophical Library, 1961.

———. *Intelligence and cultural environment.* London: Methuen, 1969.

Watson, J. B. *Behavior: An introduction to comparative psychology.* New York: Holt, 1914.

———. *Behaviorism.* New York: Norton, 1924.

Weikart, D. P. (Ed.) *Ypsilanti Carnegie Infant Education Project: Progress report.* Ypsilanti, Mich.: Ypsilanti Public Schools, 1969.

Weiskrantz, L. Sensory deprivation and the cat's optic nervous system. *Nature,* 1958, *181,* 1047–1050.

Wheeler, L. R. A comparative study of the intelligence of East Tennessee mountain children. *Journal of Educational Psychology,* 1942, *33,* 321–334.

White, B. L., & Held, R. Plasticity of sensorimotor development in the human infant. In J. F. Rosenblith & W. Allinsmith (Eds.), *The causes of behavior: Readings in child development and educational psychology.* (2nd ed.) Boston: Allyn & Bacon, 1966.

Wiesel, T. N., & Hubel, D. H. Effects of visual deprivation on morphology and physiology of cells in the cat's lateral geniculate body. *Journal of Neurophysiology,* 1963, *26,* 978–993.

Wilfram, W. *Sociolinguistic description of Detroit Negro speech.* Washington, D.C.: Center for Applied Linguistics, 1969.

Woodrow, H. The relation between abilities and improvement with practice. *Journal of Educational Psychology,* 1938, *29,* 215–230.

———. Factors in improvement with practice. *Journal of Psychology,* 1939, *7,* 55–70.

index

Guilford, J. P., 285

Hair color, 206
Haldane, J. B. S., 97–98
Hall, G. Stanley, 263–264
Harrington, Michael, 265
Hawley, A. H., 123
Haydon, John Langdon, quoted, 91–92
Head size, 206
Hebb, D. O., 8, 265
Hegmann, J. P., 98
Height, 198
Hemophilia, 121
Henmon-Nelson tests, 128–130
Heritability, 71–72, 85, 96–98, 274
Hirsch, J., 78, 274
Hitler, Adolph, 90
Holzinger, K. J., 195–196
Honzik, M. P., 189–190
Horn, J. L., 8–10
Humphreys, L. G., 286
Hunt, J. McV., 24
Hunt-Kirk Test of Information Identification, 291–292
Hydén, H., 265

Identification, racial, 244
Illness, 116
Imitation, 271–272
    see also Verbal imitation
Imprinting, ages of, 25–26
Indirect validity, 19
Inbreeding, 4, 198–203
Income, 110–112
Individualization, 248–249
Infancy, perceptual experience in, 265
Infant handling, 60
Infant mortality, 123–127
Infant reaching, 252–253
Ingle, D. J., 78
Instincts, 183
Intellectual ability, 32, 36, 51–52
    see also Accelerated children
Intelligence
    Cattell's definition of, 17
    behavioral analysis of (figure), 229
    parent-child correlation, 73
    hierarchical conception of, 283–284
    Humphreys' definition of, 31–32
    nonintellective factors of, 51
Intelligence quotient. See IQ
Intelligence tests
    breadth of, 36
    career analyses of high scorers, 234
    correlation with intelligent behavior, 52–53
    and chronological age, 224
    culture fair, 16–22

and educational diagnoses, 236
and factor analysis, 13
group differences on, 62–63
information tested by, 282–283
intercorrelations among, 32–33
norm-referenced and criterion referenced, 288–289
scores and interventional programs, 232–233
sex differences in performance on, 118–119
and sophistication, 23
standardized, 69–70
variance in scoring, 224–225
    see also specific tests
Intentions, electric recording of, 253
Interactionism, ongoing, 266
Interactions, environmental, 242
Introspection, 47
Investment theory, 13–14
Iowa Tests of Educational Development, 37
IPAT Culture Fair tests, 16–22
IQ (Intelligence quotient)
    age of lowering among poor, 270
    and consanguineous matings, 122
    and correlations among relatives (charts), 186–187
    increase in, 275
    and motivational factors, 259–260
    parent-child correlations for, 120
    prediction of, 61
    usefulness of, 54–55
Isophenes, 79

Jacobs' syndrome, 210
Jarvik, L. F., 185
Jennings, R. D., 98
Jensen, A. R.
    arguments summarized, 240–241, 267–268
    and environmental modification, 101
    quoted, 96, 231
    and racial IQ, 78, 82, 84
Jews, study of Oriental and European, 82–83
John, Vera, 276–277
Johnson, R. Peter, 104

Kamback, M. C., 253
Kirk-Hunt Test of Information-Processing Abilities, 291–292
Kit of Reference Test for Cognitive Factors, 284
Klinefelter's syndrome, 209
Knowledge, 31–32, 223
Kuznets, G. M., quoted, 119

Ladder climbing, 296
Lamarck, 263
Language competence, 276–279
Language content, 17